D1240914

THE INSIDERS' GUIDE TO
TO
Greater Indianapolis

THE INSIDERS'® GUIDE TO

·Greater Indianapolis

by
Skip Berry
&
Jolene Phelps Ketzenberger

The Insiders' Guides®, Inc.

Co-published and marketed by:
Indianapolis Newspapers Inc.
307 N. Pennsylvania Street
Indianapolis, Indiana 46204
(317) 633-1240

Co-published and distributed by:
The Insiders' Guides® Inc.
The Waterfront • Suites 12 &13
P.O. 2057
Manteo, NC 27954
(919) 473-6100

•

FIRST EDITION
1st printing

•

Copyright ©1995-96
by Indianapolis Newspapers Inc.

•

Printed in the United States
of America

•

All rights reserved. No part of this
book may be reproduced in any
form without permission, in writing,
from the publisher, except by a
reviewer who wishes to quote brief
passages in connection with a review
in a magazine or newspaper.

ISBN 0-912367-86-5

Indianapolis Newspapers Inc. Supplemental Publications

Advertising Director
Kimberly Parker

Project Manager
Laura J. Benner

Account Executives
Amy Mallett, Laura Winningham

Editor
Jeff Hauersperger

Artists
Joe Thom, Joan Presslor, Jim Halcomb

Sales Manager
Bill Legg

The Insiders' Guides® Inc.

Publisher/Editor-in-Chief
Beth P. Storie

President/General Manager
Michael McOwen

Vice President/Advertising
Murray Kasmenn

Partnership Services Director
Giles Bissonnette

Creative Services Director
Mike Lay

Online Services Director
David Haynes

Sales and Marketing Director
Julie Ross

Managing Editor
Theresa Chavez

Project Artist
Elaine Fogarty

Fulfillment Director
Gina Twiford

Controller
Claudette Forney

Preface

Welcome to Indianapolis! Whatever brings you here, it won't take long for you to realize that you're genuinely welcome. It's called Hoosier hospitality, but that isn't all our city has to offer.

Indianapolis is the 12th-largest city in the United States. It has a metropolitan population in excess of a million people. It's one of the most affordable cities of its size in the country, making it attractive to businesses and individuals looking to relocate. It's one of the key manufacturing, warehousing and distribution sites in the country. It's a vital center for medical research and amateur athletics. And, of course, it's the home of the Indianapolis 500, the largest one-day professional sporting event in the world.

Once dismissed as "Naptown" and "India-no-place," this city revived and renewed itself in the 1980s, becoming what *Newsweek* called "the Cinderella of the Rustbelt." Now, midway through the '90s, Indianapolis continues to polish its image with such projects as Circle Centre, the long-awaited mall that proponents predict will revitalize retail in the downtown district, and such endeavors as Mayor Stephen Goldsmith's nationally admired efforts to privatize many municipal services.

A book like this, which confirms the city's significance as a destination for travelers, conventioneers and relocators, is long overdue. By providing information about an array of area organizations and services, it offers access to those organizations and services — and makes clear the city's complexity and variety.

Writing any guidebook is a daunting task; writing one that provides a comprehensive, inside look at a metropolitan area the size of Greater Indianapolis is even more so. We've done our best to guide you to the best and brightest of Greater Indianapolis. We hope you'll enjoy our favorite shops, restaurants, attractions, parks, weekend getaways, etc. that we've included in this book. We've covered a wide range of topics. But we know things have been omitted, often inadvertently. If you don't find your favorite cafe in our Restaurants chapter, or if you discovered some intriguing nooks and crannies while exploring the city, please let us know. Write to us in care of:

The Insiders' Guides® Inc.
P.O. Box 2057
Manteo, North Carolina 27954

We'll be updating this book annually, so we'll have the opportunity to correct oversights and mistakes, as well as ensure the continued accuracy of existing entries.

That said, *The Insiders' Guide® to Indianapolis* is the most comprehensive guidebook to Indiana's capital city yet developed. That's not to say there aren't other good guides available — there are. But the book you're holding is the only one to assemble such a large volume and variety of information under one cover.

Don't let your *Insiders' Guide®* gather dust on a bookshelf. Use it! Stick it in your car's glovebox. Toss it in your brief-case or backpack. Scribble in the margins. Circle things that interest you. Think of it as your personal tour guide.

Use it and enjoy. We're glad you're here or are planning a trip to Greater Indianapolis. We look forward to hearing from you.

About the Authors

S. L. (Skip) Berry has lived in Indianapolis for 13 years. During that time he has freelanced for such publications as *The New York Times, Travel & Leisure* and *USAir Magazine* in addition to a number of local and regional newspapers and magazines. Currently, he is a feature writer for *The Indianapolis Star* and *The Indianapolis News*.

Berry is the author of more than a dozen nonfiction books for children and adults, including one on Indianapolis. His biography of photographer Gordon Parks was designated one of 1991's outstanding books for teens by the New York Public Library. Among his other books for young readers are biographies of poets Emily Dickinson, Langston Hughes and E. E. Cummings and books on Little League baseball and the Tour de France bicycle race.

Berry has provided freelance writing services to a variety of corporations and nonprofit organizations. He's led writing workshops for children and adults in schools, universities, libraries and museums throughout Indiana.

He lives with his wife, Margo, and their son, Tyler, in one of Indianapolis' comfortable older neighborhoods. When not writing, he enjoys walking, bicycling and gardening. He's also an avid reader and movie lover, as well as a music buff and closet musician.

Born and raised in Central Indiana, **Jolene Phelps Ketzenberger** has spent much of her writing career focusing on the Indianapolis area, first as an editor with *Indianapolis Monthly*, then as restaurant critic for *NUVO Newsweekly*. Her writing has earned numerous awards, including honors from the Hoosier State Press Association and the Society of Professional Journalists. She also teaches writing at Indiana University-Purdue University at Indianapolis.

Ketzenberger began her exploration of the city at age 18 when she lived on campus as a student at IUPUI. While there, she discovered the City Market, the Children's Museum, the Central Library and Broad Ripple — she was hooked. After finishing her journalism degree at Ball State University, Ketzenberger and her husband, John, a newspaper reporter, lived in Columbus, Indiana. They settled in Indianapolis in 1987 and have been enjoying city life while renovating their 1920s-era home. They also are raising two active young sons, Aaron and Adam, with whom they enjoy watching Indians games, playing at Holliday Park and hanging out in the backyard.

Though busy with writing and with her boys, Ketzenberger enjoys cooking, reading and traveling around the state. And although she's never been to the 500, she does know all the words to "Back Home Again in Indiana."

RE/MAX®

Realty Specialists

1-800-627-7362

99 East Carmel Drive, Carmel

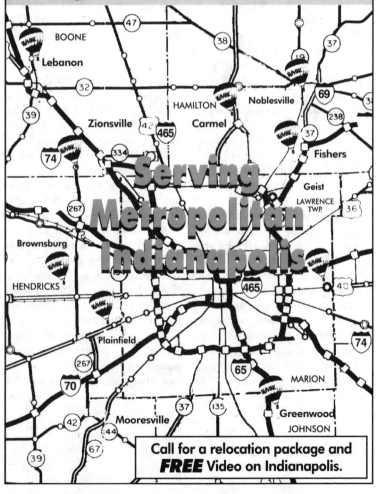

Call for a relocation package and
FREE Video on Indianapolis.

Table of Contents

Directory of Maps

Acknowledgments

Skip...

Scores of people are responsible for this book — all the people who took time to talk with me in person or on the phone, all the people who sent me information I requested, all the people who verified facts I was trying to check. I can't thank each of you by name, but I can thank all of you collectively. You helped make this book possible.

Beyond that, I offer special thanks to the following people and organizations for their help with this project: Tom Aikens, Laura Benner, Brad Carlson and the Indiana Sports Corporation, Greg Charleston and The Arts Council of Indianapolis, Indiana University, the Indianapolis Chamber of Commerce, the Indianapolis City Center, Indianapolis Downtown Inc., the Indianapolis-Marion County Public Library, the Indianapolis Project, Pat Miles and CIOCA The Access Network, the POLIS Research Center at IUPUI, and Judy Wade and her colleagues at Indy Parks.

I also want to thank my colleagues at *The Indianapolis Star* and *The Indianapolis News* for their understanding — especially Jim Lindgren who put off assigning me big sprawling articles while I was in the midst of this big sprawling project. You're a gentleman, Jim, and I appreciate it.

But most of all I want to thank Margo and Tyler, who put up with the time and energy demands that this project made on me. I know it was hard on you both, and I appreciate your love and support. You're the best.

Jolene...

I offer many, many thanks to my husband, John, for all the love, support and time; to my sons, Aaron and Adam, for trying to understand; to Sara Kendall, for her interest and enthusiasm for this project and for her unflagging willingness to try yet another restaurant; to Lisa Montgomery, for listening; to my sister, Judith Bastin, for her encouragement; and to my parents, Ed and Betty Phelps, and my in-laws, Denny and Mary Ann Ketzenberger, for their love and moral support. I'd also like to thank all the groups, businesses and individuals who answered questions and provided information for this book; *The Indianapolis Star, The Indianapolis News* and *Indianapolis Monthly* for all the background information; and the authors of *The Encyclopedia of Indianapolis* for their excellent reference book.

I also owe a big thank you to editor Theresa Chavez for her patience and to Debbie Paul, for the chance to write about Indianapolis in the first place.

Photos in this book from The Indianapolis Star & News were taken by the following: Randy Baughn, Jeff Atteberry, Frank Espich, Patty Espich, Mike Fender, Rob Goebel, Jason Koski, Matthew Kryger, Rich Miller, Jim Mellow, D. Todd Moore, Gary Moore, Susan Plageman, Guy Reynolds, Patrick Schneider, Ron Ira Steele, Kelly Wilkinson, John Warner, Jim Young, Joe Young and Jeff Hauersperger.

Greater Indianapolis

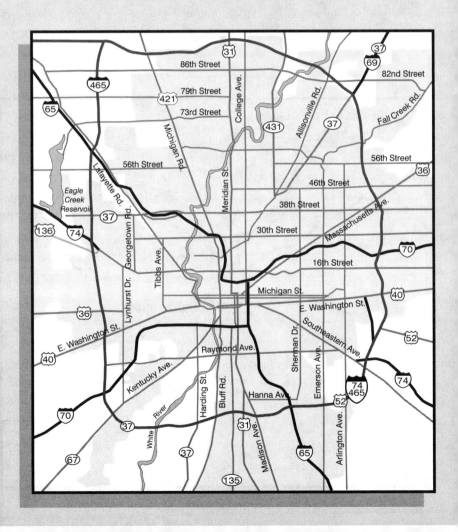

Regional
Indianapolis

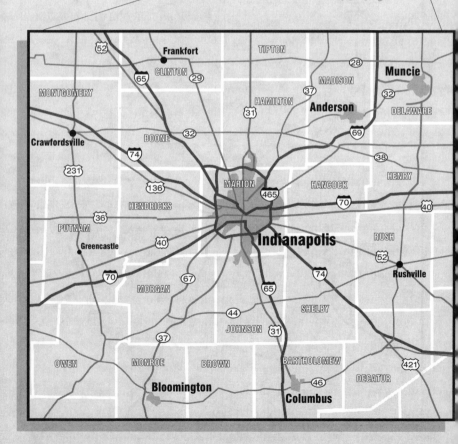

Inside
History

Novelist Kurt Vonnegut Jr. once observed that his hometown of Indianapolis is the world's largest city not on a navigable waterway. The irony of that observation lies in the fact that Indianapolis was purposely situated on the banks of central Indiana's White River because its founders believed the river would meet their transportation and development needs.

But it didn't. Then as now, the White River is too shallow most of the year for anything other than small boats to navigate safely. From the start, Indianapolis was landlocked.

The trick, it turned out, was not to focus on such an obvious liability but to capitalize on an equally obvious asset — Indianapolis's central geographic location. As roads and highways — and later railways and air routes — were mapped out, Indianapolis became a logical connecting point for east-west and north-south traffic. By virtue of a shallow river, Indianapolis became the self-proclaimed Crossroads of America.

So it goes.

Prehistory

During the last Ice Age, glaciers crept southward across what would later be Indiana, covering the top two-thirds of the state. When they finally began their retreat, they left behind a landscape with few wrinkles but plenty of lakes and rivers, streams and ponds, creeks and wetlands. And deep, rich, fertile soil, from which sprang magnificent hardwood forests.

The earliest known inhabitants of this region date to some 8,000 years ago. From that point on, archeologists believe, various indigenous peoples populated Indiana, congregating mostly near bodies of water — Lake Michigan to the northwest, the upper Wabash and Maumee rivers to the northeast, the lower Wabash and Ohio rivers to the south, and in central Indiana along the White River.

By the time European and early American explorers began venturing into the Midwest in the 17th and 18th centuries, the prehistoric Indians who had once called Indiana home had vanished. Living here in their stead were many Native Americans, most prominently the Miami and Potawatomi.

The New Purchase

Central Indiana's modern history began with the New Purchase Treaty of 1818 in which William Henry Harrison, former governor of the Indiana Territory, negotiated the acquisition of several million acres of Indian lands, primarily from the Miamis and the Potawatomis. It wasn't much of a deal from the Indians' perspective.

In return for promises of annual payments, as well as token gifts, they gave up

Photo: The Indianapolis Star & News

The state capitol was carefully planned and designed before construction began in the 1800s.

claim to land that had been their home for generations. And they agreed to either settle on plots that Harrison and his cohorts magnanimously agreed to reserve for them or to move westward — out of the way of the ever-advancing wave of white settlers.

On the other hand, Indiana, which literally (and ironically) means "land of Indians," made out like a bandit. Confined at the time to a handful of counties bordering the Ohio and the lower Wabash rivers, the fledgling state (it had attained statehood only two years earlier) gained so much territory that it more than doubled in size.

By spring of 1820, settlers started trickling into the new territory. Among them were the McCormicks — John, James and Samuel. Heading northwest out of Connersville into the New Purchase region, the McCormicks chopped a path through forests so dense that midday seemed like twilight.

When they reached the confluence of the White River and Fall Creek, the McCormicks stopped. There, John McCormick staked claim to a piece of land. The heavily forested terrain offered plentiful supplies of firewood and logs; the soil was rich and perfect for farming. James and Samuel settled close-by.

While the McCormicks busied themselves clearing their new land, Indiana's first governor, Jonathan Jennings, plotted Indiana's future. In late 1820, he sent 10 commissioners out into the New Purchase to select a site for a new state capital. At the time, the town of Corydon, in the southeast part of the newly expanded state, was the capital. Jennings and many members of the state Legislature, known officially as the Indiana General Assembly, wanted a site nearer the center of Indiana so the capital would be equally accessible to residents throughout the state. The commissioners looked at three potential locations before agreeing on the area surrounding John McCormick's cabin. Realizing the economic potential of that choice, the enterprising McCormick opened a tavern, which became one of the new state capital's earliest business success stories.

Once the site for Indiana's new capital had been chosen, the state Legislature had to give it a name. Several people suggested Indian names, but those and other suggestions were voted down. Then, in the first of what has become an Indiana tradition of choosing the obvious when it comes to naming public places, Judge Jeremiah Sullivan scribbled "Indiana" on a slip of paper. Then he added the Greek suffix "polis," which means "city." The result — "Indianapolis"— won legislative approval more by default than by delight. No one was particularly thrilled with the name, but no one had a better idea, either. Hence, the new state capital was officially dubbed Indianapolis.

Designing a State Capital

Even with a name, Indianapolis was still more of an idea than an actuality. So state officials hired surveyors Alexander Ralston and Elias P. Fordham to draw up a plan for the capital city. Ralston, who had assisted Charles L'Enfant in the planning of Washington, D.C., took one look at the heavily wooded site and said, "It will be a beautiful city — if it is ever built."

Then he designed a city modeled after Washington. He plotted a square with mile-long sides, which was as large as he envisioned Indianapolis ever becoming. In the center of the square, Ralston put a wooded knoll encircled by a wide street; four diagonal streets radiated out from it like spokes on a wagon wheel.

The plan called for the governor's house to sit atop the knoll. And between 1827 and 1839, it did, though no governor ever lived there. The idea of being on constant display in the center of the city wasn't something any governor relished. The house on the circle was torn down in 1857.

However, Ralston's legacy is still amply evident in Indianapolis today. The downtown district is known as the Mile Square, and its heart is Ralston's central circle with streets radiating outward. But the wooded knoll long ago gave way to the Soldiers and Sailors Monument, which memorializes Indiana's Civil War veterans. One of the city's best known landmarks, the monument earned the city's center the official designation of Monument Circle — though most residents today just refer to it as the Circle.

At first, Ralston's doubts about the city's future seemed prophetic. The lack of decent roads and passable waterways hampered development. The lure of building a city from scratch attracted only the most rugged settlers to the site. And those who came suffered not only primitive living conditions, but disease as well — the settlement's proximity to swampy river floodplains led to the outbreak of malaria in the summers of 1821 and 1822.

Despite the problems, the Indiana General Assembly decided to move government operations there permanently in 1824. In November of that year, Samuel Merrill, the state treasurer, loaded Indiana's stockpile of silver— as well as official documents, a printing press and his family and furniture — onto four wagons and headed north out of Corydon. Merrill's daughter Priscilla later described the 160-mile trip over rutted, muddy roads as frightening, especially when the horses and wagons would sink into the

deep water that covered much of the route. When the frazzled travelers finally straggled into Indianapolis, they found a village populated by fewer than 500 people.

But while Indianapolis wasn't quite the bustling capital city that Governor Jennings and the General Assembly had envisioned, neither was it a disaster. By 1825, it had such touches of civilization as a post office, a school building, some small shops and a courthouse. The courthouse also served as the home of the state Legislature until the first capitol building was constructed in 1835. But it wasn't until government officials and local businessmen tackled the problem of limited accessibility that Indianapolis really took shape. The key to the city's growth and prosperity, then as now, was transportation.

Transportation Hub

When the White River proved useless as a large-scale transportation route, it forced legislators and settlers alike to develop alternatives. In 1836, the Indiana General Assembly passed a piece of legislation whose title left no doubt about its intention — "The Mammoth Improvement Bill." It called for the development of roads, canals and railways throughout the state. By the mid-1830s, two major roads under development crossed in Indianapolis. The National Highway, which is now known as U.S. 40, started in Cumberland, Maryland, and ran west. The Michigan Road, which is now U.S. 421, started at the Ohio River and ran north toward Lake Michigan. The intersection of these two highways put Indianapolis on the road to its future. Over the next few years, more roads were cut through the wilderness; many of them started in, ended at or passed through Indianapolis.

Started in 1836, the Central Canal project was designed to link Indianapolis with the Wabash and Erie canals. The Central Canal began north of the city in the village of Broad Ripple. However, after only 8.8 miles of the canal had been dug, the money to pay for it dried up. Today that portion of the canal remains, running from Broad Ripple, where it's home to hundreds of well-fed ducks and geese, to downtown Indianapolis. The dirt path once trod by mules tugging canal boats is now trod by families, fishermen, runners, artists and nature lovers. In recent years, the downtown stretch of the canal got a face-lift, complete with new apartment and office buildings perched along its banks.

Work on the Madison-to-Indianapolis rail line began in 1839, but it wasn't until eight years later that the first steam train chugged into Indianapolis. Within a short time after that, railroad tracks criss-crossed the city. By 1855, Indianapolis was home to eight rail lines. The Indianapolis Union Depot was the first central railroad station in the United States: With a train shed and passenger depot that measured 420 feet long by 200 feet wide, railroad employees could service five trains and their passengers at the same time. It wasn't long before every passenger train passing through the Indianapolis region was routed through Union Depot. And the residents of Indianapolis began referring to their town as the Crossroads of America.

From Settlement to City

Indianapolis was incorporated as a town in 1832, but it wasn't until 1847 that it officially became a city with the adoption of a city charter. That same year, residents elected their first mayor — Whig Party candidate Samuel Henderson. They also voted to establish a tax to support free public schools.

Since the first school's creation in 1821, Indianapolis parents had paid for their children's lessons, sometimes using coonskins as currency. From coonskins to school taxes was a big step, and it took several years after the 1847 vote to actually establish a public school system. The first free public school in Indianapolis opened its doors in 1853, a precursor to the development of the Indianapolis Public Schools system, which now operates more than 80 schools, serving more than 45,000 students.

As transportation routes improved, the population of Indianapolis expanded. By 1850, more than 8,000 people called Indianapolis home. Many came from the bordering states of Ohio and Kentucky; others moved from Pennsylvania, North Carolina and Virginia. European immigrants also came looking for the opportunities that the new settlement offered. Two immigrant groups that had an immediate impact on life in the young city were the Germans and the Irish. As mem-

---

Wendell Willkie, a native of Elwood, was the 1940 Republican presidential candidate who lost to Franklin Roosevelt.

Insiders' Tips

bers of these two groups settled in, neighborhoods with names such as Germantown and Irish Hill evolved.

So did churches. The importance of religion to the town's immigrant residents gradually made Indianapolis a city of churches — Lutheran, Catholic, Presbyterian, Episcopal, Baptist and Methodist congregations were housed in buildings ranging from simple wooden structures to elaborate brick and stone edifices.

The love of music shared by many German and Irish residents resulted in choirs, orchestras and community bands. And their passion for politics resulted in community newspapers, public debates and political rallies.

There were only about 500 African Americans living in Indianapolis in 1850, and they were barred both by law and prejudice from participating in much of community life. As a result, they developed their own vital community, including fraternal organizations and churches. Two of the latter — the Bethel African Methodist Episcopal Church, founded in 1836, and the Second Baptist Church, founded a decade later — continue today.

Despite the General Assembly's passage in 1851 of a constitutional article prohibiting blacks from taking up residence in Indiana, fugitive slaves regularly found refuge in and around Indianapolis. And the Civil War increased still further the black population in central Indiana.

The Civil War

By the time the Civil War broke out, Indianapolis had become a bustling railway center, which in turn made it an important center of Union Army activity. Trainloads of Union soldiers on their way to or from battle stopped in Indianapolis. Restaurants, hotels and saloons were filled with bluecoats, traders, farmers, merchants and gamblers.

The city thrived as its stockyards, meat packing plants, granaries, wagon makers, clothing manufacturers and munitions factories supplied the Union forces. In 1862, Indianapolis resident Dr. Richard Gatling unveiled a hand-cranked, ten-barrel gun that fired more than 250 shots a minute. The Gatling gun became the first widely used machine gun and permanently affected both offensive and defensive battlefield strategies.

Indiana's governor during this time was Oliver P. Morton, who single-handedly directed many of the state's war efforts, including mustering up thousands of volunteers for the Union Army. Men from around the state poured into Indianapolis for training at Camp Morton, while the governor pulled strings and twisted arms to ensure that Indiana's soldiers were well-armed, well-clothed and well-fed.

One of Morton's most audacious actions was the creation of an arsenal that initially supplied munitions only to Indiana troops but later became one of the leading suppliers to the entire Union Army. That arsenal and its munitions manufacturing plant became so important to the war effort that the federal government moved it from the State House grounds to a 76-acre site just east of the Mile Square. Today, that site is home to Arsenal Technical High School, one of the city's best-known public schools.

Because of its central geographic location, Indianapolis was a hotbed of pro-North and pro-South sentiments. Heated debates flared on street corners, fueled by newspapers that cheered for one side and jeered at the other. Abolitionists such as Ovid Butler argued passionately against slavery, while pro-slavery advocates tried to use the Fugitive Slave Law to enslave local resident John Freeman, a respected black house painter. When local attorneys and businessmen rallied to support Freeman, he won his battle to remain a free man.

Meanwhile, east of the city, Hiram Bacon's dairy farm served as a way-station for the Underground Railroad. Bacon hid runaway slaves in his barn as they made their way north from Confederate states to Canada. At the same time, on the northeastern edge of the Mile Square, Camp Morton was converted into a prison camp for Confederate soldiers.

In spite of contrasting viewpoints, Indianapolis prospered during the Civil War and continued to prosper following the war's end. Ex-soldiers, freed slaves, European immigrants and newcomers from the East Coast jostled through city streets. Mule-drawn streetcars, freight wagons, farm carts and fringe-topped carriages clattered over cobblestones and crowded intersections. Business was booming.

Industrial Growth

Because it was a railway center, Indianapolis also became an industrial center in the latter part of the 19th century. Much of the credit for the city's industrial development belongs to mayor John Craven, who, during a walk one afternoon in 1876, came up with the idea of a system of railroad tracks that would encircle the city and connect with all the rail lines already in place. By 1878, a system of tracks known as the Belt Line surrounded Indianapolis, giving all freight trains coming into the city access to the stockyards, factories and warehouses that sprang up along the tracks.

The same year that mayor Craven conceived the Belt Line, a former Union Army colonel named Eli Lilly founded what would become one of the city's best-known companies — Eli Lilly and Company. Known initially as Eli Lilly, Chemist, the small pharmaceutical manufacturing operation quickly became a success, making Lilly and his heirs wealthy. Today, Eli Lilly and Company is an international corporation; its corporate headquarters, research laboratories and production facilities cover hundreds of acres of land both southeast and southwest of the Mile Square.

While Lilly became one of the industrial giants in Indianapolis, the city didn't pin all its hopes on pills and potions. The fertile soil of central Indiana had made agriculture and such related activities as meat packing, grain milling and blacksmithing important industries from the beginning. By the late 19th century, the Kingan Brothers meat packing plant was the world's largest. Van Camp Company was a leading producer of canned pork and beans. And National Starch turned corn from the surrounding farmlands into the starch that stiffened many a banker's shirt.

In addition to agricultural industries, Indianapolis was home to foundries and machine shops, carriage and wagon manufacturers, bicycle makers, distilleries, publishing companies and printing plants.

Between 1870 and 1900, immigrants continued to make their way to Indianapolis. Among their numbers were Italian tailors, shoemakers, barbers, fruit and vegetable dealers and musicians, as well as Greek mechanics and merchants. By 1910, Armenians, Hungarians, Poles, Macedonians and other eastern Europeans also had arrived, finding jobs in factories or setting up small shops.

With the growth of industry came the

trade union movement. In the late 19th and early 20th century, Indianapolis became a center of union activities when organizers such as Eugene Debs, who founded the International Workers of the World, and John L. Lewis, who founded the United Mine Workers, set up offices in the city and held rallies on the Circle. Other unions followed suit. In all, Indianapolis was home to the national headquarters of a dozen unions — though all eventually decamped for the higher profile of Washington, D.C.

Presidential Campaigning, Harrison Style

In 1888, Indianapolis attorney and U.S. Senator Benjamin Harrison (grandson of William Henry Harrison, the New Purchase Treaty negotiator and later the ninth President of the United States) became the Republican Party's challenger to unseat then-President Grover Cleveland. A reserved man, Harrison refused to take to the campaign trail, preferring instead to campaign from the front porch of his house and a platform in University Square (now University Park). Newspaper reporters then telegraphed his speeches and statements around the country.

Harrison's unorthodox tactic worked. He was elected President, serving from 1889 to 1893. During his term, he signed into law such memorable pieces of legislation as the McKinley Tarriff Act and the Sherman Anti-Trust Act. When his bid for a second term was unsuccessful, Harrison returned to Indianapolis where he lived out his life, dying in 1901. He's buried in Crown Hill Cemetery. Harrison's memory is preserved in two separate sites. His former residence at 1230 North Delaware Street now serves as his memorial and is open to the public. On the northeast side of the city is Fort Benjamin Harrison, a U.S. Army base. Unfortunately, Fort Ben, as the base is affectionately known, is scheduled to close in 1996. Its future use at this point is still being discussed.

Soldiers and Sailors Monument

When the original governor's house was torn down in 1857, the Circle became a local eyesore — livestock grazed there, and the ground was littered with trash. With the end of the Civil War came a move to make better use of the city's most visible piece of land — it was turned into a park. But in 1887, the Indiana General Assembly created a commission that was given the task of creating a monument, which was to be erected on the Circle to honor the state's Civil War veterans. Out of 70 designs submitted by architects from throughout the world, commissioners chose the work of German architect Bruno Schmitz. Work on Schmitz's monument began in 1888 and lasted until 1901. The finished monument included not only Schmitz's original concepts, but also incorporated works from three sculptors, including George T. Brewster who created "Victory," a.k.a. "Miss Indiana," which tops the monument. Soldiers and Sailors Monument quickly became (and remains) one of the city's best known landmarks — and it led to its site being officially designated Monument Circle. Flanked to the north and south by curved banks of steps and to the east and west by tiered fountains and reflecting pools, the 284-foot-tall monument is a popular lunchtime gathering place for downtown workers in the summer. Festooned with strands of lights every December, it's the city's best-known

Famous Indiana Faces

A wide variety of famous faces have been seen around these parts at one time or another. Many well-known celebrities and historical figures can claim a Hoosier heritage. Some such celebrities may return regularly, such as Indianapolis-born David Letterman, who makes an annual pilgrimage to the 500. Others barely acknowledge their Indiana roots, such Guns 'N Roses rocker and Lafayette native Axl Rose (a.k.a. Bill Bailey). Read on for a quick roundup of more than 50 famous Hoosiers.

- Former Boston Celtics star Larry Bird, "the hick from French Lick"
- Fashion designer and Fort Wayne native Bill Blass
- Presidents Nixon and Ford's secretary of agriculture Earl Butz
- Bloomington-born songwriter Hoagy Carmichael
- Singer and actor Scatman Crothers, born in Terre Haute
- Garfield creator and Marion native Jim Davis
- 1950s movie idol James Dean, also born in Marion
- Labor leader Eugene V. Debs
- "Three's Company" star Joyce DeWitt, from Indianapolis
- Bank robber John Dillinger, who grew up in Mooresville
- Chad Everett, "Medical Center's" Dr. Joe Gannon, who was born in South Bend
- Fort Wayne-area native Janie Fricke, who hit it big in Country music
- Actor and Frankfort native Will Geer who played Grandpa Zeb Walton on "The Waltons"
- Evansville native and "Barney Miller" star Ron Glass
- Architect Michael Graves, from Indianapolis
- Football Hall of Famer Bob Griese, an Evansville native

Photo: The Indianapolis Star & News

CBS funny man David Letterman (center) grew up in Broad Ripple and was once a local TV weatherman.

- Astronaut Gus Grisson, of Mitchell, who was killed during a simulation flight on *Apollo 1*
- John Gruelle, newspaper cartoonist and creator of the enduring Raggedy Ann character, who grew up in Indianapolis
- Florence Henderson, of Dale, played Carol Brady on "The Brady Bunch"
- "Artless Dodger" Gil Hodges, a native of Princeton
- The Jackson 5 began singing together in Gary in 1966
- Indianapolis native and jazz musician J.J. Johnson
- Boxing champ (and TV pitchman) Marvin Johnson
- All-American tackle Alex Karras, who played for Emerson High School in Gary
- Wolcottville native Ken Kercheval who played Cliff Barnes on TV's "Dallas"
- New York Yankee Don Larsen, from Michigan City
- Indianapolis native and former weekend weatherman David Letterman
- Actress Carole Lombard, born Jane Alice Peters in Fort Wayne
- Actress Shelley Long, also from Fort Wayne
- Evansville's Don Mattingly, who was pulled from the New York Yankee lineup in 1991 for having long hair
- Basketball player George McGinnis, from Indianapolis
- "The Magnificent Seven" tough guy Steve McQueen, born in Beech Grove
- Seymour-born singer/songwriter John Mellencamp
- Jazz great Wes Montgomery, born in Indianapolis
- Noblesville native and fashion designer Norman Norell
- Indianapolis native Jane Pauley got her start on local TV
- Lafayette-born film director Sydney Pollack, who won an Oscar for "Out of Africa," one of his many successful movies
- Songwriter Cole Porter, from Peru
- Gene Stratton Porter, who lived in Geneva and wrote *The Girl of the Limberlost*
- Dana native Ernie Pyle, a well-respected war correspondent during WWII
- Former vice president Dan Quayle
- Brazil native and popcorn king Orville Redenbacher
- Oscar Robertson began his basketball career in Indianapolis and played for Crispus Attucks High School
- Bloomington native, singer David Lee Roth, formerly of the group Van Halen
- Though he made his name with Kentucky Fried Chicken, Col. Harlan Sanders was born near Henryville
- Malden Sukilovich, who changed his name to Karl Malden and starred in "The Streets of San Francisco" before becoming an American Express pitchman, hails from Gary

- Pulitzer Prize-winner Booth Tarkington
- Chuck Taylor played for Columbus High School long before he developed his famous high-top sneakers
- Ballet dancer and choreographer Twyla Tharp, born in Portland
- Indianapolis native and bestselling author Kurt Vonnegut Jr.
- "Going All the Way" author Dan Wakefield
- Country music star Steve Wariner, from Noblesville
- Singer Deniece Williams, from Gary
- Elwood native Wendell Wilkie carried Indiana but lost to Franklin Roosevelt in 1940
- "Laugh In" regular Jo Anne Worley, born in Lowell
- Golfer and native Hoosier Fuzzy Zoeller of New Albany.

(This information was culled from a book called *Awesome Almanac Indiana*.)

Christmas symbol — the self-proclaimed "world's largest Christmas tree." The monument's observation tower, which is accessible by elevator or 32 flights of stairs, offers a panoramic view of the Indianapolis skyline.

Madame Walker and Indiana Avenue

While Eli Lilly's medicines were making him a household name, Madame C.J. Walker's hair care products for African Americans were doing the same for her. A former washer woman with limited education, Madame Walker turned her homemade hair ointment into one of the most visible black-owned companies in America. In the process, she became the country's first black female millionaire.

From humble beginnings in Walker's homes in St. Louis and Denver, the Walker System of hair care grew into a thriving enterprise, with a variety of products and services. Walker employed more than 20,000 people nationwide. In 1910, Walker moved her company to Indianapolis where she built a factory and became a well-respected local philanthropist. Six years later, Walker left for Harlem, but her company continued to operate successfully in Indianapolis.

As the local African-American population began to increase after the Civil War, a neighborhood and business district took shape northwest of the Mile Square. Indiana Avenue became the main artery in what was a thriving community of schools, churches and black-owned businesses. The rise of jazz in the 1920s, which local musicians helped create and foster, brought national prominence to Indiana Avenue. The clubs lining the Avenue booked some of the best known jazz musicians of the day, and Indianapolis became a jazz capital known throughout the country.

To commemorate Madame Walker's success, her daughter Lelia commissioned the construction of the Madame C.J. Walker Center in 1928. A block-long office and theater complex on Indiana Avenue, the Center became the centerpiece of the community and remained so until hard times hit the Avenue in the 1950s and '60s. Renovated in the late '80s, the

Walker Center, which is listed on the National Register of Historic Places, is once again a vital part of African-American cultural activities in Indianapolis.

The Auto Industry

By the late 19th century, there were several carriage and bicycle manufacturers in Indianapolis; when the automobile rolled onto the nation's streets, many of those manufacturers turned their tools and attention to making cars. In 1899, carriage-maker Charles Black became the first to do so — but he was far from the last. Between 1900 and 1936, Indianapolis was home to at least 60 different auto makers, including makers of such elegant speedsters as the Stutz, the Marmon and the Duesenberg. But when Henry Ford perfected assembly-line production in his Detroit-based factory, Indianapolis lost the race to become the country's auto manufacturing center. Ironically, however, between 1914 and 1933, Ford operated a branch manufacturing plant in Indianapolis.

As the auto industry evolved, Indianapolis retained its importance by becoming the site of factories making essential auto and truck components. And by becoming the home of the world's best-known auto racing facilities — the Indianapolis Motor Speedway.

Indianapolis Motor Speedway

Developed in 1909 by car salesman and entrepreneur Carl Graham Fisher and partners Arthur Newby, Frank Wheeler and James A. Allison, the Indianapolis Motor Speedway is actually in the town of Speedway, a couple of miles west of the Mile Square. After sponsoring several poorly attended racing events, the Speedway partners decided to host a 500-mile, $25,000-purse race on May 30, 1911. It was a gamble that paid off handsomely.

Forty cars qualified for the race, including a locally built black and yellow Marmon Wasp that Ray Harroun drove to victory in 6 hours and 42 minutes at an average speed of 74.9 miles an hour. So well received was that first 500-mile race, that it became a tradition.

In 1927, a group of investors, headed by former race car driver and World War I ace aviator Eddie Rickenbacker, bought the track. Under Rickenbacker's guidance, the track continued to thrive until World War II when gas rationing and manufacturing limitations brought auto racing to a standstill. For four years, the Speedway sat empty.

In 1945, Terre Haute businessman Anton "Tony" Hulman bought the facility. By that time, disuse had led to decline — the track was in terrible shape. Hulman spearheaded a renovation effort that restored the Speedway to its former glory— and updated it as racing needs and spectator demands dictated.

Today, the Indianapolis Motor Speedway, still privately owned by the Hulman family, hosts not only the annual Indianapolis 500, which is billed as the world's largest one-day sporting event, but also the annual Brickyard 400 stock-car race. And the track is used year-round by automakers and racing teams to test tires and engines. See our Auto Racing chapter for more information.

World War I and the American Legion

When the United States entered World War I in 1917, Indianapolis played an important role. Soldiers from throughout Indiana trained at Fort Benjamin Harrison, while local factories manufactured munitions, as well as engines for aircraft, trucks and tanks. And as in the Civil War, it was a connecting point for trains carrying troops and freight.

Following the Armistice of 1918, which officially ended the war, the American Legion was founded. In 1919, the new organization announced its national headquarters would be in Indianapolis. A year later, the Indiana General Assembly agreed to appropriate funds for the construction of a building to house the Legion, as well as for the creation of a Memorial Plaza to honor the soldiers who had served in WWI.

Today, the American Legion's national headquarters and the Indiana War Memorial stand at opposite ends of a five-block-long plaza on the northern edge of the Mile Square.

D. C. Stephenson and the Ku Klux Klan

The Roaring '20s were a dark time in Indiana and Indianapolis — it was a time defined by the presence and influence of the Ku Klux Klan. The Klan openly supported political candidates, effectively controlling congressional seats, the governor's office and the state legislature; in Indianapolis, there were Klan-backed politicians in the mayor's office and on both the city council and the school board.

Wielding its white supremacist beliefs like a club, and using racial and religious bigotry as a rallying call, the Klan became one of the strongest political and social movements in Indiana during the 1920s. In Indianapolis, whites from all walks of life — white collar and blue collar, devout Protestants and agnostics, educated and uneducated — joined the Klan.

Not everyone joined, however. The Klan met resistance from the city's powerful Catholic and Jewish communities, as well as from substantial numbers of Protestants who didn't see God's love being manifested in cross burnings and intimidation. Black residents also resisted — most who had long supported the Republican Party became Democrats when the Klan began to dictate the Republican agenda.

One of the most powerful people in the Klan during this time was Grand Dragon D. C. Stephenson, who lived in the Irvington area on the east side of Indianapolis. Stephenson was responsible for recruiting and managing Klan members in 23 states, including Indiana. As a result of selling memberships and Klan paraphernalia, he became wealthy — and egocentric. Thinking himself beyond reproach, Stephenson did what he wanted, including raping and poisoning a young woman named Madge Oberholtzer. But Oberholtzer lived long enough to identify Stephenson. Despite his many political ties, Stephenson was not only charged, but convicted of second-degree murder.

That was the beginning of the end of the Klan in Indiana. Within a very short time — thanks in part to a Pulitzer Prize-winning series of newspaper articles about the Klan in *The Indianapolis Times* —

Limestone from Lawrence County is used for landmarks throughout the state.

Insiders' Tips

membership plummeted. By 1930, the Klan's reign in Indiana was over.

Lockefield Gardens

During the 1930s, Indianapolis suffered through the Great Depression along with the rest of the nation. Still, there were bright spots, most notably the development of Lockefield Gardens, one of the first and finest public housing developments in the nation. Created by the federal Public Works Administration, Lockefield Gardens contained 24 apartment buildings, two- to four-stories tall, with a total of 748 low-cost, high-quality housing units. The complex was on 22 acres on the near northwest side along Indiana Avenue and included large, open, green spaces, shops, playgrounds and a school. It became one of the centerpieces for the African-American community in Indianapolis.

But in the 1950s and '60s new housing opportunities led to more black families moving out to the suburbs, which in turn led to the decline of Lockefield Gardens. Buildings fell into disrepair, and the complex was finally closed in the 1970s. In 1983, all but seven of the original buildings were demolished to make way for the expansion of the campus of nearby Indiana University-Purdue University at Indianapolis (IUPUI). The remaining buildings were renovated and are now part of a smaller upscale apartment complex.

World War II and Beyond

When the United States became involved in World War II, the rail system again proved important to Indianapolis. The city's central geographic location made it a logical connecting point for troops heading to bases around the country. At the same time, all of its rail lines made Indianapolis a logical place for manufacturing and shipping essential war materials.

The city became "Toolmaker to the Nation." Everyone who was old enough to hold down a job went to work. Factories ran 24 hours a day, seven days a week, turning out transportation equipment, weapons parts and aircraft equipment. General Motors' Allison Division in Speedway manufactured America's first jet engine in 1945.

A healthy economy and plentiful labor supply made Indianapolis attractive to an array of companies during and after the war. Ford, Chrysler, RCA and Western Electric opened plants. Shadeland Avenue north of Washington Street (U.S. 40) became an industrial corridor and an employment haven for job seekers.

However, as manufacturing boomed in Indianapolis in the 1950s and '60s, railroad traffic fizzled. More cars than ever before took to the nation's blossoming interstate highway system, and more people took to traveling cross-country by air. And Indianapolis's stature as the Crossroads of America shrank.

While the business climate was healthy and life was comfortable, Indianapolis began to slow down in comparison to other cities around the country. The hustle and bustle of its railroad heydays dwindled. It got a reputation as a city that woke up every May for the annual running of the Indianapolis 500 then drowsily drifted through the rest of the year. Indianapolis became known as Naptown.

Unigov

Between 1890 and 1960, the population of Indianapolis expanded nearly five-fold, from 100,000 to 476,000. With that expansion came a number of governance issues, not the least of which were the confusing (and sometimes conflicting) regulatory roles of the various city, township and county boards and agencies. While attempts to reorganize local government had been made several times throughout the city's history, it wasn't until 1969 that anything substantial happened.

Under the leadership of Republican mayor Richard Lugar (now the senior U.S. senator from Indiana and a presidential hopeful), and with the support of Republican majorities on the city council, in county offices and in both chambers of the Indiana General Assembly, reorganization legislation was drafted and voted into law. Known as Unigov (for "unified government"), that legislation consolidated some of the elected positions and administrative functions of Indianapolis and Marion County government. It also made several smaller communities in the county part of greater Indianapolis.

Unigov made Indianapolis the state's only Consolidated City and created a joint City-County Council as well as six joint administrative departments. It also extended the city's boundaries to match those of Marion County, a move that greatly increased both the city's territorial size and population. In the process, the Crossroads of America became one of America's largest metropolitan districts (the 12th largest as of 1994).

How effective Unigov has been in improving life in Indianapolis is a matter of opinion. Proponents say it has done wonders for the city's growth and development. Opponents say that rather than simplifying local government, it has complicated it. Regardless of opinions, there's no denying that Unigov set the stage for further transformation of the city.

The Business of Sports

Size isn't everything. City officials knew that having more land and more people wasn't enough to make post-Unigov Indianapolis a major player on the national scene. What they needed was an angle, something they could use to help the city shed its Naptown image. Then they hit upon sports.

It began with the Indiana Pacers. In 1973, Mayor Lugar met with a group of developers who wanted to build a new arena on the north side of the city to house the Pacers, then an American Basketball Association team. They'd been playing at the State Fairgrounds' Coliseum, and the developers felt it was time that they had a new, state-of-the-art sports venue. Lugar agreed. But he insisted that the new arena be built downtown. He saw it as the first step in what he hoped would be the revitalization of a decaying district. Market Square Arena, at the corner of Market and Alabama streets, three blocks east of Monument Circle, opened in 1974. It has been the home of the Indiana Pacers ever since.

When Lugar left the mayor's office to run for the U.S. senate in 1976, William H. Hudnut was elected to the office. And under Hudnut, who was mayor for an unprecedented 16 years, sports became the focal point of the city's downtown redevelopment efforts. Between 1979 and 1989, the city — with the help of local philanthropic giant, the Lilly Endowment, as well as other foundation and corporate investors — spent more than $126 million in the creation of world-class athletic facilities.

As a result, Indianapolis attracted an array of national and international sporting events, including the 1982 National Sports Festival, the 1987 Pan American

Games, NCAA basketball and track and field championships, ice skating competitions and Olympic trials in track and field and rowing. Impressed by the city's commitment, a number of amateur sports organizations established their headquarters here. The result of all this was a new self-proclaimed title: "The Amateur Sports Capital of the World."

But interest didn't stop with amateur sports. The city also went after professional events — and teams. In March, 1984, the NFL's Baltimore Colts moved west to become the Indianapolis Colts, playing in the newly constructed Hoosier (now RCA) Dome. The city also became an annual stop for professional golf and tennis tournaments. And in August 1994, the Indianapolis Motor Speedway hosted the first annual NASCAR Brickyard 400.

Sports have become a well-established part of Indianapolis's economic foundation and recreational scene. Naptown is once again wide-awake.

The 1990s Onward

Downtown revitalization efforts didn't stop with the construction of sports facilities. Millions of dollars have also been poured into reviving rundown buildings throughout the Mile Square, converting former warehouses and factories into apartments, condominiums and offices. Millions more have been spent erecting office towers. In the process, the Indianapolis skyline has been dramatically altered.

The latest (and one of the most controversial) downtown projects is an urban mall known as Circle Centre. Circle Centre, which opened in September 1995, is a $300 million effort to resurrect downtown shopping. More than a decade in the planning, it contains more than 100 stores, movie theaters and restaurants.

All the attention and money lavished on downtown projects attracted plenty of criticism. Some of those resources should have been directed at more pressing concerns, argued the critics — education, homelessness, low-income housing, healthcare for the uninsured, neighborhood redevelopment. These and other community concerns are now helping shape a new agenda for city officials. Under current mayor Stephen Goldsmith, efforts are being made to address some concerns by allocating more economic development resources to neighborhoods and by privatizing many government services.

The Crossroads of America is at a crossroads of its own. Figuring out how to balance ongoing development efforts with social needs and economic realities is the challenge facing city officials in the 1990s and beyond.

But at least they don't have to carve a city out of the wilderness. That part's done. And, as Alexander Ralston predicted, Indianapolis is a beautiful city. It's the trees. The city has a lot of trees. No navigable waterway, but a lot of trees. They're a legacy from the wild, wooded past. You should see this place in the autumn.

Inside
Getting Around

As you might expect from a city that bills itself as the Crossroads of America, getting around Indianapolis is fairly easy — unless you rely on mass transit . . . then it's a challenge.

Developing mass transit alternatives to auto travel hasn't been a priority — the only form of public transportation available is the Metro Bus System. (See entry in this chapter.)

However, if you've got a car, you're in luck.

Surface Streets

The surface street pattern in Indianapolis is pretty straightforward. Essentially, the entire city is laid out on a grid of north-south and east-west streets, with a few diagonals thrown in for good measure.

The downtown district, which is known as the Mile Square, originally established the street grid. Laid out by surveyor Alexander Ralston in 1821, the Mile Square's boundaries are defined by four 1-mile-long streets: North Street, South Street, East Street and West Street. In the center of the Mile Square is Monument Circle, which is bisected by Meridian Street, the city's primary north-south street. It's also the dividing line between east and west addresses. A block south of the Circle is Washington Street, the primary east-west street — and the dividing line between north and south addresses.

Photo: The Indianapolis Star & News

The Metro Bus system shuttles passengers throughout the metropolitan area.

Washington Street is also U.S. 40 — the old National Road.

Four diagonal avenues — Massachusetts, Indiana, Virginia and Kentucky — radiate out from the Square. Massachusetts and Indiana begin (or end, depending on your perspective) at New York Street, a block north of the Circle; Virginia does the same at Washington Street and Kentucky at South Street.

For nine blocks north of the Circle, all east-west streets have names. From that point on, they're numbered, starting with 9th Street. Some essential numbered streets to acquaint yourself with are 16th (home of the Indianapolis Motor Speedway), 30th (home of the Children's Museum of Indianapolis), 38th (home of the Indiana State Fairgrounds and the Indianapolis Museum of Art) and 82nd (home of the Fashion Mall and Castleton Mall, two of the city's most upscale shopping malls, as well as myriad restaurants).

A couple of cautionary notes: West of **Meridian Street**, 82nd Street becomes 86th; it confuses even the locals. And in addition to East and West Washington Street, there is North Washington Boulevard. Fortunately, the two Washingtons never intersect.

Highways

When it still bore the name the National Road, U.S. Highway 40 was the first highway to link Indianapolis with the East Coast. It's still a vital road, though its importance was diminished with the arrival of such east-west

interstates as Interstate 74, which connects Indianapolis with Cincinnati to the east and Danville, Illinois, to the west, and Interstate 70, which links Indianapolis with Columbus, Ohio, to the east and St. Louis, Missouri, to the west.

As for north-south interstates, I-65 runs north to Chicago and south to Louisville, Kentucky, while I-69 (which, depending on the direction you're heading, starts or ends at Indianapolis) runs north. There's also U.S. Highway 31, which runs north to South Bend, Indiana (home of University of Notre Dame), and south to Columbus, Indiana (home of some of the most splendid contemporary architecture in the country). U.S. 37 runs south to Bloomington (home of Indiana University) and north to Marion.

The city's bypass, Interstate 465, connects with all the major surface streets and highways. While traffic usually flows smoothly, key on- and off-ramps do back up during morning and afternoon rush hours. This is especially true for ramps at 82nd and 96th streets to the north, 38th Street to the west and Emerson and Shadeland avenues to the east. Generally, traffic peaks between 6:30 and 8:30 AM and 4:30 and 6:30 PM.

To get downtown from I-465, you have to use either inbound I-65 or I-70, or exit onto a surface street.

Parking

There are parking meters throughout downtown Indianapolis. They accept a maximum of two hours' worth of change

Insiders' Tips

Indiana drivers can turn right on a red light if there is no oncoming traffic.

The Indianapolis Heliport: Another Intersection at the Crossroads of America

One mode of transportation that might not come to mind when you hear the phrase "Crossroads of America" is helicopters. But Indianapolis is home to the most successful urban heliport in the United States.

The Indianapolis Heliport, on the southeastern edge of the Mile Square, consists of a three-story, 26,000-square-foot building with lighted touch-down pad, taxiway and a 2½-acre tie-down area. In addition to serving as a landing and fueling facility for helicopters passing through the region, the heliport provides maintenance and repair services for helicopters owned by area TV stations, hospitals, law enforcement agencies, corporations and individuals — a vital service when you realize that one definition of a helicopter is "7,000 parts flying in close formation."

A joint venture between the Indianapolis Airport Authority and the privately owned Indianapolis Heliport Corporation, the heliport opened in 1985. It was the first such facility developed under the auspices of an urban heliport program developed by the Federal Aviation Administration.

In its 1983 Rotorcraft Master Plan, the FAA projected that in the 21st century, helicopters will play an important role in interurban travel, supplanting (or at least supplementing) the current reliance on jet airliners to make short regional trips. The FAA's long-range purpose is the creation of a network of heliports throughout the country, linking the downtown business districts of cities within 300 to 400 miles of one another. For example, within a 300-mile radius of the Indianapolis facility are the downtown districts of Chicago, Cincinnati, St. Louis, Louisville, Cleveland and Detroit.

While it remains to be seen whether or not the FAA's forecast of a network of urban heliports will come to pass (there are others in New York, New Orleans and the Dallas suburb of Garland), it's clear that the Indianapolis Heliport is another instance of the value of the transportation industry to the vitality of the Crossroads of America.

For more information, call the Indianapolis Heliport, 51 South New Jersey Street, 262-3000.

(a quarter buys you 20 minutes), and they're patrolled regularly. The fine for parking at an expired meter is $12.50 if paid within 72 hours, $17.50 thereafter.

Parking garages and lots abound throughout downtown — at least until you need a space. Then, of course, every place is full. Prices are all over the map — for example, there's a surface lot southeast of Washington Street that only charges $2.50 for an entire day, but it's far enough removed from most downtown buildings that you'll have to walk a ways to get to where you're going. Then there are the of-

Photo: The Indianapolis Star & News

The best place to hail a cab is at the airport.

fice building garages that charge five or six times that for a few hours.

Indianapolis International Airport

Twelve minutes west of the Mile Square via I-70, Indianapolis International Airport serves nearly 6 million passengers a year and handles some 591,000 tons of cargo.

Designed to minimize problems for passengers and their guests, the two-story terminal is easy to get around, with all arrival services on the lower level and all departure services on the upper. To meet travelers' various needs, there are rental car counters, a travel agency, a visitors information center, bank machines and restaurants.

The terminal is also designed to efficiently accommodate physically challenged individuals. There are sloped curb cuts and elevators, motion activated doors and volume-controlled telephones, enclosed walkways and wheelchair-accessible restrooms, lift-equipped buses and van-accessible parking spaces. Wheelchairs and telecommunications devices for the deaf (TDDs) are also available. The airport's TDD number is 487-5151.

There is garage and surface lot parking for short-term stays and a remote lot with free shuttle service for multi-day parking needs. A ground transportation center provides easy access to a variety of services, including buses, hotel courtesy vehicles taxis, and limousines. Contact the center at 487-2517.

Seventeen airlines, including major carriers and their regional partners, offer passenger services at the airport. They are:

Insiders' Tips

On weekends between Thanksgiving and New Year's Day, avoid East 82nd Street between Allisonville Road and I-465 (the Castleton Mall area) — traffic is bumper-to-bumper during the pre- and post-Christmas shopping frenzy.

America West	(800) 235-9292
American Airlines/American Eagle	(800) 433-7300
American Trans Air	248-8308
Chautauqua Airlines	487-6400
Continental Airlines	(800) 525-0280
Delta Airlines	(800) 221-1212
Midstate Airlines	248-3965
Midwest Express Airlines	(800) 452-2022
Northwest Airlines	(800) 225-2525
Skyway Airlines	(800) 452-2022
Southwest Airlines	(800) 435-9792
TWA	635-4381
United Airlines	(800) 241-6522
USAir/USAir Express	248-1211
ValuJet	(800) 825-8538

For general information and paging services, call 487-7243.

In addition to being home to the nation's largest charter airline, American Trans Air, the airport also serves as a hub for both Federal Express and the U.S. Postal Service. Both American Trans Air and United Airlines have airplane maintenance operations at the airport.

Trains and Buses

For a city that once was one of the largest passenger railway centers in the country, Indianapolis now has very limited train service. **Amtrak** operates the city's only existing interstate passenger train line, an Indianapolis-to-Chicago route that departs from Union Station downtown. As of this writing, trains depart Indianapolis for Chicago twice on Monday, Thursday and Saturday mornings and once on Sunday, Tuesday, Wednes-

day and Friday mornings. For a current schedule, call (800) 872-7245.

Greyhound and **Trailways** provide interstate bus services, with a total of some 50 buses arriving from or leaving for destinations throughout the country. The Greyhound terminal is downtown at 127 N. Capitol, 267-3053. The American Trailways terminal is a few blocks farther south, 350 S. Illinois Street, 687-1111.

Mass Transit

In Indianapolis, mass transit means one thing — **Metro Bus**.

The Metro Bus system shuttles passengers throughout the metropolitan area. Fares are $1.25 on express buses, which cover longer distances with fewer stops than their non-express counterparts, $1 at peak-usage times and 75¢ off-peak for non-express buses. Transfers cost 25¢. Exact change is required at all times. For route and schedule information, call 635-3344.

Special bus services are available for physically challenged passengers. For information about Metro's open door service for the disabled, call 635-2100, extension 242.

Taxis

Unlike in many cities, taxis in Indianapolis don't usually cruise in search of fares. The best places to hail a cab are the airport, in front of major downtown hotels or at downtown taxi stands. Otherwise, you're better off calling for a taxi by phone.

During peak rush hours parking is prohibited on key downtown streets. Signs warn cars of times during which cars will be towed. Heed these signs. Towing is done regularly and within minutes of the beginning of the no-parking time period.

Insiders' Tips

Local taxi companies include **Yellow Cab**, 487-7777; **Hoosier Cab**, 243-8800; and **Metro Cab**, 634-1112.

Limousines

If you're in the mood for a mode of transportation with a bit more panache, try a limousine. Among local limo operators are **Indy Connection Limousines**, 241-6700; **Carey Limousine**, 247-7307; **Dynasty Limousines**, 241-9900; **Carte Blanche Limousines**, 867-0440; and **Personal Touch VIP Limousine Service**, 547-3325.

Carriages

For a downtown ride that's romantic and leisurely, it's hard to beat a horse-drawn carriage. The clip-clop of hooves on pavement and the gentle sway of the carriage cab take you back in time. Board a carriage outside of Union Station or at the Capitol Street entrance to the Hyatt Regency. Or hire one for an evening interlude with someone special. Then settle into a different form of getting around.

For information about rates and availability of carriages, contact **Yellow Rose Carriages**, 634-3400; **Metropolitan Carriages, Inc.**, 631-4169; or **Colonial Carriages, Inc.**, 637-2004.

Inside
Area Overviews

Fifty Fabulous Places to Raise Your Family lauds the Indianapolis area for its rapidly growing economy, affordable housing, low crime rate, great sports and overall family atmosphere. And it's all true. Visitors and newcomers are often surprised at how much house their money will buy, and that we walk around downtown or in the popular Broad Ripple neighborhood at night and enjoy solitary morning jogs at Eagle Creek Park, a huge park on the northwest side. We're not foolhardy about personal safety, of course, but we do feel a level of confidence here that residents of bigger cities cannot claim.

Just about everyone who's lived here awhile will tell you that the Indianapolis area is indeed a great place to raise a family. And the area offers such a wide range of places to call home. With the creation of Unigov, Indianapolis and Marion County merged (see our History and Government chapters for details) and have been considered one entity as far as population goes. Still, the county includes the towns of Speedway, Lawrence, Beech Grove and Southport, all of which were excluded from Unigov and retain their own individual personalities. The central city too features numerous historic neighborhoods, each with a colorful history or ethnic heritage. Across the city and county, neighborhoods such as Broad Ripple, Irvington and Woodruff Place

Photo: The Indiananpolis Star & News

Deer Creek Music Center in Hamilton County is a popular place to attend concerts by world-famous country and rock'n'roll artists.

preserve and promote their own distinct characters. (See our Neighborhoods chapter for details.)

In general, Indianapolis offers big-city amenities and a hometown ambiance, a combination that residents find hard to beat and that visitors remark upon. *American Demographics* magazine ranked the city 10th in the nation in kindness toward strangers, a helpfulness rating based on such criteria as willingness to make change for a quarter and to help a blind person cross the street. Out-of-towners, especially those from either coast, may find it odd that we actually obey the "walk" and "don't walk" traffic signals. But they appreciate our friendliness and hospitality.

If they find the city friendly, wait till they visit the surrounding counties, where life often moves at a slower pace and people still wave when they pass one another driving down a county road. Basketball hoops really do hang on the sides of barns, and high school gymnasiums are packed to the rafters for Friday night games. Farms and fruit stands offer the best the land has to offer, including incredible tomatoes, cantaloupe, watermelon and sweet corn.

But if you can't see the beauty in a freshly plowed field or in gently rolling acres of corn, you'll have a tough time appreciating the scenery. In most of our surrounding counties, farming remains an ever-present fact of life. In fact, if you drive along our state and county roads in the spring and summer, you'll eventually get stuck behind slow-moving farm equipment — until the tractor or combine driver politely pulls to the side of the road to let traffic pass.

Agriculture remains the state's No. 1 industry, and Indiana ranks among the top-five states in the nation in the pro-duction of corn, soybeans, tomatoes, cantaloupe, popcorn and, in the northern part of the state, spearmint and peppermint. Though many families nationwide lost their farms during the 1980s, 85 percent of Indiana farms remain individual operations; corporations own just 4 percent.

Central Indiana and the seven counties that surround Indianapolis — Hamilton, Johnson, Boone, Hendricks, Hancock, Shelby and Morgan — reflect these statewide agricultural trends. Farming remains vital to many of these counties; farmland accounts for 70 to 80 percent of land mass in several counties.

Area counties are easy to reach, thanks to the state's excellent highway network. Seven interstates crisscross Indiana, more than in any other state, providing easy access to most Central Indiana locations.

Two major U.S. highways also intersect at Indianapolis. U.S. 40, the old National Road (known as Washington Street within the city) runs east and west through central Indiana. Though still a busy route, the historic highway doesn't see as much of the cross-country traffic as it once did; I-70 now handles most of that. Still, vestiges of its traffic-laden past can be seen in the numerous small motels scattered along the route. In central Indiana, U.S. 40 cuts through downtown Greenfield, the Hancock County seat, continues through the middle of Indianapolis, then on into Hendricks County's Plainfield.

U.S. Highway 31 extends north and south through central Indiana is U.S. Highway 31. It cuts through Franklin and Greenwood in Johnson County, then becomes Meridian Street as it runs through the heart of Indianapolis. It continues on through Hamilton County, where Indianapolis gives way to Carmel.

Many well-maintained state roads also

provide popular routes through the counties. And, of course, the I-465 loop provides quick access around the city's periphery. Visitors can pick just about any state road exit and within minutes find themselves out in the country, driving past churches established in the 1800s, well-kept Princess Anne style farmhouses and countless front-yard fruit stands. (Stop and buy some of those fresh tomatoes. You'll never settle for the grocery-store variety again.)

In some areas, primarily in Hamilton and Johnson counties, it's tough to tell where Indianapolis ends and Carmel (to the north) and Greenwood (to the south) begin. Still, even in the more urban areas, once you turn off the main roads and get away from the upscale housing developments and strip malls, you'll find those fruit stands and antique shops.

Prop your feet up and read on for an introduction to Indianapolis' seven surrounding counties, where residents and visitors enjoy easy city access and the best in suburban, small-town and country life. (Here we give just an overview. For more information about specific restaurants, shops, festivals, etc. see our corresponding chapters throughout the book.)

Hamilton County

Just to the north of Indianapolis is Hamilton County, the state's fastest growing county in terms of population. The county experienced a 32.8 percent gain in the number of residents in the decade between 1980 and 1990, and the group with the largest increase in population was the 35- to 44-year-olds; yes, Hamilton County is home to a great many baby boomers. Restaurants, specialty shops and upscale housing developments abound.

Carmel (pronounced like the candy, with the emphasis on the Car, Kar mul), is the county's largest city and has seen plenty of growth, especially since the mid-1980s. Fishers, which by some estimates the fast-growing town in the Midwest, continues to expand. In 1970, the population of Fishers hovered around 500; a special census in 1988 counted more than 4,500 residents. By the 1990s the numbers had reached 14,000. Its convenient location (close to many northside businesses and corporations) and a well-regarded school system continue to attract young families. Though town officials have had to hustle to provide services to all these new residents, they have been determined to manage the growth. Its open space ordinance, for example, requires developers to incorporate green spaces in any new subdivision.

And there are plenty of subdivisions in Hamilton County. The median price of new homes is more than $100,000, and many go for several times that figure.

Despite its yuppie reputation, Hamilton County is more than just image. It's home to those who like its easy access to Indianapolis as well as its emphasis on top-quality education and high school athletics.

Though Hamilton County can boast plenty of amenities, once outside of

---

Check out the Sugar Grove Winery, 611 Newlin Road, in Mooresville. The area's newest winery makes a terrific stop when on a drive through Morgan County to admire the fall foliage.

Insiders' Tips

Carmel, the pricey subdivisions give way to farmland. And though Hamilton County offers shopping, sushi and such unique restaurants as Illusions, where magicians perform tableside, it's also home to Stonycreek Farm, where visitors can feed animals, pick a pumpkin or browse through the herbs and specialty items at the Buggy Barn gift shop. The county also offers at least 20 antique shops and three options for purchasing hand-made pottery: Bastine Pottery and Strawtown Pottery studios and Conner Prairie, a living history village where it's always 1836.

The Transportation Museum in Noblesville, the county seat, provides a glimpse into Indiana's railroad past. The museum also offers train rides each August to the Indiana State Fair and summertime train ride/dinner packages to such restaurants as Fletcher's of Atlanta, in a tiny town in the northern part of the county where local chef Fletcher Boyd serves up top-notch regional cuisine. Noblesville, with its busy, revitalized downtown area, also offers plenty of antique and specialty shops.

Hamilton County boasts top-notch recreational facilities as well. It is home to the 1,478-acre Geist Reservoir and the 1,800-acre Morse Reservoir, both of which are surrounded by beautiful waterfront dwellings, many costing half a million or more. The area hosts a number of special events throughout the year, including the Deer Creek Fair and Music Festival and the Amish Country Market in Noblesville.

For more Hamilton County info, contact the Carmel-Clay Chamber of Commerce, P.O. Box 1, Carmel, 46032, 846-1049; Cicero Area Chamber of Commerce, 73 W. Jackson Street, Cicero, 984-4079; Fishers Chamber of Commerce, 8710 E. 116th Street, Fishers, 578-0700; Noblesville Area Chamber of Commerce, 159 N. Ninth Street, Noblesville, 773-0086; and Westfield-Washington Chamber of Commerce, Westfield, 896-2378.

Johnson County

South of Indianapolis lies Johnson County, whose population of more than 93,000 ranks it 15th out of 92 counties in the state. The number of Johnson County residents increased by more than 26 percent in the 1970s and by more than 14 percent in the '80s. Like Hamilton County to the north, the age group in Johnson County with the greatest increase in numbers between 1980 and 1990 was the 35- to 44-year-old baby boomers.

Hamilton County's Carmel and Johnson County's Greenwood have had a long-running but good-natured feud about which boasts the best in suburban living, but the same things attract young families to the south side as to the north: low crime, convenient shopping and excellent schools. Some would say the north side is more upscale and the south side more casual, but one thing is certain: Each area has much to recommend it.

Driving south from downtown Indianapolis on U.S. 31 or I-65, the commute to Greenwood takes about 20 minutes — depending, of course, on traffic or road construction (disgruntled commuters observe that we only have two seasons around here: winter and construction). Many residents make the commute each day; the city of Greenwood is home to nearly 30,000 people. Though the Greenwood Park mega-mall, which vies with Fort Wayne's Glenbrook Square for designation as the state's largest, dominates the area's shopping scene, Old Town Greenwood offers unique shopping in the old business district as well. Check out

Helen Ellis' Apple Pie

For a real taste of central Indiana, try this prize-winning recipe, fresh from the Heartland Apple Fest's Great Apple Pie Bake-off, our favorite part of the early October festival held at Beasley's Orchard in Danville. (See our Annual Events and Festivals chapter for more information.)

Crust (makes enough for two pies):
4 cups unsifted all-purpose flour
1 $^{1/2}$ tablespoons sugar
1 $^{1/2}$ teaspoons baking powder
1 teaspoon salt
1 $^{2/3}$ cups lard
1 large egg, slightly beaten
1 tablespoon white vinegar
$^{1/2}$ cup ice water, divided

Filling (makes enough for one pie)
3 cups Jonathan apples, quartered
1 teaspoon lemon juice
1 cup sugar, divided into thirds
2 tablespoons flour, divided
$^{1/2}$ teaspoon cinnamon
$^{1/4}$ cup water
5 to 6 thin slices butter

For crust, in a large bowl, stir together flour, sugar, baking powder and salt, mixing well. Using a pastry blender, cut in lard until mixture is crumbly. Stir together egg, vinegar and water and combine with flour mixture. After the dough is mixed, divide dough in half and chill (work only with half; reserve half for another pie). Roll out bottom crust and place in deep eight-inch pie pan.

For filling, peel, core and quarter apples and sprinkle with lemon juice. Stir together $^{1/3}$ cup sugar, 1 tablespoon flour and the cinnamon and sprinkle over apples. Stir together another $^{1/3}$ cup sugar and 1 tablespoon flour and sprinkle evenly over bottom of unbaked pastry in pie pan. Arrange apples in pie pan. Sprinkle last $^{1/3}$ cup sugar on apples and dot with butter slices. Roll out and arrange top crust over apples.

Bake in preheated 400-degree oven for 15 minutes. Reduce heat to 350 degrees and continue baking until apples are tender when pierced with a fork, about 45 minutes.

Making Thyme for a variety of herbs and gift items and the Cornerstone Gallery for interior design ideas; both are located on West Main Street.

Franklin, the county seat, boasts a population of about 15,000 and can claim a gem in Franklin College. The small, four-year institution provides a cultural focal point for the town. Franklin also features the traditional courthouse square, Main Street's Artcraft Theatre and Heiskell's Restaurant, which specializes in seafood, steaks and prime rib and in its charming turn-of-the-century Victorian setting.

Recreational activities in Johnson County focus a great deal on the outdoors. The nearby Atterbury Fish and Wildlife Area near Edinburgh covers 6,400 acres and offers hunting, fishing and a wildlife viewing area. Sixteen lakes, ranging in size from three acres to 309 acres, provide even more outdoor options. Bass, bluegill and catfish are usually biting in Sugar Creek, Stone Arch and Pisgah lakes within the Atterbury area. Deer, upland game, dove and waterfowl hunting is also allowed.

Those who'd rather hunt for bargains have much territory to cover in Horizon Outlet Center near Edinburgh. Though actually in Bartholomew County, this outlet mall provides plenty of options for Johnson County shoppers.

For more information on Johnson County, contact the Greater Franklin Chamber of Commerce, P.O. Box 264, Franklin 46131, 736-6334; and the Greater Greenwood Chamber of Commerce, 300 S. Madison Avenue, Suite 420, Greenwood, 888-4856.

Boone County

Northwest of Indianapolis, Boone County remains more rural than either Hamilton or Johnson counties, though I-65 runs through the county, providing quick access to downtown Indianapolis. Despite growth in the number of high-end housing developments in recent years, the comparatively unspoiled natural beauty is a Boone County draw. More than 80 percent of the county land is farmed.

But they raise more than corn in Boone County. This is also horse country, or as near to horse country as you get in central Indiana. OK, so it isn't Lexington, but you'll still find small horse farms dotting the county. One of the area's best-known annual events (and which wins the longest name award) is the Traders Point Hunt Club Charity Horse Show and Country Fair each August.

Lebanon, with its impressive domed courthouse and 12,000-plus residents, is the county seat, but when Indianapolis residents think of Boone County, Zionsville comes to mind. This charming village of about 5,500 boasts brick streets lined with Victorian cottages, many with the requisite picket fences and flower gardens. Known for its historic ambiance, Zionsville also features numerous top-notch restaurants, including Adam's Rib, Z'Bistro and Panache. Antique and specialty shops abound, but one establishment proves especially unique: Albers Rolls-Royce — America's oldest exclusive Rolls Royce dealer.

Zionsville hosts a number of community festivals, including its Country Market art, antique and craft show and annual Fall Festival and Christmas in the Village. For a different take on tradition, Lebanon hosts the American Indian Council Annual Traditional Pow Wow each August, as well as a spring pow wow in April or May each year.

For more information, contact the Boone County Chamber of Commerce, 221 N. Lebanon Street, Lebanon, 46052, 482-1320; and the Greater Zionsville Chamber of Commerce, P.O. Box 148, Zionsville 46077, 873-3836.

Hendricks County

Hendricks County sits to the west of Indianapolis, an area that saw heavy growth from the 1960s through the '80s, as new residents sought the county's slower pace and more rural atmosphere. Even now about 70 percent of the county remains farmland. However, county residents can quickly reach Indianapolis via I-70 and U.S. 36.

Communities within the county retain a small-town feel. Plainfield is the area's largest with more than 10,000 residents and is situated on U.S. 40, the old National Road. Though considerably smaller, Danville, with its 5,000 or so residents, is the county seat.

A picture-perfect Midwestern small town, Danville boasts tidy streets, big houses and lots of red brick. The town square, where you'll find the Mockingbird Cafe (specializing in prime rib) and the Royal cinema, surrounds the handsome courthouse. For the news of the area, pick up a *Hendricks County Flyer* from a box outside the Mayberry Cafe; have a seat on the bench or head inside and peruse the paper over a cup of coffee.

In nearby Brownsburg, check out Harley's restaurant, a longtime favorite of westsiders and, in May, of Indianapolis Motor Speedway regulars. Like most area small towns, Brownsburg features a number of places to browse for antiques.

Hendricks County is also seeing more business development, and is benefiting from its proximity to the Indianapolis International Airport and that area's industrial growth. A proposed amusement park is also generating a great deal of interest in the county.

Hendricks County hosts a number of special events throughout the year that highlight its country ambiance, including the Hendricks County 4-H Fair in July and Danville's Heartland AppleFest in October, from which come the wonderful aromas of the Great Apple Pie Bake-off. (See our sidebar in this chapter.)

For more Hendricks County information, contact the Brownsburg Chamber of Commerce, P.O. Box 82, Brownsburg 46112, 852-7885; the Greater Danville Chamber of Commerce, P.O. Box 273, Danville 46122, 745-0670; and the Plainfield Chamber of Commerce, P.O. Box 14, Plainfield 46168, 839-7222.

Hancock County

Just east of Indianapolis, Hancock County is home to approximately 50,000 residents. Hancock County remains primarily rural, with more than 80 percent of the land in farms that grow corn, soybeans and winter wheat and plenty of gardens producing those luscious tomatoes. I-70 cuts through much of the farmland,

Stonycreek Farm in Hamilton County provides a great chance to get away from the fast pace of weekday life. Kids can pet the animals or pick a pumpkin in the fall.

Insiders' Tips

but you'll find more roadside vegetable stands along U.S. highways 40 and 52.

Just off I-70, Greenfield, the county seat, is home to more than 12,500 residents, many of whom are drawn by the easygoing lifestyle and the city's emphasis on historic preservation. The birthplace of famed Hoosier poet James Whitcomb Riley, who wrote such childhood favorites as "Little Orphant Annie" and "The Raggedy Man," the city takes pride in its historic heritage. James Whitcomb Riley Days, held each October, includes art, antiques and, of course, a poetry contest. Don't miss touring the Riley birthplace and the Old Log Jail Museum.

Even without a festival, antique buffs love this part of the area. Those browsing Greenfield's many shops are likely to keep on driving east on U.S. 40 to Knightstown, actually located in southeast Henry County; numerous small towns situated along U.S. 40 make up Antique Alley.

Other Hancock County towns include Cumberland (which straddles the Marion/Hendricks County line) with more than 4,700 residents, Fortville with 3,000-plus residents and New Palestine, home to about 750 people. The Hancock County 4-H Fair in July draws residents from across the county for its traditional fair food, animal judging, games and amusements.

For more information about Hancock County, contact the Greater Greenfield Chamber of Commerce, 110 S. State Street, Greenfield, 462-4188; or the New Palestine Area Chamber of Commerce, P.O. Box 541, New Palestine 46163.

Shelby County

Southeast of Indianapolis is Shelby County, a primarily rural area that is home to more than 40,000 people. Like Hancock County to its north, Shelby County retains strong ties to agriculture; more than 80 percent of its area is in farmland. I-74 provides quick access to Indianapolis, though you'll see more of the county if you head out along U.S. 421 or 52. In fact, Frank's Orchard & Farm Market, which offers a variety of fruits and vegetables throughout the season, is located at the intersection of U.S. 52 and Ind. 9.

While on Ind. 9, pull the car to the side of the road and take a look at the ostriches and emus that wander around a farm located just past County Road 350 N. Oddly enough, more ostriches can be spotted from I-74 around the Acton exit near the Shelby-Marion county line; you'll get a better view of this flock if you get off at Acton and drive along Southeastern Avenue.

I-74 takes you right to Shelbyville, the county seat, home to about 16,000 residents. Many smaller towns such as Morristown and St. Paul, with about 1,000 residents each, offer an easygoing, rural atmosphere where family and community remain the focal points.

But though some of these tiny burgs may seem frozen in time, one town capitalizes on a bygone era. The popular Boggstown Inn and Cabaret sports hearty food and a ragtime atmosphere. Daily shows feature banjos, dueling pianos and plenty of audience participation. People from all over the world have signed the guest book. Not as elaborate but still worth the drive — if you like freshly made ice cream, that is — is Shelbyville's Compton's Cow Palace. Morristown's Kopper Kettle is well-known for its family-style meals, especially its fried chicken dinners.

Special events in the area include the

Shelby County Fair in July, one of only a few in the state that still offers harness racing, and Shelbyville's Bears of Blue River Festival in late August, which celebrates the county's historic heritage as the setting for Charles Major's book *The Bears of Blue River*. The Blue River Valley Pioneer Fair in October, held at the county fairgrounds, spotlights historic arts and crafts (don't miss the traditional funnel cakes and just-pressed apple cider).

For more information about Shelby County, contact the Shelby County Chamber of Commerce, 33 E. Washington Street, Shelbyville, 398-6647; or the Morristown Chamber of Commerce, P.O. Box 476, Morristown, 46161, 763-6830.

Morgan County

Southwest of Indianapolis, Morgan County, is known for its rugged, forested scenery as well as its ultraconservative heritage (in its unseemly past, Morgan County was a hotbed of Ku Klux Klan activity).

Today, more than 58,000 people call Morgan County home, many of whom moved to the county in the high-growth 1970s. Ind. 37 and Ind. 67 provide direct routes through the county for those who work in Indianapolis; I-70 cuts through the area as well. Many of the county's residents live in Martinsville, the county seat, which boasts a population of more than 12,000. Mooresville is home to more than 5,800 people, and a number of smaller communities dot the scenic countryside. Residents enjoy the laid-back pace and small-town atmosphere characteristic of Morgan County.

They're also fond of all the outdoor recreation opportunities. The Morgan-Monroe State Forest covers more than 23,000 acres in Morgan, Brown and Monroe counties where picnicking, hiking, camping, hunting and fishing abound. Twenty area lakes also provide an abundance of fishing. Those who really like to rough it can contact the state forest at 342-4026 and inquire about reserving Draper's Cabin, a cottage in the middle of the forest without electricity or running water. Visitors are welcome to gather wood and build a fire in the cabin's stone fireplace, but they'd better bring along a sleeping bag if they want to curl up in front of the fire — there are no beds, or other furniture.

Morgan County's scenic beauty draws foliage watchers from across central Indiana who monitor the forest for the peak color in the fall. In fact, the Morgan County Fall Foliage Festival in October draws residents and visitors alike to take in the brilliant reds and yellows of an Indiana autumn. While in the county, stop by the Sugar Grove Vineyard and Winery, 611 Newlin Road, Mooresville; it offers tours and wine tastings daily.

For more information about Morgan County, contact the Greater Martinsville Chamber of Commerce, P.O. Box 1378, Martinsville 46151, 342-8110; or the Mooresville Chamber of Commerce, P.O. Box 62, Mooresville 46158, 831-6509.

Photo: The Indianapolis Star & News

Union Station, which saw 200 trains a day during the busy years of World War II, is now a festival marketplace with restaurants and specialty shops.

Inside
Accommodations

Indianapolis has plenty of room for you. In fact, it has plenty of rooms — more than 16,000 of them. Whether you're looking for a quiet little bed and breakfast or a hotel large enough to host hundreds of conventioneers, Indianapolis is very accommodating.

Hoosier hospitality isn't just a phrase — it's a fact. Enjoy your stay.

Using This Chapter

This chapter is divided into two major sections: Hotels and Motels, and Bed and Breakfasts. In turn, each of these sections are arranged geographically. This was done to help you find a place to stay that will be convenient to specific business districts and local attractions. For places that offer toll-free phone numbers, those numbers are included along with local numbers.

Each facility's entry includes a dollar sign symbol indicating the approximate price range for a one-night stay, midweek, double-occupancy. The price ranges are:

$50 or less	$
$51 to $100	$$
$101 to $150	$$$
$150 and more	$$$$

Please note that prices were quoted by a reservationist at each facility, and were current as of September 1, 1995. As always, prices are subject to change without notice. Rates are higher during times of heavy demand — major conventions and annual events (the Indianapolis 500,

Indiana Black Expo, Brickyard 400, Circle City Classic, etc.).

Also, regardless of the rate, a 5 percent local hotel tax combined with a 5 percent state sales tax will add 10 percent to your room bill. Unless otherwise noted, all establishments accept major credit cards.

In this chapter, we've tried to present you with a fairly comprehensive overview of area lodgings. But by no means is this a complete list. For other options call the Indianapolis Convention & Visitors Association (see contact information below).

INDIANAPOLIS CONVENTION & VISITORS ASSOCIATION

One RCA Dome, Ste. 100   639-4282
(800) 824-INDY

For help finding the right accommodations for your next stay in Indianapolis, this is the place to start. The Association is a central source of information about a variety of places to stay, from the plush and expensive to efficient and economical.

Hotels and Motels

Downtown

THE CANTERBURY HOTEL

123 S. Illinois St.   634-3000
$$$

Listed on the National Register of Historic Places, this 99-room, European-style hotel is one of Indiana's best facilities. Just a block from the Indiana Convention Center and the RCA Dome, it's well situated for well-heeled business travelers, conventioneers and sports fans; it's also the choice of many celebrities — Elton John, The Rolling Stones and the Rev. Jesse Jackson have all stayed there. The Canterbury has a cozy cocktail lounge, as well as an elegant dining facility known disarmingly as The Restaurant. The hotel offers limousine service to and from Indianapolis International Airport.

THE COLUMBIA CLUB
121 Monument Cir.   *635-1361*
$$$

Those who don't stay at The Canterbury probably stay here. In fact, author Tom Wolfe, in search of the perfect accommodations, once moved from The Canterbury to this 86-room private club on the Circle. Honoring club memberships from around the country, the Columbia Club provides guests with Euro-small rooms in an old-money atmosphere. As it should, given its roots.

Founded in 1889 by the Harrison Marching Society, a group of wealthy, enthusiastic supporters of local attorney Benjamin Harrison who they helped elect President of the United States in 1888, the Columbia Club has traditionally been a bastion of white, male Republican Party stalwarts. While that has gradually changed — Democrats, women and other minorities can now become members — it still retains its position as one of the city's centers of economic and political power. (Every Republican President from Harrison to George Bush has stayed here.)

Now listed on the National Register of Historic Places, the Columbia Club has four floors of guest rooms, as well as a library, a billiards room, a barbershop, a fitness center, a lounge and dining facilities.

COURTYARD BY MARRIOTT
501 W. Washington St.   *635-4443*
$$$

This 233-room facility is across the street from the Eiteljorg Museum of American Indians and Western Art, a block from the Indiana Convention Center and the RCA Dome, and two blocks from the Indianapolis Zoo. Other downtown attractions — Circle Centre, the Artsgarden, Union Station, the Indiana Repertory Theatre, and the Circle Theatre are an easy walk or a brief cab ride away.

Amenities include free parking, free airport shuttle service, facilities for the disabled, a playground, and an outdoor pool. The on-site restaurant, T.G.I. Friday's, was 1994's Franchise Restaurant of the Year— it's also a popular lunch and after-work watering hole.

CROWNE PLAZA UNION STATION
123 Louisiana St.   *631-2221*
$$$

Attached to the west end of Union Station, this 276-room hotel includes 26 rooms inside refurbished Pullman train cars. If you've ever wondered what it would have been like to travel by rail while ensconced in a private, furnished Pullman, this is your chance to find out— minus the rattles and jolts of actual train travel.

The hotel also contains an indoor pool, a whirlpool and an exercise room, as well as concierge and airport shuttle services. The on-site Louisiana Street Restaurant and Bar serves breakfast, lunch and dinner.

Across the street from the Indiana Convention Center and the RCA Dome, the

Crowne Plaza is within walking distance of Circle Centre and most other downtown attractions, as well as being a short drive from the Indianapolis Zoo, the IUPUI campus and the Children's Museum.

DAYS INN DOWNTOWN

401 E. Washington St.   637-6464
$$ (800) 325-2525

A 100-room facility adjacent to Market Square Arena, Days Inn Downtown is an easy walk away from Circle Centre, the Indiana Convention Center and RCA Dome, Union Station, Monument Circle and other downtown attractions. The hotel offers free parking and airport transportation. Complimentary continental breakfast is provided to all guests; there's also an on-site restaurant, Tommy's Fine Food & Spirits, which serves breakfast, lunch and dinner in a casual atmosphere.

EMBASSY SUITES DOWNTOWN

110 W. Washington St.   236-1800
$$$ (800) 362-2779

This 360 all-suites hotel is right in the center of the action downtown. Diagonally across Washington Street from Circle Centre and the Artsgarden, between Claypool Courts and the Indiana Repertory Theatre and just two blocks from the Indiana Convention Center and the RCA Dome, Embassy Suites is perfectly situated for both business and pleasure. A parking garage is attached to the hotel (parking is extra; valet services are available).

The hotel's suites each contain a pair of TVs, two phones, a microwave oven, a refrigerator, a coffeemaker and a foldout sleeper couch in the living room. There are also facilities for disabled persons. Every guest receives a full cooked-to-order breakfast each morning, as well as access to the two-hour "manager's reception" (re: happy hour) with complimentary beverages and snacks each afternoon. Also on-site is the cozy, elegant restaurant Ellington's. Work off the extra calories in the hotel's exercise room and indoor pool.

HYATT REGENCY INDIANAPOLIS

One S. Capitol Ave.   632-1234
$$$$

Directly across Washington Street from the Embassy Suites and across Illinois Street from Circle Centre, this 500-room facility includes a 20-story atrium, glass elevators and a waterfall. It also includes 23 grand suites, 16 shops, seven restaurants (including the Eagle's Nest, a revolving rooftop restaurant and lounge), a full-service bank and a variety of meeting and business plan rooms with phone and fax capabilities.

And because all work and no play is bad for you, the Hyatt contains the largest on-site fitness club of any downtown hotel.

Because it's less than a block from the Indiana Convention Center and the RCA Dome and only a few blocks from Market Square Arena, the Hyatt is a favorite of NFL and NBA teams, as well as of meeting planners and conventioneers. What's

May is the worst month for trying to find accommodations in the Indianapolis area. Rooms are booked months in advance by Indianapolis 500 fans. Try to make your reservations at least a year in advance.

Insiders' Tips

more, its central location makes getting most anywhere else — Eli Lilly and Company, Indianapolis International Airport, the Indianapolis Tennis Center, the I.U. Medical Center, the IUPUI campus, the Indianapolis Zoo, the Indianapolis Art Museum, the Children's Museum — a snap.

North Meridian Inn

1530 N. Meridian St.   *634-6100*
$$ *(800) 233-4639*

Just minutes from Monument Circle, this 160-room hotel offers convenience to all downtown sites, as well as to such attractions as the Children's Museum, the Indianapolis Museum of Art, the Indianapolis Motor Speedway, and the Indiana State Fairgrounds. Amenities include a pool. The on-site restaurant, Rumor's Cafe, serves breakfast, lunch and dinner— and boasts of having a menu with the city's largest selection of heart-healthy foods on it.

Omni Severin Hotel

40 W. Jackson Pl.   *634-6664*
$$$$ *(800) 843-6664*

This 423-room, highly rated facility adjacent to Union Station is a block south of Circle Centre and a block east of the Indiana Convention Center and the RCA Dome. It's also within easy walking distance of other downtown attractions. Amenities include 38 suites, a fitness club complete with indoor pool, and accommodations for people with disabilities. Dining options include the West Coffee Cafe (espresso, pastries and salads) and the Severin Bar & Grill (fish, steaks and pastas).

Ramada Plaza Hotel

31 W. Ohio St.   *635-2000*
$$ *(800) 272-6232*

A block from Monument Circle, this 371-room hotel has such amenities as a rooftop pool. Just a short jaunt away are Market Square Arena, Circle Centre, the Convention Center and RCA Dome. For casual downtown dining, the Ramada Plaza offers English's Cafe, serving breakfast, lunch and dinner.

Renaissance Tower Historic Inn

230 E. Ninth St.   *261-1652*
$$ *(800) 676-7786*

This elegant brick inn on the northeast side of the downtown district is listed on the National Register of Historic Places. It contains 80 studio suites available for both short- and long-term stays; among the amenities are free local phone service, voicemail, cable TV and on-site parking. The suites have fully equipped kitchens, including cooking and eating utensils, and there's an on-site laundry facility. All major downtown sites are just a short drive (or a healthy walk) away.

The Tower Inn

1633 N. Capitol Ave.   *925-9831*
$$

Just across the street from Methodist Hospital and 16 blocks north of the Indiana Convention Center and the RCA Dome, this facility contains 62 rooms, all nonsmoking and many equipped for handicapped individuals. There's an attached parking garage.

The inn offers easy access to all downtown sites, as well as to the Indianapolis Motor Speedway and the Children's Museum.

University Place Conference Center and Hotel at IUPUI

850 W. Michigan St.   *269-9000*
$$ *(800) 627-2700*

This highly rated facility combines a 278-room hotel with a 30-room high-tech conference center. Guests have access to

The Big Business of Conventions

Because Indianapolis is easily accessible from throughout the country, it has become a popular site for regional and national conventions, trade shows, corporate meetings and special events. According to the Indianapolis Convention & Visitors Association, between 1984 and 1994 convention business increased from 30 events to 231, and the number of people attending those events jumped from 147,000 to more than 858,000.

In addition to location, Indianapolis has equipped itself well to handle expanding convention traffic. The Indiana Convention Center and RCA Dome complex contains a combined 127,595 square feet of meeting space and more than 301,500 square feet of exhibit space. The complex has hosted the NCAA Final Four, the nation's largest African-American exhibition (Indiana Black Expo), the North American Christian Convention and the Fire Department Instructors Conference.

At the same time, there are a number of hotels within easy walking distance of the Center and Dome, as are a variety of restaurants, nightclubs, theaters and sports facilities.

And in September 1995, the missing link — downtown shopping — was forged with the opening of Circle Centre, an 800,000-square-foot retail and entertainment complex. Containing department stores (Nordstrom and Parisian), 100 speciality stores, a multi-screen cinema and restaurants, Circle Centre offers a refuge for meeting-weary conventioneers.

Photo: The Indianapolis Star & News

The RCA Dome is home to the NFL Colts and numerous other events — including NCAA Final Four games in 1997.

such amenities as a fitness facility and pool, as well as The Bistro (for breakfast) and Chancellor's Restaurant (for lunch and dinner). Covered walkways link University Place with the I.U. Medical center facilities and the I.U. Natatorium and Track and Field Stadium. Other area attractions — the Eiteljorg Museum of American Indians and Western Art, the Indianapolis Zoo, the Indiana Repertory Theatre, Circle Theatre, the Artsgarden, and Circle Centre — are easily accessible by car or on foot.

THE WESTIN HOTEL, INDIANAPOLIS

50 S. Capitol Ave.   262-8100
$$$$ (800) 228-3000

Connected by a covered skybridge to the Indiana Convention Center and RCA Dome complex, this 573-room, highly rated hotel is in the heart of downtown Indianapolis's convention, sports, shopping, and entertainment district. Its amenities include a fitness facility and indoor pool, as well as facilities for people with disabilities.

Airport

ADAM'S MARK HOTEL

2544 Executive Dr.   248-2481
$$$ (800) 444-ADAM

For luxury accommodations with easy airport access, this is it. With 407 rooms, including 44 elegant suites, this full-service hotel can accommodate everything from a couple on a weekend getaway to a banquet hall full of conventioneers. On-site facilities include 28,000 square feet of meeting space, two restaurants (Applebees's for casual dining, The Marker for more sophisticated occasions), as well as a lounge (Marker Lounge) and a nightclub (Quincy's). The hotel offers free airport shuttle service, free parking, indoor and outdoor pools and a fitness facility. Room designs accommodate people with

physical disabilities. Downtown Indianapolis is minutes away via I-70.

BUDGETEL INN

2650 Executive Dr.   244-8100
$$ (800) 428-3438

Near the airport, this 102-room facility offers easy access to west-side businesses; the downtown district is a short drive east on I-70. Rooms are handicapped-accessible. All guests receive continental breakfast delivered to their rooms.

COURTYARD BY MARRIOTT

5525 Fortune Cir. E.   248-0300
$$$ (800) 321-2211

This quiet, residential-style facility has an indoor pool and whirlpool, a fitness facility and 151 handicapped-accessible rooms. There's free shuttle service to the nearby airport, as well as an on-site restaurant and lounge.

DAYS INN AIRPORT

5860 Fortune Cir. W.   248-0621
$$ (800) 325-2525

A 238-room hotel offers guests free airport shuttle service, an outdoor pool and exercise facilities. Also on-site is P.K.'s Dining & Diversions, a restaurant and lounge serving breakfast, lunch and dinner.

HAMPTON INN HOTEL

5601 Fortune Cir. W.   244-1221
$$ (800) HAMPTON

At this 131-room hotel guests can choose among two types of rooms — those with king-size beds and those with double beds; nonsmoking rooms are available, and rooms are handicapped accessible. Among the amenities are free airport shuttle and local phone service, complimentary continental breakfast and satellite TV.

HOLIDAY INN AIRPORT

2501 S. High School Rd.   244-6861
$$$ *(800) HOLIDAY*

With a 22,000-square-foot conference center and more than 20 meeting/banquet rooms, this 274-room, full-service hotel at Indianapolis International Airport is more than a place to stay — it's also a place to work and play. Also among its offerings are airport shuttle service, free parking, an indoor pool and whirlpool and an exercise room. Guest accommodations are handicapped-accessible. On-site attractions include Chanteclair, an elegant French restaurant; The Gallery, an atrium lounge; and Benchwarmers, a sports bar.

LAQUINTA INN WEST

5316 W. Southern Ave.   247-4281
$$ *(800) 531-5900*

Only a mile from the airport, this 122-room facility offers free local phone service, satellite TV, continental breakfast, an outdoor pool and airport shuttle service. Rooms are handicapped-accessible. Downtown Indianapolis is about a 10-minute drive east.

RAMADA INDIANAPOLIS AIRPORT

2500 S. High School Rd.   244-3361
$$$ *(800) 272-6232*

This 288-room facility on the airport grounds includes some 14,000 square feet of meeting space, and offers easy access, via I-70 and I-465, to downtown Indianapolis, the Motor Speedway and other areas of the city. Among the hotel's amenities are an indoor pool, free parking and shuttle service and an on-site restaurant (Alexander's) and a lounge (Amelia's).

Northeast

AMERISUITES

9104 Keystone Crossing   843-0064
$$ *(800) 833-1516*

Situated in the upscale commercial and retail bustle of the Keystone Crossing area, this facility contains 126 two-room suites, each of which includes a refrigerator, microwave and coffeemaker. Handicapped-accessible accommodations are available. Among Amerisuites's amenities are deluxe continental breakfasts, newspapers and free local phone service, as well as an on-site fitness club and pool.

BEST WESTERN LUXBURY INN CASTLETON

8300 Craig St.   842-9190
$$ *(800) 252-7748*

This 114-room facility is near Community Hospital North and the Castleton commercial and retail district. In addition to having a pool, it offers handicapped accessibility and easy access to a variety of area restaurants, movie theaters and nightclubs.

HAMPTON INN NORTHEAST

6817 E. 82nd St.   576-0220
$$ *(800) HAMPTON*

A 130-room facility at the I-69 and I-465 junction offers handicapped-accessible rooms, an indoor pool and convenient access to the Castleton commercial and retail district.

HOLIDAY INN EXPRESS NORTHEAST

9790 North by Northeast Blvd.
578-2000
$$ *(800) HOLIDAY*

This two-story, 76-room hotel includes some rooms with whirlpool tubs, as well as handicapped accommodations. Enjoy a free continental breakfast.

HOMEWOOD SUITES AT THE CROSSING

2501 E. 86th St.   253-1919
$$ (800) 225-5466

Just west of the Keystone Crossing commercial and retail area, this 116-suite hotel is nestled in a neighborhood-like setting. Designed for both short and long-term stays, Homewood Suites offers elegantly comfortable accommodations, complete with facilities for physically disabled guests. On-site amenities include an outdoor pool and a fitness club.

KNIGHTS INN NORTH

9402 Haver Way   848-2423
$ (800) 843-5644

Just off Keystone Avenue north of I-465, this 110-room facility is near both the Keystone Crossing and the Carmel commercial and retail districts. Rooms are handicapped accessible and some include kitchenettes. There's an outdoor pool available as well as ample parking.

OMNI INDIANAPOLIS NORTH HOTEL

8181 N. Shadeland Ave.   849-6668
$$$ (800) THE-OMNI

A deluxe, full-service, high-rise hotel near the Castleton and Keystone Crossing commercial and retail districts, the Omni contains 222 rooms, a health club, an indoor pool and sauna and Abruzzi's Cafe and Grill. Rooms are handicapped-accessible.

QUALITY INN CASTLETON SUITES

8275 Craig St.   841-9700
$$ (800) 334-4460

North of 82nd Street, just west of I-69, this facility includes 163 suites, each of which contains a wet bar and refrigerator, as well as a conference table and chairs. Room rate includes free local phone service, cable TV and daily newspaper.

You'll enjoy easy access to Castleton, Fishers and Keystone office parks, as well as to nearby Castleton Square mall and an array of other area stores, movie theaters, restaurants and nightspots. Suites include handicapped-accessible facilities. The hotel offers free airport shuttle service.

RADISSON PLAZA AND SUITE HOTEL

8787 Keystone Crossing   846-2700
$$ (800) 333-3333

Twelve miles from the downtown district, this 561-room hotel is right in the heart of the Keystone Crossing commercial and retail district. It also offers easy access to the Castleton and Carmel areas. Among its amenities are an indoor pool, a fitness club, two restaurants (Keystone Cafe and Waterson's), a lounge (the Lobby Bar) and a nightclub (Whirligig's). Rooms are handicapped-accessible.

SIGNATURE INN CASTLETON

8380 Kelly Ln.   849-8555
$$ (800) 822-5252

A two-story, 123-room facility at the intersection of I-465 and Allisonville Road, this hotel is near the Castleton and Keystone Crossing commercial and retail districts. Among its amenities are meeting rooms, guest offices, free local phone service, cable TV, free breakfast express, daily newspaper and an outdoor pool. Guest accommodations are handicapped-accessible.

STUDIO PLUS

9750 E. Lakeshore Dr.   843-1181
$$

A 71-room extended-stay facility in the Keystone Crossing area, Studio Plus provides lodging that includes fully equipped kitchens, free local phone service and cable TV and an on-site laundry. There's also a pool, sauna and exercise room. Rooms are handicapped-accessible.

Northwest

BEST WESTERN
WATERFRONT PLAZA HOTEL
2930 Waterfront Parkway, W. Dr.   *299-8400*
$$ *(800) 528-1234*

Nestled beside a small lake, this 140-room hotel at I-465 and Crawfordsville Road combines business and pleasure. There's 17,500 square feet of on-site meeting space, as well as easy access to the airport and west-side commercial and industrial parks. And there's also an indoor pool, whirlpool and sauna, as well as dining (The Waterfront Cafe) and entertainment (The Excalibur II Lounge). Rooms are handicapped-accessible.

COMFORT INN NORTH
3880 W. 92nd St.   *872-3100*
$$ *(800) 228-5150*

This 58-room, three-story inn at the junction of I-465 and Michigan Road offers 22 nonsmoking rooms, as well as an indoor pool. Rooms are handicapped-accessible.

DAYS INN NORTHWEST
3740 N. High School Rd.   *293-6550*
$$ *(800) 329-7466*

This facility's 155 rooms are spread among four buildings, arranged around a central courtyard containing an Olympic-size pool. The hotel also provides free airport shuttle service. Rooms are handicapped-accessible.

EMBASSY SUITES HOTEL
3912 Vincennes Rd.   *872-7700*
$$$ *(800) EMBASSY*

This gleaming white, eight-story, 222-suite hotel looks like a transplant from southern Spain. In keeping with its setting amid the Park 100 office park area (I-465 and Michigan Road), there are meeting and banquet rooms, as well as catering services, available. Amenities include complimentary breakfast and an indoor pool and fitness club. A variety of restaurants are nearby, as is Beef & Boards Dinner Theatre. Suites are handicapped-accessible.

HAMPTON INN NORTHWEST
7220 Woodland Dr.   *290-1212*
$$ *(800) HAMPTON*

This 124-room inn near the I-465 and 71st Street junction features an indoor pool and whirlpool, a workout area, and handicapped-accessible facilities. Continental breakfast is on the house. Enjoy easy access to the surrounding Park 100 area, as well as to other north-side commercial and retail sites; the downtown district is minutes away via I-465.

HOLIDAY INN NORTH
3850 DePauw Blvd.   *872-9790*
$$$ *(800) HOLIDAY*

Near the I-465 and Michigan Road interchange, this 351-room Holidome facility offers an indoor pool, saunas, Jacuzzi, fitness equipment and putting green. Airport transportation is available, as are weekend packages. On-site restaurants and lounges include Cafe St. Paul (breakfast,

For a unique in-town getaway, book one of the railcar rooms at Union Station's Crowne Plaza hotel. The comfortable, well-appointed rooms will make you think you're in a sleeper car from days gone by.

Insiders' Tips

lunch and dinner), San Remo Grill (dinner), and Benchwarmers Sports Food & Spirits (sports bar). Situated amidst the Park 100/Pyramids business district, the hotel also offers easy access via I-465 to other north-side commercial and retail areas, as well as to downtown. Rooms are handicapped-accessible.

LEES INN INDIANAPOLIS
5011 N. Lafayette Rd.   297-8880
$$ (800) 733-5337

A 75-room facility at I-65 and Lafayette Road, Lees Inn offers free HBO and a complimentary continental breakfast. Some rooms have Jacuzzis; all are handicapped accessible. It's just minutes from downtown via I-65.

NEW ENGLAND SUITES HOTEL
3871 W. 92nd St.   879-1700
$$

The 40 two-room suites in this hotel all contain microwave ovens, refrigerators and TVs with VCRs (videotapes available). Amenities include free local phone service and breakfast. Suites are handicapped-accessible. This hotel is near northwest-side office parks.

PICKWICK FARMS
SHORT-TERM FURNISHED APARTMENTS
9300 N. Ditch Rd.   872-6506
$$ (800) 869-RENT

By the day, week or month, this apartment complex offers guests their choice of studio, one-, two- or three-bedroom furnished quarters, each with a dishwasher, microwave, stove, refrigerator, toaster and coffeemaker. Rates include all utilities, local phone service, voicemail and cable TV. Amenities include tennis and racquetball courts, workout room, indoor volleyball, bowling, a play area for children and an outdoor pool. There's also an on-site laundry.

Pickwick Farms offer convenient access to Park 100, College Park and the Pyramids, as well as other north-side business districts. Downtown is minutes away via I-465.

RED ROOF INN NORTH
9520 Valparaiso Ct.   872-3030
$$

With 108 handicapped-accessible rooms in two buildings, this facility offers economical lodgings in a location convenient to the Park 100/Pyramids business district.

RESIDENCE INN BY MARRIOTT
3553 Founders Rd.   872-0462
$$$ (800) 331-3131

This facility at 86th Street and Michigan Road has 88 suites available for either short- or long-term stays. Amenities include an outdoor pool and exercise equipment. Suites are handicapped-accessible.

ST. VINCENT MARTEN
HOUSE HOTEL & CONFERENCE CENTER
1801 W. 86th St.   872-4111
$$

Adjacent to St. Vincent Hospital, the Marten House has meeting and banquet facilities in addition to 173 handicapped-accessible guest rooms. Amenities include an indoor pool and fitness club, free parking and a host of personal guest services. The on-site restaurant, Piccard's Restaurant, serves breakfast, lunch and dinner from a menu offering an array of heart-healthy selections.

SIGNATURE INN NORTH
3910 Payne Branch Rd.   875-5656
$$

This 143-room inn at I-465 and Michigan Road offers free local phone service, cable TV and daily newspaper, as well as meeting rooms and offices for business travelers. There's an outdoor pool and free breakfast.

Photo: The Indianapolis Star & News

The Hyatt Regency Indianapolis is a 500-room facility that includes a 20-story atrium, glass elevators and the Eagle's Nest — a revolving rooftop restaurant and lounge.

STUDIO PLUS

9030 Wesleyan Rd.   872-3090
$

This 71-room extended stay hotel in the College Park area provides quarters with fully equipped kitchens, free local phone service and cable TV. Amenities include an outdoor pool and exercise facility. Daily, weekly or monthly rates are available. Rooms are handicapped-accessible.

SUPER 8 MOTEL NORTH

9090 Wesleyan Rd.   875-7676
$$ (800) 800-8000

In College Park west of the Pyramids, this 116-room motel at Michigan Road and Wesleyan Road provides complimentary breakfast. There's an outdoor pool. Rooms are handicapped-accessible.

East

BEST WESTERN INDIANAPOLIS EAST

2141 N. Post Rd.   897-2000
$$ (800) 528-1234

Convenient to both the east-side commercial district and the northeast-side commercial and retail district, this 156-room hotel at the intersection of I-70 and Post Road has an on-site fitness club and pool, as well as a restaurant and lounge.

BUDGET INN

6850 E. 21st St.   353-9781
$

Recently renovated, this 139-room facility near the intersection of I-70 and Shadeland Avenue offers access to the east-side commercial and industrial corridor. It has rooms equipped for people with disabilities. Amenities include video rentals.

BUDGETEL INDIANAPOLIS EAST

2349 N. Post Rd.   897-2300
$

This inn, which is 12 miles from the city's downtown district, contains 106 rooms. Among its amenities are free parking and valet service, nonsmoking rooms, free local phone service and complimentary continental breakfast.

FAIRGROUNDS INN

1501 E. 38th St.   926-4401
$

Across the street from the Indiana State Fairgrounds, this 147-room hotel has on-site parking, meeting rooms, an outdoor pool and a play area for children. The facility has handicapped-accessible rooms and offers free airport shuttle service. There's also a restaurant and lounge.

HAMPTON INN EAST

2311 N. Shadeland Ave.   359-9900
$$

Less than 10 minutes east of downtown Indianapolis via I-70, this 125-room inn includes an indoor pool, whirlpool and fitness area. Rooms are accessible to people with disabilities.

HOWARD JOHNSON'S EAST

7050 E. 21st St.   352-0481
$ (800) 1-GO-HOJO

This facility at I-70 and Shadeland Avenue contains 124 rooms and offers handicapped accessibility. Amenities include an outdoor pool and restaurant/lounge facilities.

HOLIDAY INN I-70 EAST

6990 E. 21st St.   359-5341
$$ (800) HOLIDAY

Eight miles east of downtown on I-70, this 184-room hotel has an indoor pool and whirlpool, a fitness facility, guest laundry, game room and in-room movies. Also available are Nintendo (say it's for the kids), free local phone service and in-room coffeemakers. Rooms are handicapped accessible. Also on-site is Damon's Restaurant (famous for barbecued ribs and chicken).

LAQUINTA INN EAST

7304 E. 21st St.   359-1021
$$ (800) 531-5900

A highly rated facility, this 122-room inn adjacent to the intersection of I-70 and Shadeland Avenue offers easy access to the east-side commercial and industrial area. Comfortable, handicapped-accessible rooms include a continental breakfast. There's an outdoor pool, an exercise facility and an on-site guest laundry.

MARRIOTT HOTEL

7202 E. 21st St.   352-1231
$$$ (800) 228-9290

Indoor and outdoor pools, as well as a fitness facility, are just some of the amenities available at this 252-room, highly rated hotel at I-70 and Shadeland Avenue. Rooms are accessible to the physically disabled. Durbin's Restaurant and Lounge offer dining and entertainment.

QUALITY INN EAST

3525 N. Shadeland Ave.   549-2222
$$ (800) 221-2222

This full-service, 123-room inn includes Jacuzzi tubs, an indoor pool and fitness room, game room and meeting rooms. There are also 12 honeymoon and executive suites with king-size waterbeds, wet bars and stereo systems. Rooms are handicapped-accessible. The on-site restaurant is Rafferty's, which serves breakfast, lunch and dinner; the lounge is the Ritz Nightclub, which offers a variety of live entertainment.

RAMADA INN INDIANAPOLIS

7701 E. 42nd St.   897-4000
$$ (800) 228-2828

Just off I-465 at the Pendleton Pike Exit, this 192-room facility also includes 11 meeting rooms, a large ballroom, indoor and outdoor pools and an exercise room. Rooms are handicapped- accessible. The Ramada offers easy access to the east-side commercial and industrial area, as well as to downtown Indianapolis.

SIGNATURE INN EAST
7610 Old Trails Rd.   353-6966
$$ *(800) 822-5252*

Primarily designed to serve business travelers, this 102-room hotel at I-465 and E. Washington Street offers free guest offices and meeting rooms, as well as free local phone service, breakfast and daily newspaper. Rooms, which are handicapped-accessible, include free cable TV; there's an outdoor pool available as well. Enjoy easy access to the east-side commercial and industrial area, as well as to the downtown district.

West

HoJo INN SPEEDWAY
2602 N. High School Rd.   291-8800
$$ *(800) 654-2000*

Conveniently sandwiched between the Indianapolis Motor Speedway (2 miles east) and Indianapolis Raceway Park (4 miles west), this 125-room facility is ideal for race fans. There's an outdoor pool and an on-site restaurant. Adjacent to the intersection of I-465 and Crawfordsville Road, the hotel offers easy access to the downtown area and the airport.

INDIANAPOLIS MOTOR SPEEDWAY MOTEL & GOLF CLUB
440 W. 16th St.   241-2500
$$

This 108-room motel on the grounds of the Indianapolis Motor Speedway offers easy access to the Speedway and the Hall of Fame Museum, as well as to the 18-hole, Pete Dye-designed Brickyard Crossing golf course. Other amenities include an outdoor pool, free airport shuttle service and an on-site restaurant (Brickyard Restaurant) and lounge (Flagroom Lounge). Rooms are handicapped-accessible.

RED ROOF INN SPEEDWAY
6415 Debonair Ln.   293-6881
$$ *(800) THE-ROOF*

This 108-room facility at the Clermont exit off I-465 is close to both the Indianapolis Motor Speedway and Indianapolis Raceway Park. The airport and downtown Indianapolis are also easily accessible. Rooms are handicapped-accessible.

SIGNATURE INN WEST
3850 Eagle View Dr.   299-6165
$$`   *(800) 822-5252*

At the intersection of 38th Street and I-465, this 99-room hotel features spacious, handicapped-accessible rooms, airport shuttle service and an outdoor pool. Other amenities include free local phone service, cable TV, breakfast express, and daily newspaper. Meeting rooms and offices are available to business travelers. Signature Inn West is convenient to the Indianapolis Motor Speedway and the airport (via I-465), the Indianapolis Museum of Art (via 38th Street E.), and downtown (via I-65).

South

ECONO LODGE SOUTH
4505 S. Harding St.   788-9361
$$ *(800) 424-4777*

Convenient to southwest-side businesses, as well as to downtown and the airport, this 150-room motel at I-465 and Harding Street offers free airport shuttle service. There's an outdoor pool, as well as an on-site restaurant and lounge. Rooms are handicapped-accessible.

COMFORT INN SOUTH
5040 S. East St.   783-6711
$$

Ten minutes from both the downtown area and the airport, this 104-room facility has both single rooms and suites; handicapped and nonsmoking accommodations are available. Amenities include free satellite TV, free continental breakfast, 24-hour hot coffee service, an outdoor pool and free parking.

DAYS INN SOUTH

450 Bixler Rd.   *788-0811*
$ *(800) 325-2525*

Five miles south of downtown, at the junction of I-465 South and U.S. 31, this facility has a meeting room with kitchen, a guest laundry and an outdoor pool and play area for children. Room rates include continental breakfast and cable TV. Rooms are handicapped-accessible.

DAYS INN SOUTHEAST

5151 Elmwood Dr.   *783-5555*
$ *(800) 325-2525*

At the intersection of I-465 and Emerson Avenue, this 119-room inn offers easy access to south-side businesses and downtown sites. Amenities include an outdoor pool. Rooms are handicapped-accessible.

HAMPTON INN SOUTH

7045 McFarland Blvd.   *889-0722*
$$ *(800) HAMPTON*

This 113-room inn provides free local phone service and cable TV, an indoor pool, and complimentary continental breakfast. For small groups in need of meeting space, Hampton Inn has a board room and hospitality suite available.

HOLIDAY INN EXPRESS

3514 S. Keystone Ave.   *788-3100*
$$ *(800) HOLIDAY*

This 62-room facility has suites with kitchenettes and whirlpools, free HBO and ESPN, free local phone service and a free breakfast bar. There are on-site meeting rooms. Guest quarters are handicapped-accessible.

HOLIDAY INN SOUTH HOLIDOME

520 E. Thompson Rd.   *787-8341*
$$ *(800) HOLIDAY*

This 184-room room facility at the junction of I-465 and U.S. Highway 31 S. is a 10-minute drive from downtown and the Greenwood Park Mall. On-site amenities include indoor and outdoor pools, a whirlpool and sauna, a health club and a play area for children. Enjoy Dining at Fountain on the Square restaurant and music and dancing in the Celebration Lounge. Free airport shuttle service is available. Also available are meeting/banquet rooms. Accommodations are handicapped-accessible.

HOLIDAY INN SOUTHEAST

5120 Victory Dr.   *783-7751*
$$ *(800) HOLIDAY*

This six-story high-rise at I-465 and S. Emerson Avenue is just minutes from downtown and the airport. Amenities include an outdoor pool, shuttle service and free parking, as well as a guest laundry and a game room. Enjoy on-site dining at Grenadyne's and cocktails at The Rusty Locker. Rooms are handicapped-accessible.

RAMADA INN SOUTH

4514 S. Emerson Ave.   *787-3344*
$$ *(800) 2-RAMADA*

This 193-room facility at the intersection of I-465 and Emerson Avenue (that translates to 8 miles southeast of the downtown district) has suites with fireplaces available for those chilly nights. Other amenities include an outdoor pool and a play area for children. Dining choices include Damon's (for ribs) and the Clubhouse (a sports bar and grill). Rooms are handicapped- accessible.

SIGNATURE INN SOUTH

4402 E. Creekview Dr.   *784-7006*
$$ *(800) 822-5252*

This 101-room hotel at I-65 and

Southport Road offers large, comfortable rooms with free local phone service, free cable TV (including HBO) and in-room recliners (when it's time to kick back and relax). Other amenities include a pool, fitness club access and on-site offices for business travelers. Rooms are handicapped-accessible. The hotel's location makes for easy access to Southport and Greenwood, as well as to downtown Indianapolis.

SUPER 8 MOTEL

4502 S. Harding St.   788-4774
$ (800) 800-8000

This 69-room motel at the intersection of I-465 and State Road 37 S. offers free local phone service and cable TV, free shuttle service to the airport and downtown and free continental breakfast. Rooms are handicapped-accessible.

Carmel

COURTYARD BY MARRIOTT

10290 N. Meridian St.   571-1110
$$ (800) 321-2211

For busy business travelers, this 149-room facility features meeting rooms, laundry and valet services and daily newspapers. And when it's time to unwind, take advantage of an indoor pool, whirlpool and fitness equipment. Other amenities include nonsmoking rooms, cable TV and free parking for cars and motorcoaches. There's an on-site restaurant/lounge and easy access to all northside commercial and retail districts.

GUEST QUARTERS SUITE HOTEL

11355 N. Meridian St.   844-7994
$$$ (800) 424-2900

This facility at the junction of I-465 and Meridian Street contains 138 suites, many of which are handicapped-accessible. Amenities include both indoor and outdoor

pools, fitness equipment and (for carb-loading) an on-site restaurant.

WYNDHAM GARDEN HOTEL

251 Pennsylvania Pkwy.   574-4600
$$

A 171-room hotel with lap pool, jacuzzi and workout room, the Wyndham also offers such amenities as coffeemakers and blow dryers in every room. Six rooms are specially designed to accommodate handicapped guests. There is a full-service restaurant and lounge on-site.

Greenwood

GREENWOOD INN FANTASUITE HOTEL

1117 E. Main St.   882-2211
Greenwood   (800) 444-STAY
$ for standard rooms
$$$ for fantasy suites

This 92-room suite hotel includes 24 fantasy suites as well as standard guest rooms. The fantasy suites bear names that reflect their theme and decor: Jungle Safari, complete with a bed enclosed in mosquito netting; Northern Lights, sleep inside an igloo; Sherwood Forest, the bed is tucked amid trees, and there's a whirlpool with a waterfall; and Alien Invasion, sleep in a flying saucer. Suites are more expensive than standard rooms, but then who among us wouldn't pay a little extra to live out our fantasies? There's also an outdoor pool.

Bed and Breakfasts

Downtown

LE CHATEAU DELAWARE

1456 N. Delaware St.   636-9156
$$-$$$

Just up the street from former President Benjamin Harrison's house, this Italian villa-like manor offers guests a choice of eight rooms, some with private baths, all furnished with either brass or poster beds and antiques. Amenities include fresh flowers in each room, daily newspapers and breakfast (homemade rolls and muffins, fresh fruit, juices, coffee). The 1,200-square-foot living room can be reserved for meetings, receptions, seminars, conferences or weddings. Le Chateau Delaware offers easy access to the downtown business district, as well as to Circle Centre, Market Square Arena and other downtown attractions.

THE HOFFMAN HOUSE
545 E. 11th St. 635-1701

An American Four-Square-style structure (c.1903), this facility offers two second-floor guest rooms furnished with antique double beds and handmade quilts. Continental plus breakfasts are served on china with silver utensils. The Hoffman House is convenient to the downtown business and entertainment district.

THE OLD NORTHSIDE
BED & BREAKFAST
1340 N. Alabama St. 635-9123
$$-$$$$ (800) 635-9127

Housed in a brick Romanesque Revival house (c. 1885) in the near-downtown Old Northside neighborhood, this bed and breakfast features original handcarved woodwork and handpainted murals on the ceilings and walls. Guests have their choice of a variety of themed rooms. The Literary Room includes memorabilia from the Golden Age of Indiana literature as well as such romantic touches as a fireplace and an extra-large Jacuzzi tub. The Theatre Room contains a large bed on a curtained stage with spotlights surrounding it, posters and playbills on the walls, and a Jacuzzi tub. The Bridal Room has a specially de-

signed shower and Jacuzzi as well as a fireplace. The 500 Room has auto racing mementos galore: For racing fans this is the ideal room to spend a night. Come prepared to eat — breakfasts here are scrumptious.

THE TRANQUIL CHERUB
2164 N. Capitol Ave. 923-9036
$$

In this 90-year-old Greek Revival-style house there are three rooms and a three-room attic suite, each with its own personality. Rogers' room includes a king-size bed with a headboard designed by innkeepers Thom and Barb Feit. The Gatsby Room features a foster-poster cannonball bed (queen-size), as well as art deco furnishings. The Victorian Room contains an antique iron and brass double bed and white wicker furniture. And Grannie's Attic, which consists of a sitting room, bath and bedroom, is furnished with an eclectic variety of antiques including a steamer trunk, a wicker baby buggy and a Victorian fainting sofa.

Breakfast consists of juice, freshly made coffee and homemade muffins or breads. This adults-only bed and breakfast offers easy access to the downtown area, as well as to the Children's Museum, the Indianapolis Art Museum, and the Speedway.

North

BOONE DOCKS ON THE RIVER
7159 Edgewater Pl. 257-3671
$$

Tucked alongside the White River in a 1920s English Tudor that many people consider a storybook house, this bed and breakfast contains a garden-level suite with private entrance and white wicker furnishings. Guests also have access to the Common Room where they can relax around a piano or beside a fireplace. There are two outside decks— the Main Deck, shaded by a huge ancient oak tree, is where breakfast is served when weather permits; the Riverside Deck, shaded by a weeping willow, is a good place to contemplate or simply to watch the heron and geese that fish the river.

Boone Docks is run by Lynne and Michael Boone. Michael is the great, great, great, great grandson of legendary pioneer Daniel Boone.

As far as credit cards go, Boone Docks on the River only accepts American Express.

THE BRICK STREET INN
175 S. Main St., Zionsville   873-9177
$$

In the heart of Zionsville's quaint village district, this romantic inn pampers guests with down comforters and gourmet breakfasts and is furnished with antiques and reproductions. There are five rooms, each furnished with antiques and reproductions. There's also a hot tub available. Cozy up to the fireplace, stroll the streets or take a twilight carriage ride.

THE NUTHATCH
7161 Edgewater Pl.   257-2660
$$

This 1920s French country cottage overlooks the White River and contains two guest rooms. There's an attached greenhouse and a private terrace — the latter is a great place to have your morning coffee or tea. The Wren's Nest is an intimate downstairs hideaway complete with private entrance. It contains a queen-size bed, a cozy sitting area, and a bath with a claw-footed tub; the decor includes stained glass and antique lighting fixtures. There's a small deck in the herb garden outside.

Breakfast choices range from Hoosier home cooking to heart-smart, vegetarian, herbal or exotic— all prepared by Joan Morris, a gourmet cook and culinary instructor, who operates The Nuthatch with her husband Bernie.

THE FREDERICK-TALBOTT INN
13805 Allisonville Rd., Fishers   578-3600
$$-$$$

Tastefully appointed in English Country decor, this inn offers guests a choice of 12 rooms complete with antique furnishings. Set in a lovely country landscape, the inn is just up the road from Conner Prairie, one of the country's premier living history museums.

South

THE RICHARDSON HOUSE
2422 E. Southport Rd.
Southport   781-1119
$$

Just 7 miles south of downtown Indianapolis, the Richardson House is a Queen Anne house (c. 1900) with three extended-stay, adults-only guest rooms, each with kitchen and bath facilities. Rental is on a weekly or monthly basis. Amenities include all cooking and eating utensils, toaster, coffeemaker, cable TV and free local phone service. The Richardson House does not accept credit cards.

PERSIMMON TREE BED & BREAKFAST
One N. Madison Ave., Greenwood   889-0849
$$

Built in the 1880s, this bed and breakfast in Greenwood's Old Town district offers rooms decorated with antiques. A wraparound veranda, beveled glass windows, claw-foot tubs, and lace curtains lend an air of old-fashioned elegance.

East

FRIENDLINESS WITH A FLAIR
5214 E. 20th Pl.   356-3149
$

Offering two lovely nonsmoking rooms, this bed and breakfast is in a residential area. Weather permitting, guests can have breakfast in a Florida room. Hostess Loretta Whitten goes out of her way to make you feel at home. Staying here is like staying in the home of an old friend.

Friendliness With a Flair does not accept credit cards.

Inside
Restaurants

As you peruse this chapter devoted to one of our favorite activities — dining out — you'll find plenty of possibilities, putting to rest once and for all that old saw about there being no place to eat in Indianapolis.

In fact, the choices prove so enticing that our favorite thing to make for dinner is reservations. Downtown and the Broad Ripple neighborhood offer an abundance of dining possibilities, and we've dedicated ourselves to trying them.

Though the choices here have traditionally been heavy on American, Italian and Chinese, within the last 10 or so years the city has seen a wider variety of ethnic cuisines, including Indian, Korean, Ethiopian and Russian. Fine dining opportunities have expanded as well. In other words, if you take the time to look, you're bound to discover lots of great food and enjoyable ambiance.

And you'll probably turn up some excellent eateries that we haven't even mentioned here. In fact, we're sure you will. We haven't included every commendable restaurant in Indianapolis for the simple reason that we haven't been to them all, at least not yet. One of our goals for the next edition is to expand this chapter with even more suggestions, including plenty from the new downtown mall, Circle Centre, which opened as we were wrapping up this edition. And if you run across a great little place we should know about, drop us a line. We'll be sure to check it out.

Photo: The Indianapolis Star & News

Dick Clark's American Bandstand Grill is a chain restaurant, and a popular one at that.

We've arranged this chapter by food category, so your favorite specialties should be easy to find. Indianapolis is such a drivable city — you can get just about anywhere in a half-hour or less. So if you have a passion for pepperoni pizza, you'll quickly find a place to satisfy your taste in the pizza category. We have, however, excluded most chain restaurants, primarily because you probably already know all about them. Here we've tried to spotlight some of our best local eateries in a wide variety of categories.

When you head out for a taste of Indianapolis, be sure to call ahead for current hours or to make reservations. Though often not needed, or even accepted, at many casual eateries, fine dining often calls for a little advance planning.

And to help with such planning, we've included a handy price guide, though remember it is only a guide — menus change and prices often fluctuate. Prices are based on dinner for two, excluding cocktails and wine, appetizers and desserts, tax and tip.

$	$12 or less
$$	$13 to $22
$$$	$23 to $39
$$$$	More than $40

(Restaurants mentioned here accept major credit cards — at least Mastercard and Visa — unless otherwise noted.)

Keep in mind that a check total jumps considerably when you add on appetizers, drinks and desserts. Likewise, you can hold down costs at a pricier place by passing on the extras or by splurging only on dessert (our favorite ploy). And prices may prove significantly lower at lunch.

So grab a friend or go alone, but be sure to explore the terrific restaurants around here. Sample the specialties, try something new and report your discoveries back to us. We're always looking for a favorite new restaurant.

Enjoy.

Afghani

KABUL

1355 W. 86th St.　　　　257-1213
$$

Check out the deliciously different Afghani fare (don't miss the aush soup) at this comfortable, casual north-side restaurant that was due to open in larger quarters just across the parking lot from its former location by late 1995.

American

BOMBAY BICYCLE CLUB

9111 N. Michigan Rd.
$$　　　　872-3446

Those who work at the nearby Pyramids office complex have made the BBC a popular spot for after-work drinks and dinner. The casual restaurant, which attracts plenty of northwestsiders on the weekends, features a varied menu with chicken, pasta, fresh seafood, steaks and daily specials.

BRICKYARD RESTAURANT

4400 W. 16th St.
$$　　　　241-2500

A trip to the Indianapolis Motor Speedway wouldn't be complete without stopping in at the Brickyard Restaurant. You're likely to see some famous faces in May; look for car owners and drivers such as A.J. Foyt. But be sure to try the specialty prime rib at this casual eatery anytime.

CORK AND CUISINE

3316 E. 86th St.　　　　846-7300
$$$

Chef Ray Pichetti, formerly of the Provincial Kitchen, now creates his seasonally changing specialties at the Cork and Cuisine. (The Provincial Kitchen has, regrettably, closed.) You'll find menu icons denot-

Chez Jean

RESTAURANT FRANCAIS ᵴᴅ INN
"Since 1957"

Serving Fresh Fish, Veal, Lamb, Shrimp, Duck & Mussels

Daily Specials – Enjoy the Same Country French
personalized service for your special luncheon or dinner

Sun. 11 a.m. to 2 p.m., Mon.-Fri. 11 a.m. to 1:30 p.m. & Tues.-Sat. 6 to 10 p.m.   VISA   MasterCard   AMERICAN EXPRESS

10 Min. from Airport on St. Rd. 67 South • 831-0870 • 20 Min. from Downtown

ing heart-healthy choices, large portions and vegetarian dishes, a carry over from the PK. The quality and creativity remain as well; Chef Pichetti has a knack for combining flavors, such as the pancetta bacon, fresh basil and sweet onions in the bucatini amatriciana. Try the steak and potato soup, Nonna's bistecca or the delicious Marco Polo: sauteed scallops and tiger shrimp with pasta.

DALTS
8702 Keystone Crossing   846-7226
$$

You may have to wait for a table at this popular Keystone at the Crossing eatery, especially at lunchtime. But once seated you'll enjoy the varied menu. The seasoned fries are always a hit, and we especially like the chicken salad quesadilla. A favorite among Fashion Mall shoppers and office workers, Dalts is also a good place to take the kids (they'll love the milk shakes).

DEL FRISCO'S
3 E. Market St.   687-8888
$$$

Overlooking Monument Circle, this second-floor restaurant occupies a prime location. Don't miss its prime cuts, but the

pasta dishes rate highly too. Reservations are a must, even at lunch, and remember it has a formal atmosphere: nice linens on well-set tables amid a power broker ambiance. Be sure to notice Monument Tower's Art Deco flourishes.

GRAFFITI'S
50 S. Capitol Ave.   231-3970
$$

So named for the paper-topped tables with crayons for doodling, this restaurant's food is hardly trivial. The Westin Hotel's second-floor eatery features American cuisine in an upscale yet casual atmosphere; you'll see diners dressed in everything from jeans to suits. Downtown power-lunchers like the convenient and tasty buffet.

DICK CLARK'S
AMERICAN BANDSTAND GRILL
3550 E. 86th St.   848-2002
$$

A chain, yes, but it's so popular we couldn't overlook it. Diners enjoy great burgers, ribs, fajitas and pasta amid the high-energy American Bandstand-themed decor. You can also purchase souvenir T-shirts, sweatshirts, jackets, CDs and other Bandstand merchandise.

THE DINER

9762 W. Washington St.   839-9464
$

If you're looking for a slice of Americana, look no further. This '50s-era dining-car-style restaurant serves up a great breakfast as well as such short order specialties as burgers, fries and tenderloins. These aluminium-clad landmarks once dotted U.S. 40 (a.k.a. the old National Road or, near the city, Washington Street), and The Diner is a reminder of a time when the route saw lots of cross-country traffic. The very reasonable prices (the $7 rib-eye dinner ranks as the most expensive) will remind you of an earlier era as well.

DODD'S TOWN HOUSE

5694 N. Meridian St.   257-1872
$$$

This N. Meridian Street landmark, wedged in among the beautiful homes in this historic neighborhood, has operated here — under different names — for 150 years. Originally the Seven-Mile Inn (because, you guessed it, the place is 7 miles from the Circle), Dodd's specializes in real American cooking. You just can't go wrong with their steaks and fried chicken. And don't miss dessert. Have a cup of coffee and enjoy a slice of blackberry or chocolate cream pie.

DURBIN'S AT THE MARRIOTT

7202 E. 71st St.   352-1231
$$

Though this hotel restaurant is a fine choice in its own right, a pleasant if typical hotel dining room, what we find special are the recipes, such as chicken velvet soup from the old downtown L.S. Ayres restaurant.

HOLLYHOCK HILL

8110 N. College Ave.   251-2294
$$$

Like Dodd's and the Iron Skillet, the popular Hollyhock Hill offers family-style

dining and plates full of fried chicken. Be sure to try the house salad dressing. Tucked into a residential area between Broad Ripple and Nora, this comfortable restaurant boasts a homey ambiance.

HOULIHAN'S

6101 N. Keystone Ave.   257-3285
$$

A mall restaurant without the mall look. Houlihan's fine food, including burgers, steaks, chicken and pasta, also belies its location, but be prepared for less than speedy service. Quick, can you find the old Chesterfield Kings advertisement among the memorabilia that fills the walls?

ILLUSIONS

969 Keystone Way   575-8312
$$$

Magic is the theme at this Carmel restaurant where magicians perform tableside at dinner (and also in the lounge). The food's great too, and the menu offers a wide enough variety that just about everyone can find a favorite amid the offerings of fresh fish, chicken, steaks and duck. School-age kids enjoy Illusions as a special-occasion treat; adults like to catch the magic acts in the bar.

IRON SKILLET

2489 W. 30th St.   923-6353
$$$

Comfort food such as well-seasoned fried chicken, pan-fried walleyed pike, New York strip and all the sides fills the menu at this restaurant set between two golf courses and across from the city's Soapbox Derby Hill. A courteous staff, that also happens to know many of the patrons, serve it all family style.

KEYSTONE COOKER

8601 Keystone Crossing   574-0790
$$

Another popular Keystone at the Crossing lunch spot, the Cooker is great for dinner too. You'll find tasty American specialties such as meatloaf, pot roast and plenty of good sandwiches and fries. But don't fill up on the delicious biscuits and butter your server will bring out (although we can't resist asking for a second basket).

MALIBU GRILL
4503 E. 82nd St.   PHONE?
$$

Voted by readers of *Indianapolis Monthly* magazine as a restaurant worth its sometimes considerable wait for a table, the Malibu Grill excels at offering something for everybody, from pizza and pasta to steak and burgers. Tasty bread with marinara for dipping is on the table right away. It's casual, trendy and comfortable.

MARBLE'S SOUTHERN COOKERY
2310 Lafayette Rd.   687-0631
$$

Marble's and mom have good food in common — that is, if you come from the South. This buffet's ribs, chops, catfish and side dishes all have that distinctive taste reminiscent of areas south of the Mason-Dixon Line. A tidy place (though on a past-its-prime thoroughfare), Marble's does a brisk business with an ever-changing menu. Don't miss the bread pudding.

NORMAN'S
39 W. Jackson Pl.   269-2545
$$

Be sure to stop in here when browsing though Union Station. It's truly a beautiful setting, with the former train station's original barrel-vaulted ceiling, terrazzo floor and leaded glass windows. The food proves excellent as well, with plenty of variety; you'll find sandwiches, steaks, seafood, pasta.

PENN ST. BAR AND GRILL
135 N. Pennsylvania St.   231-6050
$$$

If it's dessert you want, it's dessert you'll get. Renowned for its death-by-chocolate after-meal treats, this downtown restaurant also features a fine selection of pasta dishes. The chef keeps the rotating menu lively with an array of health-conscious chicken and beef entrees. But don't be afraid to loosen the belt and indulge in dessert and enjoy the stylish decor.

PLUMP'S LAST SHOT
6416 Cornell Ave.   257-5867
$$

Bobby Plump is an Indiana basketball legend. He sunk the basket that won the state championship in 1954 for Milan High School, the smallest school ever to win state. His son, Jonathan, runs this new Broad Ripple restaurant that, in addition to loads of basketball memorabilia, offers real Hoosier specialties such as venison and bluegill.

RICK'S CAFE AMERICAIN
39 W. Jackson Pl.   634-6666
$$$

An extensive menu with lots of appetizers, salads, sandwiches and such entrees as pasta, chicken, seafood and steaks, plus live jazz and a convenient and comfortable

---

Those who like to dine al fresco need only walk through the popular Broad Ripple neighborhood, where they'll find nearly a dozen restaurants that offer sidewalk cafe-style dining.

Insiders' Tips

Java Joints

Though we can't quite claim the same passion for coffee that you'll find in San Francisco or Seattle, Indianapolis boasts plenty of places to enjoy a hot cup of joe. Take along a book — or a friend — and soak up some atmosphere.

THE ABBEY

771 Massachusetts Ave.   269-8426
5909 E. 86th St.   598-9864

You'll find comfy chairs and an eclectic crowd — from college kids to retirees — and delicious pastries and desserts to enjoy along with the java.

BORDER'S BOOKS AND MUSIC

8785 N. Keystone Ave.   574-1775

A favorite bookstore expanded, and its new location includes a coffee bar, something regular patrons have been pining for since competitor Barnes and Noble opened. Expect to see all sorts of customers, from families to young professionals, since Borders has a large and loyal following.

BARNES AND NOBLE

3748 E. 82nd St.   594-7525

Featuring terrific Starbucks coffee, this massive bookstore draws plenty of professional types, reading and writing group members and a cadre of coffee shop regulars.

CAFE PATACHOU

4911 N. Pennsylvania St.   925-2823

This neighborhood cafe, which in addition to coffee also serves up excellent omelets and cinnamon toast, attracts moms with kids (there's a toy-

Photo: The Indianapolis Star & News

The original Broad Ripple Coffee Pub attracts a diverse crowd.

stocked play corner), couples sharing *The New York Times* and *Chicago Tribune* and a variety of neighborhood regulars.

CATH INC.

126 N. Delaware St.	685-0600
222 E. Market St.	634-0600
705 E. 54th St.	255-1075

With its three locations (two downtown and one in the Meridian-Kessler neighborhood) Cath serves a wide range of customers. Office workers stop in for a "Good Morning" muffin and a cup of mocha java before heading to work. The Meridian-Kessler location attracts an assortment of regulars from this diverse neighborhood.

COFFEE ZON

137 E. Ohio St.	684-0432

This downtown shop lost some of its hipness when its original owners sold and the place moved a few doors down Ohio Street. But it remains a handy spot to stop in for a cup before work.

CORNERSTONE

Coffee and Espresso Bar

651 E. 54th St.	726-1360

This newish shop, furnished in American garage-sale chic, has become popular — like Cath, its nearby neighbor — with young people from the Broad Ripple area as well as dog-walkers and baby stroller-pushers from Meridian-Kessler. (We've seen dogs waiting patiently outside the door, though there are outside tables.)

FINALE DESSERT CAFE

3953 E. 82nd St.	841-3953

The focus here is on desserts, but you'll also find excellent java to enjoy along with a serving of the supreme chocolate mud cake.

FINE GRIND

111 Monument Circle	635-2223
39 Jackson Pl. (Union Station)	635-2924

These downtown shops sell fresh roasted coffee and accessories in addition to offering walk-up counter service.

40 WEST COFFEE CAFE

40 W. Jackson Pl.	686-1414

This street-level coffee shop in the building that houses the Omni Severin offers wonderful salads, sandwiches, desserts and coffees.

ORIGINAL BROAD RIPPLE COFFEE PUB

6123 N. Guilford Ave.	254-0646

A darkened interior and wildly painted walls attract a crowd as diverse as its Broad Ripple environs.

VILLAGE IDIOT

6360 N. Guilford Ave.   257-5556

Popular among Gen-X'ers, the Village Idiot boasts good coffee, lively conversation and tasty desserts in one of the Victorian cottages that line the streets of Broad Ripple.

Union Station location make Rick's a fine choice for a casual yet cozy evening.

RICK'S CAFE BOATYARD
4050 Dandy Tr.   290-9300
$$$

This location on the water at Eagle Creek reservoir offers a nice view (especially from the outdoor deck), live music and a varied menu fresh fish, steaks, chicken and pasta. It's become quite popular; the wait for a table can be long. If it proves too long, do what we do: Find a seat in the bar, enjoy the music and order from there.

SHAFFER'S
6125 Hillside Ave.   253-1404
$$$

Shaffer's is the city's only fondue restaurant — that's right, fondue. Though perhaps reminiscent of early '70s dinner parties, Shaffer's take on this retro classic proves excellent — and a lot of fun. We're especially fond of the dessert fondues and the wine list.

TELLER'S CAGE
1 Indiana Sq.   266-5211
$$$

The food's great at the Teller's Cage (we especially enjoy the steaks, veal and lamb), but most people go to this restaurant to enjoy the view as well. The restaurant, on the 35th floor of the NBD bank tower, offers a great view of the city skyline, especially nice at night.

Steakhouses

BROAD RIPPLE STEAK HOUSE
842 Westfield Blvd.   253-8101
$$$

Featuring a Southwestern flair to the cuisine, the Broad Ripple Steak House features hand-cut steaks and a number of excellent pasta and seafood dishes. You can also enjoy outdoor dining at this popular corner establishment. Indoors, you'll find a Southwestern-inspired decor as well.

BYNUM'S STEAKHOUSE
3850 S. Meridian St.   784-9880
$$

A south-side landmark, Bynum's serves up thick, fresh-cut steaks, prime rib and lobster tail to very loyal customers in a nice-but-not-fancy setting. Situated in a residential area, Bynum's boasts a sort of antique themed decor: Old signs and tools decorate the walls. Charming glass lamps adorn each table.

Insiders' Tips

Food court fans should check out downtown's Union Station. You'll find enough fast food options at this "festival marketplace" to please the whole family.

GEORGE'S PLACE

2727 E. 86th St.   255-7064
$$$

Want an especially thick steak to-night? No problem at George's, where steaks are cut at your table to your exact specifications. Diners can also enjoy a variety of seafood selections and sample the daily special. You'll see lots of suit-and-tie types, especially at lunch; George's proves popular with Keystone at the Crossing power brokers.

MOUNTAIN JACK'S

5910 E. 82nd St.   842-5225
3650 W. 86th St.   872-4500
$$$

Both locations of this popular steakhouse serve excellent prime rib, sea-food and, of course, top-notch steaks in a casual atmosphere. We love the filet; the vegetable soup is tasty too. Servers build your salad at the table to your specifica-tions.

RUTH'S CHRIS STEAK HOUSE

9445 Threel Rd.
(96th and Keystone)   844-1155
$$$$

Yes, it's a chain, but what a chain it is. This is the place for beef, and the steaks (and everything else, including the lamb) are incredibly tender and well cooked. Service is professional and at-tentive, and the English lodge-style de-cor is handsome and classic. But cheap it's not. Everything is a la carte, and the selections do add up. This is definitely either special occasion or expense ac-count dining. Still, it's worth it.

ST. ELMO STEAK HOUSE

127 S. Illinois St.   635-0636
$$$$

Known for its mammoth, done-just-right steaks, extra spicy shrimp cocktail and impeccable black-tie service, St. Elmo

maintains nearly a century of fine dining. Next to the posh Canterbury Hotel, the downtown restaurant plays host to the city's business elite and celebrities passing through. Even Metallica stopped in. You don't have to be a rock star to afford St. Elmo but, like Ruth's Chris, this isn't an everyday kind of place. If someone offers to take you, go.

Asian

BANGKOK

7269 N. Keystone Ave.   255-7799
$$

You'll find excellent Thai fare at this unassuming strip mall restaurant. Bangkok wins plenty of local awards, and if you want to sample a variety of the tasty, sometimes spicy, dishes, try the lunch buffet. Don't miss the soup and the Thai toast.

DARUMA

3508 W. 86th St.   875-9727
$$

This Japanese restaurant offers deli-cious and unusual specialties beautifully presented. Older kids might enjoy the novelty of being seated Japanese style (see our Kidstuff chapter) and being served by the attentive, kimono-clad wait staff. Daruma offers excellent sushi, sukiyaki and tempura, as well as steak.

FORBIDDEN CITY

2605 E. 65th St.   257-7388
3837 N. High School Rd.   298-3588
3938 E. 82nd St.   845-8989
3517 W. 86th St.   872-2888
$$

If hot and sour soup is your barometer of fine Chinese food, then Forbidden City deserves your attention. The restaurant, with north and west-side locations, plus a superb north-side buffet and a northwest-side express, also does a fine job with other

Houlihan's is a mall restaurant without the mall look.

offerings from an extensive menu that offers Hunan, Szechuan and Mandarin cuisine. We especially like the green pepper beef and cashew chicken. Call ahead for dinner reservations, but you can get quick service on carry out too. Or stop in at lunchtime and enjoy an entree, soup and eggroll for a very reasonable price.

KANG'S EXPRESS
2989 W. 71st St.   297-3451
$$

The specialty at this little northwest-side establishment is the excellent Korean fare. Be sure to try the spicy kimchi (fermented vegetables) and the chop chae bab (a sweet stir fry with rice noodles). Prices are low, authenticity and quality high.

SAKURA
7201 N. Keystone Ave.   259-4171
$$

This north-side sushi bar, quite popular among the local Japanese community, serves excellent seafood beautifully presented. If sushi isn't a favorite, try the tempura; it's served in lovely lacquer boxes. But do give the sushi a try. We love the softshell crab, the futomaki and

the mackerel. If time is a concern, keep in mind that a lunch hour can easily stretch into an hour and a half (or even two if you really get into the convivial atmosphere that sharing sushi inspires).

SANSUI
1329 S. Range Line Rd.   848-9050
$$

Another good option for sushi, Sansui is large and spacious. A helpful staff will gladly explain the menu offerings and offer guidance for those unsure about what sort of sushi to try. Combination platters are a good option. Sansui also offers tasty tempura and steaks.

SIZZLING WOK/THIEN HUONG
7280 N. Michigan Rd.   298-9001
$$

Though this northwest-side eatery offers Chinese food as well, try the excellent Vietnamese fare such as sauteed beef rolls, Vietnamese pancakes and fish in clay pot. The bare bones interior is nothing fancy, but with the fresh vegetables, sophisticated flavors and cooked-just-right seafood, you won't miss a fancy place setting.

Classic Northern Italian Cuisine At Its **BEST**.

Extensive Wine Selection
Cocktails • Banquet Facilities

838 Broad Ripple Ave.
for reservations, call
253-7475

"Join Us For The Finest In Casual, Elegant Dining"

YEN CHING

1300 E. 86th St.	844-1810
8512 E. Washington St.	899-3270

$$

A local favorite, Yen Ching specializes in Mandarin and Szechuan cuisine. Try the house specials: moo shu pork, sizzling beef and Peking duck. Pricier at dinner, the lunch selections offer good value and an easy-on-the-wallet way to check out some of Yen Ching's specialties.

Cafeterias

GRAY BROS.

555 S. Indiana Ave.
Mooresville   831-3345
$

This Mooresville cafeteria is plenty popular among Indianapolis residents who don't mind the drive if the food is good. And at Gray Bros., it is. Nothing fancy, just hearty cafeteria fare served up at reasonable prices.

JONATHON BYRD'S

100 Byrd Way
Greenwood   881-8888
$

This giant among cafeterias can serve 400 diners (with banquet facilities for hundreds more). Locals of all sorts flock to this Greenwood establishment for traditional cafeteria fare: a little bit of everything.

LAUGHNER'S

General Office
4004 U.S. Hwy. 31 S.   783-2907
$

A local family began this statewide cafeteria chain around 1900. And with Hoosiers' fondness for roast beef, baked fish, fried chicken and liver and onions — not to mention macaroni and cheese, green beans and fruit pies — the chain will likely be around a lot longer.

MCL

Corporate Office
2730 E. 62nd St.   257-5425
$

An offshoot of the original Laughner clan started up another cafeteria chain, and the two restaurants serve a similar menu. Though cafeteria devotees could probably spot the subtle differences, we think MCL and Laughner's are both very good at what they do.

Bakeries

Those with a sweet tooth — or a taste for toast — will appreciate the baked goods from these local ovens.

BOYDEN'S SOUTHSIDE BAKERY

3953 S. Meridian St.   784-2992

Offering quick service on decorated cakes, Boyden's opens at 4 AM every day with plenty of doughnuts, danish and coffee cakes for early risers.

BREAD OF LIFE BAKERY

2274 W. 86th St.   872-5251

Delicious bread that makes wonderful toast is the specialty here. We especially like the honey millet variety. Atlas Supermarket also stocks the hearty loaves.

CHARLOTTE'S BAKERY

2142 N. Mitthoeffer Rd.   897-9671

Eastsiders stop in at Charlotte's for fresh doughnuts, pies, cakes and cookies.

CRAWFORD'S BAKERY AND DELI

1609 N. Capitol Ave.   924-2494

This is a popular stop for workers on their way downtown and for employees of Methodist Hospital right across the street. Regulars love the doughnuts, Danish and long Johns. And the deli serves up a great quick lunch.

GREAT HARVEST BREAD CO.

1069 Broad Ripple Ave.   251-2222
1426 W. 86th St.   872-2222
8923 S. Meridan St.   885-9999
11856 Allisonville Rd., Fishers   849-5555

The line is out the door on Saturday morning, but the fresh baked loaves are worth the wait. We're particularly fond of the sprouted wheat and cinnamon walnut. Try a slice; they give free samples.

KRISPY KREME

5060 W. 38th St.   299-3587
6706 E. 82nd St.   578-3081
1080 E. 86th St.   581-0095

This new chain has wooed plenty of local doughnut lovers since it opened, and we must admit we're converts. Don't miss the warm-from-the-oven glazed doughnuts and the apple cinnamon variety.

LONG'S BAKERY

2300 W. 16th St.	632-3741
39 Jackson Pl. (Union Station)	635-4252
2301 E. Southport Rd.	783-1442

There's nothing like a Long's doughnut and a hot cup of coffee to get you going on a cold morning.

ROSELYN BAKERIES

General Office
2425 E. 30th St.   925-8901

These corner bakeries — nearly 40 of them scattered across the city — offer great sweets. We can't get enough of the delicious powdered sugar-covered cookies called Mexican wedding cakes and the seasonally decorated goodies.

TAYLOR'S BAKERY

6216 Allisonville rd.   *251-9575*

Three generations of this family have been serving up sweet treats — and three generations have been enjoying them. Try the coffee cakes and danish.

Caribbean

CALABASH CARIBBEAN RESTAURANT

3402 N. Illinois St.   926-9751
$$

Yes, the neighborhood has seen better days, but don't let that keep you away from this tiny Caribbean eatery. The owner, born in the Virgin Islands, serves up excellent kingfish, jerk chicken, conch chowder and the "Bob Marley burger." If you're lucky, you'll get to hear some live reggae. Prices are easy on the wallet, and the Caribbean specialties, also available for carry-out, are great (so is the jungle punch).

Continental

GLASS CHIMNEY

12901 Old Meridian St.   844-0921
$$$$

Long a favorite for special occasions and expense account dinners, the Glass Chimney boasts traditional continental dining in an elegant atmosphere. Discriminating diners will also find an extensive wine list and a selection of vintage ports. For more casual dining, wine and cocktails, try the Deeter's Nasch and Nip next door. (At both you'll find excellent selections from Chef Dieter Puska.)

EAGLE'S NEST

Hyatt Regency, 1 S. Capitol Ave.   632-1234
$$$$

One of the city's most popular choices for a romantic dinner, the Eagle's Nest, atop the Hyatt Regency downtown, offers beautiful views of the city, and the rooftop room actually rotates. If you can stop staring into each other's eyes, try the prime rib, filet mignon or the salmon. If you're keeping an eye on costs, note that extras such as salads and sides are indeed extra.

THE MARKER

Adam's Mark Hotel
2544 Executive Dr.   381-6146
$$$

Service is wonderful at The Marker; relax and let them take care of everything. Don't go looking for innovative cuisine. Rather, The Marker offers classic choices such as salmon, veal, chicken and beef deliciously prepared. And everything on the dessert tray looks good too. Choose something luscious and enjoy the country lodge ambiance.

MIDTOWN GRILL

815 E. Westfield Blvd.   253-1141
$$$

Minimalist decor, attentive service and excellent food characterize the trendy Midtown Grill. The high energy level creates a vibrant atmosphere. Try the wild mushroom ravioli for a delicious vegetarian selection.

THE RESTAURANT
AT THE CANTERBURY HOTEL

123 S. Illinois St.   634-3000
$$$$

This vintage building received a facelift during Circle Centre construction. Now as beautiful outside as in, it boasts a distinctive ambiance: plush upholstery, cushy carpeting and well-set tables. This well-regarded restaurant features Continental and American cuisine; it's known for the Dover sole meuniere and rack of lamb, as well as the dessert souffles (which must be ordered in advance). Afternoon tea is served Monday through Saturday from 4 PM to 5:30 PM; be sure to make reservations.

Delis

CALIFORNIA CONNECTION

2134 E. 62nd St.   253-9993
$

This Broad Ripple deli offers a taste of the West Coast with its grilled eggplant sandwich and garden pizza with veggies and pesto. Don't go looking for brisket or a corned beef on rye with mustard and a pickle; try instead the marinated potato salad or the linguine with butter, olive oil and white wine. No credit cards are accepted.

SHAPIRO'S DELICATESSEN

808 S. Meridian St.   631-4041
2730 W. 86th St.   872-7255
$

A local landmark since 1905, Shapiro's sets the standard around here for deli fare. And "around here" means the Midwest when it comes to Shapiro's — it's that good. Patrons line up daily for fresh sliced roast beef, chicken soup with matzo balls and thick, creamy cheesecake; or you can order it all to go. You just can't beat these Kosher specialties. You can stack up the corned beef sandwich against New York's Carnegie Deli any day. No credit cards are accepted.

SCHLOTZSKY'S DELI

9605 E. Washington St.   899-3737
3958 E. 82nd St.   849-6636
$

These casual delis are, admittedly, a chain (out of Austin, Texas), but they bake their own terrific sourdough bread with which they make tasty deli sandwiches as well as pizzas. We love the smoked turkey sandwich and the chicken and pesto pizza. The soup of the day is a good bet too.

Drive-ins

BILL'S FABULOUS '50s

6310 Rockville Rd.   244-1950
$

This kitschy establishment features roller skating carhops who balance trays

Henry Grattan is a great place to enjoy a just-poured Harp and conversation.

loaded with frosty mugs of root beer, onion rings, Coney dogs and tenderloins. Turn on your headlights for service; while you're waiting, the kids can pop a quarter in the outdoor jukebox that's stocked with such titles as "Sh-Boom, Sh-Boom" and "Monster Mash." Service isn't exactly speedy, so enjoy the retro experience and check out the classic cars. Bill's doesn't accept credit cards.

Dog 'N Suds
5914 Crawfordsville Rd.   *241-4746*

You'll get surprisingly quick service at this shiny new drive-in around the corner from the Indianapolis Motor Speedway, and you'll find delicious root beer, crispy fries and really tender tenderloins. The city's newest drive-in, located in the parking lot of a busy strip mall, is quite popular, and parking places fill up fast on weekend evenings. No credit cards are accepted.

Edward's Drive-In
2126 Sherman Dr.   *786-1638*

This longtime southeast-side establishment serves up excellent jumbo tenderloins and tasty onion rings; the Coneys are pretty good too. Curbside service is quick, but you can also eat indoors. Edward's doesn't accept credit cards.

Mug 'N Bun
5211 W. 10th St.   *244-5669*

This is certainly a popular spot on weekend evenings. You won't find roller skating carhops, just good food and good service. We love the thick onion rings, rich and creamy root beer, Coneys and tenderloins — all the traditional drive-in fare. There's also a (heated) outdoor seating area. No credit cards are accepted.

Ethiopian

Queen of Sheba Ethiopian Restaurant
936 Indiana Ave.   *638-8426*
$$

Take along some friends and enjoy sharing food around the messob, a woven, lidded table upon which a platter of food is placed. All the dishes are presented atop a thin crepe-like bread called injera; diners tear off hunks of bread and scoop up bites of such Ethiopian specialties as cega (tender beef in a red pepper sauce), yemisir alecha (yellow split peas) or tekil gomen (cabbage and carrots). The food is unusual and downright delicious.

French

CHANTECLAIR
2501 S. High School Rd.   243-1040
$$$$

This is a great place to celebrate any special occasion; it's especially nice for a romantic anniversary dinner. You'll enjoy the elegant atmosphere and fine French cuisine; we recommend the sauteed shrimp and scallops. A strolling violinist adds to the romantic ambiance. Note that jackets are required for men.

CHEZ JEAN RESTAURANT FRANCAIS
9027 S. Ind. 67, Camby   831-0870
$$$$

Barbara and Jean Milesi operated this charming restaurant for more than 30 years; their son now runs this French favorite. Longtime patrons wax practically poetic over the bouillabaisse and crepes Suzette. Make reservations for dinner and also reserve a room at the adjacent inn for a close-to-home romantic getaway.

RENEE'S
839 E. Westfield Blvd.   251-4142
$$

This cozy country French restaurant consistently wins local awards for best Broad Ripple restaurant, best dessert and best carry-out. And it's deserving of such kudos. We love the chicken dijonnaise, ragout niçoise, the apple dumpling and the banana cream pie. It's also tough to top Renee's in the casually romantic category. The place is small and fills up fast; though you can probably walk in and get a table at lunch on a Tuesday, make reservations for a weekend dinner.

Z'BISTRO
160 S. Main St., Zionsville   873-1888
$$$

Another delightful country French restaurant, Z'Bistro is definitely upscale. The food is excellent, as is the wine list, and the wait staff is knowledgeable about both. Relax and enjoy the atmosphere with its fresh flowers, well-set tables and antique bar. Linger over a bottle of wine, then take a stroll through charming Zionsville.

German

CAFE EUROPA
4709 N. Shadeland Ave.   547-4474
$$

This tiny restaurant boasts excellent fare; you'll find a variety of schnitzels (try the zesty pfefferrahmschnitzel), hearty fried potatoes, sweet red cabbage, homemade spaetzel. Don't pass up the delicious apple strudel for dessert. Enjoy accordion music on weekend evenings.

GISELA'S KAFFEEKRANZCHEN
112 S. Main St., Zionsville   873-5523
$$$

This Zionsville establishment specializes in bratwurst, knockwurst, pork chops and, of course, the delicious desserts, including Black Forest cherry torte that Gisela's is known for. The charming upstairs restaurant, with its cozy dark wood ambiance, will make you believe you really are in a cozy Black Forest cafe. Regulars recommend the $15.95 Saturday night buffet.

HEIDELBERG HAUS
7625 Pendleton Pike   547-1230
$$

This east-side eatery also offers a gift shop in addition to such traditional German favorites as schnitzels, wursts and chops. You'll also find excellent breads, cakes and pastries. The food's good, and you'll enjoy browsing among the plentiful German-themed knick knacks.

HAUS ANNA
67 N. Madison Ave.   887-0439
$$

Named for the owner's mother, this little Greenwood restaurant really is in a house, though from the outside it's rather nondescript. Inside, you'll find lots of tables, walls covered in Bavarian posters, knickknacks and a cuckoo clock marking the time. Try one of the specialties from owner Edelgard Stutler's native Bavaria. We can heartily endorse the sauerbraten and spaetzel, the jaegerschnitzel and most definitely the Black Forest cherry torte.

RATHSKELLER
401 E. Michigan St.   636-0396
$$

In the Athenaeum's basement (formerly known as Das Deutsch Haus), the Rathskeller feels like a pub in the Black Forest. Dark wood, leaded glass and a fireplace complete with Faustian relief set the tone. The smell of sauerkraut and strudel complete the experience. Ask der frau for a tall stein and get ready to enjoy.

Greek and Middle Eastern

ACROPOLIS
1625 E. Southport Rd.   787-8883
$$

A fun place to take the kids (see our Kidstuff chapter), the Acropolis offers belly dancing on weekend evenings. The Greek specialties are excellent; for a real feast, try the sampler plate. We can also recommend the lamb. And if kids don't care for Greek fare, they'll find plenty of alternatives such as breaded shrimp and french fries.

AESOP'S TABLE
600 N. Massachusetts Ave.   631-0055
$$

It's fun to browse through the art galleries on Mass Ave. (see our Arts chapter), then stop in for lunch or diner at this charming Mediterranean-style cafe. It's a bit subdued compared to other Greek places. No one belly dances or shouts "Opa!" over flaming plates of saganaki, but we like it. It's casual, yet a bit sophisticated.

GREEK ISLANDS
906 S. Meridian St.   636-0700
$$

The low ceiling here is scorched from where jovial servers ignite dishes of flaming cheese with shouts of "Opa!" This place is small, crowded and boisterous, but Greek Islands is the place for authentic Mediterranean fare done well and offered with good will. And they serve up a great Greek salad.

HELLAS CAFE
8501 Westfield Blvd.   257-6211
$$

The spanikopita at this little Greek place in Nora just may be the best in town. You can also count on the leg of lamb and the souvlaki. Hellas also serves some American favorites, but we never pass up the great Greek specialties.

MEDITERRANO CAFE
5941 E. 86th St.   595-0399
$$

Be sure to try the babaganooj at this pleasant lace-curtained cafe. It's delicious, as is the lamb curry. The attentive service makes it all even better.

PARTHENON
6319 N. Guilford Ave.   251-3139
$$

The longtime Broad Ripple favorite ranks as a lot of folks' favorite restaurant. You'll see all sorts here: young parents with babies (the little ones watch transfixed as the costumes of the weekend belly dancers shimmer and jingle), artist types and office workers enjoying an outdoor lunch (in nice weather, of course). Though the gyros are especially good, we can make a meal of a maza plate and a Greek salad.

Indian

INDIA GARDEN
830 Broad Ripple Ave.   253-6060
$$

This tiny Broad Ripple restaurant specializes in authentic northern Indian cuisine. To sample a variety, try the excellent lunch buffet. Don't miss the puffy bread, baked just minutes before it appears.

STAR OF INDIA
1043 Broad Ripple Ave.   465-1100
5929 E. 82nd St.   578-4400
$$

The 82nd Street location opened in the summer of 1995, an expansion that attests to the restaurant's popularity. The bright red chicken wins rave reviews. Both locations offer delicious authentic Indian fare.

Italian

AMBROSIA
915 Westfield Blvd.   255-3096
$$$

Hidden among a row of Broad Ripple restaurants, Ambrosia is as its name implies. The place has a studio look, but it retains an intimacy unavailable at many restaurants. And you'll fall for the food. Try the pesto or the seafood fettuccine alfredo; you won't be sorry.

AMICI'S
601 E. New York St.   634-0440
$$

Off the beaten path, this old house nonetheless plays host to one of the city's finest Italian restaurants. Open a bottle of red wine, sample the sauces and pretend you're in a place only the locals who speak Italian know. They have a good jukebox too. On the menu you'll find traditional Italian specialties; we've never been disappointed in any pasta dish.

BACCO
1260 W. 85th St.   582-1362
$$$

This is an excellent little Italian place that belies its admittedly generic strip mall location. Bacco overcomes this with its decor: Photographic prints and artwork line the textured terra-cotta walls. The menu highlights seafood; be sure to try one of the seafood/pasta specialties. We like the spaghetti alla pescatora: spaghetti tossed with shrimp and clams and ringed with mussels.

BENVENUTI
36 S. Pennsylvania St.   633-4915
$$$$

This elegant restaurant, on the first floor of the Century Building, provides one of the city's best fine dining experiences. The beautiful decor, with its polished marble entryway and Brazilian rosewood paneling, creates a distinctive ambiance. Sophisticated without being stuffy, Benvenuti provides stylish, comfortable surroundings, excellent service and wonderful Northern Italian cuisine, with such excellent appetizers as homemade ravioli of lobster and a delicious roasted red bell pepper soup. Jackets are required for men.

BRAVO
8651 Castle Creek Pkwy.   577-2211
$$

This spirited restaurant proves loud and

Photo: The Indianapolis Star & News

Malibu Grill excells at offering something for everyone, from pizza and pasta to steak and hamburgers.

boisterous; the high, open ceiling contributes to the noise, but we like the high energy level. Reminiscent of a Roman cafe, Bravo offers terrific pasta dishes (some served in huge bowls). Diners will also find wood-fired pizzas and steaks. Service is friendly and efficient, and the atmosphere is conducive to lingering and enjoying the ambiance.

IARIA'S

317 S. College Ave.   638-7706
$$

One of the city's favorite Italian joints, this place is small, casual and fun. You'll see movers and shakers discussing business over their lasagne and parents with kids trying to get Junior to finish his spaghetti and meatballs. And after dinner you can wander next door to the Action Bowl (see our Parks and Recreation chapter) for a little duck-pin bowling.

MILANO INN

231 S. College Ave.   264-3585
$$$

Celebrity photographs of famous faces and local heroes line the entryway walls at Milano Inn, and the place is almost always packed. Make a reservation and come with friends to really enjoy the place. Though not especially fancy, the food is plenty good. Try the La Dolce Vita — the sweet life (veal and chicken stuffed with proscuitto and mozzarella) — or the fresh tomato pizza. For excellent take out, stop in at one of the half dozen Milano's Pasta to Go locations around town.

OGGI RISTORANTE

6101 N. Keystone Ave.   259-0222
$$$

This Glendale Center restaurant offers a wide variety of Italian dishes in comfortable surroundings. Don't skip the appetizers; the artichokes con scampi (shrimp-stuffed artichoke buttons) are particularly tasty. And the seafood dishes are nicely done as well.

OLD SPAGHETTI FACTORY

210 S. Meridian St.   635-6325
$$

We broke our rule about chain restaurants to include the Old Spaghetti Factory because it's a great place to take the family. You get your money's worth and then some.

Meals come with salad, bread (we like to slather on the garlic butter), entree, coffee and spumoni ice cream for dessert. Choices are limited primarily to pasta, after all, spaghetti is in its name, but there's plenty of variety within those parameters. We especially like the spaghetti topped with mizithra cheese and meat sauce; the tortellini and lasagna are good too.

PAPA JOE'S

2441 Lafayette Rd.   925-3593
$$

This place used to be known as Joe's Hole in the Wall, and it still has the feel of a little neighborhood joint. Nothing fancy, just good Italian classics in comfortable surroundings. Try the lasagna; we've heard customers send their compliments to the chef after indulging in this popular dish. We also like the sauce, and you can even buy it by the quart to take home.

PESTO

303 N. Alabama St.   269-0715
$$$

Regulars rave about this Lockerbie-area eatery that features excellent appetizers and entrees (and delicious bread too). Just about anything you choose from the Northern Italian menu will prove tasty at this casually elegant downtown favorite. It's not a spaghetti and meatballs kind of place; you'll find lots of cream sauces and olive oil. The pizza (we like the pesto variety) is great too. In nice weather, ask for an outdoor table. The al fresco dining area overlooks a pleasant courtyard.

TUSCANY

838 Broad Ripple Ave.   253-7475
$$$

At Tuscany part of the appeal is the streetside Broad Ripple location. The Northern Italian specialties, steaks and seafood prove consistently good, and the atmosphere is tough to beat — especially if you get a table near the sidewalk, order a nice bottle of wine and dig in to a plate of pasta.

VITO PROVOLONE'S

8031 S. Meridian St.   888-1112
$$

This little south-side place offers a nice variety of standard Italian dishes in a cozy setting. There's not much room to wait for a table, but once you're seated, you'll enjoy the food. Try the mix-and-match "pastabilities" and pair up some fettuccine with Vito's vodka sauce. Or maybe some linguine with pesto.

Mexican

ACAPULCO JOE'S

635 N. Illinois St.   637-5160
$$

Joe, before he died, would burst into the restaurant and sing "God Bless America" at least twice an hour. Now Kate Smith does it via record, but little else has changed. "Aca Joe's" remains a hit with the downtown office crowd for the simple reason that the tacos and tostadas (and everything else) taste good and are priced right. Make sure you munch on the fresh chips and squirt-bottle salsa.

EL SOL DE TALA

2444 E. Washington St.   635-8252
1353 W. 86th St.   255-4300
$$

You'll miss El Sol if you're not careful, but this near east-side eatery is worth finding. The authentic Mexican food earns universal raves among those who find it (though the neighborhood doesn't). Still, many of the city's most prominent citizens know where it is, and they also know not to miss the guacamole and the chile rellenos. And now a north-side location, situated amid the many 86th Street strip mall restaurants, carries on the tradition.

LA JOLLA

921 Broad Ripple Ave.   253-5252
$$

One of the best things about this popular Broad Ripple restaurant is the porch. It's great to grab a table outside, sip a Margarita and watch the goings on in this eclectic neighborhood and nightlife district. Oh, and the food's good too. La Jolla offers a healthful take on traditional Mexican.

ZORRO'S

1300 E. 86th St.   571-1001
$$$

Don't come looking for refried beans or a giant chimichanga. Zorro's specializes in Pacific Mexican cuisine, with an emphasis on seafood preparations almost tropical in origin. The fish and shrimp in banana leaves is excellent; so is the classic chicken mole. A stylish decor and reasonable prices also make this new restaurant appealing.

Pizza

ARNI'S

3443 W. 86th St.   875-7034
$$

A great family choice (see our Kidstuff chapter), Arni's has won "best decor" awards from *Indianapolis Monthly's* People's Choice poll for six years running. The bar is full of lifesize cutouts of celebrities; the dining rooms boast bicycles on the ceiling. And the pizza and salads are great.

BAZBEAUX

334 Massachusetts Ave.   636-7662
832 E. Westfield Blvd.   255-5711
$$

The city's original gourmet pizza joint, Bazbeaux remains one of the most interesting, due primarily to its locations. The tiny house in Broad Ripple sees crowds hanging around the sidewalk waiting for tables; admire the wall paintings at the trendy Mass Ave. address. Whichever location you try, don't miss the quattro formaggio (four cheese) pizza.

PUCCINI'S SMILING TEETH

1508 W. 86th St.   875-9223
3944 E. 82nd St.   842-4028
$$

Two locations offer easy access to this north-side favorite where you'll find a variety of gourmet pizzas as well as several pasta dishes. We like the barbecue chicken and smoked gouda pizza; traditionalists opt for the "ultimate warrior" with pepperoni, sausage, onions and much more. And the "veg head" is a tasty vegetarian alternative.

SOME GUYS

6235 Allisonville Rd.   257-1364
$$

The gourmet pizza here proves great; we especially like the barbecue chicken variety. And the logo — a face on a pizza slice — is cool too.

UNION JACK PUB

924 Broad Ripple Ave.   257-4343
6225 W. 25th St.   243-3300
$$

The incredibly thick Chicago-style pizza at Union Jack is sure to fill you up; in fact, you'll probably have to ask for a box for the leftovers. These popular pizza joints boast somewhat different crowds: The west-side location tends to be rowdier, the Broad Ripple crowd more given to conversation.

Pubs

(Check out our pub listing in the Nightlife chapter for more entertainment-oriented information about Pubs.)

ARISTOCRAT

5212 N. College Ave.   283-7388
$$

Though the Aristocrat does indeed feel like a pub, with dark wood and a cozy bar, it offers family dining and a very popular Sunday brunch. In nice weather, ask for a table outside; the sidewalk landscaping makes this a very pleasant option.

BROAD RIPPLE BREW PUB

842 E. 65th St.   253-BREW
$$

In addition to terrific beers (we especially enjoy the redbird ale), this microbrewery offers great fish and chips, daily specials and a number of excellent vegetarian dishes. Note that kids are welcome (in the front dining room, which is separate from the bar).

CORNER WINE BAR

6331 N. Guilford Ave.   255-5159
$$

Not really a pub, the Wine Bar is just what its name implies: a great place to sit outside in popular Broad Ripple, sip a Cabernet, nibble on fruit and cheese and watch the world go by.

ELBOW ROOM

605 N. Pennsylvania St.   635-3354
$$

The quintessential pub, this popular downtown spot does a brisk business; it's tough to get a table at lunch. After work you'll see tables full of friends and coworkers hashing over the day's events. The burgers are great here; an order of nachos is huge. You'll find plenty of sandwiches and some steaks on the menu.

HENRY GRATTAN

745 Broad Ripple Ave.   257-6030
$$

This Irish bar is a great place to enjoy a just-poured Harp and some conversation.

The food, mostly traditional pub specialties, is pretty good, the service friendly and the atmosphere inviting. It's has a traditional pub-style ambiance with lots of dark wood and plenty of old photographs lining the walls.

LEGAL BEAGLE

20 N. Delaware St.   266-0088
$$

As its name implies, this place is a lawyer hangout. And why not? It's across from the City-County Building. But don't let that scare you away. Regular folks will find the standard bar fare done well and the legal-themed decor pleasant. If you listen carefully, you might hear the inside dope about the latest big trial.

LOUGHMILLER'S

301 W. Washington St.   638-7380
$$

First, don't mispronounce the name. It's a hard consonant: Lock-miller's. Second, don't miss the club sandwich. And third, the salads are splendid. Loughmiller's is a lunchtime favorite among state employees, politicos and conventioneers (it's across the street from the Statehouse and behind the Westin Hotel), and it has a fine beer selection.

MELODY INN

3626 N. Illinois St.   923-4707
$$

"The Mel," as it's affectionately known, has a storied past and a cameo in Dan Wakefield's book *Going All The Way*. Popular among all types of folks, from college kids and softball teams to the after-work crowd and neighborhood regulars, the Mel offers the standard bar fare served in plastic baskets that won't disappoint. Plus, the beer is cold, and the shots are affordable.

OAKEN BARREL BREWING CO.

50 Airport Pkwy.
Greenwood   887-2287
$$

The area's most recent entry into the microbrewery business (also see the Broad Ripple Brew Pub entry), this south-side place has much more of a family atmosphere than the Brew Pub. But the food's good, and the beers are great; try the raspberry wheat variety.

PAWN SHOP

5906 N. College Ave.   251-1111
$$

This classic Broad Ripple pub remains extremely popular and features a varied menu. The chili is always good, the fries are plentiful and you'll find some surprises, such as the vegetarian water buffalo sandwich. Often crowded, this comfortable neighborhood hangout is a great place to get together with friends.

Regional

FLETCHER'S OF ATLANTA

185 W. Main St., Atlanta   292-2777
$$$$

This small eclectic eatery run by local chef Fletcher Boyd boasts excellent service and a creative menu. Its location in the tiny northern Hamilton County town of Atlanta might be a drawback to some, but it really is worth the 45-minute drive (take U.S. 31 north to County Line Road then east to Atlanta). You'll enjoy a casual, hip ambiance; there's artwork on the walls (and more in an upstairs gallery), beautifully set tables and a crowd dressed in everything from jeans to evening wear. You'll also find a seasonally changing menu and top-notch service. We can heartily recommend Hog Heaven, a marinated pork chop and pork loin dish. Salads prove excellent as well. Fletcher's is expensive, but worth it.

PANACHE

60 S. Elm St., Zionsville   873-1388
$$$

This tiny Boone County town boasts plenty of excellent restaurants, and Panache, which specializes in seasonal modern American food, is certainly among them. The small, casual restaurant features an interesting menu that changes periodically, but if you see a lamb dish, try it. Attentive service makes the dining experience even more enjoyable.

PETER'S RESTAURANT AND BAR

8505 Keystone Crossing   465-1155
$$$$

Chef Peter George is very well-regarded around Indianapolis, and plenty of patrons would call his restaurant the best in the city. Making use of seasonally available herbs and produce, he creates excellent regional American dishes — lamb, game and fresh fish. His restaurant is upscale, yet casual, with a beautiful open kitchen and inviting bar. Call for info on kids' night; Peter's kitchen staff can whip up a tasty macaroni and cheese with the best of them.

Russian

MOSCOW NIGHTS

3532 W. 86th St.   875-0777
$$

Though the modern, minimalist decor doesn't look particularly Russian, the food certainly is. An interesting menu includes caviar-stuffed eggs, Russian-style perogy and delicious borscht.

RUSSIA HOUSE

1475 W. 86th St.   876-7990
$$

You'll feel like a Cold War-era spy sitting in this tiny cafe, with its lace curtains and fabric-draped walls. The borscht is excellent here, as are the Siberian pelmeni, small meat-filled dumplings. If you're lucky, you'll get to hear a sultry chanteuse sing Russian ballads on weekend evenings. It'll help you keep up the James Bond masquerade.

Seafood

FISHERMAN'S DOCK

3451 W. 86th St.	876-FISH
3838 E. 82nd St.	578-FISH
$$	

Fresh fish is flown in daily for lunch and dinner at this restaurant, which also features hand-cut steaks, poultry, pasta and even a kids' menu. Two north-side locations offer plenty of convenience.

HOT TUNA

40 W. Jackson Pl.	687-5190
$$$	

Though we can't help thinking of the early '70s rock band when we think of this place, the name refers to the food, not the music. A relaxed hotel dining room on the first floor of the downtown Omni Severin, Hot Tuna is relaxed and casual, yet it offers professional, attentive service. Enjoy the complimentary appetizer your server will bring out, but be sure to try the lightly breaded fried calamari; it's some of the best in town, extra tender and done just right. The pan-browned walleye is great too.

KEYSTONE GRILL

8650 Keystone Crossing	848-5202
$$$	

Popular for lunch among Keystone at the Crossing office workers, the Keystone Grill remains a good choice for dinner as well, especially if you have a yen for fresh seafood. Though the menu changes, look for such specialties as rainbow trout, grilled Norwegian salmon or farm-raised catfish. You'll find a number of steak and poultry dishes as well; one of our favorites is the linguine with mussels and clam sauce.

KEY WEST SHRIMP HOUSE

39 Jackson Pl.	635-5353
6714 E. 82nd St.	635-5353
$$$	

This longtime local landmark moved north from the near south-side, and you can now enjoy its traditional seafood specialties at Union Station (and in Castleton as well). The restaurant kept the traditional nautical theme as much as was possible in Union Station's grand hall; even the 45-year-old captains' chairs remain. Regulars enjoy the variety of shrimp dishes, fresh seafood, lobster and oysters (though you'll also find steaks, chicken and pasta).

KONA JACK'S FISH MARKET AND SUSHI BAR

9413 N. Meridian St.	843-2600
$$$	

Kona Jack's advertises the city's freshest fish and seafood, and the north-side establishment has won over plenty of locals who appreciate the wide selection and the staff's willingness to slice an order to fit the requirements of your favorite recipe. The sushi bar proves popular as well, the atmosphere upscale but inviting.

THE MAJESTIC OYSTER BAR AND GRILL

47 S. Pennsylvania St.	636-5418
$$$	

This elegant downtown establishment boasts a number of excellent seafood dishes served by a knowledgeable wait staff in comfortable surroundings. Plenty of windows look out onto the street; tables are nicely set. Dinner entrees, especially such fresh seafood options as salmon and orange roughy, are well-prepared; lunch is considerably less expensive.

NEW ORLEANS HOUSE

8845 Township Line Rd.   872-9670
$$$

Come to this seafood buffet ready to indulge, and be sure you have plenty of time set aside to really enjoy it (the menu suggests a two-hour dinner, and we agree). Eat your fill of steamed shrimp, oysters on the halfshell, smoked salmon, clams and crab legs. And don't miss the frog legs that servers bring around for diners to try. Enjoy the bountiful buffet as well as the relaxed country club sort of atmosphere.

Soups/Salads/Sandwiches

BAY WINDOW

202 W. Main St.   882-1330
$

This homey, cozy little spot in Old Towne Greenwood is a great place to stop after browsing through the old downtown area (see our Shopping chapter). You'll find a tasty selection of sandwiches and soups; we like "Mary's Favorite" a turkey and cranberry sauce combo on dark rye paired with a cup of the homemade cream of broccoli soup. Try the ooey-gooey butter cake or the pumpkin crunch pie for dessert.

BENVENUTI THE BAKERY

I N. Pennsylvania St.   686-9615
$

Though Benvenuti, the "parent" restaurant to this bakery, is quite posh, this offshoot offers the same excellent quality in a casual lunch and carry-out location. Everything in the display case looks great; be sure to sample the salads and some focaccia. And if you really want to indulge, try the tiramisu and one of the tiny chocolate cream puffs for good measure.

BETWEEN BREAD

136 N. Delaware St.   638-4174
$

If gazpacho is on the menu, order it. If not, then any of the soups will please. But, as the name implies, sandwiches star here, and patrons line up daily at this restaurant in an alley near the City-County Building. Be patient, the line moves quickly, and it's worth the short wait. No credit cards are accepted.

BROTHER JUNIPER'S

339 Massachusetts Ave.   636-3115
150 E. 16th St.   924-9529
$

A religious order runs the place (hence the name), and the whole-Earth food tastes divine. Fresh soups and sandwich combinations fuel many a downtown worker, and the pies are wonderful. It's a miracle, though, that fights don't break out over tables at the always busy Mass Ave. location. Herron art school students run in for a sandwich at the 16th Street address. No credit cards are accepted.

CITY MARKET

222 E. Market St.   634-9266

At this historic downtown marketplace, lunchtime diners find a wide variety to sample. Libby's Deli offers great sandwiches and deli sides, Pameer serves up delicious Afghani fare, the Rice Bowl has terrific eggrolls, and you'll find plenty more food stands throughout the market. For dessert, stop by Cath for cookies, muffins or coffee, or pick up some fresh fruit at Constantinos (also see our Shopping chapter). Inside dining is at a premium, but on sunny days the outdoor tables, benches and ledges offer great spots to enjoy lunch and people-watch. Many stands do not accept credit cards.

ILLINOIS STREET FOOD EMPORIUM
5500 N. Illinois St.   253-9513
$

In the heart of the Butler-Tarkington neighborhood you'll find a great little shopping district, the Shoppes at 56th Street (see our Shopping chapter). And within that is the Illinois Street Food Emporium, which offers great deli fare and excellent pastries and desserts. We can heartily recommend the avocado-and-turkey croissant; you'll also find plenty of heart-healthy options. The side salads are great too; try the wild rice variety. Grab a table inside, eat outdoors or enjoy a walk through the neighborhood.

PETITE GRILL
443 N. Pennsylvania St.   631-3500
$

This long, narrow space in a downtown office building is indeed petite, but the Petite Grill can satisfy any appetite. From it's big-as-the-plate tenderloin to the crunchy onion rings, the food is good, so be ready to eat. For lesser appetites there is lighter fare; early risers will find breakfast too.

Vegetarian

ESSENTIAL EDIBLES
429 E. Vermont St.   266-8797
$

Very popular among the downtown lunch crowd, Essential Edibles is known for its creative approach to vegetarian cuisine. You find such specialties as grilled eggplant sandwiches, mushroom pâtes and a range of pasta and grain salads. And if you see a flier advertising an upcoming cooking class, sign up.

ESSENTIAL EDIBLES TOO
115 E. 49th St.   931-1080
$

This carry-out cafe brings the best stuff from the downtown location to the popular Meridian-Kessler neighborhood. Be sure to try the focaccia, the herb breads and the vegan cookies. They'll make a believer out of you.

Inside
Nightlife

Your work is done, and now you're ready to have some fun. Where do you go? What can you do? Well, it just so happens that those questions are the core of this chapter.

What follows is a look at some of what Indianapolis has to offer in the way of live music, dance clubs, pubs and movie theaters.

To help you navigate through the choices, we've primarily arranged this chapter geographically. For example, if you're downtown and want to check out the nightlife there, flip to our "Downtown" section and read through our Jazz and Blues, Rock/Pop, Dance Clubs, Pubs and Comedy categories. You can do the same for Broad Ripple and the Northwest, Northeast, South, East and West sides of town. If, however, you're looking for a particular concert venue or want to take in a movie, turn to our separate "Concert Venues" and "Movie Theaters" sections at the end of the chapter.

Go now. A good time awaits.

Where to Start

In addition to this chapter, which provides specifics in terms of names, addresses and telephone numbers, the following publications provide schedules of events and activities on a weekly basis.

Weekend, 633-9079, a weekly arts and entertainment insert appears in the Fri-

The Vogue is the place to see and hear the best in local and regional bands, while C.T. Peppers offers live music that defies categorizations. In between these two spots is Broad Ripple Comedy Club.

day editions of *The Indianapolis Star and the Indianapolis News*. It includes movie listings, live music schedules for both concert venues and clubs, and information about performing arts events, stage productions, museum exhibitions, lectures and so forth.

NUVO, 254-2400, a free weekly newspaper, which is published each Thursday, covers news, public issues and arts and entertainment. In the case of the latter, *NUVO* provides a comprehensive schedule of events as well as a detailed list of area clubs and the performers appearing at them.

Downtown

When it comes to nightlife, downtown offers something for everyone. From cozy hotel lounges to smoky blues clubs, hot dance spots to chummy little pubs, you're bound to find someplace you like. And since the downtown district is relatively compact, you can walk from one place to another until you do.

Jazz and Blues

CHATTERBOX TAVERN
435 Massachusetts Ave.   636-0584

For classic jazz in a classic jazz setting, this tiny, smoky, hole-in-the-wall bar in the Mass Avenue arts district is it. Some of the city's best musicians show up to play at the Chatterbox after midnight, once their early evening gigs are over.

RICK'S CAFE AMERICAIN
39 W. Jackson Pl.   634-6666

On the second level of Union Station, this restaurant/bar features jazz that's as tasty as its entrees.

SLIPPERY NOODLE INN
372 S. Meridian St.   631-6974

This place just south of Union Station is Indiana's oldest (c. 1850) continually operating tavern. With blues performers on stages upstairs and down, it's also the best place in town to hear local, regional and national blues. And if all that great music makes you hungry, the Noodle's full-service kitchen is open well past midnight.

Rock/Pop

AMERICA LIVE!
39 W. Maryland St.
Ste. H-7 Circle Centre   630-LIVE

Occupying nearly 50,000 square feet on the fourth floor of the downtown mall, America Live! is an entertainment complex containing three nightclubs — Gator's, Flashbaxx and World Mardi Gras — as well as a beer pub, a coffee shop and two restaurants. Based on a beach theme, Gator's is a high-energy dance club featuring state-of-the-art audio, video and lighting. Done up in 1970s-style decor, Flashbaxx is a dance club that features '70s and '80s music. For live music, World Mardi Gras combines a New Orleans atmosphere with local, regional and national performers. The music here ranges from jazz to rhythm 'n' blues to rock.

But if all you want is someplace to have a beer and shoot some pool, try JA Flats. With more than 80 varieties of beer on hand, along with an array of pool tables and electronic games, it's designed for fun.

There are also two full-service on-site restaurants — The Big Easy Cafe and Sports City Cafe — for those times when having too much fun makes you hungry. When you want a shot of caffeine to perk you up, try Juke 'n Java coffee shop.

Voted best comedy club 4 years in a row!

CRACKERS™

*Our 14th Year
as Indy's Original
All Comedy
Night Club*

**CALL
317/846-2500
FOR
RESERVATIONS**

See Tomorrow's Stars Today!

8702 Keystone Crossing at the Fashion Mall

THE COZY

115 E. Wabash St.   *638-2100*

A combination restaurant and nightclub, this place is tucked away in an alley-like street off Pennsylvania, making it a bit hard to find. But it's worth the search. The Cozy has a large dance floor, as well as pool tables and TVs throughout broadcasting sports. There's live music — blues, rock and funk — on the weekends, a mixture of recorded music the rest of the week.

CULTURE CLUB

235 S. Meridian St.   *756-1588*

With three floors of live and recorded reggae, house and Top 40 music, this club attracts a multicultural crowd that comes to dance the night away.

IKE & JONESY'S

17 W. Jackson Pl.   *632-4553*

Offering a mix of live and recorded music — '60s rock, R&B and Top 40 stuff — this c. 1950s-style diner is a favorite after-work watering hole for downtown workers looking to unwind. It's an uninhibited kind of place, and it's loud. But you can have yourself a good time here without much effort. (A word of advice: Don't wear your favorite clothes here unless you're prepared to overlook the spills that happen in crowded bars.)

LIL' DITTY'S

39 W. Jackson Pl.   *687-0068*

Although this is a piano bar of sorts, it certainly isn't your ordinary piano bar. The bar's two pianos are fingered by players who view entertainment as a birthright — and sing-alongs as opportunities to be rowdy, bawdy and loud. From college fight songs and TV theme songs to those camp songs your parents warned you not to sing in the car, don't expect sedate decorum here — this is where people go to have some real fun.

Every Friday evening from 6 to 10 PM, the Madame Walker Urban Life Center hosts "Jazz on the Avenue," which features local, regional and national musicians.

Insiders' Tips

PLAYERS

39 W. Jackson Pl.   *687-0068*

Sharing a place inside Union Station with Lil' Ditty's, Players has an old-fashioned wood-and-brass bar atmosphere that belies its live music mix — everything from '60s rock covers to contemporary Afro-Latin, acoustic to electric.

SPORTS, A BAR & GRILL

225 S. Meridian St.   *631-5838*

With two stages, two DJs and two levels with five bars, this place is nothing if not busy. There are also plenty of TV screens throughout the place for keeping an eye on college and professional sports action. The music runs the gamut from alternative rock (covers and originals) by local and regional bands as well as classic rock, techno dance and industrial.

Dance Clubs

In addition to the dancing at the previously mentioned live music clubs, the following clubs offer dancing to recorded music.

FACES NIGHT CLUB

2145 N. Talbott St.   *923-9886*

While you'll see members of other races and ethnic groups in the crowd, this club 2 miles north of downtown is predominantly an African-American nightspot — and an elegant one at that. This is a no-jeans-and-T-shirts kind of place. Faces' patrons dress to go out. From very nice casual clothes to beautifully tailored suits and dresses, the people who go to Faces jump sharp. The music here ranges from rhythm 'n' blues to jazz, sometimes live, sometimes not. In either case, there's room to dance.

JACKSON STREET BAR

234 S. Meridian St.   *266-8444*

In a New Orleans-style setting, the music, which is primarily dance pop from the '80s and '90s, motivates until the wee hours — or until your feet weep for relief.

UNION STATION ORIGINAL SPORTS BAR

39 W. Jackson Pl.   *687-0068*

A companion to Lil' Ditty's and Players, this Union Station bar contains not only a dance floor and high-quality sound and video systems, but also dart boards, pool tables and a basketball free-throw court. This place was designed to induce serious fun.

Pubs

For food-related information, please see our "Pubs" category in the Restaurants chapter.

THE ELBOW ROOM

605 N. Pennsylvania St.   *635-3354*

A downtown landmark for decades, The Elbow Room is as much restaurant as pub, but that doesn't diminish its value as a place to relax for an evening over a good imported beer. The music emanating from speakers throughout the place ranges from '70s radio hits to contemporary stuff.

FILIBUSTERS

Westin Hotel
50 S. Capitol Ave.   *262-8100*

Sit and sip in the pub where the pols do — this hotel pub is across the street from the State Capitol and the state office complex, so it attracts its fair share of state and local government officials. And plenty of weary conventioneers from the nearby Convention Center.

Indianapolis Jazz Greats

When you're sitting in one of the local jazz clubs, soaking up the ambiance and the music, consider this: Indianapolis has long been an important contributor to American jazz. In fact, from the 1920s through the mid-1960s, the city was one of the centers of jazz in this country, on a par with other jazz hotspots such as Chicago and St. Louis.

And the city's roster of significant jazz artists, past and present, includes names known to any jazz buff. Among them are:

David Baker: Chair of Indiana University School of Music's jazz department, Baker, a trombonist, has played with the likes of Stan Kenton and Quincy Jones. As a composer and arranger, he's both highly regarded and in constant demand.

Erroll Grandy: Known as the "godfather of Indianapolis jazz" for his affect on the local jazz scene of the 1940s, '50s and '60s, Grandy was both a gifted pianist and an inspiration to several generations of jazz musicians. At various times, he backed such well-known figures as Dinah Washington, Billie Holliday and Count Basie.

Slide Hampton: An innovative trombone player and acclaimed jazz composer, Hampton played with and arranged music for some of the best-known names in jazz: vibes player (and distant cousin) Lionel Hampton, Maynard Ferguson and Art Blakey, among others. Today, he's one of the international jazz world's most respected figures.

Freddie Hubbard: A major player in the development of jazz in the second half of the 20th century, trumpet player Freddie Hubbard, both solo and in tandem with others, influenced the sound and stretched the boundaries of modern music.

J.J. Johnson: Another innovative trombonist, Johnson more than any other player affected the evolution of the instrument in contemporary

Photo: The Indianapolis Star & News

Jazz trombonist J.J. Johnson is a native of Indianapolis.

music. From the way he played to what he played, Johnson explored the potential of his instrument in a manner that redefined what a trombonist can do.

Wes Montgomery: One of the 20th century's most influential jazz guitarists, Montgomery won accolades from musicians, critics and fans for his inventive playing. Guitarists today continue to sing his praises and study his techniques, while fans continue to listen to such Montgomery recordings as the 1965 Grammy Award winner "Goin' Out of My Head" and 1967's best-selling jazz LP *A Day in the Life*.

Today, Wes (who died in 1968) is memorialized both in a namesake park at 34th Street and Hawthorne Lane and in the annual Wes Montgomery Jazz Festival held in Washington Park each August.

Monk Montgomery: Wes's older brother Monk was the first jazz musician to record with an electric bass, which he did in 1953. A member of Lionel Hampton's band in the early 1950s, Monk also played with Wes and their younger brother, Buddy, in the Wes Montgomery Trio, as well as with a variety of other musicians.

Buddy Montgomery: Younger brother of Wes and Monk, Buddy played piano with Miles Davis as well as with his brothers in the Wes Montgomery Trio. Today, he remains a widely respected composer and player, occasionally returning to Indianapolis from his home in Oakland, California, for concerts.

LOUISIANA STREET BAR

123 W. Louisiana St.   *631-2221*

This street-level bar in the Crowne Plaza hotel offers a respite after a hard day. Its kitchen serves a variety of food until midnight, so you can have a late dinner as well as a nightcap.

Comedy

INDIANAPOLIS COMEDY CONNECTION

247 S. Meridian St.   *631-3636*

A local downtown comedy classic, the Comedy Connection hosts a variety of the nation's best touring comedy talent. Past acts have included such rising starts as Tim Allen, Rosie O'Donnell and Ellen DeGeneres.

Broad Ripple

This is entertainment central. In just a few square blocks, this north-side village contains more nightlife options than any other section of town. While there's something going on in Broad Ripple seven nights a week, the busiest nights are Thursday, Friday and Saturday. That's when it's clear that Broad Ripple is clearly an ancient Sumarian term for party.

Jazz

JAZZ COOKER

925 E. Westfield Blvd.   *253-2883*

If you can't get down to New Orleans for the real thing, this place is a good alternative — order up some red beans and rice, then kick back for some Big Easy jazz.

THE JAZZ KITCHEN
5377 N. College Ave.   253-4900

This is the city's hottest jazz club, a place where the best local, regional and national musicians come to cook. You can see everyone from local favorites such as Affinity and Steve Allee to performers of international stature such as Maynard Ferguson.

MIDTOWN BAR & GRILL
815 E. Westfield Blvd.   253-1141

In the heart of Broad Ripple, this place offers cool jazz in an intimate environment. This is a tablecloths-and-candles kind of place where a throaty sax or some smoothly fingered ivories remind you how sensuous jazz can be.

Pop/Rock

THE VOGUE
6259 N. College Ave.   259-7029

Let's start with the king. This former movie theater is the state's top spot on the rock club circuit — *the* place to see (and hear) the best in local and regional bands as well as national acts the caliber of Taj Mahal, Buddy Guy and Johnny Cash.

The Vogue is a great place to see performers at their best — or in some cases, their worst, but that's not the club's fault. It's hard to beat a table by the balcony railing: You can see everything going on on-stage without having to crane to see around anyone. The only problem is ordering; when the band's cranked up, communicating with your waitress can be a challenge. Just wave your bottle around and point at it, then hold up the appropriate number of fingers.

On Sunday nights, The Vogue hosts "Boing," an alternative dance party popular with the local gay community.

C.T. PEPPERS
6283 N. College Ave.   257-6277

Live music that defies categorization, including rock, jazz, blues and reggae, along with pool, darts and electronic games make this Vogue neighbor a local favorite. And Peppers' kitchen cooks up great chow.

THE PATIO
6308 Guilford Ave.   253-0799

A smaller version of The Vogue, this cramped club is the kind of place your mother would frown upon— the floor's too sticky, the air's too smoky and the music's too loud. In other words, it's perfect. At The Patio, you're apt to hear anything from punk to funk — and apt to see anyone from polo-shirted frat boys to totally tatooed bikers.

J.C. BISTRO
838 Broad Ripple Ave.   255-8755

On the main drag through the village, this club is a contemporary version of the fern bars of the 1970s. Though festooned with mirrors and hanging plants, it manages to book some of the best acts in the area. The music here ranges from radio covers to alternative tunes, reggae to acoustic.

Every Thursday evening in August, Ameritech teams up with the Indianapolis Zoo to present "Animals and All That Jazz," a combination of live jazz, good food and all the Zoo's attractions. It's a favorite of families looking for something different to do.

Insiders' Tips

Dance Clubs

EDEN

6235 N. Guilford Ave.   *475-1588*

For "a different point of view from the top of Broad Ripple," this club inside a former VFW hall is home to cutting edge dance music. The patrons here run the gamut from smartly dressed to multiply pierced. Rave on, Garth.

LANDSHARKS

810 Broad Ripple Ave.   *254-8157*

A mix of live and recorded music, along with a beach party atmosphere, makes this a place "where good fins get together." If you can't make it down to the islands, this is an inexpensive alternative, unless you're looking for some sun. But then, who goes to a nightclub for that?

Pubs and Bars

For food-related information, please see our "Pubs" category in the Restaurants chapter.

AVERAGE JOE'S

816 Broad Ripple Ave.   *253-5844*

MINESHAFT SALOON

812 Broad Ripple Ave.   *253-5844*

ROCK LOBSTER

820 Broad Ripple Ave.   *253-5844*

These three clubs, which bill themselves as "Broad Ripple's Party Trifecta," offer re-corded music, pool tables, air hockey, video games and sports TV. Take advantage of domestic and imported beer specials throughout the week and spicy chicken wings for sustenance.

BROAD RIPPLE BREW PUB

840 E. 65th St.   *253-2739*

In a manner of speaking, this is the test-ing facility for the on-site microbrewery.

Freshly brewed beers in several varieties, including seasonal brews, are available in a relaxed pub setting.

THE CORNER WINE BAR

6331 Guilford Ave.   *255-5159*

For those times when you'd like to sit and sip a glass of wine while talking with a friend, this place at the corner of Guilford Avenue and Westfield Boulevard is perfect. Domestic and imported wines and beers are available.

HENRY GRATTAN

745 Broad Ripple Ave.   *257-6030*

No this isn't some guy's house — it's a pub, complete with brass rails and dark wood. It's the kind of place that beckons on a rainy afternoon.

THE PAWN SHOP PUB

5906 N. College Ave.   *251-1111*

Sometimes you find a place that feels like home the minute you walk in the door — a "Cheers" sort of place. This is one of those places. The Pawn Shop is where you go when you want to while away a few hours shooting the breeze.

THE RED KEY TAVERN

5170 N. College Ave.   *283-4601*

This is the classic neighborhood bar: Formica-topped tables and vinyl chairs, a jukebox in the corner, a bar lined with regu-lars. It's a great place to spend an evening alone or with a friend.

UNION JACK PUB

924 Broad Ripple Ave.   *243-3300*

This place is reminiscent of those oak-and-brass bars you find in college towns everywhere. The collegial atmosphere is ideal for quaffing a few brews along with some of the great pizza this place is famous for (yeah, yeah, the British aren't exactly known for their pizza, but it's just the name

KITTLE'S
INDIANA'S LEADING FURNITURE STORE

Whether it's a single piece or an entire houseful of furniture, you'll find the right furniture at the right price at **Kittle's**. At our two Indianapolis-area super stores you can choose from an incredible selection of the best *fashion* and values in home furnishings and accessories. At Kittle's you'll find LEADING AMERICAN makers such as, Thomasville, Henredon, Sealy, Lane, Broyhill, Kincaid, Barcalounger, Hancock & Moore and Richardson Brothers.

The Right Furniture at the Right Price!

KITTLE'S CASTLETON SUPER STORE • 8600 ALLISONVILLE ROAD
KITTLE'S GREENWOOD SUPER STORE • 665 U.S. 31 NORTH

10202 E. Washington St.
(317) 899-4567

38th & Lafayette Rd.
(317) 291-6390

CASTLETON SQUARE

82nd St. & Allisonville Rd.
(317) 849-9993

It's hip to be "Square" in Indianapolis

Washington Square Mall is conveniently located on the eastside of Indianapolis. Washington Square offers 120 fine stores including Lazarus, L.S. Ayres, Sears, Montgomery Ward and JCPenney. Easily accessible from I-465 and I-70.

Castleton Square Mall is located on the fast growing northeast side of Indianapolis. Castleton Square is served by I-69, I-465 and Allisonville Road. Over 125 stores including six major department stores.

Lafayette Square Mall is part of the strong tradition of the Indianapolis westside which includes the Indianapolis Motor Speedway. Lafayette Square can be conveniently reached from I-65 and I-465. Over 97 fine stores including L.S. Ayres, Sears, Lazarus, JCPenney, and Montgomery Ward.

GRAHAM'S CRACKERS
& Other Collectables

Voted Best!

- Indianapolis Gift Shop
- Indianapolis Card Shop
"By Indianapolis Monthly Readers"

Visit us for any gift giving occasion.
We'll help you make it special!

5981 E. 86th Street • Indianapolis, IN
North of Castleton Square Mall • 842-5727 • 1-800-442-5727

of the place, not it's culinary identity). See the "Pizza" category in our Restaurants chapter.

Comedy

BROAD RIPPLE COMEDY CLUB
6281 N. College Ave.   *255-4211*

This club upstairs from C.T. Peppers features a variety of regional and national comedians, including such favorites as Michigan's own Heywood Banks and song parodists Pinkard and Bowden. On the third and fourth Mondays of each month, BRCC hosts Comedy Showcase, which features local and regional acts.

Northwest

Rock/Pop

SHOOTERS II
5522 Georgetown Rd.   *388-0022*

Tucked away in a strip mall, this live music club features a wide variety of bands from classic rock and Top 40 to the blues.

Dance Clubs

MEMORIES
79th St. and Michigan Rd.   *879-0759*

This is a place where the past and the present combine to create the time of your life. Enjoy DJ dancing every Thursday, Friday and Saturday, plus a game room and big screen sports. This is home of the Notre Dame Club of Indianapolis, so be prepared to cheer on the Fighting Irish during football season.

Pubs and Bars

For food-related information, see the "Pubs" category in our Restaurants chapter.

BENCHWARMERS SPORTS FOOD AND SPIRITS
3850 DePauw Blvd.   *872-9790*

A congenial sports bar inside the Holiday Inn North, Benchwarmers has TVs throughout for those crucial sporting events, as well as billiards, shuffleboard and NTN (a sports and trivia game). On Saturday nights, there's a DJ and dancing.

Northeast

Rock/Pop

COCKTAIL COVE
82nd St. and Allisonville Rd.   *576-9800*

Live music and televised sports — need we say more? When you're looking for a port to ride out a storm, anchor yourself here.

WHIRLIGIG'S
8787 Keystone Crossing   *846-2700*

This high-energy club inside the Radisson Hotel features both local bands and DJs. On weekends, this place really hops, and the dance floor's packed. Dress up a little, and lighten up a lot.

Pubs and Bars

LEGENDS SPORTS BAR & GRILL
8250 Center Run Rd.   *576-9238*

With a DJ pumping out dance tunes every night, it's easy to see why Legends is, well, legendary for fun. If you're rhythmically challenged, you can spend your time shooting pool, eating (the food here is also, uh, legendary), or just leaning back in your chair working on your smile.

Photo: The Indianapolis Star & News

Wes Montgomery.

Comedy

CRACKERS COMEDY CLUB
Fashion Mall
Keystone at the Crossing   846-2500

Featuring such hilarious comedians as Brad Garrett, Crackers is longtime staple of the local nightlife scene. And its upscale setting makes it easy to sell to affluent northsiders.

South

Jazz

THE JAZZ CELLAR
522 E. Raymond St.   788-4521

This club, which is on the lower level of the Fireside South Restaurant, features a variety of local and regional jazz artists.

JAZZ IN ACTION
1105 Prospect St.   686-6006

Ensconced on the fourth floor of the Fountain Square Theatre, this club offers great music and a good view of the historic area around it. Here you'll hear everything from covers of jazz classics to new compositions and improvisations.

Rock/Pop

CELEBRATION LOUNGE
520 E. Thompson Rd. 787-8341

Inside the Holiday Inn South, this club features live music on the weekends, including classic rock, country, funk and '50s goldies. During the week, there's a DJ. And there's a jukebox, along with a buffet, in the back of a fin-tailed Cadillac.

THE FOUNTAIN ROOM
1103 S. Shelby St.   686-6010

This place in the Fountain Square area offers patrons a chance to time travel back to the 1950s for a weekend sock hop. Dance to live and recorded music.

LADY LUCK BILLIARDS
911 N. State Rd. 135
Greenwood   885-1962

In the downstairs portion of this two-level club you can catch a potpourri of area bands and musical styles including rock, reggae, funk, etc. Upstairs, you can shoot some pool. And all over the place, you can keep an eye on televised sports.

Comedy

ONE-LINERS COMEDY CLUB
50 Airport Pkwy.
Greenwood   889-LAFF

Owned in part by local comedian Dave "The King" Wilson, this south-side club is a great spot to catch local and regional acts.

East

Rock/Pop

ZANIES TOO
5914 E. 10th St.   357-6022

This club defines intimate. It's small enough that when a band's on stage, you can count the change in the bass player's pocket. The music here is primarily rock and blues, both acoustic and electric.

Dance Clubs

RITZ NIGHTCLUB
3525 N. Shadeland Ave.   549-2222

Inside the Quality Inn East, you'll find this club, home of DJ'd dance tunes, six nights a week. Nobody sits (for long) at the Ritz.

Comedy

RITZ NIGHTCLUB
3525 N. Shadeland Ave. 549-2222

Every Monday evening at this club inside the Quality Inn East is "Comedy Nite," with comedian Ty Wilson hosting the open-mike festivities.

West

Country

A LITTLE BIT OF TEXAS
111 N. Lynhurst Dr. 487-9065

Inside a building the size of an airplane hanger, this club near the airport is home of the Texas two-step and host to some of country's best up-and-comers. Join in free dance lessons. And if all that dancing makes you hungry, this is the only nightclub in the country with a Taco Bell inside it.

WESTERN STAR DANCE HALL
6447 W. Washington St. 486-8100

Part of a dining-dancing establishment, the hall has a 1,500-square-foot, hardwood dance floor as well as a high-quality sound and light system. Eat what you like in the Western Star Dinner House, then work it off in the dance hall.

Rock/Pop

QUINCY'S
2544 Executive Dr. 248-2481

Hear some of the best live sounds around in this club in the Adam's Mark Hotel. Performers range from Top 40 and classic rock cover bands to local Afro-Caribbean mambo maniacs, Dog Talk.

And when there isn't a band on stage, the DJ's working hard to keep the beat.

Comedy

COMEDYSPORTZ ARENA
3121 W. 30th St. 926-3368

This is improvisational comedy up close and personal. Teams of "actletes" create scenes based on audience suggestions while a ref regulates the humor (as in keeping it clean yet funny).

QUINCY'S COMEDY CABARET
2544 Executive Dr. 248-2481

Every Tuesday evening, this nightclub in the Adam's Mark Hotel hosts a comedy night.

Concert Venues

CIRCLE THEATRE
45 Monument Cir. 262-1110

Home of the Indianapolis Symphony Orchestra, this former movie theater is now a gorgeous concert hall. When not in use by the ISO, it is occasionally used for other classical or jazz performances. (Also see entry in The Arts chapter.)

CLOWES MEMORIAL HALL
4600 Sunset Ave. 283-9696

This performance hall on the campus of Butler University is Indianapolis's version of the Kennedy Center for the Performing Arts. In the acoustically marvelous Clowes auditorium, you can see Broadway shows, operas, jazz ensembles, rock groups, dance performances, readings and lectures by well-known writers. (Also see entry in The Arts chapter.)

DEER CREEK MUSIC CENTER
12880 E. 146th St. 841-8900

One of the premier amphitheaters in the Midwest, Deer Creek is set amid 220 acres of beautiful countryside about 15 miles north of Indianapolis. During its season (May through October), it hosts an array of performers. The 1994 roster included such diverse acts as the Allman Brothers, Santana, Blues Traveler, Sheryl Crow, Diana Ross, Soul Asylum, R.E.M., Jimmy Buffett, The Grateful Dead and Hank Williams, Jr. At Deer Creek, you can hear the stars beneath the stars. (Also see entry in The Arts chapter.)

INDIANA ROOF BALLROOM
140 W. Washington St.   *236-1870*

On the fourth floor of the Indiana Repertory Theatre building downtown, the Spanish-style ballroom was built in the 1920s. Since being renovated in the early 1980s, the Roof has become a popular site for Big Band dances as well as dinners, receptions and occasional concerts by such performers as Harry Connick Jr. (Also see entry in The Arts chapter.)

MURAT THEATRE
502 N. New Jersey St.   *635-2433*

In this wonderful old theater inside the Murat Shrine Temple, you can catch an array of acts. Performance artist Laurie Anderson, singers Tony Bennett and Sarah McLachlan, and jazz saxophonist Branford Marsalis have performed at the Murat. Currently under renovation, it is one of downtown's truly wonderful music venues.

MADAME WALKER
URBAN LIFE CENTER & THEATRE
617 Indiana Ave.   *236-2099*

Built to commemorate Madame C. J. Walker, creator of the Walker System of hair care products and America's first black female millionaire, this beautifully restored building houses both a ballroom and a theater. The center offers events year-round, including Jazz on the Avenue, performances by local, regional and national musicians every Friday evening; and the Walker Repertory Showcase, a series of stage productions by and about the black experience. (Also see entry in The Arts chapter.)

Movie Theaters

Out-of-the-Ordinary Theaters

HOLLYWOOD BAR & FILMWORKS
247 S. Meridian St.   *231-9255*

If your idea of heaven is having someone serve you food and drinks while you watch a movie, then the door to this downtown establishment may just be the Pearly Gates. The Filmworks features new and classic films in a high-tech cinema setting complete with at-your-seat food and beverage service. One of the city's best-kept secrets, the Filmworks is fast gaining popularity among people who appreciate first-rate movies, atmosphere and service.

IRVING THEATER
5507 E. Washington St.   *357-3792*

This small two-screen theater on the east-side shows both second-run Hollywood releases and independent films. It also has great popcorn.

The first Friday of every month, the Indianapolis Museum of Art hosts "First Friday," a combination of live jazz, wine and hors d'oeurves and admission to the museum's galleries. It's a popular event with singles hoping to meet someone interesting amid all the music and art.

Insiders' Tips

GENERAL CINEMA CASTLETON SQUARE
North Parking Lot   *849-3471*

The three screens in this small complex show a combination of offbeat Hollywood and independent films. It's long been among local film buffs' favorite cineplexes.

UNITED ARTISTS THEATRES
Circle Centre, fourth floor
49 W. Maryland St.   *237-6356*

While this nine-screen cinema complex is a lot like other first-run multiple-screen complexes in the area, it includes some elements that set it apart, namely motion simulators and virtual reality theaters. While you can go watch a movie in the same old static setting you're used to, you can also go watch a virtual reality movie that will literally move you (and your seat).

First-Run Theaters

General Cinema Corporation, Clearwater Crossing (12 screens), 82nd Street and Dean Road, 595-6234

Eastgate Mall (six screens), Shadeland Avenue and Washington Street, 377-1117

Glendale Center (three screens), 5988 N. Rural Avenue 253-6491

Greenwood Park Mall (seven screens), 1251 U.S. 31, Greenwood, 888-7224

Lafayette Square (five screens), 3919 Lafayette Road, 293-6200

Sony Cherry Tree (10 screens), 9529 E. Washington Street, 357-3792

Sony College Park (10 screens), W. 86th Street and Michigan Road, 872-4345

Sony Greenwood (10 screens), U.S. 31 and Fry Road, 881-3905

Sony Lafayette Square (eight screens), Lafayette Road and Georgetown Road, 299-0852

Sony Norgate (four screens), Keystone Avenue and 73rd Street, 253-1201

Village Park Plaza (12 screens), U.S. 31 N., Westfield, 843-1666

Second-Run Theaters (a.k.a. "cheap seats")

Greenbriar Cinema (two screens), W. 86th Street and Ditch Road, 253-3015

Woodland Cinema, N. Keystone Avenue and 116th Street, 846-2425

Cinemark Theatres, Greenwood Corners (eight screens), U.S. 31 and Stop 11 Road, 882-0202

Washington Market (eight screens), 10455 E. Washington Street, 898-1990

Drive-Ins

ABC Drive-In Theatre, junction of State Roads 37 and 32, 767-5812

Clermont Deluxe Outdoor Theatres I & II, 10310 E. U.S. Highway 136, 291-1560

Tibbs Drive-in, 480 S. Tibbs Street, 343-6666

Twin Drive-In Theatre, 3000 Southeastern Avenue, 631-8494

Inside
Shopping

Local residents once complained that they had to travel to Chicago to find decent shopping. If that ever was true it's certainly no longer the case. Indianapolis has seen an exciting growth of shopping possibilities in the past five years or so. A Fashion Mall expansion brought Jacobson's, and later Parisian, to the city, and now, with the opening of Circle Centre, residents and visitors are able to enjoy the well-known customer service of Nordstrom and the variety of The Limited stores, as well as an additional Parisian location, not to mention the 100 or so specialty shops that fill Circle Centre.

Excellent shopping can be found all across the city. You'll discover tiny shopping districts tucked into neighborhoods, vibrant collections of specialty stores and enough strip centers and shopping malls to keep you busy year round — and especially during the holidays.

Except for malls and a few special categories, shopping is grouped here by location. Indianapolis is a very drivable city; you can get from one side of town to the other in less than 30 minutes. So hit the bank machine, grab the credit cards and head out to explore the city with a shopping bag in hand.

Just don't forget where you parked the car.

Shopping Districts

Downtown

With the opening of **Circle Centre**,

Photo: The Indianapolis Star & News

Keystone at the Crossing boasts several fine restaurants and stores.

in September 1995 (see sidebar), downtown is experiencing a renewed emphasis on shopping. But in addition to the new mall, the area around Monument Circle offers lots of terrific specialty shops such as **Bash Seeds**, 103 N. Delaware Street, a downtown mainstay since 1902, which stocks an extensive selection of seeds as well as garden accessories in an old-fashioned interior. The **Rocky Mountain Chocolate Factory**, 28 Monument Circle, sells such sinful specialties as fudge, truffles and marvelous caramel apples. For an indulgence of a different sort, check out the custom designs at **Reis-Nichol's Jewelers**, 47 S. Pennsylvania Street; **Goodman Jewelers**, 30 Washington Street, a full-service jeweler, has been a downtown mainstay for years and has hung in there throughout all the construction. **Redwood & Ross** men's clothiers, 11 S. Meridian Street, has also seen its share of nearby construction as Circle Centre has gone up.

Even with the construction, just about everything downtown is easy to get to. A short walk on Pennsylvania Street will take you to **Architectural Center Bookstore**, which stocks an interesting selection of interior and graphic design titles as well as books on restoration and home repair. **Indiana News**, 14 W. Maryland Street, offers a wide selection of magazines, books and newspapers from across the country. Writing — or writing instruments, to be exact — remains the focus at the **Hoosier Pen Company**, 155 W. Washington Street, where you'll find a wide selection of both fountain and ballpoint pens.

And even though it's not right downtown, **Odyssey Map Store**, at 902 N. Delaware Street, is worth a quick drive (or a long walk). The shop stocks thousands of maps, as well as globes and travel guides — a must for anyone dreaming about a getaway.

UNION STATION
39 W. Jackson Pl.   267-0701

This beautifully renovated train station offers buyers and browsers an interesting array of specialty shops including **The Great Train Store** for model trains and railroad-themed books and gifts; **Scents and Soaps**; **Pewter Junction**, which handles works by artist/sculptor Michael Ricker; **Sandcarvers**, a shop that offers personalized gifts, collectibles, ornaments and more; and **Hats Where It Is**, stocking — you guessed it — hats and other accessories.

The station, billed as a festival marketplace, also houses a number of fine dining places (see our Restaurants chapter), as well as an expansive food court ringed by an upper level arcade.

CITY MARKET
222 E. Market St.   634-9266

A market at this site was planned by the city as early as 1821, and the original building, completed in 1886, still boasts food stalls and produce stands, though the emphasis these days is on eating rather than shopping. Lunchtime is the best time of day to visit; the market is crowded with downtown workers who want to grab a corned beef at **Libby's Delicatessen**, Chinese food from the **Rice Bowl** or Afghani fare from **Pameer** (see our Restaurants chapter). Still, the market is a great place to pick up fresh produce at **Constantino's**, imported olive oil at **Aesop's Kitchen and Cupboard** or health food from **The Good Stuff**. Whatever you find, stop for a while and enjoy a cup of coffee and a pastry at **Cath Inc.** or take it outside on the plaza, where tables and benches provide a place to people watch.

Reis - Nichols

Manufacturer • *Designer* • *Importer*

Award-winning customer designs in gold and platinum, with the largest selection of loose diamonds in the state!

Fine Swiss watches from
Rolex • Cartier • Baume & Mercier
Ebel • Raymond Weil

47 South Pennsylvania   2nd Floor Majestic Building
635-4467   One Block East of Circle Centre

MASSACHUSETTS AVENUE
From New York St. to College Ave.

The downtown section of this diagonal street has become something of an art district, with a variety of small galleries representing plenty of talented, innovative artists (see The Arts chapter for more information).

In addition to art, the street offers a number of restaurants as well as interesting shops (see our Restaurants chapter). The shops include: **Stout's Shoes**, a traditional full-service shoe store with an old-fashioned but still-operational system of baskets and pulleys to retrieve selections from the stock area. The **Mass. Ave. Knit Shop** offers all the raw materials necessary for a terrific afghan. Farther down the street, near the corner of College Avenue, **Chatham's on the Avenue** offers a browsable mix of fine cards and gifts (the store takes its name from the neighborhood Chatham Arch). Don't miss the delicious desserts at **The Abbey** coffeehouse next door. Or come back to the area around midnight and hear some great jazz at the **Chatterbox**.

Around Town

OLD TOWNE GREENWOOD
Downtown along Main St.

Though the community of Greenwood has become known for its massive Greenwood Park Mall, you'll find a small but charming area in the old business district downtown. **Making Thyme** offers herbs and related gift items. **Kooler's Boutique** is a traditional dress shop, and **Bauman Interiors** offers beautiful home furnishings and accessories. You'll also spot the **Bay Window**, a small lunch place with excellent soups and sandwiches. Don't miss the well-regarded **Kids Ink** bookstore around the corner on Madison Avenue.

THE SHOPPES AT 56TH AND ILLINOIS
5600 block of Illinois St.

This small shopping district in the Butler Tarkington neighborhood offers considerable convenience, with a handy supermarket and liquor store, plus a variety of specialty shops. The locally owned **Tarkington Tweed** offers fine clothing for women and men including an impressive array of ties. You'll also find fashions at the **Oxford Shop**. The nearby **G. Thrapp Jew-**

Book Nooks

At Insiders' Guides® we have a penchant for bookstores, and in a city like Indianapolis, with a wide variety of top-notch offerings, we couldn't help sharing our favorites with you. For information about the city's vibrant literary life, please see our Literary Life chapter.

General Interest Bookstores

B. DALTON BOOKSELLER

Castleton Square	849-6240
Glendale Square	257-1373
Washington Square	899-4150
Greenwood Park Mall	888-4436

One of the original chains, B. Dalton has downsized many of its stores in recent years. Still, the local outlets regularly stock some 25,000 titles, including a good selection of computer books. There are also in-store newsstands that carry a selection of mainstream magazines and newspapers. B. Dalton stores are open seven days a week.

BARNES & NOBLE BOOKSTORE

3748 E. 82nd St.   594-7525

This store in the Clearwater Crossing complex contains thousands (it claims more than 100,000) of new and backlist books as well as a large remainder section. The magazine racks are jammed with a huge assortment of popular and offbeat publications. Buy a couple and plop down at a table in the in-store coffee shop, order a cappuccino and relax.

Barnes & Noble also hosts a number of book discussion groups (see entry in the "Reading Groups" section of The Literary Life chapter), as well as book signings and other writer-related events. Call or drop by for more information.

Barnes & Noble is open seven days a week.

BOOKLAND

137 W. Market St.   639-9864

This small store just east of the State Capitol building carries one of the largest stocks of newspapers and magazines in Indiana along with an array of paperback books. It's open seven days a week, 6 AM to 7 PM.

BORDERS BOOK SHOP

5612 Castleton Corner Ln.   849-8660

For several years, this has been the place that serious readers go. With more than 125,000 titles in stock, as well as a well-informed and well-read staff, it's the store that all the others in town have to compete with. It's a reader-friendly place, with chairs, benches and couches scattered throughout the store to encourage book browsing and conversation.

It, too, has an extensive selection of magazines and newspapers, including a special section just for literary publications. Border's hosts a variety of public events, including book signings, readings and reading groups (see entry in the "Reading Groups" section of The Literary Life chapter).

Borders is open seven days a week.

BORDERS BOOKS AND MUSIC

8675 River Crossing Blvd.   *574-1776*

This is the new kid in town, having opened for business in September 1995. In nearly 33,000 square feet of space, it contains not only 100,000-plus books, but also more than 50,000 music selections, more than 8,000 videotapes, and some 2,000 CD-ROMs and floppy disks. It also contains an in-store espresso bar, Cafe Espresso, which serves a Borders blend of coffee (strong enough to keep you awake so you can read one more chapter!). Like it's older, well-established predecessor (see previous entry), this Borders hosts readings, book signings and other literary activities. It's open seven days a week.

CHAPTERS BOOKSHOP

8660 Purdue Rd.   *872-2665*

While not as large as Barnes & Noble or Borders, this locally owned northwest-side store has a reputation as a place where a staff that knows about books takes good care of customers who care about books. What it lacks in size, Chapters tries to make up for in service and attractions. Though small, it manages to snare its share of writers on book tours, hosting several book signings every year. Chapters is open seven days a week.

COOPERSMITH'S

The Fashion Mall
Keystone Crossing   *574-9718*

An upscale bookstore in an upscale mall setting, Coopersmith's is a comfortable place to browse the latest releases and bestsellers. It, too, is open seven days a week.

DOUBLEDAY BOOK SHOPS

Circle Centre
39 W. Maryland St.   *632-4910*

With 17,000 titles lining the shelves in a home-library type of setting, this store in Circle Centre caters to an upscale crowd. There are special sections devoted to fiction, cooking, travel, lifestyles, art and children's books. Armchairs allow you to relax and peruse books, while free gift wrapping makes giving a book as a present an easy decision. It's open seven days a week.

INDIANA NEWS CO. INC.

14 W. Maryland St.   *636-7680*

In a funky old building across the street from Circle Centre, Indiana News carries a huge selection of out-of-town and foreign newspapers and magazines as well as sports publications, racing forms and paperbacks. It's open seven days a week from 6 AM to 6 PM.

WALDENBOOKS

Castleton Square	849-2175
National City Bank Plaza	632-2478
Washington Square	898-5537
Greenwood Park Mall	882-0270
1430 S. Range Line Rd., Carmel	575-0062

A longtime rival of B. Dalton, Waldenbooks has also undergone some downsizing in the past few years. Still, the local outlets remain viable sources for recently published fiction and nonfiction titles as well as for mainstream magazines and newspapers. Hours vary according to location.

Specialty Bookstores

ARCHITECTURAL CENTER BOOKSTORE

47 S. Pennsylvania St.   634-3871

For books on architecture, interior and graphic design, restoration and repair, landscaping and related subjects, this small shop is a gold mine. It's open Monday through Friday, 11 AM to 4 PM.

DOWNTOWN COMICS

111 N. Pennsylvania St.   237-0397
5767 E. 86th St.   845-9991

Both locations carry new and collector comics, graphic novels, role playing games and trading cards. Hours vary by location.

DREAMS & SWORDS BOOKSTORE

6503 Ferguson St.   253-9966

This "feminist family bookstore" in Broad Ripple is a good source of books on women's issues — social, political and sexual.

KIDS INK CHILDREN'S BOOKSTORE

5619 N. Illinois St.   255-2598

A real success story, local-style, Kids Ink is one of the Midwest's most respected children's book retailers due to the efforts of owner and founder Shirley Mullin. It's also a real find for aspiring authors of children's or young adults' books. In addition to selling such books, Kids Ink also hosts book signings and helps coordinate Butler University's annual children's literature conference (see the "Literary Events" section of The Literary Life chapter).

MURDER AND MAYHEM BOOKSTORE

6411 Carrollton Ave.   254-8273

This Broad Ripple shop stocks mystery, horror and adventure books for adults and children. It's open Monday through Friday, 11 AM to 6 PM; Saturday, 11 AM to 5 PM; and Sunday, noon to 4 PM.

PASITU ENTERPRISE

309 W. 42nd St.   927-9297

This small shop specializes in Islamic and African-American literature.

X-PRESSION

5912 N. College Ave.   257-5448

This shop specializes in ethnic books and gifts. It's also a great place to meet African-American writers on book tours.

Religious Bookstores

ABBA CHRISTIAN BOOKSTORE

3330 N. Emerson Ave.   546-4406

This small store specializes in African-American art and history, as well as theology and used/rare books.

AGAPE BOOKSTORE

2131 Mitthoeffer Rd.   894-1110

This east-side shop carries Christian books, music, cards, and gifts.

BEREAN CHRISTIAN STORE

8811 Hardegan St.   888-0682

This County Line Mall store stocks Christian books, Bibles, music, videos and Sunday School supplies.

FAMILY BOOKSTORE

10202 E. Washington St.   897-9908

In Washington Square between JCPenney and L.S. Ayres, this shop stocks a variety of Christian books, music, gifts, Bibles and church supplies.

HERALD DISCOUNT

Christian Bookstore
7850 E. 96th St.   842-8942

For 10 percent to 50 percent off religious books, Bibles, music and cards, this is the place to shop.

JOHN 3-16 CHRISTIAN STORE

1056 Broad Ripple Ave.   253-9114

Here you'll find Bibles, books, music, cards and gifts.

KRIEG BROTHERS

Catholic Supply House
119 S. Meridian St.   638-3416

A downtown institution for years, Krieg Brothers specializes in religious books as well as in a variety of Catholic supplies.

LIGHT & LIFE BOOKSTORE

5062 Pike Plaza Rd.   293-9922

From books and Bibles to robes and church supplies, this northwest-side store carries a wide assortment of religious items.

ROMAR CHRISTIAN BOOK STORE

7767 U.S. 31 S.   882-3006
5458 E. 82nd St.   842-5115

Both Romar sites stock books, music, cards, Bibles and church supplies.

UNITY BOOKSTORE

907 N. Delaware St.   635-4066

This downtown shop is a good source of metaphysical, New Age and self-help books and tapes.

Used and Rare Books

ALL-ABOUT BOOKS

5136 N. Keystone Ave.   475-1869

This shop buys and sells rare, used and collectible books.

BLUE RIVER BOOKS

6219 Guilford Ave.   254-3031

A wonderful Broad Ripple place, Blue River specializes in Indiana history, modern first editions, military history, Americana and biography. In addition to books, the shop also deals in historical prints and ephemera.

THE BOOK RACK

8013 E. Washington St.   897-2173
6144 W. 25th St.   297-8968
3780 S. East St.   783-2473
County Line Mall, Greenwood   881-3010

These shops buy, sell and trade used paperbacks.

BOOK SHOP — BARELY USED BOOKS

616 Station Dr., Carmel   843-1855

This store in the Target Mall deals in both hardcover and paperbacks as well as used records.

BOOK WORLD, INC.

5620 Crawfordsville Rd.   241-4000
7775 E. Washington St.   359-0099

Both Book World locations buy, sell and trade used paperbacks and comic books.

BROAD RIPPLE BOOKSHOP

6407 Ferguson St.   *259-1980*

When you visit Broad Ripple Bookshop, you'll enter an old house stacked high with wonderful texts — a book lover's paradise. This shop deals in old, rare and out-of-print books in such subject areas as Indiana, Civil War, Americana and art. You'll also find children's books and modern first editions.

FOUNTAIN OF MYSTERY BOOKS

1119 Prospect St.   *635-2583*

This is a good source for mysteries, true crime and science fiction.

HALF-PRICE BOOKS

8316 Castleton Corner Dr.   *577-0410*
1551 W. 86th St.   *824-9002*
844 N. U.S. 31, Greenwood   *889-1076*

Local outlets of this national used book chain, these three stores buy and sell books, magazines, CDs, LPs and audio and video tapes.

OLD LIBRARY BOOK SHOP

6219 Guilford Ave.   *254-3031*

Actually housed in the former site of the Broad Ripple Library (it's now a few blocks east in Broad Ripple Park), this shop is actually a used book cooperative of some 20 dealers. Here you'll find art books, children's books, American literature and general interest books. It's open Monday through Saturday, 11 AM to 6 PM.

---

elers manufactures beautiful designs in-house. Other shops include **Charles Mayer & Co.** gifts, **Reardon Tennis** and **Kids Ink** bookstore as well as **Kincaid & Sons** meat market, **Banura** for Middle Eastern food and the **Illinois Street Food Emporium** for sandwiches, salads and bakery items.

PENNSYLVANIA AND 49TH STREET SHOPS
Corner of Pennsylvania and 49th

Another small neighborhood shopping area, this little enclave is situated in the midst of the Meridian Kessler neighborhood. Here you'll find **Cafe Patachou**, a popular European-style coffee shop, and **Essential Edibles Too**, a vegetarian carry-out cafe. Antique lovers enjoy **Hope's**

Shop, and just across the street is **Collections Antiques Etc.** Neighborhood residents also patronize **Hamaker Pharmacy** and **Friendly Foods**.

BROAD RIPPLE
Broad Ripple Ave. between
College Ave. and Westfield Blvd.

You could easily spend a whole day — and evening — in this arty, eclectic neighborhood exploring its many shops, galleries and restaurants (see our Restaurants and Nightlife chapters as well). The area is compact enough to explore on foot, though parking — available along the streets and in one lot — is at a premium. Finding a spot on a warm weekend night, when the neighborhood is full of people milling about the sidewalk cafes and walking from one nightspot to another, can be a real challenge. You'll have less trouble during the day, though the neighborhood is still a busy place.

Shops abound. Many are in older Victorian cottages, and the best way to find them is simply to wander the side streets. You'll discover unusual fragrances at **Moorman's Perfumes**, offbeat fashion designs at **Dinwiddie's**, useful art and home accessories at **The Bungalow**, cards and gifts at **Chelsea's**, and furniture from the 1920s through the '50s, as well as glass, pottery and accessories at **Blue Sun Gallery**. **Turandot** stocks unusual and artistic gifts and home accessories. **Artzy Phartzy** offers an array of clothes, art and gift items. **Sitzmark** carries sporting goods and ski wear. **Artifacts** specializes in original art and gift items, and **Marigold** stocks unique women's apparel.

Many more shopping possibilities exist in and around Broad Ripple, including a number of resale boutiques and bookstores (see our sidebar in this chapter).

SOUTH BROAD RIPPLE
College Ave. between 46th and 54th Sts.

The SoBro area, situated along the College Avenue corridor, features a number of interesting shops, most of which are clustered around intersections. In addition to several antique shops, a branch of **Habig's Garden Shops** and **Modern Times** bookstore, the neighborhood boasts one of the city's best gourmet groceries, **Atlas Supermarket**, where Indianapolis native David Letterman worked as a bag boy. You'll find African-American books and gifts at **X-Pressions**, children's "gently worn" clothes at **Casey's Closet**, distinctive timepieces at **Clockworks**, used furniture and antiques at **Bluemingdeals** and delicious desserts at the **Broad Ripple**

Pie Company, **Cath** and **Cornerstone Coffee and Espresso Bar**.

NORA
86th St. between Meridian St. and Westfield Blvd.

Though Nora remains a residential area as well as a shopping district, it is also home to a considerable variety of specialty shops. In addition to grocery and discount store shopping, you'll find gift items at **Perry Luggage & Gifts** and **The Accent Shop** and original jewelry designs at **Aronstam**. Look for fashionable kidswear at **The Blue Bear** and **New Generation Kids**. Those with a green thumb will want to check out **Habig's Garden Shop** and its **Garden Cottage** expansion right across the street.

CLEARWATER SHOPPES AND CLEARWATER CROSSING
82nd St. between Keystone Ave. and Allisonville Rd.

This area has burgeoned in the last few years and now boasts quite a sizeable and varied selection of stores and restaurants. You'll find kids' clothes at **Chocolate Soup**, fine wines and spirits at **The Wine Gallery**, a **Barnes and Noble** bookstore complete with an espresso bar, **Leland's** fireplace accessories, **Expressions Custom Furniture**, **Houseworks** home decor and accessories and many more.

CASTLETON
82nd St. and Allisonville Rd.

By the early 1990s what was once a small village had become the county's most intensively developed shopping district. Indeed, Castleton boasts nearly 20 shopping centers within just 2 square miles. You can find just about anything you want, from party supplies to sporting goods, computers to kidswear. Though the many strip centers boast a multitude of small shops, some of the major area stores are **Graham's**

Photo: The Indianapolis Star & News

City Market is a favorite place for workers and downtown shoppers to meet for lunch.

Crackers, 5981 E. 86th Street, which stocks a huge inventory of collectibles and gifts, and the expansive **Kittle's Home Furnishings**, 8600 Allisonville Road, which boasts an Ethan Allen gallery and its in-house design studio. And in the midst of it all is Castleton Square Mall.

WEST 86TH STREET
Between Meridian St. and N. Michigan Rd.

Work your way west along this stretch of very busy street where you'll find several popular strip malls and such stores as **Courtyard Cottage**, which specializes in intimate apparel; **Mary V**, offering fine women's wear in larger sizes; **Arnold's Men's Store** for updated traditional clothing; **Collections 94** with its out-of-the-ordinary fashions; **Little Women and Company** for girls' special occasion dresses — as well as tea parties. And **Wells Flower & Gift House**, across from St. Vincent Hospital, offers browsers a great selection of gift items.

ZIONSVILLE
Northwest of Indianapolis off N. Michigan Rd.

This charming village, with its bricked Main Street, distinctive boutiques, restaurants and specialty shops, provides a good day's worth of shopping. Like Broad Ripple, which was itself once a separate village, Zionsville is compact enough to be explored on foot. Here you'll find a number of antique shops (see our "Antiques" section in this chapter), as well as **Potpourri**, **Stacy LaBolts**, **Lilly's Boutique Gallery** and the **Children's Clothier** for fine apparel; and the **Tin Soldier**, the **Gift Horse** and the **General Store** for unusual gift items and home accessories. Other specialty stores include **Avalon Jewelers**, the **Village Clock** shop, **Ironwood** book shop, **My Mother's Doll Shop** and the **Rug Gallery**. Refer to our Restaurants chapter for the scoop on Zionsville's many excellent eateries.

Malls

The Greater Indianapolis area boasts malls on all sides of town, and all are easily worth a morning or afternoon of browsing. You'll find major department stores, specialty shops, theaters and plenty of dining options, from sit-down restaurants to grab-a-sandwich food courts.

Downtown Goes
Uptown with Circle Centre

Wow! That's the reaction many people have the first time the see Circle Centre. And who can blame them? This 800,000-square-foot, four-level shopping and entertainment complex in the heart of downtown Indianapolis, which opened for business on September 8, 1995, is no run-of-the-mill mall.

In addition to including the only Nordstrom department store in Indiana, Circle Centre includes an array of other upscale retailers — the city's second Parisian department store (the other is at the Fashion Mall on the north side), an FAO Schwartz toy store, The Museum Company, Doubleday Book Shops, The Body Shop, Guess Home Collection and Kitchen Express. It also includes a variety of restaurants and nightclubs, as well as a United Artists cineplex with nine theaters and a virtual reality arcade.

In all, there are nearly 100 Circle Centre tenants, making it the retail/entertainment complex that city planners long envisioned as an essential component of downtown revitalization. Its construction capped a two-decade-long effort to once again make downtown Indianapolis an inviting place for residents and visitors.

With other components already in place — sports and performing arts venues, hotels, a convention center, a zoo, museums and housing — what was needed to round out downtown redevelopment was a project that would revitalize the once-bustling shopping district.

As in other cities around the country, most of Indianapolis's major retailers had abandoned the downtown area for suburban shopping malls. The stores that remained— a handful of clothing and shoe stores, some jewelers, a few newsstands and book shops — survived due to patronage by downtown office workers.

But on evenings and weekends, no one shopped downtown.

Yet as the convention business boomed, and as sports venues sprouted, people began coming downtown on Saturday and Sunday afternoons. And civic leaders took a look at what was missing: a place for all these people with time on their hands and money in their pockets to go either before or after their events. Why not send them shopping?

That was the genesis for one of the largest construction projects in Indiana's history. Circle Centre was conceived and constructed to lure shoppers — including out-of-town conventioneers and area residents — to the downtown district.

With a $310 million price tag, the project was developed by a joint public-private partnership between the City of Indianapolis and Circle Centre Development Company, which is itself a partnership between real estate development and management company Simon Property Group Inc. and 19 corporate investors. According to the International Council of Shopping centers, a corporate collaboration of this magnitude was unprecedented in retail development.

Designed by the New York firm Ehrenkrantz & Eckstut Architects, Circle Centre's architecture combines the facades from eight older buildings with new construction to achieve a graceful, elegant appearance that's both comfortable and contemporary. Inside, arched skylights running the length of the mall allow natural light in, and storefronts run the gamut from elegantly understated (Coach, Ann Taylor) to unexpectedly funky (Junkyard, a unisex clothing store). The overall effect is urban and urbane — at once cosmopolitan, metropolitan and fun.

THE STORES

The largest of the mall's tenants, and one of its two anchor stores, is **Nordstrom**, which is housed in a 28,000-square-foot facility. Famous for customer service (there's an in-store concierge), the Seattle-based department store carries very high quality merchandise, including more than 150,000 pairs of shoes (including hard-to-find sizes) in five shoe departments as well as 35 specialty departments offering designer clothing and accessories for men, women and children. Elegant is the operative word at Nordstrom.

Parisian, a Georgia-based department store chain, is the second anchor. It covers 145,000 square feet and specializes in fine-quality clothing, shoes and accessories for men, women and children. One innovative touch for restless kids is an in-store jungle gym, while for harried adults the store offers personal shopping services. Like Nordstrom, Parisian prides itself on customer service.

In addition to the anchors, Circle Centre contains stores that cater to a wide variety of needs and desires. At **Abercrombie & Fitch Co.** you'll find rugged, contemporary sportswear for men and women, while at **Banana Republic** the clothes for both sexes are classic and comfortable. For women, there's **Everything But Water** that sells swimwear; in a somewhat drier mode, there's **Bebe**, which offers a private collection of business and casual clothes.

Men can drop by **Structure**, which sells European-design sportswear, or **Britches Great Outdoors**, home of both casual and business clothes. For kids, the mall offers **Baby Guess?** and **Guess? Kids** as well as **Gap Kids**.

If you've got a hankering for chocolate, there's **Godiva Chocolatier**, where you'll find more than 70 types of freshly made candies. Or if you prefer smelling sweet things to eating them, try **The Body Shop** or **Garden Botanika**, both of which deal in natural hair and body products.

If it's art you're after, take a peek inside **The White River Trader**, a store operated by the local Eiteljorg Museum of American Indians and Western Art, and Niang African Art and More. Also, stop by **Papyrus** for handmade greeting cards, imported gift wrap and collector-quality fountain pens.

If you're an avid reader (you're reading this, right?), the **Doubleday Books Shops** offer more than 17,000 fiction, travel, cooking, lifestyle and children's books, while at **Sam Goody** you'll find more than 35,000 CDs and cassettes as well as videotapes, laserdisks and computer software.

In other words, there's something for everyone at Circle Centre.

PARKING

Realizing that the success of Circle Centre would in part depend on overcoming central Indiana residents' reluctance to venture downtown where parking could sometimes be a problem, mall developers included underground parking garages in its design. Well-lit and well-marked with icons to help you find your car again once you've finished shopping, Circle Centre's garages contain 2,700 spaces. For maximum safety, the garages are patrolled regularly by a private security company. The cost for up to three hours of parking is $1.

HOURS

Circle Centre is open Monday to Saturday, 10 AM to 9 PM, and Sunday, noon to 6 PM. Individual tenants — notably restaurants, nightclubs and movie theaters — are open on different schedules.

CASTLETON SQUARE

82nd St. and Allisonville Rd.   849-9993

Situated near one of the city's busiest intersections, Castleton Square Mall remains a very popular shopping destination. Anchored by a new **L.S. Ayres**, as well as **Lazarus, JCPenney, Sears** and **Montgomery Ward**, the mall also offers a dozen shops unique to the city. Serious browsers can relax with a cup of coffee from **Barnie's** or enjoy an above-it-all view at **Lazarus' Top of the Mall** restaurant, where window-side tables overlook the mall below. Or take in a movie; Castleton's cinema is known for its highbrow and offbeat flicks. The area around the mall along 82nd Street abounds with strip centers; nearby you'll find everything from natural foods to doughnuts, from computer gear to sporting goods.

EASTGATE CONSUMER MALL

7150 E. Washington St.   352-0951

This east side bargain-hunter's dream offers plenty of off-price possibilities, though few of the traditional mall extras such as fountains and fancy food courts. Here you'll find **Burlington Coat Factory**, which in addition to coats stocks good quality menswear, dresses, kids' clothes and even baby furniture.

THE FASHION MALL

Keystone Ave. and 86th St.

Anyone looking for the unusual, the designer name, the out of the ordinary has to hit the Fashion Mall. Anchored by **Jacobson's**, which offers a Chanel boutique, and **Parisian**, the mall's two upscale department stores are linked by loads of small and not-so-small shops specializing in designer labels, distinctive accessories and other pricey items. Here's where you'll find such national names as **Banana Republic, Eddie Bauer, Abercrombie & Fitch, Crabtree & Evelyn** and **The Sharper Image**. Local retailers such as **N. Theobald** and **J.T. Meusing** feature fine gifts, china and crystal, while **M.G. Tates** stocks great kitchen gadgets and home accessories, and **Kits & Kaboodle** features unique, collectible and educational toys. The mall offers food court dining as well as the always-popular **Dalt's** and **TGI Friday's**, both excellent lunch spots (though you may have to wait for a table). The adjacent **Radisson Plaza Hotel** also offers fine dining at **Waterson's** and a more casual atmosphere at the **Keystone Cafe**. **Keystone at the Crossing** (where Keystone crosses 86th Street), as the area is called, boasts several other fine restaurants, and a new shopping area is under construction.

GLENDALE CENTER

6101 N. Keystone Ave.   *251-9281*

One of the city's oldest enclosed malls, Glendale is anchored by **L.S. Ayres** and **Lazarus** and is home to 100 specialty shops. Stores include **This End Up** furniture, **Lechter's** housewares, **African Art and More** and **Watercolor Indiana**, as well as plenty of specialty clothiers. **Kits & Kaboodle** toy shop, with its unique collectibles, educational and science-related toys, teddy bears and Brio train sets, is also here. The mall also houses longtime favorite **Houlihan's** restaurant, **Swensen's** ice cream and sandwiches and newcomer **Oggi Ristorante**. You can also catch a first-run flick or a bargain movie, and the unique shops and nightlife of Broad Ripple are nearby.

GREENWOOD PARK

1251 U.S. Hwy. 31 N.
Greenwood   *881-6758*

This south-side mega-mall has it all:

movies, plenty of specialty shops, restaurants and such major department stores as **L.S. Ayres**, **Lazarus**, **JCPenney**, **Sears** and **Montgomery Ward**. Billed as the state's largest mall (though Fort Wayne's Glenbrook Square also claims the title), this is where TV stations go to shoot videotape of the holiday shopping crush. The massive parking lots really do fill up; just try to find a space the weekend after Thanksgiving. But for an all-day mall extravaganza, you can't beat it. And the whole mall area offers one strip center after another providing even more possibilities.

LAFAYETTE SQUARE

38th St. and Lafayette Rd.   *291-6390*

West-side shopping focuses on Lafayette Square, where nearly 100 stores, including **L.S. Ayres**, **Sears**, **Lazarus**, **JCPenney** and **Montgomery Ward**, offer buyers a wide variety of shopping options. In addition to the standard mall theater and specialty shops, you'll even find **G.C. Murphy's**, a traditional dime store complete with a lunch counter and deliciously sticky caramel corn. The immediate area, along both Lafayette Road and W. 38th Street, provides plenty of strip center shopping; you'll find shops specializing in fabric, menswear, ceramic tile, garden supplies and more.

WASHINGTON SQUARE

10202 E. Washington St.   *899-4567*

Especially popular among eastsiders and those who live in nearby Hancock and Shelby counties, Washington Square pro-

---

Prowl around the streets of the Broad Ripple neighborhood; you'll find excellent art galleries, bookstores and gift shops (and plenty of good restaurants too).

Insiders' Tips

vides shoppers with 120 stores, including the major anchors of **L.S. Ayres, Lazarus, Sears, Montgomery Ward** and **JCPenney**. You'll find housewares, gift shops, specialty clothiers, shoe stores, movies and plenty of fast food options. E. Washington Street offers an abundance of shopping; you could spend a day working your way east, stopping at huge furniture stores, small dress shops, discount dens and other emporia.

Antiques

Read on and you'll soon see that Greater Indianapolis has plenty to offer any antique buff.

There's also the renowned 35-mile stretch of U.S. 40 extending east from Knightstown to Richmond that might just be heaven on earth. Known as Antique Alley, this highway stretch provides access to some 700 antique dealers. If you're in the mood for a drive, you won't want to miss it.

Indianapolis

ANTIQUE BARN VILLAGE/
BARN VILLAGE ANTIQUES
5209 N. College Ave.   283-5011

In the area where Broad Ripple meets Meridian Kessler (called "SoBro" for South Broad Ripple), this shop buys and sells a little bit of everything — furniture, clocks, dolls, signs, music boxes, antique toys, art deco radios, pottery, patio furniture, paintings, rugs and statuary. It's a browser's paradise that's open seven days a week.

THE ANTIQUE CENTRE
3422 N. Shadeland Ave.   545-3879

With 75 showcases of collectibles and 10,000 square feet of furniture and accessories, it's easy to see why this place bills itself as "the place to start your treasure

hunt." You'll also find American Indian artifacts and antiquarian books. It's open Tuesday through Sunday.

ANTIQUES N MORE
3440 N. Shadeland Ave.   542-8526

From sterling flatware to oak and mahogany armoires, tables and more, this place sells it — and buys it, including entire estates. It's open seven days a week.

BLUE SUN GALLERY
922 E. Westfield Blvd.   255-8441

This Broad Ripple area shop carries furniture from the 1920s to the 1950s as well as glassware and pottery. It's open Tuesday through Saturday and is closed Sunday and Monday.

COLLECTIONS ANTIQUES, ETC.
113 E. 49th St.   283-5251

With a focus on 19th-century European furnishings and accessories, Collections is an upscale shop in the heart of the Meridian Kessler neighborhood. It's open Monday through Saturday, and is closed on Sunday.

COLONIAL ANTIQUES
5000 W. 96th St.   873-2727

Specializing in architectural antiques — fireplace mantles, doors, windows, pillars, etc. — this northwest-side shop also buys and sells a variety of other items. It's open Friday and Saturday, noon to 5 PM and Monday through Thursday, by chance or appointment.

EARL'S AUCTION COMPANY
5199 Lafayette Rd.   291-5843

You'll find antique furniture, firearms, tools and a live auction every Tuesday. It's open for inspection of goods Monday through Saturday; the auction is Tuesday at 4 PM.

Photo: The Indianapolis Star & News

Glendale is one of the city's oldest enclosed malls.

FINDS ANTIQUES
1764 E. 86th St.   571-1950

This shop in the Northview Mall caters to an upscale crowd. Here you'll find period furniture, porcelains, lamps, Oriental rugs and decorative accessories. If you've got something to sell (or something you're curious about, Finds offers professional appraisals. It's open Tuesday through Saturday and is closed Sunday and Monday.

FOUNTAIN SQUARE ANTIQUE MALL
1056 Virginia Ave.   636-1056

With more than 70 dealers, this is the largest two-story antique mall in the city. Looking for an old oak hutch? An antique watch? A tin milk box? Look here. It's open seven days a week.

HOPE'S SHOP
116 E. 49th St.   283-3004

Specializing in glass, china, kitchenware and dolls, this small Meridian Kessler shop also offers expert appraisals. It's open Tuesday through Saturday; it's closed Sunday and Monday.

IN PRAISE OF THE PORCH
1764 E. 86th St.   571-1950, 675-9485

Across the street from North Central High School, this shop deals in antique wicker furniture and accessories. It's open Tuesday through Saturday and is closed Sunday and Monday.

INDIANAPOLIS DOWNTOWN ANTIQUE MALL
1066 Virginia Ave.   635-5336

In the historical Fountain Square district (c. 1870, the oldest continually functioning commercial district in Indiana), this mall consists of 40 shops on two floors. Here you'll find everything from Depression glassware and American art pottery to furniture, quilts and Hummel figurines. It's open seven days a week.

QUALITY ANTIQUES
1105 Shelby St.   686-6018

This store in the Fountain Square Theatre Building specializes in lamps, furniture and barware from the '50s. You'll also find deco-era items and primitives, as well as other collectibles and rare oddities. It's open seven days a week. (If shopping makes you hungry, right next door you'll find the Fountain Diner, an authentic 1959 diner.)

RECOLLECTIONS

5202 N. College Ave.   283-3800

From antique toys and musical instruments to hand tools and costume jewelry, this shop's got it. It's open Monday through Saturday and is closed Sunday.

RED ROSE VINTAGE CLOTHING

834 E. 64th St.   257-5016

There's used clothing and there's *vintage* clothing — this Broad Ripple shop buys and sells the latter. This is where to go if you're in need of a genuine flapper dress or 1940s suit. It's open Monday through Saturday and is closed Sunday.

SHADELAND ANTIQUE MALL

3444 N. Shadeland Ave.   542-7283

The oldest and largest antique mall in the city, this east-side facility contains 99 dealers who buy and sell a range of antique items — furniture, musical instruments, radios, toys, books, sheet music, lamps, china, glassware, rugs, jewelry, etc. It's open seven days a week.

SOLOMON-JONES

2850 N. Meridian St.   926-5555

Offering antiques, traditional interior design assistance and appraisal service, Solomon-Jones focuses on an upscale clientele. It's open Monday through Saturday and is closed Sunday.

TRASH TO TREASURES

5505 N. Keystone Ave.   253-2235

Operated by longtime Indianapolis antiques dealer Virginia Lucas, this shop is a stockpile of both stuff and knowledge. Whether you're looking for a table, a lamp or someone who knows antiques, this place is worth a trip. It's open Thursday through Saturday.

Boone County

BROWN'S ANTIQUE SHOP

315 N. Fifth St.
Zionsville   873-2284

Established in 1945, Brown's consists of three buildings filled with furniture. It's open seven days a week.

THE SOW'S EAR

76 S. Main St., Zionsville   873-2785

Specializing in Hummel figurines, Lalique glassware, music boxes, slot machines and art glass, this shop is open Monday through Saturday.

Hamilton County

ACORN FARM ANTIQUES

15466 Oak Rd., Carmel   846-2383

This shop in a 10-room Colonial house is home to a variety of quality items — furniture, brass, silver, copper, glass, china and paintings. It's open Tuesday through Saturday.

ANTIQUE EMPORIUM

1055 S. Range Line Rd.   844-8351

Here you'll find fine quality furniture from country casual to formal as well as handmade Oriental rugs and accessories. It's open Tuesday through Saturday.

ANTIQUES GALORE & MORE

110 E. Main St., Westfield   867-1228

When you're looking for Victorian furniture, art glass, art pottery and Indiana art, stop by this place that specializes in the unique and unusual. It's open Wednesday through Saturday and by appointment.

THE ANTIQUE MALL OF CARMEL

622 S. Range Line Rd.
Carmel   848-1280

This mall features 30 booths of quality antiques and collectibles. It's open seven days a week.

ANTIQUES & STUFF
18386 Moontown Rd.
Noblesville   896-3416

Whether you're in the mood for an old steamer trunk, a ceramic water jug or a rolltop desk, this shop is worth a stop. A bit off the beaten path, but it's worth the trek to find out what owner Judy Williams has on hand. It's open evenings and weekends.

R. BEAUCHAMP ANTIQUES
16405 Westfield Blvd.
Westfield   896-3717

With more than 16,000 square feet of American and European antique furnishings, Oriental rugs and accessories, this shop claims to have one of the largest selections of goods in the Midwest. It's open Tuesday through Saturday.

BOUND TO BE FOUND ANTIQUES
74 N. Ninth St.
Noblesville   776-1993

With stock that runs the gamut from old toys and advertising ephemera to military items and primitives, this place on the east-side of Noblesville's square is bound to be found by serious antiquers.

THE COLLECTOR'S DOOR
44 S. Eighth St., Noblesville   773-4777

A man's antique shop, this place stocks tools and nautical instruments as well as sports- and travel-related antiques. Open Monday through Friday.

LAZY ACRES ANTIQUES
77 Metsker Ln., Noblesville   773-7387

Inside a c. 1872 barn and carriage house, this shop specializes in American, primitive and folk art. It's open seven days a week.

NOBLESVILLE ANTIQUE MALL
20 N. Ninth St., Noblesville   773-5095

Within the walls of this restored 1880s building are three floors of furniture, glassware, art, jewelry and antiquarian books. It's open seven days a week.

STRAWTOWN POTTERY & ANTIQUES
12738 Strawtown Ave.
Noblesville   984-5080

Offering a selection of quality antique furniture, handmade pottery and Native American artifacts, this shop is open Tuesday through Saturday.

UNION STREET ANTIQUES/THE JONATHON WESTFIELD COMPANY
120 N. Union St.
Westfield   896-3566

From Windsor chairs and tin lighting to folk art and handmade furniture, you're apt to find it here. It's open Monday through Saturday.

Hendricks County

GILLEY'S ANTIQUE MALL
1209 W. Main St.
Plainfield   839-8779

This mall, which consists of two buildings and more than 250 booths, is open seven days a week. During the summer, Gilley's also hosts weekend flea markets.

Specialty Stores

Gourmet Groceries

Looking for hoisin sauce, tahini, Stilton or an exotic spice for your favorite recipe? You're sure to find them at one of these specialty food stores. (But don't forget the major chains. You'll find a good selection of specialty items at Cub, Marsh and Kroger

— all have locations around town — as well.)

A-1 Oriental Supermarket

3709 N. Shadeland Ave.   546-5252

This specialty grocery, one of the state's largest, stocks foods items from China, Japan, Korea, the Philippines, Thailand and Latin America.

Atlas Supermarket

5411 N. College Ave.   255-6800

This full-service grocery, where David Letterman worked as a bagboy, stocks the usual stuff in addition to a wide variety of specialty ingredients and gourmet and imported foods. You'll find shoppers crowding through the narrow aisles and clustered around the popular deli counter.

The Cheese Shop

8702 Keystone Crossing   846-6885

Check out the Cheese Shop in the Fashion Mall for a variety of fancy imported foods and gourmet take-out in addition to the specialty cheeses.

Marsh

Locations all over town
Corporate Offices
9800 Crosspoint Blvd.   594-2100

You'll find these expansive well-stocked stores all across the city. They boast excellent bakeries and delis. Don't pass by one when you're looking for specialty ingredients.

Meijer

1425 W. Carmel Dr.	573-8300
72 N. Ind. 135	885-3000
5349 Pike Plaza	387-2400
11351 E. Washington St.	894-6700

Though not really what we call gourmet, Meijer gains inclusion here due to its unique grocery/department store stock (shoes, clothes, toys, hardware and household goods in addition to grocery and fresh produce) and its 24-hour-a-day schedule.

Nuts Plus

4217 Lafayette Rd.	299-4628
11554 Westfield Blvd.	575-8952

Here you'll find an assortment of imported foods and spices from India, Pakistan and the Middle East.

O'Malia's Food Market

General Office
867 W. Carmel Dr.   573-8088

These full-line upscale groceries stock plenty of specialty foods amid very pleasant surroundings — carpeted floors, attractive decor. Check out the baked goods and meat counters. Though primarily on the north side, O'Malia's maintains a store — complete with a cooking school kitchen — in downtown's Lockerbie neighborhood.

Sakura Mart

2450 E. 71st St.   254-9598

This offshoot of the popular Sakura Japanese Restaurant sells an array of imported Asian ingredients as well as fresh seafood and sushi-to-go.

Jewelers

Hofmeister Personal Jewelers

3809 E. 82nd St.   577-7070

In this lovely Lake Clearwater building, you'll find a small staff of professionals, including five full-time goldsmiths, dedicated to customer service. Hofmeister, a family business, offers everything from simple engagement rings to lavish custom designs. Manufacturing of the firm's award-winning designs is done in-house. It's also an official Rolex dealer.

Reis-Nichols Jewelers

47 S. Pennsylvania St.   635-4467

This family-owned business stresses personal service and designs and manufacturers its award-winning designs at its downtown facility. It also handles Masonic, emblematic and award jewelry and employs a certified Rolex watchmaker.

Outdoors and Recreation

GAYLAN'S
Castleton Corner Shopping Center
Allisonville Rd. and 86th St.   842-9606

Galyan's sporting goods supermarkets, with several locations in the metropolitan area, stock just about anything you'd need for just about any sport. The north-side location even includes a wall to simulate rock-climbing and the instruction to learn to do it.

OUTDOOR VENTURES
73 E. Epler Ave.   784-1255

Stocking new and used military surplus, camping, caving and rapelling gear, this shop also offers training classes and adventure trips.

PLAY IT AGAIN SPORTS
2110 Broad Ripple Ave.   257-0036

These shops at several locations in the metropolitan area buy and sell new and used sporting goods, and you can often get good deals on secondhand equipment, stuff maybe used a few times before its former

owner decided that perhaps rock climbing was a bit too strenuous.

SITZMARK
924 Westfield Blvd.   251-8557

Perhaps known primarily as a ski outfitter, Sitzmark also carries backpacking, hiking, rock climbing and in-line skating gear.

DON'S GUNS
96th St. and Keystone Ave.   574-0800

You'll see Don Davis' cheesy ads on late-night TV hyping his shops that sell an array of firearms as well as hunting and fishing supplies at several locations. The stores also boast indoor shooting ranges.

FALL CREEK BAIT & TACKLE
4215 E. Fall Creek Pkwy. N. Dr.   251-9229

This longtime landmark offers hunting and fishing supplies for the serious sportsperson.

FLYMASTERS
1001 E. 86th St.   255-3597

The city's only store specializing in fly fishing offers a course to introduce novices to the sport.

Photo: The Indianapolis Star & News

The Indiana Soldiers and Sailors Monument stands in tribute to the more than 210,000 Hoosiers killed during the Civil War and the more than 4,000 Hoosiers killed in the War with Mexico.

Inside
Attractions

Attractions in Indianapolis boast a certain historic flair, and visitors and newcomers remark upon the city's many monuments, statues and historical markers. We like to commemorate people and events around here. Scattered throughout downtown you'll find statues immortalizing the likes of the young Abe Lincoln and such sculpture as "Jammin' on the Avenue," a free-form collage of musical instruments in the Lockefield Gardens area. And of course, Miss Indiana herself, the statue named Victory that tops the Soldiers and Sailors Monument. You get a great sense of history by walking up to some of these monuments, touching them, reading the inscriptions and getting a feel for what earlier residents thought was important enough to immortalize. Most of our museums also offer a historical perspective, though you can find plenty of modern galleries as well (see our Arts and Culture chapter).

Indianapolis features numerous examples of historic architecture; indeed, a stroll through downtown is a veritable walking tour — if you know where to look. Use the following descriptions as a guide and pick up a detailed map from Landmark Tours, 340 W. Michigan Street. Those who prefer to tour in style can take a horse-drawn carriage; many drivers can tailor a tour to suit your interests. You'll see these Hansom cabs all over downtown on weekends and can almost always find them waiting outside Union Station or at the Capitol Street entrance of the Hyatt Regency Hotel.

While we've tried to highlight our major attractions here, you'll also find some listed elsewhere in this book as well. The Children's Museum, for example, certainly ranks as one of the city's top attractions, but for a detailed discussion of its many wonders, see our Kidstuff chapter. Ditto for the Indianapolis Zoo and Conner Prairie. And don't forget to check our Sports chapter for a look at some of the venues that earned Indianapolis its "amateur sports capital" label.

Visitors — and even longtime residents — may be surprised at the variety of sights to see in the Indianapolis area. From Rembrandts to railroads, local museums

---

When ogling the exterior of our impressive Statehouse, don't be too startled by a sudden burst of loud, raucous laughter when you think no one else is around. The recorded noise is just the state's nonviolent way of shooing away pigeons.

Insiders' Tips

offer something for every interest. Some, such as the Eiteljorg, the Indiana State Museum and the National Art Museum of Sport, lie within walking distance of downtown, but most others, including the Indianapolis Museum of Art, require at least a short drive. Our notable monuments, historic sights and architectural attractions however, clustered as they are in the downtown area, can be easily toured on foot, if you have plenty of time and some comfortable shoes. A few exceptions, including Crown Hill Cemetery and historic North Meridian Street, require transportation for more comfortable sightseeing. What follows is a guide to the museums, monuments and historic sights that make Indianapolis something to see.

General Attractions

INDIANAPOLIS CITY CENTER
201 S. Capitol Ave. 237-5200

Any sightseeing should really begin at the Indianapolis City Center.

Need some help getting the lay of the land? Take a look at the 13-by-13-foot model of downtown. Touch a button and local landmarks light up, allowing you to see just how far Union Station is from Monument Circle (not far at all — an easy walk) or from Indiana Avenue (a healthy hike). The place offers plenty of souvenirs as well, including the requisite selection of mugs, T-shirts and tote bags. You could easily fill one of those bags with brochures; the City Center offers more than 300 highlighting local and statewide attractions.

INDIANAPOLIS/
MARION COUNTY PUBLIC LIBRARY
40 E. St. Clair St. 269-1700

This beautiful building, with its impressive lobby and seductive book stacks,

ranks as many people's favorite downtown spot. Situated as it is near the American Legion Mall, the library offers a great view of downtown from the front steps. Inside are more than 1.5 million books and plenty of out-of-the-way reading spots in which to enjoy them. The Riley Room on the lower level offers a great children's collection. Plenty of special events, such as lectures, film series, readings, small-scale theater productions, etc., are offered here at the Central Library as well as at the many branches across the city. The library opens 9 AM to 9 PM Monday through Friday, 9 AM to 5 PM Saturday and 1 PM to 5 PM Sunday. The library is closed on major holidays as well as over the Memorial Day weekend, when the 500 Festival Parade that takes place nearby makes it nearly impossible to reach the door.

INDIANAPOLIS ZOO
100 W. Washington St. 630-2001

You'll find this beautiful downtown zoo within walking distance of the Statehouse and the Eiteljorg Museum. Its centerpiece, an $8.5 million waters building, offers piranhas, penguins and even underwater viewing of polar bears at play. See our Kidstuff chapter for more details.

CANAL WALK
Ohio and West sts. 632-1824

Situated below street level, this stretch of the renovated Central Canal provides a lovely spot for walking or jogging, and on any nice day you'll see loads of downtown workers doing both. The areas designated by the purple Canal Walk signs feature beautiful landscaping, fountains, bridges — and plenty of people enjoying them during lunch. The State Office Building cafeteria opens onto the Canal; you can eat indoors or tote your lunch

Be There When History Comes Alive At Conner Prairie

Go For A Ride In The Past Lane.

Take a time trip at the 1836 Village of Prairietown. Everyone in the histroic Village seems to be expecting you, and they're ready to chat about their lives in early Indiana.

Have Lunch With The Governor.

A trip to Conner Prairie is not complete without lunching at Governor Noble's Eating Place, overlooking the rolling prairie.

13400 Allisonville Road
Fishers, IN 46038
(317) 776-6000

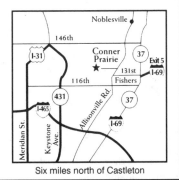

Six miles north of Castleton

out to one of the handy picnic tables. It's a pleasant spot to rest after touring of the Statehouse or the Eiteljorg. Kids like the pedal boats; see our Kidstuff chapter for details.

CAPITOL COMMONS
Corner of Washington St. and Capitol Ave.

This beautiful park, reminiscent of a formal English garden, boasts a huge fountain as its centerpiece. Surrounding the fountain are grassy areas, flower beds, walkways and seating areas. Across Washington Street is the Statehouse; beneath the garden is an underground parking garage.

Museums and Monuments

INDIANAPOLIS MUSEUM OF ART
1200 W. 38th St.   *923-1331*

The 152 acres along White River and the Central Canal where the Indianapolis Museum of Art is located may be one of the prettiest spots in the city. The wooded grounds feature trails, gardens, a greenhouse and numerous statues scattered about — as well as the huge Robert Indiana "LOVE" sculpture (the letters L, O, V and E are stacked atop each other). Don't miss a stroll outside before or after visiting the museum itself. Four pavilions house the museum's collections, which include Renaissance works, Old Masters, 19th century French pieces and outstanding collections of Asian and African art. A recent expansion enlarged the museum's capacity considerably, and it boasts plenty of flexibility for showcasing the many traveling exhibits the IMA hosts. The building is also home to Civic Theater. The IMA opens 11 AM to 5 PM Tuesday through Sunday; you can usually join a docent-led tour at 2 PM. Contributions are encouraged. Special exhibits often require admission.

THE CHILDREN'S MUSEUM
3000 N. Meridian St.   *924-5431*

You don't need a kid in tow to take in the incredible array of attractions at the Children's Museum; you'll see plenty of adults wandering about on their own or showing their spouses exhibits they remember from their own childhood (the huge stuffed polar bear is a longtime museum favorite). Refer to our Kidstuff chapter for detailed information on this local landmark.

CONNER PRAIRIE
13400 Allisonville Rd., Fishers   *773-0666*

Another notable sight highlighted in our Kidstuff chapter, Conner Prairie interests history buffs of all ages. A living history museum showcasing Indiana life in 1836, the village wins kudos for authenticity. In addition to its impressive historical details, Conner Prairie is also noted for its handmade salt glaze pottery and the winter Hearthside Suppers held in the restored Conner home. See our Festivals and Events chapter for more information on the January through March Hearthside Suppers.

INDIANA STATE MUSEUM
202 N. Alabama St.   *232-1637*

The former Indianapolis City Hall building is home to the Indiana State Museum, which often hosts traveling exhibits from the Smithsonian. On permanent display are geological and historical exhibits highlighting life in Indiana. Don't miss the huge Foucault pendulum that — due to the Earth's rotation — endlessly knocks down strategically placed wooden pegs. See our Kidstuff chapter for more information.

EITELJORG MUSEUM OF AMERICAN INDIANS AND WESTERN ART
500 W. Washington St.   *636-9378*

Art and artifacts of the American West are exhibited in this beautiful museum. The building's design was inspired by Southwest-

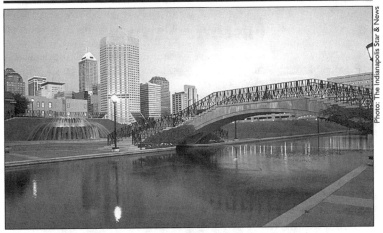

Situated below street level is the Canal Walk that provides a breathtaking view of the city.

ern adobe architecture, but the native wildflowers and prairie grasses that grace the eastern side of the building are pure Indiana. Inside, the museum showcases works by such artists as Georgia O'Keefe and Frederick Remington as well as works by Taos group artists Joseph Henry Sharp and Victor Higgins. Displays also include excellent examples of Native American textiles, pottery, basketry and beadwork. Stop in at the topnotch gift shop, the White River Trader (there's also a Circle Centre location as well; see our Shopping chapter). The Eiteljorg is open 10 AM to 5 PM Tuesday through Saturday and noon to 5 PM Sunday. It also opens Mondays in July and August but closes Thanksgiving, Christmas and New Year's Day. Admission is $2 for adults, $1.50 for seniors, students and children ages 13 to 18 and $1 for children ages 4 to 12. (See The Arts chapter for more details.)

NATIONAL ART MUSEUM OF SPORT AT UNIVERSITY PLACE CONFERENCE CENTER
850 W. Michigan St.   274-2339

Housing what is thought to be the nation's largest collection of fine art depict-

ing athletics, this museum includes works representing 40 different sports. Included in the collection is a series of Winslow Homer wood engravings of mid-19th century leisure sports and a group of works depicting the games of the Inuit people, as well as a few oddities such as a silkscreen print done by Muhammad Ali. The museum can accommodate most visitors during regular business hours, but because of its location within the University Place Conference Center, groups should call to schedule a visit. Admission is free.

INDIANA TRANSPORTATION MUSEUM
Forest Park On Ind. 19
Near downtown Noblesville   773-6000

Although plenty of adults visit this Noblesville museum on their own, check our Kidstuff chapter for more information on exploring the steam, diesel and electric trains of the past.

INDIANAPOLIS MOTOR SPEEDWAY HALL OF FAME MUSEUM
4790 W. 16th St. (Gate 2)   241-2500

An Indianapolis must-see is the Hall of Fame Museum at the track. Though the

Historic Stores

When Circle Centre, Indianapolis' new downtown mall, opened, it included historic elements unusual in mall design. Ehrenkrantz & Eckstut Architects of New York, specialists in historic renovations, designed the new mall to incorporate eight storefronts from the late 1800s.

Though most of the facades are purely ornamental, three function as either entrances or exits. Enter through the former House of Crane storefront, an Italianate Revival-style facade, and you'll find yourself in one of Nordstrom's espresso bars. This building front was the only one to be restored without being taken down. Most of the others, which include the Chicago School-style J.F. Darmody Building, the impressive black art deco Rost Jewelers on Illinois Street, the Italianate Revival Rothschild Building and the Italian Commercial Revival P.W. Jackson Building on Meridian Street, were disassembled and stored. The cast iron facades of the Wilking and the Levey Brothers buildings, for example, were taken apart and stored on the ground of Central State Hospital.

The storefronts camouflage the mall in places and create the feel of separate buildings. Carefully reassembled and skillfully incorporated into the mall's design, the historic facades provide a reminder of the area's past as the city's warehouse district.

Photo: The Indianapolis Star & News

Historic storefronts are part of Circle Centre. The facades were preserved even though the original buildings were destroyed.

raucous fans who gather outside the Speedway the night before the race may offer more excitement, anyone who's heard Paul Page announce "a new track record" will want to view the museum's collection of antique race cars and racing memorabilia.

Included in the exhibit is Ray Harroun's yellow Marmon "Wasp," winner of the first Indy 500 in 1911. Visitors can also take a guided spin in a tour van around the famous oval — if it's not in use for racing or testing. An adjacent memorial area honors

Louis Chevrolet and other racing pioneers, and the Speedway Hotel and Brickyard Restaurant offer convenient dining and accommodations.

The 18-hole Brickyard Crossing, a championship course designed by Pete Dye, features holes 7, 8, 9 and 10 in the track's infield. The museum is open from 9 AM to 5 PM every day except Christmas. Admission is $2 for adults; kids younger than 16 get in free.

HOOK'S HISTORIC DRUG STORE AND PHARMACY MUSEUM
1202 E. 38th St.   925-1503

Now a part of the Revco chain, Hook's drugstores have been a part of Indianapolis since John Hook opened his first store here in 1900. This little museum, with its reproductions and antique pharmacy memorabilia, earns mention in our Kidstuff chapter for its soda fountain and candy counter. See that chapter for more details and be sure to sample a traditional chocolate soda.

INDIANA MEDICAL HISTORY MUSEUM
Old Pathology Building
3000 W. Washington St.   635-7329

This museum, once a part of Central State Hospital, remains the oldest surviving pathology lab in the country and was built to study the causes and effects of mental illness. Listed on the National Register of Historic Places, the museum boasts 15,000 medical artifacts such as 19th-century surgical equipment, patent medicines and a Civil War doctor's kit and 19 rooms, including labs, a library and lecture hall. The museum opens 10 AM to 4 PM Wednesday through Saturday or by appointment. Admission is $3 for adults; kids 6 and younger get in free.

WISHARD MEMORIAL HOSPITAL NURSING MUSEUM
1001 W. 10th St.   630-6233

This museum, housed in two rooms in the older section of Wishard Hospital, chronicles the advances in nursing since 1883. Take a look at the antique hypodermic needles, which are lots larger than those used today, and the 1920s-era surgical amphitheater to see how much medical equipment has — thankfully — changed. Though the museum is open 9:30 AM to 11:30 AM Wednesdays only, call 630-6432 to set up a group tour from 9 AM to 4 PM weekdays. Admission is free.

AMERICAN LEGION MALL AND HEADQUARTERS MUSEUM
700 N. Pennsylvania St.   635-8411

This fourth-floor museum displays the outfit and equipment of a doughboy along with dioramas of World Wars I and II and the Vietnam Conflict. History buffs and veterans will enjoy the military artifacts. It's free and open from 8 AM to 4 PM weekdays, but the grassy, sunken mall is open at all times. The inviting green space is a favorite among the lunchtime crowd and

---

For a beautiful view of the Statehouse, go to the south end of the Capitol Commons garden and look north. For an excellent view of Downtown, stand on the steps of the Indianapolis-Marion County Public Library and face south. Don't forget your camera! Both are great photo opportunities.

Insiders' Tips

those looking for some shade on a hot, sunny day.

INDIANA SOLDIERS AND SAILORS MONUMENT
Monument Cir.
Meridian at Market St. 233-3247

"To Indiana's Silent Victors," the monument stands in tribute to more than 210,000 Hoosiers killed in the Civil War and more than 4,000 killed in the War with Mexico. A basement museum features photographs, weapons and uniforms from the War Between the States. Atop the monument's limestone shaft, up 330 steps, is an observatory with a striking view of downtown. The monument's base provides another haven for lunchers who enjoy sitting next to bubbling fountains that drown out city noises. Admission is free, and it's open daily except some holidays.

WORLD WAR MEMORIAL
431 N. Meridian St. 232-7615

Built on a hill over an underused and acoustically perfect auditorium, the war memorial's awe-inspiring Shrine Room reminds visitors of attractions in the nation's capital. Multicolored light refracted through stained glass illuminates a huge American flag suspended over an alter commemorating fallen war heroes. Built as the centerpiece of a five-block plaza, the war memorial also features the statue "Pro Patria" on its south steps. Inside, a collection of wartime relics dates back to Indiana's founding, and listings of the state's war dead line wide staircases. This memorial is open daily from 8 AM to 4:30 PM, except July 4th, Thanksgiving, Christmas and New Year's Day. The monument was built, as its inscription reads, to "vindicate the principles of peace and justice in the world."

VETERANS MEMORIAL PLAZA
Between Meridian and Pennsylvania sts.
Between the old Federal Building and American Legion Headquarters

This five-block park anchored by the War Memorial provides a calming haven when downtown work gets too hectic. University Park, south of the memorial, features a lively fountain, full of prancing nymphs and sprites, and monuments to Benjamin Harrison, Abraham Lincoln and Schuyler Colfax (Grant's vice president). In Obelisk Square to the monument's north is another fountain, this one with a miniature black-and-gold Washington Monument in the center as well as the country's 50 state flags, placed in order of when the states entered the Union. For those who don't work downtown, the park's a nice place to stroll, feed the squirrels or do a little people-watching.

Historic Sights

Those who enjoy walking tours can easily spend a day or two exploring downtown Indianapolis. Keep in mind that most of these historic attractions lie within the downtown Mile Square, and none are too terribly far apart.

MADAME WALKER URBAN LIFE CENTER
617 Indiana Ave. 635-6915

This beautiful building, with its Egyptian and African design motifs, was built to house the business of Madame C.J. Walker, America's first African-American female self-made millionaire. The restored structure houses the impressive Walker Theater; an hour-long tour of the building is available; call to schedule one. Combine a tour with the a Friday night *Jazz on the Avenue* show and really get a feel for the place and neighborhood, which once featured numerous jazz joints that at-

Photo: The Indianapolis Star & News

Arts and artifacts of the American West are exhibited in the Eiteljorg Museum.

tracted the biggest names in the business. Most of the historic Indiana Avenue neighborhood has given way to IUPUI, but you can tour the Walker building 8:30 AM to 7 PM Monday through Saturday; admission is $2 for adults and $1 for seniors older than 65 and kids younger than 19. Be sure to call for reservations.

INDIANA STATEHOUSE
Market St. at Capitol Ave. 232-8880

Before its centennial renovation in 1988, prison inmates occasionally painted the Statehouse's interior walls a drab green, and little attention was given to its historic features. The renovation, which cost five times the original $2 million price tag, renewed the original hand-painted details, beautiful brass chandeliers and marble floors. From the governor's office, which features a desk made of teak decking from the USS *Indiana*, to the Supreme Court chambers with original brass spittoons, the Statehouse now evokes a feeling for the city's long history as a seat of government. The Indiana General Assembly still meets here beginning in early January each year for either a short or long session. Guided tours are available by appointment between 9 AM and 3 PM weekdays or stop at the information desk on the rotunda's north side for pamphlets that provide a self-guided Statehouse tour.

INDIANA THEATRE
134 W. Washington St. 635-5252

Home to the Indiana Repertory Theatre, the state's only professional resident theater company, the Spanish Baroque Indiana Theatre building was a 1920s movie palace. Now it features three stages and a variety of performances. The elaborate Indiana Roof ballroom on the sixth floor, with its star-studded domed "sky" and decor that recalls a Spanish village, is a wonderful place to enjoy a concert or dance to nostalgic Big Band music. New Year's Eve dinner-and-dancing celebrations are a great way to ring in the New Year. Tours of the IRT and "The Roof" are available by appointment. (See The Arts chapter for more information.)

UNION STATION
39 Jackson Pl. 267-0700

Built on the site of the nation's first Union

station, the current building was erected in 1888. Though in disrepair when renovation began in the early 1980s, the station saw 200 trains a day during the busy years of WWII. It's now a festival marketplace loaded with restaurants and specialty shops; upstairs a food court and arcade offer plenty of amusements for the kids (see our Kidstuff chapter for more details.)

CIRCLE THEATRE
45 Monument Cir.   262-1110

You wouldn't guess it now, but 20 years ago a down-at-the-heels Circle Theatre — the city's first movie palace — was showing Beatles film festivals. Now restored, the impressive building is home to the Indianapolis Symphony Orchestra and provides a wonderful venue for its many musical events. Families especially enjoy taking the kids to the Yuletide Celebration concert. Tours of the building can be arranged in advance; cost is $1 per person.

CHRIST CHURCH CATHEDRAL
125 Monument Cir.   636-4577

This beautiful Gothic church (the subject of Eli Lilly's book *The Little Church on the Circle*) is worth a quick peek or a formal tour, which are usually available after services or by calling ahead to schedule a group visit; the church is often open for touring during downtown festivals. The oldest Episcopal congregation in the city still worships here at the Circle's only remaining church. It's a lovely setting for services or for the church's many music programs. See our Places of Worship chapter for more information.

CITY MARKET
222 E. Market St.   634-9266

Completed in 1886, the historic central building still houses fruit stands, meat markets and a variety of specialty food stalls.

Don't miss the Greek imports at Aesop's Kitchen & Cupboard, gourmet coffee and pastries at Cath Inc. and what may be the city's best coney dog at Libby's Deli. Though seating is limited, you can scout out a table on the upper level balcony and listen to midday concerts by local musicians. Or take your lunch outdoors and enjoy it on the plaza. Teens find the place entrancingly bohemian (you'll find it listed in our Kidstuff and Restaurants chapters as well). The market opens 6 AM to 6 PM Monday through Friday and 6 AM to 5 PM Saturday.

JAMES WHITCOMB RILEY HOME AND LOCKERBIE SQUARE
528 Lockerbie St.   631-5885

Riley lived here for 23 years until his death in 1916 and penned much of his poetry here. The 1872 house is furnished with period pieces. Riley's room includes some of his personal effects: clothes, top hat, a self portrait and his pen, with which he may have composed such famous poems as "Little Orphant Annie" and "When the Frost is on the Punkin." The home opens 10 AM to 4 PM Tuesday through Saturday, noon to 4 PM Sunday. The museum closes on most holidays, but opens with free admission on the poet's October 7th birthday. Otherwise, admission is $1 for adults and 25¢ for kids ages 12 to 15.

The surrounding Lockerbie Square neighborhood, with its cobblestone streets and charming homes, is considered one of the best Victorian restorations in the country and is bounded by Michigan, New York, Davidson and East streets. (See our Neighborhoods chapter for more details.)

ATHENAEUM
401 E. Michigan St.   636-0390

This 1892 landmark began as a social

club and illustrates the city's German heritage; indeed people with a German background still make up the city's largest ethnic group. The Rathskeller's dark wood and Faustian ambiance evoke an Old World feel; stop in for lunch and try the brats and sauerkraut (see our Restaurants chapter for details). The Athenaeum now houses the American Cabaret Theatre and a YMCA.

MURAT SHRINE TEMPLE
510 N. New Jersey St. 635-2433

Looking like you took a turn at the Athenaeum and ended up in the Sahara, this more than 85-year-old building on the National Register of Historic Places boasts a definite Middle Eastern motif, especially the Egyptian Room. Hour-long tours will guide you through the historic structure, which some say houses a resident ghost. Stories of a semitransparent spectre appearing in a box seat, footsteps crossing the stage, doors slamming shut and lights turning on by themselves have spooked visitors and workers alike. Some think it is the ghost of Elias J. Jacoby, a former potentate of the shrine. He died in 1935 while getting ready for the shrine's New Year's Eve Party. The lights that some insist they've seen have appeared to rise from Jacoby's favorite box seat. To try to see for yourself, call the shrine and arrange a visit. You can tour the shrine on Monday, Wednesday and Friday from 9 AM to 3 PM.

SCOTTISH RITE CATHEDRAL
650 N. Meridian St. 262-3100

Kids think this Tudor Gothic structure looks like a castle, and they're right. The impressive Masonic temple building, built in 1929, has been deemed by an international architectural association as one of the most beautiful buildings in the world. The temple's magnificent details, such as the ballroom's black-and-white walnut parquet floor and the rare Russian white oak used in the auditorium enhance the impressive architecture. An hour-long tour is available by checking in with the guide at the North Street door. Stop by 10 AM to 3 PM Monday through Friday; groups should call ahead.

KEMPER HOUSE
1028 N. Delaware St. 638-5264

Called "the wedding cake house," this 1873 home was built as a wedding present. This really will remind you of a wedding cake, with its many columns and gingerbread trim. Restored by Eli Lilly, the home now houses the offices of Historic Landmarks. Three small rooms are filled with Victorian furnishings and can be rented for meetings and such. Though the home doesn't open for tours, those who really want to view the interior can call to make special arrangements.

BENJAMIN HARRISON HOME
1230 N. Delaware St. 631-1898

Our country's 23rd president lived here from 1875 to 1901, and many of the original Victorian furnishings can be seen during a one-hour tour of the home. Knowledgeable guides will fill you in on the life of Benjamin Harrison

---

Take the lobby elevators of the City-County Building, 200 E. Market Street, to the top floor observation deck for a bird's-eye view of downtown.

Insiders' Tips

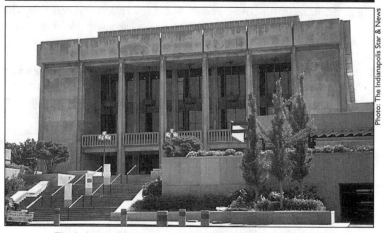

The Indianapolis Museum of Art has four pavilions that house the museum's collections.

as well. The Fourth of July Ice Cream Social is a popular summertime celebration. The president himself (well, a believable costumed interpreter) attends the annual community event. The home is open 10 AM to 4 PM Monday through Saturday and 12:30 PM to 4 PM Sunday; it's closed on major holidays and during the first two weeks in January. Admission is $2 for adults and $1 for students.

MORRIS-BUTLER HOUSE
1204 N. Park Ave.   *636-5409*

This 1866 home was restored by Historic Landmarks and gives modern-day visitors a glimpse into a Victorian Indianapolis home, complete with lace curtains at the windows and an Indiana-made Wooton desk. A tour takes an hour, and the home is open 10 AM to 4 PM Tuesday through Saturday and 1 PM to 4 PM Sunday; groups should call ahead for an appointment. The home is closed on holidays and during January.

A Short Drive Away...

CROWN HILL CEMETERY
700 W. 38th St.   *925-8231*

This is the nation's fifth largest cemetery, and its rolling, expansive grounds can provide a morning or afternoon's worth of history. You'll find the graves of bank robber John Dillinger, President Benjamin Harrison and Hoosier poet James Whitcomb Riley. In fact, Riley's memorial is atop Strawberry Hill (also known as "the crown"), the highest natural point in the city, one that offers a great view of the downtown skyline. You can pick up a tour map at the gatehouse; the grounds are open every day. (See our Literary Life chapter for additional information on Riley.)

MANSIONS AT MARIAN COLLEGE
3200 Cold Spring Rd.   *929-0299*

On the grounds of this private college northwest of downtown are two notable mansions that provide an inside look at how local movers and shakers once lived. Built for one of the Speedway founders, the James A. Allison Mansion, called Riverdale, boasted a pipe organ and an indoor pool. Much of the first floor has been restored; some of it is furnished with the original custom-made furniture. Also on the grounds is the Wheeler-Stokely Mansion, dubbed Hawkeye, and built for another Speedway founder. Pick up the *Mansions of Marian* booklet, available at the college, for more details, and book the $2 per person tours in advance.

MERIDIAN STREET

38th to 56th Sts.

This historically designated stretch of U.S. Highway 31 boasts some of the city's most beautiful homes. Many of these "Meridian Street mansions" date from the 1920s, and residents take great pride in the historically accurate restorations. Beautiful yards, especially in the spring, make this neighborhood perfect for a stroll. You can also see plenty of sightseers driving slowly past the magnificent houses. Several tours, including Meridian in Bloom, spotlight the area that often hosts the annual Decorators' Show House.

Photo: The Indianapolis Star & News

Saddle up, kids, for some Indianapolis fun.

Inside
Kidstuff

One refrain you'll hear over and over in Indianapolis is that it's a great place to raise a family. And indeed it is. It's a backyard-barbecuing, softball-playing, bicycle-riding kind of town. Many of our most popular events boast a definite family flair, and Indianapolis offers enough attractions to provide weekends full of kid-oriented sightseeing, plus plenty of activities to keep youngsters occupied year round.

Not only can we claim the world's largest children's museum and one of the biggest city parks in the nation, but also the area abounds with opportunities for kids to participate in sports, the arts and the community. Even most restaurants — except the poshest, of course — are kid-friendly as well. Indeed, a trip to an ethnic restaurant, where kids can try to eat with chopsticks or watch wide-eyed as jingling, scarf-draped belly dancers perform, can be great fun for the whole family.

In fact, many of the attractions listed in this chapter could have easily been included elsewhere and just might keep the grownups amused as well. The Children's

Museum, for example, is a guaranteed crowd-pleaser, and we know plenty of parents who relish an opportunity to slip on some knee-pads and crawl through indoor playgrounds right behind Junior.

This chapter's suggestions include a variety of possibilities, from kid-pleasing stores and restaurants to unique museums and outdoor activities. Though by no means all-inclusive, our suggestions include well-known, can't-miss attractions as well some out-of-the-ordinary options. At any rate, this list will certainly get you started exploring the city from a kid's point of view.

Of course, it helps if you have at least one youngster tugging you along.

Attractions and Museums

Here are our picks for the city's best sights from a kid's perspective. Don't be surprised if they ask to go to some of these places again and again. Say yes; they're all worth a return trip.

CHILDREN'S MUSEUM
3000 N. Meridian St.   924-5437
This is it, the primo point of interest for kids in Indianapolis. The Children's Mu-

Kids tune in to AM 810 for *Radio Aahs*, where the Children's Radio of Indianapolis offers cool daily programming from dawn to dusk.

Insiders' Tips

seum ranks as the largest such facility in the world, and the place is filled with exhibit after exhibit highlighting science, cultures, history, the arts and just plain fun. The best part is that things are designed to be touched, examined, climbed on and crawled through.

Generations of kids have stared in awe at the enormous stuffed polar bear; youngsters often ask their parents if they remember seeing it when they were kids (this writer certainly does). And the place really must be seen to be believed! A recently renovated entrance features the world's largest water clock, and kids are fascinated with the bubbling timepiece. Of course, they also dig the Indy race car, the carousel, the planetarium and the computers. And due to open in 1996 is a large-format CineDome theater.

Around here, parents start bringing the kids to the Children's Museum even before they can walk, and there's stuff even for the tiniest ones to do. **Playscape**, a gallery for the preschool crowd, includes water and sand play, a tiny log cabin, art supplies, animal costumes to dress up in and plenty of things to climb in, around, under and over. There's also an extra-soft area for babies to explore.

In other galleries, school-age kids will love exploring a replica of an Indiana limestone cave, slipping into a real submarine and wondering about Wenuhotep, a 2,500-year-old Egyptian mummy. Teenagers can work on academic and community projects in CFX, the Eli Lilly Center for Exploration.

During October, the Children's Museum also operates a haunted house. One of the city's best (and least gory), it also offers lights-on tours for little ones.

The museum is open 10 AM to 5 PM Tuesday though Sunday; it's open the same hours on Mondays from Memorial Day through Labor Day. The museum is closed on Christmas and Thanksgiving. Though subject to change, at the time of this writing admission fees are $3 for youths ages 2 to 17; $6 for adults 18 to 59; and $5 for seniors. The museum is open late, and admission is free the first Thursday evening of each month from 5 PM to 8 PM. Annual family passes can be purchased for $40. Theater, SpaceQuest Planetarium, computer center, carousel and haunted house tickets must be purchased separately.

INDIANAPOLIS ZOO

1200 W. Washington St.   630-2001

Designed as a zoo without cages, the Indianapolis Zoo provides a wide-open look at wildlife from the jungles, plains, deserts and oceans. Home to more than 3,000 creatures, the zoo features a world-class Waters Complex with penguins, polar bears and daily dolphin shows. The Deserts Biome provides an arid environment for birds, lizards and tortoises to fly, slither and creep across your path. And, of course, lions, tigers and bears — even eagles — can be spotted outdoors. For a little more interaction, kids (and grownups too) can ride camels and elephants; a train takes visitors around the park in a more conventional manner.

It's a beautiful facility, with well-designed and well-maintained walkways throughout. It's especially festive when decked out with thousands of lights for Christmas at the Zoo, but note that lines can be long for this popular holiday outing.

The zoo opens at 9 AM year round; closing times vary seasonally from 4 PM to 5 PM. Admission is currently $9 for adults, $5.50 for kids 3 to 12 and $6.50 for seniors; parking costs an additional $3.

The Children's Museum ranks as the largest such facility in the world, and the place is filled with various exhibits.

EITELJORG MUSEUM OF
AMERICAN INDIANS AND WESTERN ART
500 W. Washington St.   *636-9378*

The Eiteljorg offers one of the finest collections of Native American and Western art in the nation (see our Arts and Attractions chapters), and kids will enjoy the artist-in-residence series that features Native American artists demonstrating their work.

The museum, which is within walking distance of downtown, is open 10 AM to 5 PM Tuesday through Saturday and from noon to 5 PM Sunday; it's also open Mondays from June through August. It's closed on Thanksgiving, Christmas and New Year's Day. Admission is $3 for adults, $1.50 for kids 5 to 17 and for full-time students, and $2.50 for seniors; family admission is $10.

CONNER PRAIRIE
13400 Allisonville Rd., Fishers   *776-6004*

Ranked by *Midwest Living* as among the best Midwest historical sites and by *Vacations* magazine as one of the 10 best U.S. family vacations, Conner Prairie is indeed one of the area's most interesting attractions. The living history village frozen in time offers visitors the chance to experience life in 1836 and watch as costumed interpreters go about their business. Visit the schoolhouse, the blacksmith shop or watch village residents celebrate a typical 1836 wedding (in June). Visitors can also tour the original Conner home, built by settler and statesman William Conner, which has been restored and furnished; it now looks as it might have when it was built in 1823. Kids used to overflowing toy boxes and bookshelves will be surprised at the nursery, where they can look around a 19th-century kid's room.

In addition to touring the historic areas, visitors can also experience hands-on activities such as candle-dipping and soap-making in the Pioneer Adventure Area. The modern Museum Center houses exhibits, a gift shop, bakery and Governor Noble's Eating Place, a fully modern and casual dining room. Special events are planned throughout the year. Some of the most popular include the summertime Symphony on the Prairie series; the Apple

A recreated turn-of-the-century village with covered bridges greets visitors to Billie Creek Village in Parke County.

Store produce market, open in September and October; the Headless Horseman at Conner Prairie during October; and Conner Prairie by Candlelight and the Festival of Gingerbread in December.

The historic areas are open April through November. Hours in those months are 9:30 AM to 4 PM Wednesday through Saturday, and 11:30 AM to 4 PM Sunday. From May through October, the museum is open Tuesdays as well. The village celebrates Independence Day each year with A Glorious Fourth in Prairietown and is open on Memorial Day and Labor Day; Conner Prairie is closed on Easter and Thanksgiving. During the winter, it opens only for special events. Admission is $9 for adults, $8.50 for seniors and $6.50 for kids 6 to 12; tours of the William Conner home cost an additional $1.50. Conner Prairie is 6 miles north of Indianapolis near the community of Fishers.

INDIANAPOLIS MOTOR
SPEEDWAY HALL OF FAME MUSEUM
4790 W. 16th St.   484-6747

Racing fans of all ages will get a kick out of visiting the Indianapolis Motor Speedway (see our Attractions and Auto Racing chapters), where they can gaze at speedsters of the past and imagine themselves behind the wheel of the Marmon "Wasp," winner of the first 500-Mile Race in 1911.

The museum is open from 9 AM to 5 PM every day except Christmas. Admission is $2 for adults 16 and older.

INDIANA STATE MUSEUM
202 N. Alabama St.   232-1637

Highlighting the state's natural and cultural history, the Indiana State Museum (see our Attractions and Arts chapters), offers kids a glimpse into Indiana's Ice Age past as well as daily life in historic Indianapolis. Kids (OK, grownups too) stand around watching the 85-foot Foucault pendulum that, due to the Earth's rotation, continuously knocks over little wooden pegs placed on the floor. Freetown Village, a living history exhibit at the Indiana State Museum, was created in 1982 to teach African-American history. Costumed interpreters present a view of daily African-

American life in Indianapolis in 1870. (See the "Seasonal Specialties" section later in this chapter for information on the winter holidays' Toy Soldiers Playground.)

The Indiana State Museum is open 9 AM to 4:45 PM Monday through Saturday; noon to 4:45 PM Sunday. Admission is free.

HOOK'S HISTORIC
DRUG STORE AND PHARMACY MUSEUM
1202 E. 38th St.   *924-1503*

The main attraction here for kids is the soda fountain and candy counter that came from an Indiana ice cream shop. They can enjoy an old-fashioned ice-cream soda while Mom and Dad browse through the outstanding collection of pharmacy and drug store relics (see our Attractions chapter).

The drug store is at the Indiana State Fairgrounds and is open 11 AM to 5 PM Tuesday through Sunday.

INDIANA TRANSPORTATION MUSEUM
Forest Park, on Ind. 19
Near downtown Noblesville   *773-6000*

Even in these days of cyberspace, kids remain fascinated by railroads, and at the Indiana Transportation Museum in nearby Noblesville, they can examine steam, diesel and electric trains and even take a ride on the former Nickel Plate Railroad (rides are offered on weekends only and require an additional fare).

The museum is open 10 AM to 5 PM Tuesday through Sunday from Memorial Day through Labor Day; it opens on weekends in May and from Labor Day through

Halloween. Admission is $4 for adults and $2 for seniors and for kids 4 to 12.

INDIANA STATE POLICE YOUTH
EDUCATION AND HISTORICAL CENTER
8500 E. 21st St.   *899-8293*

Offering one of the nation's finest collections of police-related paraphernalia, the Historical Center features vehicles, firearms, photos, displays and souvenirs. State Police officers often conduct tours; call for details.

The center is open 8 AM to 11 AM and 1 PM to 4 PM Monday through Friday; it's also open 9 AM to 4 PM every third Saturday from April through October. Admission is free, though donations are accepted.

GEOKIDS
Indianapolis International Airport   *487-7243*

This interactive exhibit, developed in conjunction with the Children's Museum, aims to teach school-age kids about geography, weather and travel with such appealing displays as a 6-foot rotating globe and a 3-D floor map of the United States.

Stuff to do Downtown

Even if they're stuck downtown, surrounded by conventioneers, with no hope of ever getting more than walking distance away from the hotel, kids (and their parents) can still find plenty to do. Here are a few of our favorite outings.

INDIANA SOLDIERS
AND SAILORS MONUMENT
Monument Cir.   *233-3247*

Challenge the kids to climb the 330 steps

Sign the kids up for the Indianapolis Indians' Knot Hole Club. For one low price, they get in to all home games and receive an Indians T-shirt too.

Insiders' Tips

to the enclosed balcony for a great view of downtown; you can take the elevator and beat them there. In warm weather, locals enjoy lunch on the Monument steps. The kids won't be able to resist a trip inside the Rocky Mountain Chocolate Factory, 28 Monument Circle, which boasts a delicious assortment of chocolates and caramel apples.

CITY MARKET
222 E. Market St.   *634-9266*

This historic market, with fresh fruit and meat stands, ethnic food shops, gourmet coffees and some of the city's best deli fare, can seem like the most bohemian place in the world to a kid. Local musicians often perform during the weekday lunch rush when the market is most exciting (see our Restaurants and Shopping chapters). Get in line, get some food and find a table along the upstairs balcony or take some sandwiches outside and enjoy lunch on the open-air plaza. Many City Market stands are open 6 AM to 6 PM Monday through Friday and 6 AM to 5 PM Saturday.

UNION STATION
39 Jackson Pl.   *267-0700*

This train station houses a festival marketplace (see our Restaurants, Shopping and Nightlife chapters). It boasts specialty shops, nightclubs and sit-down restaurants, but the best parts from a kid's point of view are the food court and the upstairs arcade.

INDIANA WORLD SKATING ACADEMY
201 S. Capitol Ave.   *237-5555*

A competition site for the 1987 Pan Am Games, these two indoor ice-skating rinks across from Union Station offer year-round public skating (call for a schedule) as well as lessons, private parties and hockey, figure skating and speed skating camps and clinics.

CANAL WALK
West and Ohio Sts.   *632-1824*

This urban oasis sits below street level and offers a handy place to rest if you've been touring the Statehouse or the Eiteljorg. Kids, however, aren't big on cooling their heels, so load the family onto a pedal boat and cruise along the canal. The boats, which seat up to five passengers, are available 10 AM to 6 PM on weekends from mid-April through mid-May and mid-September through October. During the summer, you can pedal along from 4 to 9 PM Monday through Friday and 10 AM to 11 PM Saturday and Sunday. Boats cost $6 per half-hour or $10 per hour (plus a 5 percent sales tax).

AMERICAN LEGION MALL
700 N. Pennsylvania St.

Though kids might not dig poking among a bunch of war mementos in the Legion museum, they might appreciate the chance to throw a Frisbee or toss a football around the expansive grassy areas of the American Legion Mall. We even see kite flyers here on blustery March afternoons. The mall area is great for picnic lunches; kids love stopping at one of the hotdog vendors who park their carts in the area.

INDIANAPOLIS-MARION COUNTY LIBRARY
40 E. St. Clair St.   *269-1700*

Just across St. Clair Street from the American Legion Mall is our impressive public library. Take the kids to the ground-level Riley Room, a relaxing spot (complete with rocking chair) to read a book with the little ones.

Holliday Park, perhaps the best park in Indianapolis, features three separate play areas.

Stores and Restaurants

Though you can find great shopping and dining possibilities all over town, here we offer some bona-fide, kid-tested suggestions.

Shops

TOYS R US

8250 Castleton Corner	841-9334
4575 W. 38th St.	297-0338
9251 E. Washington St.	897-0320
1650 E. County Line Rd.	882-5838

Yes, it's a chain, but this mega-store is a kid's paradise, with aisles upon aisles of toys, games and electronics. Here you can find everything from traditional Barbies and GI Joes to the latest in Sega and Nintendo. Selection remains excellent even at Christmastime, when stores stay open into the wee hours to accommodate sneaky parents playing Santa.

KITS & KABOODLE

8701 Keystone Crossing	574-3333
6101 N. Keystone Ave.	255-3448

This shop exudes personality and of-fers a gold mine of unusual gift ideas for your favorite kid. While you may not find the ubiquitous Little Tikes line, you will find shelves stocked with a wide variety of cool stuff, including science-related toys, traditional teddy bears, collectible dolls, stamp pads and stickers galore. Looking for paper dolls, Brio or those doctor office bead mazes? This is the place.

KIDS INK CHILDREN'S BOOKSTORES

5619 N. Illinois St.	255-2598
13632 N. Meridian St.	844-6516
199 Madison Ave.	882-1090

One of the Midwest's leading kid's-only book retailers, Kids Ink stocks more than 15,000 children's books, plus hundreds of toys and cassettes. The knowledgeable staff will help you find whatever you're looking for, from *Pat the Bunny* to *The Babysitters' Club*. The stores also schedule story hours and special events.

THE GREAT TRAIN STORE

39 Jackson Pl.	634-6688

This Union Station shop is the place for model train enthusiasts as well as for fans of Thomas the Tank Engine, star of

Photo: Billie Creek Village

The state's largest Civil War re-enactment is one of the many special historical events at Billie Creek Village west of Indianapolis in Parke County.

PBS's *Shining Time Station*. Railroad-themed books and accessories make this a favorite of parents, and little ones like to watch as real electric trains (situated up high and out of reach) run through the place.

COMIC CARNIVAL AND S-F EMPORIUM
Information Hotline   257-1450

With locations all over town, this popular comic book shop caters to X-Men fans of all ages. It stocks a wide variety of titles, both new and traditional, including a top-notch science fiction selection.

PACERS HOME COURT GIFT SHOP
300 E. Market St.   263-2164

Pro-sports fans can stock up here, and after two straight seasons with the Pacers in the NBA Eastern Conference playoffs, Pacer paraphernalia have become hot items. You can find a good variety of T-shirts, sweatshirts and other game gear in this downtown shop at street level beneath Market Square Arena.

Restaurants

CHUCK E CHEESE'S
5501 E. 82nd St.	849-7324
8804 U.S. 31 S.	887-0646
4910 W. 38th St.	299-2544
8109 E. Washington St.	897-2751

Kids love this place more for the games than for the pizza, and it's almost always full of token-toting tots clamoring for just one more game of Skee-Ball or Whack-a-Mole. Some parents get a headache just pondering such an excursion, but birthday parties at Chuck E Cheese's remain extremely popular. And while it ain't gourmet, the pizza really isn't bad at all.

ARNI'S
3443 W. 86h St.   875-7034

The pizza is really good at Arni's, and the restaurant offers a wide variety of sandwiches, salads and specialty items as well. But it's still a kid kind of place, and youngsters love the decor, which features bicycles on the ceiling and scooters on the walls. It's loud, comfortable and casual, and no one cares if a little one drops pizza on the floor.

BILL'S FABULOUS '50s
6310 Rockville Rd.   244-1950

This west-side drive-in features roller-skating carhops balancing trays full of icy root beer mugs and greasy onion rings. You turn on your lights for service, and while you wait, the kids can pop a few quarters in the outdoor juke box; they can select from such vintage titles as "Purple People Eater" and "Monster Mash." A few Hula-Hoops are usually lying around in case Mom or Dad feel like demonstrating how it's done. Bill's is a silly, kitschy kind of place, but it's a summertime hangout for classic car buffs who like to park their '57 Chevys and kibbitz with other motorheads.

THE OLD SPAGHETTI FACTORY
210 S. Meridian St.   635-6325

A downtown family favorite, the Spaghetti Factory offers good food, ample portions and low prices in an offbeat building full of fringed Victorian lamps and monstrous chandeliers. Kids enjoy eating in the trolley car situated in the middle of the restaurant. Be warned that the wait for a table can be quite long; although the restaurant doesn't take reservations, you can call ahead to put your name on the list.

ACROPOLIS
1625 E. Southport Rd.   787-8883

This family-oriented south-side restaurant boasts authentic Greek fare as well as more standard menu items; just about anyone can find something they like if gyros, moussaka and other Greek specialties don't

appeal. But everyone is sure to enjoy the belly dancing offered on weekend evenings. The whole place will be clapping along.

DARUMA
3508 W. 86h St.   875-9727

Though not recommended for the youngest of kids, Daruma nonetheless offers older ones a unique dining experience that includes sitting on the floor in traditional Japanese style. Beautifully prepared and deliciously different, the food—brought to the table by kimono-clad servers — is sure to intrigue young diners.

WOK 'N' ROLL
1041 Broad Ripple Ave.   257-3663

This isn't China, the menu says, and while you won't discover authentic Oriental fare at this tiny Broad Ripple eatery, you will find such fun and tasty specialties as Cashew-Cashew Geshundeit Chicken and A Hunka Hunka Burnin' Love. The award-winnning interior is decorated with woks and Chinese checkerboards; the order counter looks like a giant take-out box.

Back to Nature

When the kids tire of tagging along while Mom and Dad browse through yet another museum or antique shop, take them outdoors and turn 'em loose for a while. Here are a few places to soak up some sunshine.

EAGLE CREEK PARK
7840 W. 56th St.   327-7110

This huge northwest-side park is one

For some low-tech, low-cost fun, grab a loaf of bread, head to Broad Ripple and feed the ducks. The Central Canal is home to a permanent and always hungry flock.

Insiders' Tips

of the perks of living in Indianapolis (see our Parks and Recreation chapter). It's big, beautiful and loaded with stuff for kids to do. Situated along Eagle Creek Reservoir, the park includes a sandy beach, a marina where you can rent a Sunfish or windsurfer, lots of hiking trails, smooth paved roads for biking or jogging, a nature center, playgrounds and picnic areas. As part of the parks department, it also offers classes, camps and programs for all ages. An admission fee ($2 per vehicle on weekdays and $3 per vehicle on weekends) is charged.

MAROTT PARK
7200 block of N. College Ave.

This park and nature preserve, located surprisingly enough between the busy shopping districts of Broad Ripple and Nora, offers a small open area for picnicking or Frisbee-playing, but its main draw are the wooded trails leading down to White River, where kids can skip stones, wade and watch for wildlife (see our Parks and Recreation chapter).

GARFIELD PARK & CONSERVATORY
2450 Shelby St.   327-7184

Garfield Park's formal sunken gardens are being restored, and the renovated conservatory, a warm, tropical oasis especially appealing in the winter, is scheduled to reopen in late 1995. Kids love the jungle atmosphere, and a 15-foot waterfall completes the rain forest illusion (see the Parks and Recreation chapter). The conservatory is open 10 AM to 5 PM Tuesday through Saturday and noon to 5 PM Sunday; admission is free.

CENTRAL CANAL
Westfield Blvd. in Broad Ripple

The Central Canal is home to a large year-round community of ducks and geese who waddle up on shore at the first sign of a human with a loaf of bread. Though several Broad Ripple businesses sell little bags of high-priced bread crumbs, stop in at the Kroger store, 6220 Guilford Avenue, in the middle of Broad Ripple and pick up a couple loaves of white bread for less than a buck. The birds will eat it up. In fact, some of the geese are bold enough to take a slice right out of your hand. But remember that a big hissing goose can scare the littlest kids and intimidate older ones as well; just shoo the flock away or empty out the bread bag if the birds get too demanding.

HOLCOMB GARDENS
4600 Sunset Ave.   940-9351

Located on the Butler University campus, this beautiful area is great for biking and strolling along the Central Canal. The Holcomb Observatory and Planetarium, 940-9333, are cool too. The facility offers public shows at 7 PM and 8:15 PM on Friday and Saturday.

Playgrounds and Water Parks

When the kids are bouncing off the walls and need to burn off some excess energy, it's time for a trip to a playground or water park. And the choice isn't necessarily determined by the season. Indianapolis kids can play and swim all year round. In addition to commercial facilities, the parks department offers plenty of options. While you can find great city parks and aquatic centers all over town, here are some favorites.

HOLLIDAY PARK
6349 Spring Mill Rd.   327-7180

Probably the best playground in the city, Holliday Park (see our Parks and Recreation chapter) features three separate play areas designed for different ages. A fenced area for the littlest ones includes a low, wooden climbing and sliding structure, but

The dolphin show is one of the highlights during a trip to the Indianapolis Zoo.

kids seem more interested in the bigger ones that include tubes, ladders and terrific slides. A climbing feature that kids refer to as "that spiderweb thing" provides plenty of places to perch and survey the action. And though you won't find teeter-totters or merry-go-rounds, the park does boast swings: baby swings, tire swings, even swings that accommodate wheelchairs. A group called Friends of Holliday Park has put a lot of effort into refurbishing the play area and the trails that lead down to White River. As at Marott Park, kids love to wade along the shallow riverbanks. As they splash around looking for minnows and snail shells, you'll find it hard to remember you're in the middle of the city.

INDY ISLAND AQUATIC CENTER
8575 E. Raymond St.   862-6867

Though nearly a dozen city parks boast swimming pools, the parks department now offers six aquatic centers with water slides, sand play areas and lap pools (see our Parks and Recreation chapter). However, Indy Island, at the new Warren Middle School at the corner of Post Road and Raymond Street, is the state's only indoor water park.

It wins rave reviews — especially in the middle of winter — for its 150-foot water slide, a water playground, geysers and a meandering lazy river. Indy Island hours are noon to 5 PM and 6:30 PM to 9:30 PM Monday through Friday, noon to 5 PM and 6 PM to 8 PM Saturday and Sunday. Admission is $4 for adults during the day and $2.50 in the evening; $3 for children during the day and $1.75 in the evening.

DISCOVERY ZONE
5926 Crawfordsville Rd.	244-4386
1238 U.S. Highway 31 N.	889-7529
3720 E. 82nd St.	577-1565
9493 E. Washington St.	899-4386

"DZ," as it's called, always seems frenzied, but the kids love the maze of tubes, tunnels, ball bins and bungee rooms. Kick off your shoes, rent some knee pads and take off after the kids as they climb, crawl and slide through these top-notch indoor playgrounds. Though adults may prefer to sink into the ball pit and stay there, kids love climbing across ropes and discovering new places to hide. They also enjoy the roller slide, which can prove a bit much for grown-up posteriors. When the going gets tough, Mom and Dad can adjourn to the quiet room — no kids allowed — or relax a bit in the less-frenzied tiny tot play area.

Local Discovery Zones are open 10 AM to 8 PM Monday through Friday, 10 AM to 10 PM Saturday and 10 AM to 7 PM Sunday. Admission is about $6 for kids 3 to 12 and around $3 for tots 2 and younger. Accompanying adults are admitted free.

THUNDER ISLAND
WATER & RECREATION PARK
19830 U.S. Highway 31 N.
Westfield 896-5172

Kids can cool off with bumper boats, a water slide and children's pools as well as enjoy miniature golf and go-carts. Thunder Island also features an adult pool and a driving range. The park opens 10 AM to 7 PM daily for golfing and go-carts starting April 1. Kids can make a splash from 11 AM to 7 PM daily from Memorial Day weekend and through the end of August (plus Labor Day weekend). Admission is $10.75 for adults; $9.50 for ages 4 to 12.

The Sporting Life

In a state like Indiana, where many kids pick up a basketball before they learn to walk, you'd expect sports to be popular. And you'd be right. But kids around here do more than just practice their free throws. You'll find youngsters on the baseball diamond, the tennis court, the soccer field and the water learning to sail. And, yes, you'll find kids as young as 3 hustling up and down a court with a pint-sized round ball learning basketball basics even before they head off to preschool.

But for many kids, school teams provide their primary opportunity to participate in sports. Local public schools and most private schools offer a variety of sports activities. Churches also sponsor teams and leagues, and some programs have grown quite large. **Tabernacle Presbyterian Church**, 926-9426, the **Jewish Community Center**, 251-9467, and the **First Baptist Church of Indianapolis**, 844-3559, work with thousands of kids. In Hamilton County, the **Carmel Dads Club**, 846-1663, organizes leagues in several sports.

Here are a few more of our favorite ways to build team spirit.

Boys and girls ages 8 through 18 can sign up to play baseball on one of the city's more than 16 **Little League** teams; more than 400 sluggers participate each season, which lasts from early May through mid-August. Call 897-6127 for sign-up info. **Indy Parks and Recreation**, 327-0000, also sponsors baseball and softball leagues.

Older boys — ages 15 through 18 — can participate in **American Legion** baseball leagues. Call 654-8135 for information. And the **Indiana Amateur Baseball Association**, 923-3484, sponsors leagues that allow high school- and college-age young men to hone their skills in hopes of winning a college scholarship.

The **Amateur Softball Association**, an Olympic-affiliated group, organizes leagues across the city for both kids and adults. Call 783-9644 with kid-related questions (881-5170 if Mom and Dad want to play).

Though the first experience many youngsters have with organized basketball is in elementary school, Indy Parks and Recreation runs leagues and clinics — some for kids as young as 3 or 4. And local **YMCAs** offer plenty of opportunities to shoot hoops as well as to play soccer, racquetball and volleyball, swim and do gymnastics and aerobics — you name it. Call the Y's general office at 266-9622.

Those who prefer swinging a racquet

to dribbling a ball can participate in **Washington Township Schools' Community Tennis Program**, which boasts an excellent reputation. Taught by professional instructors and top high school and college players, these summer clinics offer all levels of instruction — even a basic skills class for preschoolers. The popular program is held at the North Central High School Community Tennis Center, 1801 E. 86th Street, 259-5377.

When it comes to sports camps, local parents know to call Butler University, 283-9375, where kids can participate in a wide range of day and overnight sport camps. Youngsters can spend part of their summer vacation honing their skills in baseball, football, soccer, volleyball and gymnastics.

For kids who'd rather be sailing, Eagle Creek Park offers a sailing day camp through **Indy Parks and Recreation**. And for those who prefer a horse of a different color, Indy Parks offers a **Galloping Guys and Gals** camp. Call the parks department at 327-0000 for details.

For those who'd rather watch, the Indianapolis Indians sponsor a **Knot Hole Club** for kids 14 and younger. For an annual price of about $8, kids get free general admission (when accompanied by an adult), plus a newsletter and a T-shirt. Kids especially enjoy games when the Famous Chicken or the Philly Phanatic perform. A new baseball stadium is under construction downtown, but the Indians may begin their 1996 season still playing in historic Bush Stadium, 1501 W. 16th Street. Call 269-3545 for details.

The Indiana Pacers, who play at Market Square Arena, 300 E. Market Street, also sponsor a kids' program, and the group now sports a new name: **Boomer's Buddies** (Boomer is the Pacers mascot). For about $10 per child, kids age 6 though 14 receive a number of ticket discounts, coupons good at concession stands and at the Home Court Gift Shop and usually a Pacers T-shirt or hat. Call 263-2100 for information.

Seasonal Specialties

Indianapolis kids often judge the passing of time by the changing festivities. Though you'll find some of these (and many more) in our Events and Festivals

Photo: The Indianapolis Star & News

The YMCA has more than a half-dozen sites around town.

chapter, here's a quick year-round guide to kids' favorite seasonal events (organized from a kid's perspective, starting when school begins).

August

WENS SKYCONCERT
Downtown on the banks of
White River   266-9700

Everyone knows that a kid's year really begins when summer ends and school starts, usually the third or fourth week of August. Marking the end of summer is the WENS Skyconcert on Labor Day weekend. Families find a place to park on the west side of downtown, tune their radios to 97.1 and settle back for a super fireworks display synchronized to music.

October

October, a favorite month among the preschool and elementary-school crowd, brings plenty of Halloween-related festivities.

HAYRIDES
Kids and their families can enjoy hayrides at Conner Prairie, where the Headless Horseman makes a visit. The fun rather than frightening performance is a hit with younger kids. Call **Conner Prairie** at 776-6000. **Eagle Creek Park**, 327-7110, also offers autumn hayrides through a spooky (if you use your imagination) setting, though you'll find no one galloping around without a head. Hamilton County's **Stonycreek Farm**, 773-3344, offers hayrides as well. Call ahead to make reservations.

PUMPKIN PATCHES
Stonycreek also boasts a pumpkin patch where kids can select just the right

gourd to carve. **Waterman's Farm Market** at 7010 E. Raymond Street, also offers pumpkin picking. Call 356-6995 to see when the potential jack-o'-lanterns are ready. For a pleasant autumn drive in addition to a pumpkin, head west to Danville's **Beasley's Orchards and Gardens**, 2304 E. Main Street, 745-4876; or east to Greenfield's **Tuttle Orchard**, 5717 N. County Road 300 W., 326-2278. If you decide to brave the crowds of Brown County during autumn, you'll find a good selection of already-picked pumpkins (as well as apples and cider, Indian corn and decorative gourds) in Bean Blossom, a wide spot in the road on Ind. Highway 135 before you get to Nashville.

November

CELEBRATION OF LIGHTS
Monument Cir.   237-2222

Once Halloween is over, kids can begin looking forward to winter holidays. The Celebration of Lights, held on Monument Circle the Friday night after Thanksgiving, includes the lighting of the 284-foot-tall Soldiers' and Sailors' Monument, turning it into the world's largest Christmas tree.

CHRISTMAS TREE FARMS
Choosing their own evergreen at a tree farm can be fun for kids, and by Thanksgiving weekend, many tree farms around the county are ready to hand you a saw and let you cut down your own. A favorite is **Watt's Christmas and Train Shop**, 9180 Hunt Club Road (in the Zionsville area), 873-2365.

TOY SOLDIERS PLAYGROUND
At the Indiana State Museum
202 N. Alabama St.   232-1637

Also opening the weekend after

Thanksgiving is the Toy Soldiers Playground. The Santaland Express train, which many adults remember from the former downtown L.S. Ayres, chugs through the museum's display of mechanical figures and Christmas scenes.

CHRISTMAS AT THE ZOO
1200 W. Washington St.   *630-2001*

Also running throughout December is Christmas at the Zoo, a celebration that turns the Indianapolis Zoo into a twinkling wonderland of light displays.

HANUKKAH

Children also enjoy the many activities surrounding Hanukkah, the Jewish festival of lights, held at local synagogues (see our Places of Worship chapter).

KWANZAA
Crispus Attucks Middle School
1140 Martin Luther King Jr. St.   *226-4611*

Indianapolis Public Schools' Kwanzaa Celebration includes a candle-lighting ceremony as well as singing, storytelling, dancing and drumming. Call for details on the time and date.

February

KIDSFEST
100 S. Capitol Ave.   *637-4574*

This late February event fills the RCA Dome with kid- and family-oriented displays. Hands-on activities in arts, sports, education and recreation offer plenty of excitement.

March

High school basketball fans become increasingly frenzied throughout March as Hoosier Hysteria takes hold of just about everyone — especially high school students. The late-March Indiana High School Athletic Association boys basketball championships determine the state's best team and signal an end to winter in Indiana, although bad weather and basketball often go hand-in-hand around here. We generally expect snow during the sectional, regional, semistate and state finals; it's more of a surprise when the white stuff doesn't fall. (Easter egg hunts, held at parks around the city, serve as a more reliable harbinger of spring.)

EASTER EGG HUNTS
Indy Parks and Recreation, 327-0000, sponsors great Easter festivities. Check out the Broad Ripple Eggstravaganza and Eagle Cree Park's Easter Egg Hunt (kids are separated into age groups). You'll also find good hunts at J.T.V. Hill, Watkins Park and Municipal Gardens; all are part of Indy Parks.

ST. PATRICK'S DAY PARADE
Downtown

Even though it's quite possible that March 17 will prove snowy and blustery, kids welcome the downtown St. Patrick's Day parade as a bona-fide sign of spring in Indianapolis. They enjoy the kilt-clad pipe and drum bands, floats and clowns. Maybe they'll catch a green bagel tossed by the O'Malia Supermarket employees who always participate in the parade.

Summer

Though school isn't quite out yet (most continue into the first week of June), the Memorial Day weekend — and of course the 500 Festival Parade and the race — mark the first real weekend of summer. Although it's just about as likely to be cool and rainy as hot and sunny, this is also when the outdoor pools in local parks open — another landmark in the year of a kid.

In June, U-pick farms, often the same that offer pumpkins in October (see earlier entry), feature ultra-fresh strawberries and, a bit later, blackberries and raspberries. But you'd better hurry; by July, the berries are just about gone. But that's OK. Fourth of July celebrations mark the apex of a kid's summer, and there are plenty of opportunities to celebrate.

Conner Prairie hosts its Glorious Fourth (see our Festivals and Events chapter) and downtown's Fourth Fest brings thousands of families to the sidewalks and parking lots around town to watch the fireworks that start about 9 PM.

Though they may not be as ingrained as 500 activities, Brickyard 400 events in early August, including Circlefest and the race itself, are sure to become signposts that, even though temperatures may reach the 90s, a kid's summer is winding down and school is just around the corner.

Out-of-Town Options

Though Indianapolis boasts plenty to do, sometimes a special trip is in order. And while our Daytrips and Weekend Getaways chapter offers plenty of possibilities, here are a few that will especially please the kids.

BILLIE CREEK VILLAGE

U.S. 36, Rockville   569-3430

West of Indianapolis in Parke County (known for its autumn covered-bridge festival), Billie Creek Village features a recreated turn-of-the-century village with 30 historic buildings, a tree-lined creek, covered bridges and one of the Midwest's largest consignment craft shops. Plenty of special historical events, such as the state's largest Civil War re-enactment, are held here, in addition to craft fairs, ice cream socials

and music festivals. Some of the kids' favorites include the Maple Fair, when you can watch maple syrup being made, and Halloween "fright rides." They also like the General Store, with its 20-foot candy counter, homemade fudge and the old-fashioned Coke machine that vends those little kid-size glass bottles.

The whole county just crawls with cars during the October covered-bridge festival; traffic can be heavy, and kids can get impatient. It may be advisable to schedule a visit to avoid the mid-October festival; the bridges can be seen year round, and Billie Creek Village itself proves more enjoyable for kids when it's less crowded.

Located 1 mile east of Rockville, Billie Creek Village opens from Memorial Day through Halloween and for special events; it offers limited operation the rest of the year. Admission is free during the week; on weekends it's $3.50 for visitors age 4 and older. You can also purchase a $20 annual pass.

CARTHAGE, KNIGHTSTOWN & SHIRLEY RAILROAD

112 W. Carey St.
Knightstown   345-5561

The CK&S Railroad offers hour-long rides on tracks that were once part of the Big Four Railroad (Cleveland, Cincinnati, Chicago and St. Louis Railroad). Passengers board the vintage coach car at the former site of a New York Central freight and passenger station in Knightstown, about 30 miles east of Indianapolis off I-70. The coach, caboose and open platform car travel south to Carthage, crossing the old National Road (U.S. Highway 40) and passing under the old "Pennsy" railroad bridge. The engine is "run around" for the return trip. Both depots offer refreshments, railroad-related memorabilia and equipment displays to

Photo: Conner Prairie

It's always 1836 at Conner Prairie, the living history village that's frozen in time.

examine. (As a special bonus for parents, Knightstown is loaded with antique shops.)

Trains depart Knightstown on weekends May through October at 11 AM Friday; and 11 AM, 1 and 3 PM Saturday and Sunday. Round-trip fares are $6 for ages 12 to adult, $4 for kids 3 to 11.

OLD INDIANA FUNPARK

7230 N. County Rd. 350 W.
Thorntown 873-4141

Old Indiana bills itself as a "fun-n-water park," and this small amusement park boasts seven water slides, including kiddie slides with the bonus of heated water. It also offers more than 30 rides and attractions. It's a bit hokey, especially the song-and-dance shows, but kids will enjoy Splashdown Mountain and Lazy River.

Old Indiana is off I-65 midway between Indianapolis and Lafayette at Ind. Highway 47. The park is open weekends mid-May through mid-September; it's also open Wednesday, Thursday and Friday from June through August. Admission is $13.95 for ages 3 and older, $9.95 for kids under 48 inches tall (who can't ride all the rides and water slides), $7.95 for seniors.

HOLIDAY WORLD/SPLASHIN' SAFARI

Hwy. 162 (800) GO-SANTA

For years known as Santa Claus Land, Holiday World is one of the country's oldest amusement parks. More elaborate than Old Indiana, Holiday World boasts the largest wooden roller coaster in Indiana and Kentucky, bumper boats, a white-water rapid-style ride and all the traditional amusement park favorites. And, of course, Santa himself, who reads to kids in the Storytime Theater.

It also offers its own water park, called Splashin' Safari, which includes a wave pool (with free use of inner tubes), a 350-foot water chute, a 300-foot water tunnel, plus (and this is what distinguishes Splashin' Safari from other water parks) two areas — Butterfly Bay and Crocodile Isle — for the littlest kids.

Though Holiday World offers a fun, kid-oriented weekend getaway, it's not especially convenient to Indianapolis. It's way down in southern Indiana, 7 miles south of I-64. But the kids will think it's worth the drive.

Holiday World opens weekends in May, September and October and every day during June, July and August; Splashin' Safari opens weekends in May and September and every day during June, July and August. General admission is $17.95; $11.95 for seniors and kids under 48 inches tall.

INDIANA STATE PARKS
Department of Natural Resources 232-4125

Indiana boasts a wonderful network of state parks (see our Parks and Recreation chapter), and any of them can provide a day or weekend of fun for families. Recreation guides that detail operating hours and amenities of each state park, reservoir, forest, fish and wildlife area and historic site are available free from the DNR. Here are some highlights.

Brown County State Park is probably the most popular among Indianapolis residents. On Ind. Highway 46 near artsy-craftsy Nashville, Brown County State Park is sometimes crowded, and its housekeeping cabins are often booked two years in advance. But except for the busiest holiday weekends, you can almost always find a camp site (there are more than 400 available). For those who prefer a little less nature, the park offers a very comfortable inn, the Abe Martin Lodge. There's also a pool, great scenery and plenty of wildlife (but please don't feed the deer).

McCormick's Creek State Park, Indiana's first state park, is just as beautiful as Brown County and somewhat less crowded. Situated 14 miles northwest of Bloomington on Ind. 46, the park provides rugged terrain, caves and scenic waterfalls — perfect for hiking. Again, cabins are often booked way in advance, but more than 300 campsites are available. And the Canyon Inn offers cozy accommodations (and — just in case you can't get the campfire going — a great breakfast buffet).

Turkey Run State Park offers a great

chance to take the kids canoeing. Sugar Creek runs right through it and boasts great views of sandstone ravines and shady forests. Rent a canoe at one of several liveries near the park; they'll drop you off and pick you up later. Southwest of Crawfordsville on Ind. 47, Turkey Run provides plenty of activities within the park as well, including horse and bicycle rentals, and — a plus for the kids — Turkey Run Inn has an indoor pool.

For Teens

Though it's a great place to be a kid, Indianapolis doesn't especially cater to teenagers, and unless they're involved in sports, many claim to have a tough time finding something to do. They like to hang out in offbeat Broad Ripple, but they have no real place to go there; restaurants prove pricey and the many nightspots are strictly for the 21-and-older set. Coffee shops such as the Village Idiot, where you don't need an ID, just a taste for java, has become favorites of older teens and the much ballyhooed Generation X crowd. And though skateboarders love to cruise the streets north of Broad Ripple Avenue, a no-skateboarding ordinance was in the works at the time of this writing.

Parents may have to do some digging, but activities do exist for those kids too old for playgrounds but too young for college. Best bets include teen classes at the Indianapolis Art Center and those sponsored by Indy Parks and Recreation, as well as programs offered by local YMCAs.

INDIANAPOLIS ART CENTER
820 E. 67th St.   *255-2464*

The art center offers kids and teens lots of creative options. Past classes have included puppetry, collage, ceramics and printmaking, all taught in the center's studios. The center also sponsors a fine arts summer day camp. Costs for week-long classes and camp do prove pricey; most cost more than $100 for art center members. Family memberships are available for $40. The center offers a terrific array of adult classes as well (see our Arts chapter).

INDY PARKS AND RECREATION
1426 W. 29th St.   *327-0000*

New classes begin every few months with each new season (see our Parks and Recreation chapter), and the *Fun Guides* list the many options sponsored by Indy Parks. The guides are available free from the parks department; call to add your name to the mailing list. Teens (and younger kids too) enjoy the sports clinics, dance classes, cooking courses, photography and art instruction.

YMCAs
General Office
615 N. Alabama St.   *266-9622*

With more than a half-dozen locations around town, the Y offers convenience coupled with a great variety of fitness, culture and arts-related courses. Membership is required for full access to all the facilities, but limited memberships are available (for summertime swimming, for example).

Runners get set to take off running for the annual Indianapolis
500 festival Mini-Marathon.

Photo: The Indianapolis Star & News

Inside
Festivals and Events

To get to know an area, you just have to attend its festivals. Sample the food, watch the people and get a feel for what makes a region special. Indianapolis is no exception. Around here, fairs and festivals highlight our history and ethnic heritage as well as our love for sports. Pick any month and you'll find plenty going on around the city. Art fests begin in May and continue throughout the summer, and food fests — where the focus is on eating — begin with Holy Rosary's Italian street fair in early June and continue 'til September's Greek Festival. Food vendors abound at Midsummer Fest and Circlefest, and, speaking of food, plenty of locals eat their way through the State Fair in August, filling up on such specialties as hot buttered corn on the cob, Hoosier rib-eye sandwiches and warm, sugary elephant ears.

Fall yields apples, and plenty of nearby orchards and small towns celebrate with fresh-pressed cider and just-picked Winesaps and Granny Smiths. The holiday season, which seems to begin just after the haunted houses close their creaky doors, brings plenty of activity as well. Flipping through our local calendar, you'll also find an abundance of sports-related events, from the Indiana High School Athletic Association's basketball finals to Olympic trials (also see our Sports chapter). In May, of course, the action at the track is the main topic of conversation, and you'd better pull together at least one black-and-white outfit to have ready for the many 500-related parties and events.

To really find out what's going on in Indianapolis, get involved with some of the organizations that put on these annual shows. Regardless of the fair or festival, you'll meet a bunch of dedicated volunteers who'll help introduce you to what happens behind the scenes, where the action really is. We've noted whether an event charges an admission fee. Call ahead for specific rates.

January

HEARTHSIDE SUPPERS
13400 Allisonville Rd., Fishers
Conner Prairie   776-6000
Admission fee
Guests to the historic William Conner home at Conner Prairie, a living history

Be sure to stop by the Lions Club tent at the Indiana State Fair for hot buttered corn on the cob, what we call "roastin' ears."

Insiders' Tips

village north of the city, help prepare authentic 19th-century dinners and learn to eat with a knife (forks weren't in use yet, and everything at Conner Prairie is authentic). After the dinners, which despite the low-tech cooking methods really are delicious, guests play old-fashioned parlor games and tour the restored home. Reserve early for these popular dinners that run through March.

GREATER INDIANAPOLIS GARAGE SALE
Indiana Convention Center
100 S. Capitol Ave.   632-2666
Admission fee

This popular annual event is a must for bargain hunters across the city. Scour the more than 700 booths for all sorts of treasures — who knows what you'll find.

INDIANAPOLIS HOME SHOW
Indiana State Fairgrounds
1202 E. 38th St.   298-7111
Admission fee

Anyone building, remodeling or just dreaming about it will want to check out this venerable home show that includes as a centerpiece a home built indoors. You'll find lots of booths, vendors and tons of home improvement options. Crowds are largest on weekends when lines to tour the home can be quite long.

KID'S FEST
RCA Dome
100 S. Capitol Ave.   637-4574
Admission fee

The dome is home to a working carousel during this kidstuff extravaganza. Hands-on sports and arts activities offer plenty for kids and parents to do, and 100 exhibitors showcase children's products and services.

February

THE ANNUAL
CARQUEST WORLD OF WHEELS
Indiana Convention Center
100 S. Capitol Ave.   632-2666
Admission fee

Car collectors, shade-tree mechanics and motor heads of all ages descend upon the Convention Center to scope out the custom cars, trucks and specialty vehicles that make this show an annual favorite.

INDIANA BOAT,
SPORT AND TRAVEL SHOW
Indiana State Fairgrounds
100 S. Capitol Ave.   632-2666
Admission fee

The city's oldest sport show draws outdoor enthusiasts inside to check out the latest in hunting, fishing, camping and boating equipment. Take a stroll through the displays, poke your head into a lavish RV and make plans for your summer vacation.

IHSAA GIRLS' BASKETBALL FINALS
Market Square Arena
300 E. 38th St.   846-6601
Admission fee

Hoosier Hysteria starts early when players from across the state square off in this annual contest to determine the best in girls' basketball.

March

NCAA DIVISION I MEN'S
AND WOMEN'S INDOOR TRACK
AND FIELD CHAMPIONSHIPS
RCA Dome
100 S. Capitol Ave.   632-2666
Admission fee

Spectators will find plenty to watch during this two-day exhibition of athletic prowess as the top collegiate competitors

Paintings, drawings and sculptures are just a sample of the variety available at the annual Talbott Street Art Fair in early June.

Photo: The Indianapolis Star & News

from across the country vie for All-America honors.

1996 OLYMPIC SWIMMING TRIALS
IU Natatorium
901 W. New York St.   274-3364
Admission fee

The top-notch facilities of the Natatorium are put to use when the country's best swimmers compete for a spot on the U.S. Olympic swim team.

FLOWER AND PATIO SHOW
Indiana State Fairgrounds
1202 E. 38th St.   255-4151
Admission fee

Just when you think spring will never arrive, this terrific annual event offers showgoers a chance to stop and smell the daffodils. Visitors can wander through numerous garden displays designed by area landscape professionals, pick up pointers from local gardening guru and Marion County Extension Agent extraordinaire Dick Crum, purchase English ivy or an African violet or join a local garden club.

ST. PATRICK'S DAY PARADE
Downtown   237-3855
Free admission

Put on something green and head downtown for this festive hour-long parade. Office workers on their lunch breaks vie with kids clutching green balloons for the best curbside spots to watch one of the city's favorite parades. Catch green bagels tossed to the crowd by O'Malia Supermarket employees or scramble with the kids for candy. Or you can just enjoy the spectacle — and the Gordon Pipers as they fire up their bagpipes.

IHSAA BOY'S BASKETBALL FINALS
RCA Dome
100 S. Capitol Ave.   846-6601
Admission fee

The state's top four teams compete in this annual example of Hoosier Hysteria at its most rampant. Sold out for more than 60 years, the event draws more than 40,000 spectators, and downtown crawls with wild-eyed basketball fans.

Pack Up the Car.
Let's Go to a Festival!

Though we have plenty of terrific festivals in Indianapolis, it's fun to experience some in other parts of the state. Here's a handful of Indiana festivals worth the drive.

MAPLE FAIRS

The last weekend of February and the first weekend of March finds Parke County dripping with maple syrup. At Billie Creek Village, a mile east of Rockville on U.S. 36, visitors can view a primitive maple camp and sample maple candy and maple cream (and enjoy wagon rides, crafts and more good food as well). Admission charge. Call 569-3430 for details.

Parke County also hosts maple sugaring demonstrations at sites throughout the county (no admission charge). Call 569-5226 for information.

WILDFLOWER FORAYS

Usually held the last weekend in April, this celebration of spring shows off acres of flowers at the **T.C. Steele State Historic Site**, off Ind. 46 near Nashville. Visitors can tour the gardens and enjoy plenty of musical entertainment with no admission charge. Call (812) 988-2785 for information.

You can usually count on plenty of blooms during the last weekend in April and the first weekend in May in Madison, and the **Madison in Bloom Festival** celebrates the spring color. Visitors can tour private gardens not generally open to the public in Madison's historic district. There is an admission charge. Madison is in south central Indiana, east of I-65, on the Ohio River. Call (812) 265-2335 for details.

WEEKEND WARRIORS

Mid-May in Blackford County, northeast of Indianapolis off I-69, sees hundreds of costumed participants arrive for the annual **Civil War Reenactment.** Watch battles and a wedding; enjoy afternoon tea, and witness a re-enactment of the 1862 draft riot. There is an admission charge. Call 348-2938 for more information.

The Memorial Day weekend draws plenty of history buffs to Vincennes, on U.S. 41 in southwestern Indiana, for its well-known **Spirit of Vincennes Rendezvous**. The event features 1700-to-1840-era artists and craftspeople at work and includes early American foods, kids' games and battle re-enactments. There is an admission charge. Call (812) 882-7079 for information.

PICKIN' AND GRINNIN'

Visitors to Petersburg, a small community in southern Indiana, will get an earful the first weekend in June when the town hosts the **Indiana State**

Even rain cannot keep art patrons and browsers from filling Talbott Street during the annual Talbott Street Art Fair.

Pickin' and Fiddlin' Contest. Musicians will compete in guitar, mandolin, banjo, harmonica and fiddle, and visitors can sing along to the old-time bluegrass music. There is an admission charge. Call (812) 354-8155 for details.

For another bluegrass get-together, head to Bean Blossom, south of Indianapolis on Ind. 135, to the mid-June **Annual Bluegrass Festival**. The longest-running bluegrass event in the country will mark its 30th year in 1996. There is an admission charge. Call (615) 868-3333 for more information.

SOMETHING FISHY

Here are three choices for those eager to sample a real Hoosier tradition: the annual community fish fry. In late June, anyone hungry for wall-eye and codfish sandwiches, generally served up with coleslaw and fruit pie, can head to **Fairland**, a tiny burg in Shelby County; call 835-7744; **Palmyra**, a tiny burg in Harison County; call (812) 364-6122; or **Jonesville**, a tiny burg in Bartholomew County; call (812)-522-7728. At all three you'll find live music, entertainment and craft booths with no admission charge.

A WEEK IN FORT WAYNE

After the Fourth of July celebrations are over, Fort Wayne gears up for its huge **Three Rivers Festival**, a week-long extravaganza with a parade, lots of art, children's events and fireworks. There is an admission charge for some events. Call (219) 745-5556 for details.

But if you miss Three Rivers, catch Fort Wayne's mid-July **Indiana Highland Games**. This celebration of Scottish heritage, with pipe and drum bands, Highland dancing and clan tents is held at Zollner Stadium at Concordia Lutheran High School. Call (219) 436-0705 for information.

HISTORIC HERITAGE

Enjoy great food and admire the work of 350 artists and crafters at the mid-August Amish Acres Arts and Crafts Festival in Napanee in northeastern Indiana. You'll also find two entertainment stages and plenty of great food (see our Daytrips and Weekend Getaways chapter for more on Amish country and call (219) 773-4188 for more information).

For another angle of history, attend the mid-to-late-August **Annual Traditional Pow-wow** at the Boone County 4-H Fairgrounds in Lebanon, northwest of Indianapolis off I-65. You'll enjoy Native American dancing, singing, food and arts and crafts. Call 482-3315 for details. There is an admission fee.

For a look at Indiana's automotive heritage, head to Auburn, off I-69 in DeKalb County during Labor Day Weekend. Tour the art-deco **Auburn Cord Duesenberg Museum**; Saturday afternoon brings scores of antique cars for **Parade of Classics**. Check out how much such antiques go for at the classic car auction. There is an admission charge for some events. Call (219) 925-3600 for information.

EVEN MORE HISTORY

Early October brings visitors to Greenfield, east of Indianapolis in Hancock County, to celebrate Hoosier poet James Whitcomb Riley during James Whitcomb Riley Days. Visitors enjoy arts and crafts, a fine arts show and, of course, a poetry contest. There's no admission charge. Call 462-4188 for more information.

Enjoy a re-created gathering of French and Indians at Fort Ouiatenon Historic Park near Lafayette in west central Indiana during the **Feast of the Hunters Moon**. Peruse authentic crafts, enjoy military demonstrations and indulge in tasty cooked-outdoors food. There is an admission charge. Call 742-8411 for details.

April

CHILDREN'S FOLK DANCE FESTIVAL
Indiana Convention Center
100 S. Capitol Ave. 924-7060

Chase away the tax-time blues with the 1,400 elementary school students who learn about ethnic customs and dances. Sponsored by the Indianapolis Department of Parks and Recreation, this mid-April event offers plenty of high-spirited dance demonstrations.

DECORATORS' SHOW HOUSE
Location to be announced
St. Margaret's Guild, P.O. Box 40793
Indianapolis 46240
Admission fee

The volunteers of St. Margaret's Hospital Guild organize this late-April through mid-May showcase for local interior designers to benefit Wishard Hospital. As the show house nears completion, motorists will notice the many signs along Meridian Street marking former show homes. Decorators often transform a Meridian Street mansion — and sometimes two — though both the Stokely and Allison mansions at Marian College have served as show houses as well.

500 FESTIVAL OF THE ARTS EXHIBIT
Children's Museum
3000 N. Meridian St.   636-4556
Admission fee

More than 4,000 Marion County students from grades K-12 submit artwork for this juried competition, and all entries are displayed during May at the Children's Museum. It's fun to peruse the paintings and drawings as you go from level to level at the museum.

May

INDIANAPOLIS LIFE
500 FESTIVAL MINI-MARATHON
Monument Cir.   636-4556
Entry fee for participants

If you want to watch rather than participate in this early May event, dubbed the country's largest half-marathon, tag along with someone who works in a downtown high-rise — preferably one with lots of windows. The more than 14,000 registered participants in the mini, which now attracts top runners from across the country, start at Monument Circle, and it's great fun to watch the masses move down the streets. While race car drivers hope for warm, dry days in May, those participating in the mini long for overcast skies or even a light drizzle.

If you want to enter the race, you can

receive an entry form by sending a self-addressed stamped envelope requesting an entry to 201 S. Capitol Street, Indianapolis, 46225. No entries are accepted after April 1.

QUALIFICATIONS
Indianapolis Motor Speedway
4790 W. 16th St.   481-8500
Admission fee

Those who decline to join the 400,000 or more spectators who attend the race each year can still experience some racing excitement by attending the qualifications, which draws a smaller crowd — just a quarter-million fans on the first day. The two weekends leading up to the race determine the starting positions for the 33-car field, and everyone who's in a race pool monitors the action to find out where their driver will start.

BROAD RIPPLE ART FAIR
Indianapolis Art Center grounds
820 E. 67th St.   255-2464
Admission fee

If, for some unfathomable reason, you're not either attending or listening to qualifications, check out the season's first art fair, usually the weekend before the race. The weather is notoriously unpredictable this time of year, however, and though last year's fest saw warm temperatures and clear skies, it's just as likely to be rainy in May, much to the chagrin of both artists and race car drivers. But with a little sunshine, this 26-year-old art festival offers a great opportunity to browse the booths, sample gourmet food and enjoy live music. The

Indiana Black Expo's Summer Celebration in July is the largest event of its kind in the nation and draws visitors — some famous — from across the country for its annual array of festivities focused on African-American culture.

Insiders' Tips

Art Center is just north of Broad Ripple off College Avenue, but fair-goers can often find a better spot at Broad Ripple Park and catch a shuttle to the Art Center.

INDIANAPOLIS 500 CARBURETION DAY
Indianapolis Motor Speedway
4790 W. 16th St.   481-8500
Admission fee

OK, so today's high-tech race cars don't have carburetors anymore. This last practice day, the Thursday before the race, still boasts its traditional name. Popular among those who don't mind calling in "sick" and showing up at work the next day with a sunburn, Carburetion Day includes semifinals and finals of the Miller Genuine Draft Pit Stop Contest between four racing teams.

HULMAN HUNDRED
Indiana State Fairgrounds
1202 E. 38th St.   927-7500
Admission fee

Ever-popular A.J. Foyt presents this dirt car race on the State Fairgrounds' oval the Friday night before the 500. The 100-mile competition, which attracts more than 30 cars, is part of the USAC Silver Crown series.

DELCO ELECTRONICS 500 FESTIVAL PARADE
Downtown   636-4556
Admission fee for reserved seats

More than 150,000 spectators attend this annual day-before-the-race extravaganza, which features floats, bands and, of course, the 33 race car drivers. Grandstands are set up along the route for ticketholders, who are issued props and costumes to interact with the parade units, turning the event into the nation's only participatory parade. Though grandstands full of ticketholders fill some of the best viewing areas, plenty of spectators tote along lawn chairs and pick

their own perfect spot to watch the festivities.

INDIANAPOLIS 500-MILE RACE
Indianapolis Motor Speedway
4790 W. 16th St.   481-8500
Admission fee

Called the world's largest one-day sporting event, the greatest spectacle in racing attracts nearly a half-million people to the track in late May. The infield area, which once hosted race-day denizens who arrived early and spent the day drinking and ogling the opposite sex, has earned the moniker "the snakepit." Efforts to tone down some of the more, shall we say, exuberant fans resulted in a reduction of some of the shenanigans. Those heading to their seats in the grandstands should be sure to bring along the de rigeur fried chicken box lunch and plenty to drink. But keep in mind: It's a long way to the restrooms.

June

BALKAN FESTIVAL
Sts. Constantine and Elena Romanian Orthodox Church
3237 W. 16th St.   638-4162

Forget the fighting in the Balkans for a while and soak up that area's culture as those of Serbian, Romanian and Macedonian descent share their music, food and dance at this two-day festival in early June.

ITALIAN FESTIVAL
Holy Rosary Church
520 Stevens St.   636-4478

You just can't beat the combination of a warm early June evening, a cup of cappuccino and a plate of pasta — unless maybe you add some cannoli. Festival-goers, some 30,000 each year, can also en-

Photo: The Indianapolis Star & News

The Starquest Gospel competition is just one of the many events during the Indiana Black Expo Summer Celebration that attracts visitors from throughout the United States.

joy music, a traditional religious procession and church tours.

TALBOTT STREET ART FAIR
Talbott between 16th and 19th Sts. 257-4687

One of the city's oldest festivals, it was established in 1955 by Herron art students as a way to sell their work at the end of the semester. Now, usually the second weekend after the 500, more than 200 artists working in a variety of media sell their wares in the historic Herron-Morton neighborhood, an area known for its artistic ambiance. You'll find plenty of top-notch artwork — no junk — at this popular fest, one of the last free art fairs around. (See our sidebar in this chapter.)

GUS MACKER
3-ON-3 BASKETBALL TOURNAMENT
IUPUI campus
425 University Blvd. 687-6064
Entry fee for participants

Approximately 8,000 Hoosier hoopsters participate in this annual roundball roundup that matches competi-

tors according to skill level. Anyone who's ever played driveway basketball will love it. Temporary courts are set up all over IUPUI parking lots for the mid-June double-elimination competition.

MERIDIAN-KESSLER
HOME AND GARDEN TOUR
Various homes in the Meridian-Kessler neighborhood
38th St. to Kessler Blvd. and Meridian St. to Winthrop Ave. 283-1021
Admission fee

Get a glimpse inside one of the city's oldest and most prestigious neighborhoods as eight homes and gardens open for tours. The neighborhood is beautiful in the spring, and this tour, which also includes Friday night dinner and dancing, highlights some of the area's best. Walk from house to house to really get a feel for this expansive neighborhood.

STRAWBERRY FESTIVAL
Christ Church Cathedral
55 Monument Circle 636-4577

Nearly 20,000 people stand in line on

Monument Circle to buy these sweet treats during this popular day-long berry bonanza in mid-June. Enjoy the sweet taste of an Indiana summer as the Cathedral Women of Christ Church Cathedral dish up homemade shortcake, ice cream, strawberries and whipped cream to raise money for charities. Downtown workers often designate one person to make a strawberry run for the whole office, and the sweet servings are worth the wait.

DEER CREEK FAIR

Deer Creek Music Center
12880 E. 146th St.
Noblesville   776-3337
Admission fee

The whole family can enjoy this celebration of music, sports and art. You'll find a full midway, arts and crafts demonstrations and sport competitions at this mid-June festival.

MIDSUMMER FEST

Monument Circle   637-4574
Admission fee

Celebrate the summer solstice on the Circle with continuous entertainment, lots of music and food, food, food. More than 30 local restaurants and caterers set up booths, and festival-goers can find everything from bratwurst to eggrolls.

July

A GLORIOUS FOURTH

Conner Prairie
13400 Allisonville Rd., Fishers   776-6000
Admission fee

Celebrate the Fourth at this living history museum where it's always 1836. Even though Independence Day wasn't yet a national holiday in 1836 (the year represented in Conner Prairie's living history village), visitors to Prairietown can still enjoy a day of patriotic celebration, complete with wa-

termelon, homemade ice cream, a reading of the Declaration of Independence and a noon militia muster.

FOURTH FEST

Pan Am Plaza
201 S. Capitol Ave.   633-6363
Free admission to some events

Music, food and fireworks, all the makings of a perfect Fourth of July, characterize this day-long downtown festival. The fireworks begin after dark, so there's plenty of time to find the perfect place to ooh and ahh. Those who work downtown often set up lawn chairs atop parking garages, while others scout out spots around the American Legion Mall and the World War Memorial. What you want is a clear view of the NBD bank tower, from which the fireworks are launched. We prefer to find a piece of grass and spread a blanket somewhere on the IUPUI campus. The near-downtown university offers vast parking lots and is far enough away from the action to muffle the loudest booms (a plus for those with skittish kids) and to reduce the post-fireworks traffic jams.

INDIANA BLACK EXPO SUMMER CELEBRATION

Indiana Convention Center
100 S. Capitol Ave.   925-2792
Admission fee to some events

The diverse offerings of this well-known late-July event attracts visitors from across the country. The nation's largest and longest-running celebration of African-American culture and heritage, this festival includes an ecumenical service, music festival, boxing tournament, health fair, youth summit and an art competition and exhibition. Though much of the festivities take place at the Convention Center, other sites across the city also host Expo events.

WOODRUFF PLACE
HOME AND GARDEN TOUR
Woodruff Pl.
Between 10th and Michigan Sts. 685-0571
Admission fee

This neighborhood, developed in the late 1800s by James Woodruff, features fountains, statuary, grassy esplanades and grand old mansions. Take this early-July opportunity to tour some of the restored homes in this historic near-east side neighborhood.

COUNTY FAIRS

For a real taste of small-town Americana, visit any of central Indiana's county fairs. Most have a week-long run in July, and you likely could spend the whole month tromping through county fairgrounds with an elephant ear in hand admiring livestock and canned goods, playing carnival games and riding the Tilt-A-Whirl. The Shelby County fair also offers harness racing, and though gambling on the trotters is not allowed at the fair (head to Hoosier Park in Anderson for that), top-notch driver Brian Barnes is the one to watch. The Marion County Fairgrounds are at 7300 E. Troy Avenue, 353-2444. Each county around Marion also hosts a fair; see our Area Overview chapter for county information and chamber of commerce numbers. There are admission fees to some fairs.

HOOSIER STATE GAMES FINALS
Various locations 237-5030
Entry fee

The Hoosier State Games, one of the largest amateur multisport festivals in the country, offers athletes of all ages and skill levels the chance to compete in this statewide competition. The games spotlight 19 sports, from bowling to water polo, and include traditional Olympic-style opening and closing ceremonies. The goal of the Games is to promote health and fitness for all Indiana residents and to provide an Olympic-type experience for participants. You must be an Indiana resident for at least 30 days prior to your first competition to enter. You must also be an amateur.

KROGER CIRCLEFEST
Monument Circle 237-2222
Admission fee

More than 30,000 visitors flock to the Circle in late July for this family-oriented festival, which offers plenty of food and music for Mom and Dad, plus a children's entertainment area for the kids. Now a part of the Brickyard 400 Festival, Circlefest kicks off this still-new NASCAR celebration.

August

BRICKYARD 400
Indianapolis Motor Speedway
4790 W. 16th St. 481-8500
Admission fee

Local race fans wholeheartedly welcomed this new Speedway event in early August 1994, when the first race resulted in a purse of $3.2 million, the richest in NASCAR history. Those who want to find out what stock car racing is all about before the big event can check out qualifications, when the cars will be on the oval for two days of practice prior to the race. (See the "May" section of this chapter and our Auto Racing chapter for more information.)

BRICKYARD CROSSING CHAMPIONSHIP
Brickyard Crossing Golf Resort and Inn
4400 W. 16th St. 484-6709
Admission fee

This Senior PGA Tour tournament is played on the course that winds in and around the Indianapolis Motor Speedway. (See our Sports chapter for more information.)

RCA CHAMPIONSHIPS
Indianapolis Tennis Center
755 University Blvd. 632-8000
Admission fee

Big names in men's professional tennis hit town in mid-August for this nine-day event. (See our Sports chapter for more information.)

INDIANA STATE FAIR
Indiana State Fairgrounds
102 E. 38th St. 927-7500
Admission fee

August in Indiana means the State Fair, and that means corn on the cob, Hoosier rib-eye sandwiches, pork chops, lamb kabobs, elephant ears and lemon shake-ups. And all that food means more than one trip — it's at least two trips' worth of stuff to see. Of course, there're the animals, which according to surveys is the No. 1 attraction. Be sure to check out the world's largest male hog — a huge creature — and the tiny piglets born each year during the fair's two-week mid-August run. Watch 4-H'ers spend hours fluffing fleece and combing manes to ready their animals for competition; these dedicated kids often camp out in the animal barns to be near their charges. (But don't get fooled by the plastic spider — attached to a string thrown over the rafters — that kids have been spotted using to startle unsuspecting fair-goers.)

In addition to the animals, kids can't resist the midway; there are plenty of kiddie rides for the little ones as well as scarier contraptions for daredevils. Free stages offer plenty of entertainment, the Pepsi Coliseum usually hosts a rodeo, and such performers as Randy Travis, Clint Black and

Dolly Parton have filled the Grandstand. So have another elephant ear and enjoy!

TRADERS POINT HUNT CLUB CHARITY HORSE SHOW AND COUNTY FAIR
Wild Air Farm, 7750 E. Hunt Club Rd.
Zionsville 873-5552
Admission fee

This highly regarded mid-August horse show features hunters, jumpers, a children's horse show and a county fair.

AMISH COUNTRY MARKET
Hamilton County Fairgrounds
2003 E. Pleasant St. 545-1970
Admission fee

Come early to beat the crowds of shoppers at this late-August market that snap up Amish baked goods, craft items and one-of-a-kind gifts at the county fairgrounds in Noblesville. Several buildings house the goodies, but be prepared for crowds everywhere. If you're taking the kids, note that the market gets so packed with browsers that baby strollers must be parked outside the buildings.

INDIANA AVENUE JAZZ FESTIVAL
Madame Walker Urban Life Center
617 Indiana Ave. 236-2099
Admission fee for some events

Local and national jazz artists perform on the Avenue, a street with a rich music history, during this week-long event that includes an all-day festival with street food, art booths and clothing vendors.

September

WENS SKYCONCERT
Banks of White River
West side of downtown 266-9700

The "lite rock" radio station, WENS, broadcasts music synchronized to a spectacular fireworks display Labor Day

Street Art

What began as a way for Herron art school students to sell their work at the end of the semester has evolved over the years into a popular weekend street fair that stretches along three blocks of one of the city's unique historic areas. Talbott Street Art Fair, usually held in early June, stretches for several blocks, beginning at the Herron School of Art building at 16th and Talbott streets.

When it began in the late '50s, patios were turned into display areas, and artists hung their canvases on carriage house walls. Now, more than 250 craftspersons from 21 states exhibit their wares in this well-regarded juried show. When you walk along Talbott Street during the rest of the year, you can see little painted lines on the streets marking booth space; you'll see many familiar faces if you attend the fair regularly.

Be prepared for crowds. Go with the flow and wander through the displays. You find ceramicists, painters, metalworkers, sculptors, wood carvers and just about every other artistic specialty imaginable — and some you couldn't even imagine. It's all good though; you'll find no hokey junk.

Talbott Street Art Fair turned 40 in 1995, and the venerable art fest, the oldest of its kind in the state, remains one of the best. Traditionally held the second weekend after the Indy 500, the weather is often hot, but participating artists prefer high temperatures to the spring-in-Indiana thunderstorms that keep browsers and buyers away. There is no admission charge.

weekend. Head over to the west side of downtown, find a patch of grass along the river (or, as mentioned before, on the IUPUI campus), turn up the car radio and enjoy the show.

NHRA U.S. NATIONALS

Indianapolis Raceway Park
9901 Crawfordsville Rd.   *291-4090*
Admission fee

Approximately 150,000 fans crowd into Raceway Park each Labor Day weekend for this popular end-of-summer drag, the richest in the Winston Drag Racing Series. These high-powered monsters reach speeds of 300-plus mph and travel a quarter-mile in four seconds. Admittedly exciting, all that horsepower can also be deafening, so take along some ear plugs.

OKTOBERFEST

German Park
8600 S. Meridian St.   *888-6940*
Admission fee

We know it's not October yet, but forget the calendar and join in this traditional fall favorite complete with beer, brats and oompah bands. Stretching over two weekends in early September, it's part of the state's largest celebration of German culture.

GREEK FESTIVAL

Holy Trinity Greek Orthodox Church
4011 N. Pennsylvania St.   *283-3816*
Admission fee

One of the city's most popular food fests, visitors to the church grounds in the Meridian-Kessler neighborhood enjoy homemade gyros, shish kabobs and baklava at this early-September event.

Sample baked goods and watch as parish children in traditional garb demonstrate Greek folk dances.

PENROD ARTS FAIR
Indianapolis Museum of Art
1200 W. 38th St.   923-1331
Admission fee

Attracting nearly 20,000 people, this juried fine arts fair in early September spotlights the work of more than 200 artists, dancers, actors and other performers. The 30-year-old festival is held on the beautiful 152-acre IMA grounds.

FIESTA
American Legion Mall
Downtown   636-6551
Free admission

This day-long mid-September party celebrates traditional Hispanic culture of North and South America with music, dancing, craft booths and plenty of food vendors.

HOOSIER STORYTELLING FESTIVAL
Indianapolis Art Center
820 E. 67th St.   255-7628

Bring the kids to this late-September festival and enjoy imaginative yarns from a variety of storytellers plus workshops on telling your own tales.

October

COCA-COLA CIRCLE CITY CLASSIC
RCA Dome
100 S. Capitol Ave.   237-5222
Admission fee

This contest spotlights two historically black colleges and has grown to include more than 20 related events, including a princess pageant, golf tournament and parade. One of the highlights of the early-October game is the halftime show when the McDonald's Battle of the Bands pro-

vides plenty of high-stepping, hand-clapping entertainment.

BLUESFEST
Indianapolis Art Center
820 E. 67th St.   255-2464
Admission fee

Local blues bands jam on the banks of the White River at the beautiful outdoor facilities of the Art Center. Spread out on the sheets and enjoy the tunes.

THE HEADLESS HORSEMAN AT CONNER PRAIRIE
Conner Prairie
13400 Allisonville Rd., Fishers   776-6000
Admission fee

This amusing — not scary — evening includes a hayride through Conner Prairie's apple orchard where visitors may catch a glimpse of the headless horseman, watch costumed interpreters perform the *Legend of Sleepy Hollow* and enjoy an animated version as well.

ANNUAL HAUNTED HOUSE
Children's Museum
3000 N. Meridian St.   924-5431
Admission fee

The museum guild sponsors this October tradition that opens mid-month and boasts a different creepy theme each year. Last year's was dubbed the International House of Haunts, with spooky displays including the Amazon "Brain" Forest. Much less gruesome than many local haunted houses, the Children's Museum's exhibition even offers lights-on tours for the littlest kids.

HALLOWEEN ZOOBILEE
Indianapolis Zoo
1200 W. Washington St.   630-2001
Admission fee

Kids dressed as goblins, ghouls or even Power Rangers can participate in a costume contest, go trick-or-treating, roast marshmallows and enjoy a hayride.

HEARTLAND FILM FESTIVAL

Various locations   464-9405
Admission fee for some events

Recognizing "life-affirming" filmmakers, the festival awards $100,000 in cash prizes and offers screenings, workshops and special events (see our sidebar in The Arts chapter for more information).

November

CHRISTMAS GIFT AND HOBBY SHOW

Indiana State Fairgrounds
1202 E. 38th St.   927-7500
Admission fee

Get in the Christmas mood early at one of the season's biggest bazaars. For more than 40 years, this annual extravaganza, billed as the world's largest, has been providing crafts, gift ideas and holiday food to its faithful visitors, many of whom come back year after year.

TOY SOLDIERS PLAYGROUND

Indiana State Museum
202 N. Alabama St.   232-1637
Free admission

Gather up the kids and take along a camera. This exhibit, which traditionally opens the weekend after Thanksgiving, features the old L.S. Ayres Santaland Express train that many locals remember from their own childhoods. Enjoy carolling choirs in the rotunda while little ones give Santa their wish lists.

CELEBRATION OF LIGHTS

Monument Circle   237-2222
Free admission

For more than 30 years, Indianapolis residents have been braving the cold on the Friday night after Thanksgiving to watch the lighting of "the world's largest Christmas tree." Strung with lights, the monument does indeed resemble a tree, and the whole family will cheer as a local child flips the switch that lights up the 284-foot-tall monument.

HOLIDAY MUSIC FESTIVAL

Union Station
40 Jackson Pl.   267-0701
Free admission

Get into the Christmas spirit with the more than 300 music groups, choirs and bands from across the state that perform at Union Station during the holiday season.

December

CHRISTMAS IN THE VILLAGE

Main St., Zionsville   873-3836
Free admission

Stroll the streets of this charming Boone County town during the holidays and enjoy specialty shops, unique restaurants and plenty of festive holiday decorations.

KROGER CHRISTMAS AT THE ZOO

1200 W. Washington St.
Indianapolis Zoo   630-2001
Admission fee

All through December the zoo sparkles

Zionsville's Christmas in the Village, with its quaint brick streets, unique shops and thousands of twinkling lights, is guaranteed to put just about anyone in the Christmas spirit.

Insiders' Tips

with more than 150,000 twinkling lights and animated displays. Lines can be long (and the weather chilly) for this popular holiday event where kids can ride a camel, see real reindeer and enjoy a special holiday dolphin show.

CONNER PRAIRIE BY CANDLELIGHT
Conner Prairie
1300 Allisonville Rd., Fishers   776-6000
Admission fee

Walk through Prairietown during December and talk with costumed interpreters who explain Christmas celebrations c. 1836. Christmas wasn't the extravaganza it is today, and kids will likely be surprised at the simplicity of the holiday observation.

HOLIDAY CANDLELIGHT TOUR
Various locations   638-5264

Enjoy a Historic Landmarks walking tour that takes visitors to the Morris-Butler, Kemper and President Benjamin Harrison homes, all decorated for a Victorian holiday.

GARFIELD PARK
CONSERVATORY POINSETTIA SHOW
Garfield Park and Conservatory
2450 S. Shelby St.   783-3044
Free admission

This traditional holiday poinsettia show has continued for nearly 60 years, and

though the conservatory closed for seven months for renovation, it was due to re-open just in time for the 1995 show. Later in the month you can get a good price on the poinsettias during the annual sale.

INDIANAPOLIS AUTO SHOW
100 S. Capitol Ave.
Convention Center and RCA Dome 262-3410
Admission fee

Traditionally held the weekend after Christmas, the Auto Show provides a place to go to escape a houseful of visiting relatives when not much else is going on. Lust after the latest in automotive technology and plan next year's Christmas wish list.

NEW YEAR'S EVE CELEBRATION
Union Station
40 Jackson Pl.   267-0701
Admission fee

The historic festival marketplace is packed with holiday revelers who enjoy a variety of music, food and dancing. Spill outdoors to join in a Times Square-like countdown and fireworks display at the clock tower. Even if you don't buy a ticket for the indoor festivities, it's fun to walk around downtown as the New Year is rung in.

Inside
The Arts

First, let's acknowledge the obvious: When it comes to the arts, Indianapolis is no New York. But it is the hub of artistic activity in Indiana. The arts are well represented here, at least insofar as the mainstream is concerned.

If you're looking for avant garde, cutting-edge stuff, you'll have to look hard. Experimentation happens here, but not to the extent that you'll find in more cosmopolitan cities. Chalk that up to Midwestern conservatism, both in attitude and in funding. Corporate and foundation coffers tend to open more freely if the artist or organization requesting help is producing safe, noncontroversial art. Still, safe as most of it is, the art being produced here on many fronts is high quality — a reflection of the caliber of the artists and the arts organizations in the community. Sometimes on extremely tight budgets, creators and presenters alike not only find ways to make ends meet but also to produce credible, commendable works of art.

The arts are having a significant impact on the local economy. According to a study commissioned by the Arts Council of Indianapolis and conducted by Indiana University's Center for Urban Policy and the Environment, the total annual impact of the arts on the city's economy is $46 million. What's more, there are some 4,000 people employed by

Photo: Indianapolis Symphony Orchestra

The ISO presents several programs throughout the year, including its six-week Symphony on the Prairie Series.

200 local arts organizations — and they account for a payroll of $35 million. Clearly, the arts are more than window-dressing in Indianapolis: They're a vital part of the city's economic infrastructure and a vital part of people's lives. Arts organizations report a collective attendance total of nearly 5 million people annually. The arts are alive and well in Indianapolis.

But don't take our word for it. Go see and hear for yourself.

Support Organizations

INDIANA ARTS COMMISSION (IAC)
402 W. Washington St.   232-1268

This state agency is responsible for promoting the arts and providing financial assistance to arts organizations and artists throughout Indiana. Using funds from the National Endowment for the Arts, as well as those allocated to it by the state legislature, the IAC operates a number of programs ranging from artists fellowships to a popular and widely admired arts education program that puts painters and poets, potters, percussionists and a potpourri of other artists into classrooms statewide.

INDIANA HUMANITIES COUNCIL (IHC)
1500 N. Delaware St.   638-1500

Using funds from the National Endowment for the Humanities as well as from contributions made by corporations, foundations and individuals, the IHC funds the development of programs and projects — lectures, discussion groups, film series and readings — aimed at exploring the cultural and academic life of Indiana. One such program is the popular biannual WORDSTRUCK a weeklong celebration of Indiana's literary life. (For more on this, see our Literary Life chapter.)

THE ARTS COUNCIL OF INDIANAPOLIS
47 S. Pennsylvania St., No. 703   631-3301

This private, nonprofit organization is charged with providing financial, planning, programming and management assistance to arts organizations, artists and the local community. It also operates the city's newest arts facility — the Artsgarden, Circle Centre's arts information center inside the glass-enclosed arch that spans West Washington Street (see the sidebar in this chapter).

INDIANA ADVOCATES FOR THE ARTS/ INDIANA CITIZENS FOR THE ARTS
47 S. Pennsylvania St.   638-3984

These jointly run organizations are nonprofit, volunteer-driven arts advocacy groups that lobby the state Legislature on behalf of the arts, work within communities around the state to promote and raise awareness of the arts, and stress the value of arts education for children and adults alike.

VERY SPECIAL ARTS OF INDIANA INC.
1605 E. 86th St.   253-5504

Dedicated to making the arts accessible to very special audiences — children and adults with physical and/or mental disabilities — this organization funds hands-on arts programs and projects. It also conducts workshops to train artists and teachers how to create arts activities for people with special needs.

YOUNG AUDIENCES OF INDIANA INC.
3050 N. Meridian St.   925-4043

Affiliated with Young Audiences, a national arts education organization, this nonprofit operation provides schools, community centers, parks, libraries and

The Sound of the City

The internationally-acclaimed 88-member Indianapolis Symphony Orchestra invites you to experience the real joy of musical excellence. One of America's few 52-week orchestras, there are always concerts, some 200 every year, for all audiences.

The Classical Series
Highly celebrated maestro Raymond Leppard conducts the Orchestra for these concerts, right in the heart of downtown.
Circle Theatre on Monument Circle, September through June.

The Pops Series
Erich Kunzel conducts and the Orchestra swings for these evenings of outstanding entertainment. *Circle Theatre; September through June.*

Ameritech's "Yuletide Celebration"
The sights, sounds and smiles of the season come to life through music, singing, giant puppets and dancing.
Circle Theatre; December.

Marsh "Symphony on the Prairie" Series
Food, families, fun, familiar favorites, even Fourth fireworks,all under the fantastic sky at Conner Prairie.
North on Allisonville Road; June through August.

Enjoy other ISO performances in the Sound of the City, Young People's Discovery, Family and Indiana series in the Circle Theatre, other locations around Indianapolis and throughout the State of Indiana. The Indianapolis Symphony Orchestra can be heard on *Koss Classics* compact discs and on national and regional radio broadcasts.

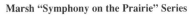

For complete concert information, call the ISO box office.
In the Indianapolis area **639-4300**; or call toll free **1-800-366-8457**.

INDIANAPOLIS SYMPHONY ORCHESTRA
Raymond Leppard, Music Director

museums statewide with arts programs for school children. The roster of Young Audiences of Indiana usually contains some 60 visual artists, storytellers, dancers, actors, musicians and writers from throughout the state.

PENROD SOCIETY

P.O. Box 40817
Indianapolis 46240   252-9895

Named for Penrod Schofield, the hero of local author Booth Tarkington's *Penrod* stories, this organization promotes and supports various arts events and activities in Indianapolis. One of its most visible activities is its annual fund-raiser, the Penrod Arts Fair (see separate entry in the "Arts Events" portion of this chapter). Beneficiaries of the society's largesse include the Indianapolis Museum of Art, the Indianapolis Symphony Orchestra, the Indiana Repertory Theatre and Dance Kaleidoscope.

ARTS INDIANA INC.

47 S. Pennsylvania, Ste. 701   632-7894

This is the corporate entity responsible for publishing *Arts Indiana*, the only statewide publication devoted exclusively to reporting on the arts and cultural life in Indiana. Published monthly from September through June, *Arts Indiana* explores the human, social and political aspects of the arts — literary, performing and visual. Lively writing and uncluttered design make reading this magazine a pleasure — and its statewide focus make reading it a must if you want to feel at all informed about what's going on not only in Indianapolis but throughout Indiana.

"Making art accessible" is a facet of many an arts organization's mission statement — *Arts Indiana* does exactly that.

Performing Arts

Facilities

CIRCLE THEATRE

45 Monument Cir.
Offices   262-1110
Box office   639-4300

Home of the Indianapolis Symphony Orchestra, the Circle Theatre is the second-oldest building on Monument Circle. Originally built in 1916, it was the city's first facility devoted exclusively to showing movies. But by the time it closed in 1981, the Circle Theatre had degenerated to the kind of place that attracted customers who wore overcoats year-round.

The theater didn't sit vacant long before supporters of the Indianapolis Symphony Orchestra arranged to buy it and renovate it as the orchestra's permanent home. The renovation process, with such painstaking tasks as recasting plaster moldings, involved scores of local construction and craftspeople.

In 1984, the ISO staged its first concert in the theater's gorgeous (and acoustically wonderful) auditorium. In the years since, the Circle Theatre has reclaimed its role as one of the city's premier venues. On evenings when the orchestra is performing, the sidewalk in front of the Circle Theatre is thick with a lively mix of concert-goers, from formally clad socialites to blue-jeaned music students.

CLOWES MEMORIAL HALL

4600 Sunset Ave.   283-9696

Prior to its move to the Circle Theatre, the ISO called Clowes Memorial Hall, on the campus of Butler University, home for 20 years. Often referred to simply as Clowes, this facility was built in the early 1960s with donations from the family of the late George Henry Alexander Clowes, a wealthy businessman and local arts supporter.

While no longer the home stage for the ISO, the acoustically superb Clowes auditorium continues to feature an array of performing arts, including the road versions of Broadway shows, chamber music and choral groups, ballets, and operas, as well as pop, rock and jazz artists.

MURAT TEMPLE
510 N. New Jersey St.   *635-2433*

The local headquarters for the Shriners, the Murat Temple is renowned for its theater. Built in 1910, it's the oldest surviving downtown stage; the Egyptian-influenced architecture provides an exotic counterpoint to the eclectic mix of performers who appear at the Murat — from Tony Bennett to Laurie Anderson, the theater hosts a variety of acts year-round.

The Murat's a funky alternative to the Circle Theatre, and the hope is that it will remain so even after the completion of an extensive repair and renovation project currently in the works. (The roof leaks, the carpeting and seats are worn, but it's still a wonderful place to see live acts.)

MADAME WALKER URBAN LIFE CENTER
617 Indiana Ave.   *236-2099*

Another downtown theater that's a great discovery is the one inside the Madame Walker Urban Life Center. The Walker Building was originally built in 1927 to commemorate the late Madame C.J. Walker whose Indianapolis-based cosmetics manufacturing firm had made her America's first black female millionaire. Over the years, neglect took its toll on the structure, but in 1979 efforts began to save it. After an extensive $5 mil-

lion renovation, the building became the Madame Walker Urban Life Center, opening for business in 1984. Four years later, the 950-seat, fourth-floor Walker Theatre opened.

The Walker Theatre, once the site of performances by such renowned black artists as Louie Armstrong and Lena Horne, now hosts Jazz on the Avenue concerts every Friday night. It's also the site for the annual Indiana Avenue Jazz Festival, a four-day celebration of jazz that features well-known musicians. Additionally, other local and national jazz events, as well as gospel, rhythm 'n' blues, and urban-music performers appear at the Walker.

In addition to music, the Walker hosts stage plays and films. It's home to the Walker Repertory Showcase, which provides opportunities for local African-American theater companies to present productions in conjunction with the Walker Theatre. It also houses a youth arts program for young actors, writers, dancers, musicians and visual artists.

RUTH LILLY THEATER
3000 N. Meridian St.   *921-4000*

This 350-seat facility, named for local arts and education patron Ruth Lilly, is on the first level of the Children's Museum of Indianapolis. It offers a variety of family fare ranging from children's music favorite Raffi to local and national children's theater productions. (For more information on the museum and its many programs and attractions, see our Kidstuff chapter.)

THE WARREN PERFORMING ARTS CENTER
Warren Central High School
9500 E. 16th St.   *898-9722*

This is one of the city's most techno-

If you only have time to shop one place in Indianapolis... shop The Fashion Mall.

THE FASHION MALL
KEYSTONE AT THE CROSSING
Keystone Avenue & 86th Street

Monday – Friday 10 a.m. – 9 p.m. Saturday 10 a.m. – 6 p.m. Sunday Noon – 5 p.m. 317-524-4000

Located on the north side of Indianapolis–just 20 minutes from downtown and less than 30 minutes from the airport logically advanced arts facilities. Constructed in 1983 at a cost of $10.5 million, it's comprised of a 1,000-seat grand auditorium, a 150-seat studio theater, a dance studio and several rehearsal halls. While used on a daily basis by the school's drama and music classes and groups, the center is the site of school-related concerts and theater/dance productions as well as of community and off-Broadway shows.

CHRISTEL DEHAAN FINE ARTS CENTER
University of Indianapolis
1400 E. Hanna Ave.   *788-3368*
The city's newest arts venue, the DeHaan Fine Arts Center is named for local arts patron and businesswoman Christel DeHaan. The center includes the two-tiered Ruth Lilly Performance Hall, an art gallery, art studios, sound-isolated practice rooms for instrumental and vocal musicians and an 80-seat lecture hall.

Considered the equal of any concert hall in the country, the center's performance hall utilizes 28-inch-thick walls, a sound-reflecting chandelier and acoustic drapes that can be adjusted for specific types of performances from symphonic orchestras to electronic music. During its first year of operation, the center presented a variety of performing arts productions ranging from student and faculty recitals to modern dance, from folk singer/storyteller Jean Redpath to poet Carolyn Forche.

DEER CREEK MUSIC CENTER
12880 E. 146th St.   *776-3337*
Since it opened in 1989, this facility has earned a reputation among performers and fans alike as one of America's best amphitheaters. Situated on 220 lovely, rolling acres in Hamilton County, Deer Creek contains 6,200 pavilion seats and 81 corporate boxes, as well as room for another 14,000 people on the surrounding lawn. During any given May-to-September season, you can catch pop, rock, heavy metal, jazz and country performers on the Deer Creek stage. It also hosts the week-long, family-oriented Deer Creek Festival every June (see our Annual Events chapter for more information).

INDIANA ROOF BALLROOM
140 W. Washington St.
Office   *236-1870*
Events line   *236-1877*
On the top floor of the Indiana Repertory Theatre (see separate entry under the "Theater Companies" portion of this chapter) is the Indiana Roof Ballroom. Under its 40-foot-high domed ceiling, which is dappled with stars and clouds, audiences attend performances by the likes of jazz guitarist Earl Klugh or glide across the floor to the music of Guy Lombardo's Royal Canadians (yes, Guy's gone, but his band plays on). In addition to buying tickets to Roof events, you can also buy packages that include dinner and a room at the adjacent Embassy Suites hotel. Call the Indiana Roof's office for details.

MARKET SQUARE ARENA
300 E. Market St.
Box office information   *639-2121*
While clearly not designed for the nuances of a piano sonata or the subtleties of classical ballet, Market Square Arena (or MSA, as it's known locally) does serve as a venue for rock, pop and country performances, as well as for assorted productions by such road companies as Disney, Jim Henson's Muppets and, yes, the ubiquitous Mighty Morphin Power Rangers.

Theater Companies

INDIANA REPERTORY THEATRE

140 W. Washington St.

Offices	924-6770
Box office	923-4597

If you spend any time wandering around the stretch of W. Washington Street between N. Illinois and N. Capitol, you'll spot the Indiana Repertory Theatre. Looking every bit the gorgeous c. 1927 movie palace that it is, the IRT building houses a professional theater operation that presents both classic and contemporary stage productions. During its October-to-May season, this is the place where works by Shakespeare and Moliere rub shoulders with those by Neil Simon and August Wilson.

The IRT is actually three theaters in one: a 600-seat mainstage, a 250-seat upperstage and a 150-seat cabaret. Situated in the heart of downtown's hotel, retail and convention district, the IRT attracts more than 100,000 theater-goers every year, while its educational outreach program provides another 40,000 school children opportunities to experience live theater.

The IRT offers a variety of series: the Mainstage Series; a Senior Discount Series; the Culture Collection, which is a miniseries featuring African-American playwrights and actors; an American Sign Language/Audio described series for patrons who are hearing- or sight-impaired; a Student Series; an Opening Night Series; and an Upperstage Family Series. There are also Saturday Brunch, Sunday Tea Talk and Tuesday Pub Night series. Ticket prices for these options vary, and series packages are available. To learn more, contact the IRT box office.

THE PHOENIX THEATRE

749 N. Park Ave.

Offices	635-2381
Box office	635-7529

As the city's premier site for contemporary theater productions, the Phoenix offers issue-oriented dramas and comedies that are apt to make you think about what you've seen. In addition to staging productions, the Phoenix also hosts workshops and classes for aspiring playwrights and actors, as well as sponsoring the Festival of Emerging American Theatre, an annual playwriting competition that attracts entries from around the world.

Season subscriptions are available, as are single-admission tickets. For a season schedule and ticket prices, contact the Phoenix box office.

BEEF & BOARDS DINNER THEATRE

9301 N. Michigan Rd.	872-9664
Group reservations	876-0503

Since 1973, Beef & Boards has been home to Broadway-style plays and musicals. As the only year-round Equity theater in town, it recruits professional performers both locally and nationally. In addition to productions of such stage gems as *West Side Story* and *Brigadoon*, B&B also hosts concerts from the likes of B.B. King and the Wright Brothers.

Ticket prices vary; season discount memberships are available, as are group rates for parties of 20 or more. A table for two will cost you five bucks extra.

AMERICAN CABARET THEATRE

401 E. Michigan St.	631-0334

If you too think that "Life is a cabaret," then the American Cabaret Theatre, inside the turn-of-the-century Athenaeum Turners building, is for you.

The Heartland Film Festival

Tired of gratuitous sex and violence? Yearning for movies that aim higher than daredevil chases and explosions? Looking for films that aspire to enrich or enhance viewers' lives rather than merely titillate or thrill? Then you're ready for the Heartland Film Festival.

Since its debut in 1992, the Heartland Film Festival has become a well-respected addition to the national film community. Created as a vehicle for honoring life-affirming films — that is, films that illuminate and celebrate the best in human nature — the four-day-long October festival has attracted such movie world luminaries as directors Robert Wise and Sydney Pollack, film critics Jeffrey Lyons and Michael Medved, and producers Don Hahn (*The Lion King*) and Branko Lustig (*Schindler's List*) to Indianapolis for workshops and screenings.

Founded by Jeffrey Sparks, who now serves as its artistic director, the Heartland makes good use of the talents and connections of Indiana natives who've gone on to success in Hollywood. Writer/producer Matt Williams (*Roseanne* and *Home Improvement*), as well as director David Anspaugh and screenwriter Angelo Pizzo (*Hoosiers* and *Rudy*) have contributed time and energy to the festival.

As it has gained exposure, the Heartland has also gained access to the works of both independent and mainstream filmmakers. At the 1994 festival, for example, Walt Disney Studios' film *Squanto: A Warrior's Tale*, premiered, as did Miramax Family Films', *Gordy*. At the same time, the festival featured such independently produced documentaries as *Satya: A Prayer for the Enemy* about Tibetan nuns' nonviolent response to the Chinese occupation of Tibet, and *Moving the Mountain*, which is about one of the Tienneman Square protest leaders. (*Moving the Mountain*, produced by rock star Sting's wife, Trudi Styler, went on to win the festival's top prize, the Crystal Heart, which is literally that, along with a check for $25,000.)

The festival's films are shown at a variety of sites ranging from the Madame Walker Urban Life Center and the Circle Theatre to the Hollywood Bar & Film Works and Union Station. Ticket prices vary, and festival packages are available. For information, contact the Heartland Film Festival, 613 N. East Street, 464-9405.

Founded in New York in 1975, ACT moved to Indianapolis in 1990. Since then, it has gained a reputation for presenting high-energy, professionally staged musical productions. Call for a schedule and ticket information, then get ready for a good time.

INDIANAPOLIS CIVIC THEATRE

1200 W. 38th St.
Offices   924-6770
Box office   923-4597

Founded in 1914, the Indianapolis Civic Theatre is the oldest continuously operating community (nonprofessional) theater in the United States. Inside a facility on the lower level of the Indianapolis Museum of Art, the Civic's small, paid staff works with a cadre of volunteer actors and technicians to produce musicals, dramas and comedies for its 700-seat mainstage theater, as well as experimental productions in a separate 90-seat theater known as Studio C.

The Civic Theatre also sponsors the Junior Civic, one of the city's longest-running youth theater programs. It offers classes to kids in 1st through ninth grades. There are various ticket options and prices. To learn more, contact the Civic's box office.

ASANTE CHILDREN'S THEATRE
P.O. Box 22344   638-6694

Speaking of kids, the Asante Children's Theatre is one of the city's new bright lights. Founded in 1991 by veteran actress Deborah Asante, the group is based at the Christamore House, a community center on the near-east side. Created as a means of educating children about both theater and African culture, Asante Children's Theatre holds annual city-wide auditions to fill the 30 slots it has open for children between the ages of 8 and 18. During its September-to-June season, the troupe stages three productions at the Madame Walker Urban Life Center, 617 Indiana Avenue. For information, call Asante Children's Theatre.

THEATRE ON THE SQUARE
627 Massachusetts Ave.   637-8085

This small but well-respected theater dedicates its seven-production season to contemporary and lesser-known plays and musicals, presented in intimate settings. Housed in a renovated building on the northeast edge of the Mile Square, Theatre on the Square consists of a 150-seat main stage and an 80-seat cabaret.

A schedule and ticket information are just a phone call away.

EDYVEAN REPERTORY THEATRE AT CTS
1000 W. 42nd St.
Offices   927-8052
Box office   923-1516

In its theater on the campus of the Christian Theological Seminary (CTS), the Edyvean features both classical and contemporary stage plays and musicals during its six-show season. In 1992, it introduced Indiana's first audio description service for visually impaired audience members. The 425-seat theater also contains FM sound enhancement equipment for the hearing impaired.

Making theater accessible to adults with disabilities has long been important at the Edyvean. Since 1982, the theater has been home to the Jumping Mouse Players, a nonprofessional troupe open to anyone 16 or older who is physically, mentally or developmentally challenged. The group creates its own material, utilizing acting, dance, mime, song and improvisation to entertain and educate its audiences. The Jumping Mouse Players perform in schools and churches, at colleges and for civic groups and clubs statewide. For more information on the Jumping Mouse Players, call 927-8054. For information on the Edyvean's season, contact the box office.

NAPI REP/
NEW ARTISTS PRODUCTIONS
3909 N. Meridian St.
Offices   923-4581
Box office   547-6338

NAPI REP is a professional, non-union theatre company established specifically to assist African-American playwrights, actors, directors, craftspeople and technicians in their efforts to learn about and work in live theater. The company's season runs September to June, during which time it presents five productions on the IRT's upperstage and cabaret.

Photo: The Indianapolis Star & News

The Walker Theater hosts Jazz on the Avenue concerts every Friday night.

In 1993, NAPI REP was one of 20 theater companies in the United States selected to perform at the National Black Theatre Festival; that same year, the company also performed at the International May Time Festival in Ireland. NAPI REP is an offshoot of the African-American production company New Artists Productions. To learn about forthcoming productions, call the NAPI office.

FOOTLITE MUSICALS

1847 N. Alabama St.   **926-6630**

Since 1956, Footlite Musicals has been dedicated to presenting musical theater to central Indiana audiences. On its home stage in the Hedback Theatre, this all-volunteer community theater group produces four shows a year. In 1991, Footlite was designated the No. 1 community theater in America when its production of Stephen Sondheim's *Into the Woods* won the American Community Theatre Association's national competition. Judge Footlite's quality for yourself; call for a schedule and ticket information.

Music

INDIANAPOLIS SYMPHONY ORCHESTRA

The Circle Theatre, 45 Monument Cir.
Box office   639-4300
Offices   262-1100

The Indianapolis Symphony Orchestra (a.k.a. ISO) is one of the few professional symphony orchestras in America that operates on a full 52-week schedule, performing nearly 200 concerts a year. It's also one of the few orchestras that owns and maintains its own concert hall, the aforementioned Circle Theatre. The orchestra also performs in parks and other public sites throughout Indiana and at Conner Prairie (see the Attractions and Kidstuff chapters) during the annual Symphony on the Prairie summer series.

Since 1987, the ISO's conductor has been internationally acclaimed maestro Raymond Leppard. Under his direction, the orchestra has attained international acclaim of its own, performing to critical accolades throughout the United States and Europe and releasing several well-received recordings. (In 1994, the ISO began a series of one-hour syndicated radio programs; called *Indianapolis On The Air*, the 13-week series is heard on more than 175 radio stations nationwide.)

The ISO presents several programs throughout the year. In addition to its 21-week Classical Series and its seven-week Symphony on the Prairie Series, there is a Pops Series conducted by Erich Kunzel; a Studio Series that combines Maestro Leppard's analysis with performances of classical masterworks; a Family Series; the always popular Yuletide Celebration performance; and the Sound of the City and Indiana series that take the ISO out to parks and community centers throughout Indianapolis and the state.

Ticket prices vary, and subscription packages are available. Discounts are available for seniors, students and children.

INDIANAPOLIS SYMPHONIC CHOIR
4600 Sunset Ave.   921-4641

Founded in 1937 by Fabien Sevitzky, music director of the ISO, and Elmer Steffen, music director of the local Roman Catholic archdiocese, the Indianapolis Symphonic Choir has become one of the city's musical treasures. Comprised of some 120 trained singers, the choir not only performs with the ISO but also stages concerts on its own, including the popular holiday presentation, *Festival of Carols*. In addition to appearances throughout Indiana and nearby states, the choir has performed at Carnegie Hall in New York City and the Kennedy Center in Washington, D.C. Call for a schedule and ticket information.

INDIANAPOLIS OPERA
250 E. 38th St.
Offices   283-3531
Box office   921-6444

If its arias you crave, the Indianapolis Opera will be happy to oblige. Since its founding nearly 20 years ago, this renowned company has garnered praise for its high musical and production standards. Under the guidance of general director Nando Schellen, former artistic director of Amsterdam's Sweelinck Conservatory and associate director of the Netherlands Opera, Indianapolis Opera stages four productions each season at Clowes Memorial Hall, three with the Indianapolis Symphony Orchestra and one with the Indianapolis Chamber Orchestra. To ensure the quality of the productions, singers are selected through national auditions.

And to ensure audience understanding, the company hosts pre-performance discussions of an opera's plot and characters as well as of opera history in general. Ticket prices vary, and subscription packages are available through the Clowes box office.

INDIANA OPERA THEATRE INC.
2825 E. 56th St.   253-1001

While formally known as the MacAllister Awards and Festival Opera Theatre, this organization is still widely known by the name under which it operated for well more than a decade — Indiana Opera Theatre. Regardless of its name, it has earned a reputation for imaginative stagings of operatic works — its production of Gilbert and Sullivan's *Trial by Jury*, for instance, was performed in a local courtroom.

This organization is also the sponsor of the well-respected MacAllister Awards, which, through a series of nationwide auditions, recognizes the skills of young (younger than 36) opera singers. The annual competition, which is named for local businessman and arts patron P.E. MacAllister, includes divisions for professional singers, college singers (younger than 25) and youth (ages 13 to 18).

For schedules and ticket information, contact the opera's office.

INDIANAPOLIS CHILDREN'S CHOIR
Butler University
4600 Sunset Ave.   283-9640

From the moment of its first meeting in 1986, the Indianapolis Children's Choir has been an unqualified success. Founded by Henry Leck, former assistant director of the Indianapolis Symphonic Choir, the Children's Choir has become a well-respected part of not only the Indianapolis musical community but the world's as well.

With 700 members between the ages of 9 and 14, the ICC is actually a collection of 10 choirs, organized according to youngsters' levels of musical comprehension and ability. In addition to performing locally, the ICC has sent touring contingents to Europe, Australia and New Zealand; it has also done a number of recordings, including one with the Canadian Brass. The choir has performed at places as diverse as Carnegie Hall and the former Nazi concentration camp at Dachau.

To get a sense of how popular the ICC is in this town, count the number of cars and minivans you see bearing the Indianapolis Children's Choir sticker in a window or on a bumper. You'll be surprised how quickly they add up.

Contact the ICC office for schedules and ticket information.

CATHEDRAL ARTS INC.
47 S. Pennsylvania St., No. 401   637-4574

Cathedral Arts acts as an umbrella organization for a number of musical programs and events, including two chamber ensembles, Suzuki & Friends and the Ronen Chamber Ensemble, as well as the acclaimed International Violin Competition.

Founded in 1980 by Indianapolis Symphony orchestra concertmaster Hidetaro Suzuki, the eponymous Suzuki & Friends has attracted a loyal and enthusiastic following. The ensemble usually performs five concerts each year in the Ruth Lilly Theater at the Children's Museum of Indianapolis. They also occasionally perform at other sites, including the Circle Theatre and the Christel DeHaan Fine Arts Center on the campus of the University of Indianapolis.

The Ronen Chamber Ensemble, which was also founded by ISO members (principle clarinetist David Bellman and cellist Ingrid Bellman), performs wind instrument selections. Ronen concerts are held in the Wood Room of the Circle Theatre.

One Cathedral Arts program that attracts significant attention internationally is the quadrennial International Violin Competition. The brainchild of the late violin master and Indiana University Music School professor Josef Gingold, the IVC brings 50 of the world's finest young violinists to Indianapolis every four years for two weeks of intense competition. The results are cash prizes as well as performance and recording contracts that are the richest in the history of violin competitions.

While the IVC is popular locally, it's even more popular outside the state. In 1982, a PBS documentary on the competition won a number of prestigious television awards; four years later, the BBC broadcast a seven-part series of excerpts from the 1986 contest. American Public Radio and the Voice of America both broadcast the violinists' stage performances.

The next International Violin Competition will be held in Indianapolis in 1998.

The Indianapolis Artsgarden

Arching like a crystalline bridge across the downtown intersection of Washington and Illinois streets, the Artsgarden is the newest addition to the Indianapolis arts scene. This $12 million, 12,500-square-foot glass and steel structure, which is owned and operated by the Arts Council of Indianapolis, was designed to serve both as a venue for showcasing area performing and visual artists and organizations and as a clearinghouse for information about local arts events.

At its apex, the Artsgarden curves 95 feet above street level, making it one of the downtown's architectural focal points, along with, of course, Circle Centre, the city's new downtown shopping and entertainment complex. The Artsgarden links Circle Centre with the National City Bank/Hyatt Regency Hotel and office complex and the Claypool Court/Embassy Suites Hotel shopping and entertainment complex. Literally and symbolically, the Artsgarden serves as a bridge between the arts and commerce.

At least, that's the hope — the facility, which opened in September 1995, has only begun trying to fulfill its mission as a presenter of performances and exhibitions and as a purveyor of information about area arts events. (Given its accessibility, the Artsgarden is a one-stop-shopping center for schedules, tickets, calendars, maps, and directories related to local arts organizations and events.)

While clearly one of the city's most visible — and visually arresting — arts facilities, the Artsgarden has attracted its share of criticism. Several area performing arts groups have lamented the fact that they weren't consulted during the structure's design stage; as a result, they predict that poor

Photo: The Indianapolis Star & News

The Artsgarden is the newest addition to the arts scene in Indianapolis. The Artsgarden is a 12,500-square-foot glass-and-steel structure that spans Washington and Illinois streets.

acoustics will prevent it from being a viable site for musical or theatrical activities. Likewise, visual arts organizations have expressed concern about the effects of harsh light and heat upon art works. (In their defense, the architects have pointed out that the structure's 26,000 square feet of glass is tempered to reduce noise and tinted to reduce light and heat.)

Despite criticisms, proponents insist that the Artsgarden, which includes a portable stage, theatrical lighting and acoustics, dressing rooms and exhibition cases, will ultimately enhance visibility and public awareness of arts organizations and events and artists. And, in a manner of speaking, it already has.

Since the initial unveiling of the design and the ground-breaking ceremonies (presided over by Jane Alexander, chair of the National Endowment for the Arts) in 1994, throughout the ten-month-long construction process, and right on up to the September 1995 opening, the Artsgarden generated plenty of publicity and attracted plenty of public attention— always with the reminder that its purpose is to showcase the arts.

For information about the Artsgarden, contact the Arts Council of Indianapolis, 631-3301.

To get schedules and ticket information for any of these Cathedral Arts programs, contact the organization.

INDIANAPOLIS CHAMBER ORCHESTRA INC.

4600 Sunset Ave.   *283-9607*

Founded in 1984, this nonprofit 32-member orchestra is modeled after London's renowned chamber orchestra, the Academy of St. Martin-in-the-Fields. Under the baton of conductor Kirk Trevor, the orchestra performs an annual six-concert series at Clowes Hall, which also serves as its headquarters. Contact the Clowes box office for ticket information.

INDIANAPOLIS ARTS CHORALE

P.O. Box 17446   *787-1874*

If you're a choral music fan, lend an ear to the Indianapolis Arts Chorale. Consisting of 40 singers — doctors, teachers, ministers, executives and homemakers — the chorale performs a variety of vocal mu-sic ranging from the compositions of Haydn and Brahms to excerpts from Gilbert and Sullivan in settings that include high school auditoriums, churches, the Indianapolis Museum of Art and the Indiana Statehouse.

A subscription to the Chorale's six-concert, October-to-May program is available by contacting the Chorale directly — or you can buy single-event tickets before each performance.

CARMEL SYMPHONY ORCHESTRA

P.O. Box 761, Carmel 46032   *844-9717*

Largely a volunteer organization (only 15 of the orchestra's 63 musicians are paid), the Carmel Symphony Orchestra still manages to produce a full season, including family concerts, orchestral concerts, chamber music concerts and educational concerts. Events take place at various sites, including churches, high school auditoriums and area parks.

This is a community orchestra that, due to central Indiana's large contingent of well-trained musicians (many of whom are graduates of Indiana University's prestigious school of music), doesn't sound like a community orchestra. These folks got chops! For a schedule and ticket information, contact the orchestra's office at the telephone number listed above.

DRUMS OF WEST AFRICA

4037 Graceland Ave.   283-7681

Guided by founder Prince Julius Adeniyi, Drums of West Africa utilizes a variety of authentic African percussion instruments to showcase the rhythmic traditions of West African cultures. In appearances before audiences from elementary school children to adults, in settings from school gymnasiums to concert halls, Drums of West Africa offers living proof that music is at once personal and universal. Watch for newspaper announcements of a performance, then go: Just be prepared to be wowed both by the music and by Adeniyi's infectious joy.

THE FESTIVAL MUSIC SOCIETY

6741 N. Central Ave.   251-5190

Since its founding in 1961, this nonprofit organization has been staging annual performances of early classical music, that is, music from the Medieval, Renaissance, Baroque and Classic periods. The organization's program, which is held each July, includes both concerts and lectures, bringing in such noteworthy performing groups as the Cologne Chamber Orchestra, the Paris Consort and Hesperus (the ensemble-in-residence at the Smithsonian Institution's National Museum of American History).

Contact the society for a schedule and ticket information.

AMERICAN PIANISTS ASSOCIATION

4600 Sunset Ave.   283-9945

The American Pianists Association,

which has its headquarters at Clowes Hall on the Butler University campus, hosts two significant biennial musical events in the city: the National Piano Fellowship Auditions and the American Jazz Piano Competition. The Ninth Biennial National Piano Fellowship Auditions will be held in 1997, while the Third Biennial Jazz Piano Competition is in April 1996. In addition, the winners of the National Piano Fellowship Auditions appear annually at PianoFest, a series of piano performances held at the Circle Theatre's Wood Room and at the Indianapolis Museum of Art.

FINE ARTS SOCIETY OF INDIANAPOLIS

1400 E. Hanna Ave.   788-3291

Since 1968, this organization has been a leader in the production of classical music radio in Indianapolis. A public charitable trust, the society broadcasts more than 100 hours of classical music programming each week on WICR (88.7 FM), a noncommercial radio station operated by the University of Indianapolis. In 1986, the society received a George Foster Peabody Award for excellence in broadcasting.

In addition to its radio programs, the society also sponsors a variety of fine and performing arts events and annually honors a civic leader for contributions to the cultural life of the community with its Diploma of Honor.

Dance

DANCE KALEIDOSCOPE INC.

4600 Sunset Ave.

Office   920-6555
Civic Theatre box office   923-4597

Dance Kaleidoscope (or DK as it's known in dance circles) is Indiana's only professional, modern dance company. Under the direction of world-renowned dancer and choreographer David Hochoy, the eight-member troupe stages a full professional season, performing at the Indianapolis Civic Theatre, on the lower level of the Indianapolis Museum of Art, 1200 W. 38th Street.

DK's repertoire consists of pieces choreographed by such leading modern dance pioneers as Martha Graham as well as by such contemporary artists as Fred Mathews. In addition to its concerts, DK also conducts workshops and demonstrations in schools throughout Indiana. The company also offers the Jaffee-Hall Emerging Indiana Artist Award, which gives Indiana dancers a chance to be part of a professional dance company for a season. For a DK season schedule and the lowdown on tickets, contact the Indianapolis Civic Theatre's box office.

INDIANAPOLIS BALLET THEATRE INC.
502 N. Capitol Ave., Ste. B

Office	637-8979
Box office	921-6444

If ballet is your pleasure, Indianapolis Ballet Theatre is your ticket. Around since 1959, IBT has gradually transformed itself from a struggling local ballet troupe into a high-quality touring company and a major regional ballet company.

Stylistically patterned after the Ballet Russe de Monte Carlo, IBT mixes classic ballets with contemporary and original works. That means that, in addition to traditional ballets, you can see works by such 20th-century choreographers as Jose Limon and George Balanchine. You'll also enjoy the Christmas classic, *The Nutcracker*.

In addition to performing locally at Clowes Memorial Hall and the Warren Performing Arts Center, the IBT tours extensively. To date, it has danced for more than 65,000 people in 24 states and in Canada. And the IBT Academy, housed in the company's downtown facilities, offers students professional training.

For a performance schedule and ticket information, contact IBT's offices.

INDIANAPOLIS DANCE COMPANY
P.O. Box 30345   *846-2441*

The Indianapolis Dance Company (IDC) combines a variety of dance styles — modern, ballet, jazz, ethnic and avant-garde — in eclectic performances intended to challenge traditional notions of what dance is (or should be). Under the guidance of founder and artistic director Gregory Hancock, the IDC uses dance to address social, political, religious, cultural and historical issues as well as to entertain. The company's productions are staged at Caleb Mills Auditorium, inside Shortridge Junior High School, 3401 N. Meridian Street. The IDC's programs also include a company specifically for high school and college dancers (called IDC ALSO), the annual staging of a modern version of *The Nutcracker* entitled *The Nutcracker?*, and a month-long summer dance academy for young dancers.

BUTLER BALLET
Jordan College of Fine Arts
4600 Sunset Ave.   *283-9346*

Housed in a contemporary building tucked away on the northeastern corner of Butler University's campus, the Butler Ballet is a troupe of college-age dancers that performs publicly a few times each season. Additionally, the company's facilities serve as a training ground for a variety of young dancers from throughout the community. There are dance classes available for different age and skill levels.

Visual Arts

Museums

INDIANAPOLIS MUSEUM OF ART
1200 W. 38th St.   923-1331

Founded in 1883, the Indianapolis Museum of Art (a.k.a. IMA) is one of the oldest art museums in the country. Set amid the beautifully landscaped riverside splendor of the former estate of Josiah K. Lilly Jr. (grandson of pharmaceutical company founder Eli Lilly), the IMA is home to superb collections of J.M.W. Turner watercolors and drawings, Old Master paintings and contemporary art, and unparalleled collections of Chinese and African art.

The 152-acre site also exemplifies landscape design and botanical gardening at its best. The onsite greenhouse facilities sell flowers, herbs and plants and host year-round gardening and landscaping lectures and workshops.

In addition to the museum's natural appeal to art students and art lovers, the beauty of the surrounding grounds attracts picnickers and nature lovers.

During the summer, the IMA hosts musical performances and movies in its outdoor terraced amphitheater. Every September it also hosts the Penrod Festival (see the "Arts Events" portion of this chapter), the city's best-attended outdoor art fair. Throughout the year, the museum is the site of the popular first-Friday program, which offers after work jazz and wine on the first Friday of each month. This program is particularly popular with singles who see it as opportunity to mingle and meet amid arty environs.

There is also a wonderful museum shop on the parking garage level. There you'll find everything from prints and art books to handpainted clothing and fine art jewelry. And if browsing makes you hungry, check out the cafe on the first floor or the Garden on the Green restaurant, which is just down a winding drive north of the museum.

The IMA is open Tuesday, Wednesday, Friday and Saturday from 10 AM to 5 PM, Thursday from 10 AM to 8:30 PM and Sunday from noon to 5 PM. It's closed on Mondays, Thanksgiving, Christmas and New Year's Day. Admission is free; however, there is a charge for admission to special exhibitions within the museum (except on Thursdays when admission to all exhibitions is free). Members are admitted free to all exhibitions. Membership information is available by calling the main switchboard number listed previously.

EITELJORG MUSEUM OF AMERICAN INDIANS AND WESTERN ART
500 W. Washington St.   636-9378

It isn't what you expect to find, but on the western fringe of the downtown district, a pale pink building rises like a mesa amid the bustle of Washington and West streets. With a design as contemporary as the gleaming office towers a few blocks east yet as ancient as adobe pueblos, the Eiteljorg Museum of American Indians and Western Art is a Southwestern gem in a Midwestern setting.

The museum is named for its chief benefactor Harrison Eiteljorg, a local industrialist and philanthropist, whose multimillion-dollar collection of Native American and Western artworks and artifacts form the core of its bounty. In addition to Eiteljorg's collection, the museum exhibits traveling shows that focus on Indian and/or Western subjects; it also hosts a variety of community-oriented events ranging from lecture and film series to workshops, tours and an annual chili cook-off. Its artist-in-residence series features

Native American artists demonstrating various arts and crafts.

If museum shops excite you, don't miss the Eiteljorg's. It's filled with Western and Southwestern treasures ranging from gorgeous turquoise and hammered silver jewelry to handwoven blankets and one-of-a-kind baskets.

The Eiteljorg is open Tuesday through Saturday from 10 AM to 5 PM and Sunday from noon to 5 PM. It's closed on Monday except for June, July and August when it's open Monday as well. It's closed on Thanksgiving, Christmas and New Year's Day. Admission is $3 for adults, $1.50 for full-time students and for children 5 to 17, and $2.50 for seniors; family admission is $10.

INDIANA STATE MUSEUM
202 N. Alabama St. 232-1637

The Indiana State Museum (ISM), housed in the former city hall building, contains wonderful examples of Indiana-related artworks, including an unrivaled collection of paintings and drawings by well-known turn-of-the-century Indiana artist T.C. Steele. (The museum also owns and cares for Steele's former Brown County residence, known as the House of the Singing Winds.)

In addition to Steele, the ISM contains artworks from other notable Indian artists — J. Otis Adams, William Forsyth, Frank V. Dudley and Adolph Shulz. In keeping with its commitment to collecting and showing Indiana art, the museum also presents exhibitions by various contemporary artists and photographers.

The ISM is open Monday through Saturday from 9 AM to 4:45 PM, and on Sunday from noon to 4:45 PM. It's closed on Thanksgiving, Christmas and New Year's Day. Admission is free.

Galleries

Downtown

HERRON GALLERY
1701 N. Pennsylvania St. 920-2420

Herron Gallery, which is part of Indiana University's Herron School of Art, focuses on contemporary art produced within the past decade. The home of student and faculty shows, as well as local, regional, national and international exhibitions, this gallery features artwork that varies from representational to abstract. Herron specializes in exhibitions of contemporary works that you won't likely see anywhere else in the city.

RUSCHMAN ART GALLERY
421 Massachusetts Ave. 634-3114

Owner Mark Ruschman focuses on exhibiting and selling the work of regionally and nationally known artists such as local painter James Wille Faust and sculptor James Tyler. Exhibitions change monthly.

IN VIVO GALLERY
326 E. Vermont St. 630-9640

For contemporary art with an edge and an attitude, this is the place.

CHATHAM GALLERY
702 Massachusetts Ave. 637-0444

Home of contemporary photos, sculptures and paintings, this gallery offers a lively mix of the familiar and the challenging, and it does it all in a comfortable setting in the refurbished Catham Arch area.

HOT HOUSE GALLERY
546 S. Meridian St., Ste. 511   *686-0895*

Here you'll find the work of the local artists who have studios in this old industrial warehouse known as the Faris Building. There are also periodic open houses in the building. Call for information.

THE STUTZ BUSINESS CENTER
1036 N. Capitol St.   *767-0518*

Once the home of the Stutz Automobile Company, this beautiful old brick structure has been refurbished as an office/warehouse/light manufacturing center, with a number of the rental units being appropriated by artists for use as studios. While there's an annual open house, individual artists also allow visitors to drop by.

VAN RIPER GALLERY AND SPECIALTY FRAMING
1036 N. Capitol St., Ste. 220   *488-8848*
    684-9471

In this gallery, housed in the Stutz Business Center, you'll find abstract oils, limited-edition prints, serigraphs and antique furniture. This is also where you can have your prized artwork mounted in museum-quality frames. Be forewarned: This place is open by appointment (or by chance) only.

THE BUSHMAN LOFTS
470 Fort Wayne Ave.   *926-2980*

This is where you can feast your eyes on *A Moveable Feast*, an ever-changing (artists, media, even location) bounty of conceptual and expressionistic art. There's no telling who or what you'll find — or when you'll find it. Call ahead for schedules, artists and other vital details.

UTRILLO'S GALLERY
2630 E. 10th St.   *684-9883*

In a small brick building on the near-east side, Utrillo's challenges conventional ideas about what is or is not art by exhibiting fine art side-by-side with objects d'art and thrift (some would say junk) art. Owner Greg Brown also hosts a local cable access program called ARTV, which features homemade art videos as well as performances by poets and musicians.

THE 703 GALLERY FOR THE ARTS
703 E. 30th St., Ste. 15   *925-1500*

This gallery specializes in originals and prints by African American artists.

THE WEST 22ND STREET ART GALLERY
8 W. 22nd St.   *923-1152*

Here's where you'll find work by African American and Asian artists as well as optic and paper-sculptured art.

Broad Ripple

INDIANAPOLIS ART CENTER
820 E. 67th St.   *255-2464*

As the largest fine arts facility in this part of town, the Indianapolis Art Center anchors the Broad Ripple art scene. The center showcases the work of local and regional artists and artisans and offers more than 90 different art classes for all ages and skill levels. Classes are available in watercolor and oil painting, drawing, photography, jewelry-making and ceramics.

Organized in 1934 as the Art League, the Center has grown to its present status as one of the area's most respected community arts resources. In fact, the demand for more classroom and gallery space fueled a fund-raising effort that is resulting in the construction of a $7.2 million facility adjacent to the center's current building. Designed by internationally known architect and Indianapolis native, Michael Graves (who graduated from nearby Broad Ripple High

School), the new structure is scheduled to open in 1996.

The Art Center also hosts a number of community events throughout the year, most notably the annual Broad Ripple Arts fair, a weekend-long affair during which some 200 artists display and sell their artwork (see listing under the "Arts Events" portion of this chapter), and the annual Children of Color Festival, a one-day arts celebration of diversity for children (and their parents).

The center also has a riverside stage where local and regional jazz, blues and rock musicians perform. Additionally, it periodically hosts storytellers, film series and theater performances.

Admission to the Center's exhibitions is free. All classes require payment of tuition fees, and for other events the Center usually charges admission fees. Call for a schedule of events and exhibitions, information about classes and gallery hours.

Fox Studios Inc.

5901 N. College Ave.   *253-0135*

This combination design studio and showroom at the corner of N. College and Kessler Boulevard creates custom stained, beveled and etched glass lamps, windows, sculptures, awards and decorations.

Hoosier Salon Gallery

6434 N. College Ave.   *253-5340*

A showcase for the work of Indiana artists since 1925, this gallery features a solo exhibition by a different artist each month. It also presents an annual juried show at the Indiana State Museum.

Byron and Sons Gallery

6434 N. College Ave.   *257-6741*

Housed in the same building as the Hoosier Salon, this gallery also specializes in Indiana artists, specifically those working from 1880 to 1940.

911 Gallery

911 E. Main St.   *257-8350*

Electronic media mix with fine arts in 911 Gallery where shows can include everything from computer graphics and ink jet prints to digital video and interactive computers. This gallery was the first in the city to go on the World Wide Web; you can contact it via computer at http://\\ww.iquest.net\911\911.html.

Artifacts Gallery

6327 N. Guilford Ave.   *255-1178*

Artifacts offers an array of contemporary artwork— paintings, prints, drawings, jewelry, ceramics, glass and sculpture — along with such services as design, custom framing and installation.

Eckert Fine Art

726 E. 65th St.   *255-4561*

For 19th- and 20th-century American and European art, try Eckert Fine Art. This is where you can buy paintings by Hoosier Group members T.C. Steele and Otto Stark as well as the work of more contemporary artists.

Crystal Mountain Jewelry

6314 Winthrop Ave.   *251-3528*

If you're looking for exquisite gold and silver jewelry, stop by Crystal Mountain, where handmade means high-quality. In at least three shows annually, Crystal Mountain features the handiwork of jewelers, metalsmiths and artists whose artistry extends to carving precious and semiprecious gems as well as shaping precious metals.

DER GLASS WERKS STAINED GLASS
833 Westfield Blvd. E. 257-7603

Since 1921, Der Glass Werks artisans have been designing and manufacturing beveled, etched and stained-glass windows, panels and other objects that meld artistry with utility.

G. C. LUCAS GALLERY
6219 N. Guildford Ave. 254-6460

With an emphasis on contemporary realism, G.C. Lucas Gallery displays the work of current artists alongside select pieces from modern American artists from earlier this century.

SIGMAN GALLERY
930 Broad Ripple Ave. 253-9953

This gallery offers contemporary art by local and regional artists, including originals, limited-edition prints and posters.

YAEL'S ATELIER
6528 N. Ferguson St. 255-5528

Here you'll find a working artist's studio, which includes one of the largest privately owned metal-forging furnaces in the country. There are also several presses that Yael uses to create her large copper enamel sculptures and prints, many of which can be found in corporate and private art collections throughout the world.

BROAD RIPPLE GALLERY AND FRAMING
720 E. 65th St. 475-9845

For contemporary glass, clay and fiber works done by artists from around the country, look to Broad Ripple Gallery and Framing. This gallery also carries graphics, prints and antique etchings and engravings.

PROTOCOL GALLERY
6317 Guilford Ave. 254-1778

If you'd rather wear art than contemplate it, Protocol fits the bill. Here you'll find innovative, artist-designed clothing and accessories.

CENTER FOR CREATIVE ARTS
6263 N. Carrollton Ave. 255-9633

CCA is a nonprofit, artist-run gallery where you'll find paintings, prints, pottery, woodwork and jewelry done by the 45 artists who own and operate CCA. It's art in action.

THE BUNGALOW
6367 N. Guilford Ave. 253-5028

The focus at The Bungalow is on contemporary handicrafts by Indiana and nationally known artisans.

FOLK ARTS IMPORTS
6503 N. Carrollton Ave. 257-7602

This is where you'll find folk art with a global outlook— handicrafts, jewelry, musical instruments and clothing from Asia, Africa, Mexico and South America. Take a peek upstairs and see the large African tribal pieces.

THE POTTER'S HOUSE
6503 N. Carrollton Ave. 253-4178

This is the home of clay wares — mugs, bowls, vases and planters — handmade by potter Karen Van De Waile.

WINTHROP ART GALLERY
6224 Winthrop Ave. 255-1127

Here at the oldest art gallery in Indianapolis, owners John and Andie DeCosta specialize in 19th- and 20th-century American paintings. They also offer art and frame restoration services as well as art appraisal.

North Side

EDITIONS LIMITED
GALLERY OF FINE ART
4040 E. 82nd St.   842-2626

The emphasis at Edition Limited is on contemporary art — from abstracts to realism — in a variety of media, done by local, national and international artists.

DETAILS
1516 W. 86th St.   872-2626

At this shop in North Willow Commons, you'll find ordinary items such as jewelry, pottery, glasswork and greeting cards that are extraordinarily well done.

RENDITIONS FINE ART GALLERY
8702 Keystone Crossing   848-5205

For wildlife art, including originals and limited-edition prints, that lives up to its designation as art, trek to Renditions in the Fashion Mall. From local to international, this place features artists whose work combines artistry with appreciation for wildlife.

Arts Events

PENROD ART FAIR
Indianapolis Museum of Art
1200 W. 38th St.   923-1331

This is the granddaddy of local art fairs in Indianapolis. Started in 1966 as a means of raising money for the Indianapolis Museum of Art, the Penrod Art Fair has become an end-of-summer institution. Held the first Saturday after Labor Day on the grounds of the Indianapolis Art Museum, it includes some 280 arts, crafts and food booths as well as performances by area musicians. The fair attracts thousands of people, many of whom come just to people-watch and wander the museum's beautifully landscaped grounds. This is the place to be and be seen for artists, arts administrators, arts patrons and just plain old art appreciators.

Admission is $10 in advance (from the IMA or Marsh Supermarkets) or $15 at the gate. Children 14 and younger are admitted free when accompanied by an adult.

THE BROAD RIPPLE ART FAIR
Indianapolis Art Center
820 E. 67th St.   255-2464

From its inception in 1970 during the hippie heydays of sand candles and tie-dyed T-shirts, the Broad Ripple Art Fair has evolved into one of the Midwest's best-known art fairs. Held on Memorial Day weekend, this two-day event on the grounds of the Indianapolis Art Center includes some 200 artists displaying (and selling) paintings, sculptures, ceramics, drawings, prints, photographs and clothing. There are also food and drink vendors as well as live music from a variety of local bands.

While the crowds aren't as thick as those at Penrod, this fair attracts thousands of visitors, including everyone from gallery owners and serious collectors to babies in strollers (moms and dads in tow, of course) and dogs sporting bandanas. It's a good time for all. Admission is $5 advance, $7 at the gate and $1 for children younger than 12.

TALBOTT STREET ART FAIR
Talbott St. between 16th and 19th Sts.

Though somewhat smaller than the Broad Ripple fair, this early June event (usually held the second weekend of the month) also attracts large numbers of art patrons and browsers during its weekend-long run. Held on a blocked-off portion of Talbot Street adjacent to the Herron School of Art and Gallery, the fair consists of scores of artists displaying their works and wares. Crowds are often elbow-to-elbow throughout the fair, so be prepared for some jostling as you try to maneuver over to a display you want to see. But it's a friendly environment, so you'll make it— just remember to use your manners. Admission is free.

HANNAH ARTS DAY
Hannah House, 3801 Madison Ave.

Held on the first Saturday in June, this event on the city's south side is the most recent (c. 1994) entry in the art fair lineup. As such, it's not yet as large as the preceding three fairs, but it's gaining momentum. Like the other events, it features artists' displays, food and entertainment. Hannah Arts Day takes place on the grounds of the Hannah House, a historic landmark, which is in itself a work of art. Admission is $5 for adults, $4 for seniors and free for children younger than 12.

INDIAN MARKET
Eiteljorg Museum of American Indians and Western Art
500 W. Washington St.   *636-WEST*

With more than 90 booths displaying the jewelry, pottery, basketry, weavings and carvings of 80 Native American artists, the Indian market is in an art fair category of its own. Add in Native American drums and dances, as well as food and children's activities and you've got a great day out. This, too, is a June event, usually the third weekend of the month. Admission is $5 for adults; children younger than 12 are admitted free. Call the Eiteljorg for details.

Inside
The Literary Life

Is there literary life in Indianapolis? Yes, most definitely. There are a number of literary groups and events for writers and readers alike. There is a superb public library system as well as a wonderful state library and some fine university libraries. And there are plenty of very good bookstores. You'll find a lot of writers living in and around Indianapolis: poets and novelists, children's authors and journalists, historians and playwrights, screenwriters and biographers, authors of romances and mysteries and science fiction.

Yes, there is literary life in Indianapolis, and there always has been. In fact, the city was once (and many maintain, may yet be again) *the* literary center of the Midwest.

A Brief History

Since the city's founding, literature has played a significant role in the cultural life of Indianapolis. When Indiana's first state treasurer, Samuel Merrill, left the old capital of Corydon for Indianapolis in 1824, he brought with him the contents of the state library, as well as those of his own personal book collection. To Merrill, life without literature was unthinkable.

So unthinkable that in 1850, he bought one of the city's two existing bookstores and increased its inventory. He also established the Merrill Publishing Company, which initially focused on producing law books but eventually expanded into trade books. By the early 20th cen-

Photo: The Indianapolis Star & News

The James Whitcomb Riley House was the Hoosier poet's home for 23 years and is a city landmark and listed on the National Register of Historic Places.

tury, the firm, which through a series of mergers became Bobbs-Merrill, was one of the leading trade publishers in the United States. On its roster were such bestselling Indiana authors as James Whitcomb Riley, Meredith Nicholson, George Ade and Booth Tarkington, who collectively were known in publishing circles as "The Big Four."

In fact, those four writers, along with other Bobbs-Merrill authors such as Maurice Thompson (*Alice of Old Vincennes*) and Charles Major (*When Knighthood Was in Flower*), were important contributors to an era known as Indiana's Golden Age. Comprised roughly of a period from 1880 to 1920, the Golden Age was a time when Indiana and Indianapolis gained and sustained national attention for their contributions to American culture, politics and commerce. (While Bobbs-Merrill is no longer in operation, Indianapolis is currently home to a number of other publishing firms.)

The literature produced by Indianapolis writers in the Golden Age ranged from scholarly nonfiction to mystery and romance. Attorney and politician Albert Beveridge's four-volume biography, *The Life of John Marshall,* published in 1916, garnered widespread acclaim. Meredith Nicholson's *The House of a Thousand Candles* mixed mystery with romance to become a national bestseller.

The Golden Age ended with World War I, and Indianapolis lost its position as the literary center of the Midwest to Chicago. But the city continued to contribute to American literature. In fact, two of the most significant figures in the development of contemporary writing were Indianapolis natives and members of the famous Lost Generation in post-WWI Paris.

Margaret Anderson, an Indianapolis native and founder of the *Little Review*, a literary magazine based at various times in Chicago, New York and Paris, was an early supporter and publisher of such rising literary stars as Ernest Hemingway and James Joyce. And her friend Janet Flanner, who often wrote under the pen name of Genet, was a regular contributor to *The New Yorker*, as well as the author of a number of widely respected books including *An American in Paris* and *Paris Journals*.

Another Indianapolis-bred writer who gained national stature in the wake of a war — this time World War II — was novelist Kurt Vonnegut Jr. The son of a prominent Indianapolis architect, Vonnegut witnessed the horrors of war firsthand, including the firebombing of Dresden, Germany, an event that colored his outlook on war and on America. In the 1960s and '70s, Vonnegut's biting satire and black humor, evident in such books as his anti-war masterpiece, *Slaughterhouse Five*, made him one of the country's most popular writers.

The roster of significant 20th-century writers from Indianapolis also includes novelist and nonfiction writer Dan Wakefield, poets Etheridge Knight and Mari Evans, fiction writer and essayist Susan Neville and historian Alan T. Nolan.

Reading

For avid readers, Central Indiana is a gold mine of book discussion groups, some independent, others hosted by branch libraries or by bookstores, that meet regularly throughout the area. And there are a number of reading and lecture series sponsored by the Indianapolis-Marion Public Library, the Writers' Center, the Butler University Writers' Studio and the Indiana Humanities Council.

And finally, Indianapolis can claim dozens of bookstores ranging from large general interest stores such as Borders, Barnes & Noble, and B. Dalton to small, specialized shops dealing in children's books, mysteries, religious books, feminist books or comic books.

Whether you yearn to write a book or just like to keep your nose buried in one, Indianapolis has something for you. Read on.

Bookstores

You can learn a lot about the vitality of a community's literary life by the number and variety of bookstores it contains, and by this measure Indianapolis is in good shape. At last count, there were some 60 bookstores, including those with more than one location, in the Greater Indianapolis area. (For a detailed listing, see our sidebar in the Shopping chapter.)

Reading Groups

Like the literary salons and clubs of the past, reading groups (a.k.a. book discussion groups) bring book lovers together to talk about books and authors. In Indianapolis, there are dozens of these groups, many of which are privately run. But there are also many more that are open to the public, namely those operated by area libraries and bookstores.

If you like to talk about what you read, maybe even engage in a friendly debate now and then, the following groups welcome newcomers. (Meeting days and

times are subject to change, so check with individual locations for confirmation.)

Library Groups

Several reading groups meet at Indianapolis-Marion County Public Library branches. Each of the following groups is general in interest — that is, they read a range of books, fiction and nonfiction, rather than focusing on specialized types of books. Some people attend more than one group, others prefer to find a group they're comfortable with and leave it at that. The choice is yours.

THE BROAD RIPPLE BOOK DISCUSSION GROUP
Broad Ripple Library 1550
Broad Ripple Ave.   269-1791
This groups meets the second Tuesday of each month from 10:15 AM to 11:15 AM.

THE BROWN LIBRARY BOOK REVIEW GROUP Brown Library
5427 E. Washington St.   269-1864
This groups meets six times a year, usually in the spring and fall, on the second Thursday of the month from 1:30 PM to 2:30 PM.

THE NORA BOOK DISCUSSION GROUP
Nora Library
8625 Guilford Ave.   269-1830
This group meets the first Tuesday of each month from 10:15 AM to 11:15 AM.

The achievements of Indiana's pioneer poet laureate, Sarah T. Bolton, are remembered with a bronze plaque in the rotunda of the State House.

Insiders' Tips

The Merrill Legacy

No family had more of a cultural impact on 19th-century Indianapolis than the Merrills, especially the father-daughter duo of Samuel and Catharine Merrill. Their combined influence on the city's literary life was significant and lasting.

Indiana's first state treasurer, Samuel Merrill (1792-1855) transported the contents of both the state treasury and the Indiana State Library from Corydon to Indianapolis in 1824. But it wasn't just state-owned books and papers that Merrill brought along on the move. He also brought his personal library. An educated man, he cherished books, and he lent them freely to friends and acquaintances.

When the demand for books outstripped his supply, Merrill bought one of the city's two bookstores and increased its stock. What's more, he also established a publishing company, the Merrill Publishing Company. Though initially it concentrated on publishing mostly law books, that firm was the precursor of the Bobbs-Merrill Company, one of the country's leading trade publishers in the late 19th and early 20th centuries.

Catharine Merrill (1824-1900) inherited her father's love of literature and turned it into a career as a teacher and author. First as the headmistress of her own private school, the Catharine Merrill School, then later as an instructor in the English department of Butler University, she was credited with introducing innumerable young people to the wonders of books.

So widely known and respected was Catharine that at the end of the Civil War, Indiana's governor, Oliver P. Morton, personally recruited her to write a history of Indiana's soldiers in the war. The result was a two-volume set, *The Soldier of Indiana in the War of the Union,* which earned accolades for its comprehensive, biographical approach to recounting history.

Catharine didn't have to look far to find a publisher for her work— the Merrill Publishing Company took it on gladly. Following the Civil War, the Merrill family ceased direct involvement with the company. It went through a series of mergers, becoming first Merrill, Meigs and Company, then the Bowen-Merrill Company, and finally in 1903 the Bobbs-Merrill Company.

Regardless of its name, the company began gradually to expand its operations into the trade book field. Its first breakout success came when the firm teamed up with local poet James Whitcomb Riley whose folksy poetry made him one of the country's most popular writers in the late 19th century. Among the company's other bestselling authors were Meredith Thompson (*House of a Thousand Candles*) and Maurice Thompson (*Alice of Old Vincennes*).

In the 20th century, Bobbs-Merrill made successful forays into children's literature with its popular *Childhood of Famous Americans* series and into the movie business in the 1920s; the firm sold more of its authors' works to Hollywood than all other U.S. publishers combined.

In 1958, another local publisher, Howard W. Sams, bought Bobbs-Merrill and concentrated on its educational division, which became one of the nation's leading suppliers of textbooks to schools and colleges. In the meantime, Bobb-Merrill's trade publishing division lost importance. One of its last big successes was Ayn Rand's novel *The Fountainhead*.

The Sams purchase marked the end of Bobb-Merrill as a force in trade publishing. Eventually the imprint itself disappeared, and in 1985 MacMillan Company bought the Bobbs-Merrill backlist. The company was officially dead.

But the Merrill legacy lives on in the impact that Samuel and Catharine individually, and the Bobbs-Merrill Company collectively, had on local and national literary history.

THE SOUTHPORT LIBRARY BOOK DISCUSSION GROUP

Southport Library
2630 E. Stop 11 Rd.   269-1873

This group meets on the fourth Monday of each month from 7 PM to 8 PM.

Bookstore Groups

Bookstores have a vested interest in hosting reading groups because they attract regular groups of avid readers to their sites and promote reading. Both of these are pluses for booksellers. But the real point is getting books into the hands of people who want to read and talk about them is.

What sets bookstore groups apart from the library groups is that they tend to be focused on specific topics or interests. Two of the city's largest bookstores also host some of its liveliest specialized reading groups.

BORDERS BOOK SHOP

5612 Castleton Corner   849-8660

Long a popular haunt for true book lovers, Borders has a really knowledgeable staff (as in, people who read books as well as sell them) and a browser-friendly environment. Because of its popularity, it was a natural place for reading groups to congregate, and they do.

The **Classics Club** meets on the second Wednesday of each month at 7:30 PM.

The **Mystery Club** meets on the third Wednesday of each month at 7:30 PM.

The **Military History Club** meets on the first Thursday of each month at 7:30 PM.

The **Contemporary Fiction Club** meets on the fourth Wednesday of each month at 7:30 PM.

The **Lavender Book Club**, which deals with gay and lesbian topics, meets on the third Thursday of each month at 7:30 PM.

BARNES & NOBLE BOOKSTORE

3748 E. 82nd St.   594-7525

A relative newcomer to the local literary scene (this store opened in 1994), Barnes & Noble has attracted a loyal following, in part for its friendly atmosphere and in-store coffee shop, which invites customers to relax and read over a cup of joe. Like Borders, B&N hosts a variety of reading groups.

The **African American Discussion**

Group meets on the first Thursday of each month at 7:30 PM.

The **Indy Fiction Lovers** meet on the first Tuesday of each month at 7:30 PM.

The **Coffee and Book Chat** groups meets on the second Monday of each month at 10 AM.

The **Women's Issues** group meets on the third Thursday of each month at 7:30 PM.

The **Singles Who Love Books** group meets on the third Thursday of each month at 7:30 PM.

The **Literature and Medicine** group meets on the fourth Thursday of each month at 7:30 PM.

The **History Reading Group** meets on the fourth Wednesday of each month at 7:30 PM.

The **Blue Blazer International Reading Group**, which reads and discusses titles from the Great Books program, meets quarterly. Call Barnes & Noble for the date, time and topic.

Literary Organizations, Facilities and Programs

INDIANA ARTS COMMISSION (IAC)
402 W. Washington St.   *232-1268*

This statewide arts agency promotes and sponsors several programs of interest to writers, including biannual fellowship grants to help writers underwrite the costs of writing projects and the artists-in-education program, which provides matching grants to schools for writing residencies. The IAC also helps underwrite reading and storytelling series as well as literary events and publications.

INDIANA HUMANITIES COUNCIL (IHC)
1500 N. Delaware St.   *638-1500*

In addition to helping fund reading and lecture series, this statewide organization, an affiliate of the National Endowment for the Humanities, is the sponsoring agency for the biannual WORDSTRUCK literary festival (see the "Literary Events" section of this chapter).

BUTLER UNIVERSITY WRITERS' STUDIO
4600 Sunset Ln., Jordan Hall 304   *283-9861*

Founded by award-winning fiction writer and essayist Susan Neville, a member of Butler's English department, the Writer's Studio provides students direct access to the experience, skills and advice of area poets, novelists, journalists and playwrights through its fellowship program. The studio also sponsors the annual Visiting Writer Series that presents lectures and readings (most of which are open to the public) by nationally known writers such as Grace Paley and hometown hero Kurt Vonnegut Jr. (see our Literary Stars sidebar in this chapter), along with such Indiana favorites as Michael Martone and Scott Russell Sanders.

INDIANAPOLIS-MARION COUNTY PUBLIC LIBRARY
40 E. St. Clair St.   *269-1700*

Standing on land donated by local literary legend James Whitcomb Riley (see our Literary Stars sidebar in this chapter), the Indianapolis-Marion County Public Library's downtown facility, which is known officially as the Central Library, is one of the city's architectural and literary treasures. Inside this lovely old building (Greek Doric style, c. 1916), you'll find some 1.7 million books, as well as magazines, newspapers, audio tapes, CDs, films, videotapes, artwork and other items.

There were two or three early and unsuccessful attempts at creating librar-

The Ruth Lilly Poetry Prize

It's no secret that poets don't get rich, at least not from writing poetry. But a select few do once in a while win prizes that enrich both their reputations and, to some degree, their bank accounts. The Ruth Lilly Poetry Prize is one such prize.

In fact, it's one of the most desirable prizes in the literary world, in so far as its cash value is concerned. Established in 1986 by wealthy arts patron and poetry fan Ruth Lilly, a member of the Eli Lilly and Company founder's family, the annual prize includes a $75,000 honorarium. That makes it one of the richest literary awards in the world.

Chosen by a three-member panel — the editor of the Chicago-based *Poetry* magazine and two poets of the editor's choice — the Ruth Lilly Poetry Prize recipient is judged on the merits of his or her body of work. The official citation reads that the prize is given "to an American poet whose accomplishments warrant extraordinary recognition."

Since its inception, the list of Lilly prize winners reads like a Who's Who of American poetry: Hayden Carruth, Adrienne Rich, Donald Hall, David Wagoner, Philip Levine, Mona Van Duyn, Anthony Hecht, John Ashbery and Charles Wright. (Of that list, only Wagoner has connections to Indiana, having been born in the northwestern town of Whiting.)

Apart from its generous honorarium, the Ruth Lilly Poetry Prize is important for another reason. In an era when poets and poetry are increasingly devalued, the prize bestows a sense of value to an ancient and honorable literary art form.

Photo: The Indianapolis Star & News

David R. Wagoner, poet and novelist, grew up in the 1930s in Whiting.

ies in Indianapolis before an impassioned sermon by Rev. Hanford A. Edson of the Second Presbyterian Church on the Thanksgiving Day of 1868, on the need for a free, public library led 113 citizens to form the Indianapolis Library Association. After four years of fund-raising and policy-making, the Indianapolis Public Library opened in one room of a school at the intersection of Pennsylvania and Michigan streets. Its collection consisted of 12,790 books.

From that early effort, the library began to grow, including expanding its service area in 1968 to all of Marion County (except Beech Grove and Speedway, which maintain their own community libraries). Today, in addition to the Central Library, the Indianapolis-Marion County Public Library system contains 21 branch libraries and an extension services division that provides library programs to neighborhood community centers.

Among the library's many programs are several of interest to writers and readers, including readings and workshops presented by local and national writers. Every March, the library hosts the Marian McFadden Memorial Lecture, which, on alternate years, features a renowned author of adult or children's books, such as Saul Bellow, Chris Van Allsburg, Madeline L'Engle and Tom Wolfe.

Several of the branch libraries also host book discussion groups (see entries under the Reading Clubs section of this chapter) for readers who like to talk about books as well as read them. And for those whose love of literature outpaces their finances, six times a year the library holds used book sales at the Extension Services building at 2450 N. Meridian Street.

For information on the schedule of specific events and activities, pick up a copy of the library's bimonthly newsletter, *Reading in Indianapolis*, which is available at the Central Library and all branches. The Central Library is open Monday through Friday, 9 AM to 9 PM; Saturday, 9 AM to 6 PM; and Sunday 1 to 5 PM. Branch library hours vary by site.

THE WRITERS' CENTER INC.
3200 Cold Spring Rd.   929-0625

From its headquarters in St. Francis Hall on the campus of Marian College, the Writers' Center — which is Indiana's only comprehensive community-based literary organization — offers workshops, special-interest writing groups, educational programs and readings by regionally and nationally prominent poets, fiction and nonfiction writers. Among its programs are the annual Naptown Invitational Reading Series and the Visiting Writers Series. The Center also plays an active role in the planning and development of the biannual Wordstruck literary festival (see related sidebar in this chapter). Additionally, it hosts open readings at The Slippery Noodle Inn, a downtown blues club.

The Writers' Center publishes *Literally*, a quarterly newsletter, which provides up-to-date information about literary events in the area, as well as information about upcoming writing contests and publications that are seeking submissions. The Writers' Center Press offers Indiana writers opportunities to publish in its semiannual magazine, *The Flying Island*, as well as in occasional chapbooks and through various competitions.

The organization's Marian College office houses a resource library of literary publications, writers' aids and reference books, as well as an informal meeting space for Center members.

Membership to the Writers' Center is $30 per year for individuals in Marion and adjoining counties, $20 for nonlocal, students and seniors.

Whether you're interested in poetry, scriptwriting, fiction or nonfiction, chances are the Writers' Center offers a workshop, discussion group or publication that will meet your needs. Call for a schedule of classes and events.

INDIANA STATE LIBRARY
140 N. Senate Ave.   232-3675

Established in 1825, this state-run institution is the central repository of all documents and publications pertaining to Indiana's government as well as a regional repository for U.S. government documents. Additionally, it's a treasure trove of materials, including books, maps, letters, pamphlets, brochures, newspapers, magazines, manuscripts and photographs, from the state's territorial days to the present. The on-site genealogy division is a popular resource for writers, scholars, historians and families. The library's staff is both knowledgeable and helpful in seeing that writers and readers make best use of the available resources.

In addition to housing the library collections, the State Library building, which is just west of the State Capitol, is also home to the Indiana Center for the Book (see following entry) and the Indiana Historical Society (see separate entry in the Book Publishers section of this chapter). The State Library is open Monday through Friday, 8 AM to 4:30 PM; the genealogy department is open Saturdays from Labor Day to Memorial Day, 8 AM to 4 PM.

INDIANA CENTER FOR THE BOOK
140 Senate Ave.   232-3569

Established in 1989 to stimulate public interest in books, reading, publishing and literacy throughout the state, the Indiana Center for the Book periodically sponsors programs, discussion groups, lectures and exhibitions. Affiliated with the Library of Congress's national Center for the Book, the Indiana Center works with writers, educators and librarians to develop projects aimed at encouraging appreciation for books from both an aesthetic and an educational perspective.

UNIVERSITY LIBRARY AT IUPUI
755 W. Michigan St.   274-0551

One of the first libraries in the United States designed for the electronic information age, this new facility (c. 1993) on the campus of Indiana University-Purdue University of Indianapolis (IUPUI) contains a fiber optics network that allows voice, video, data and graphics to be transmitted to multimedia stations throughout the library. There are also 100 on-site workstations that provide patrons with free access to the World Wide Web and the Internet.

Of course, the library also contains

The former home of author Meredith Nicholson, 1500 N. Delaware Street, houses the Indiana Humanities Council.

Insiders' Tips

more traditional resources as well — a half-million books, an extensive microfilm and microfiche collection and a periodicals department that subscribes to 3,000 magazines and newspapers from around the world, including an array of popular and obscure literary publications.

The library, which is open to the general public as well as to IUPUI students and staff, is open Monday through Thursday, 8 AM to 11 PM; Friday, 8 AM to 9 PM; Saturday, 8 AM to 7 PM; and Sunday, 10 AM to 11 PM.

Literary Events

WORDSTRUCK
Indiana Humanities Council
1500 N. Delaware St.   638-1500

Produced biennially by the Indiana Humanities Council, in cooperation with more than two dozen area cultural organizations, WORDSTRUCK is a free, citywide event that celebrates the power and pleasure of books and reading through public programs such as lectures, readings and workshops by regionally and nationally known writers. In the past, the four-day event has attracted such notables as Kurt Vonnegut Jr. and Dan Wakefield, both products of Indianapolis. (See our Literary Stars sidebar.)

BUTLER UNIVERSITY MIDWINTER CHILDREN'S LITERATURE CONFERENCE
4600 Sunset Ave.   940-9861

Since 1991, this annual conference has been held on the campus of Butler University each February. Conference participants attend presentations and workshops given by internationally known, award-winning children's book authors and illustrators, as well as by children's book editors and agents, university professors, book critics, teachers, and librarians. Past speakers have included Avi, Kathryn Lasky, Jerry Pinkney and conference organizer (and acclaimed local author) Valiska Gregory.

In addition to conference activities, there are a variety of other community activities — readings, lectures and book signings — that are open to the public, free of charge.

VISITING WRITERS SERIES
Butler University Writer's Studio
4600 Sunset Ave., Jordan Hall 304   283-9861

In keeping with its on-going commitment to the city's literary life, Butler University hosts this series that brings poets, novelists and nonfiction writers to town for readings and lectures throughout the fall and winter. The events are held on the university campus, either in Robertson Hall or Clowes Memorial Hall, and most are open to the public. In the past, such notable writers as Grace Paley, Robert Bly and P.J. O'Rourke have taken part in the series. Contact the Butler Writer's Studio to be put on the series mailing list, or watch the events calendars in *The Indianapolis Star* and *The Indianapolis News*.

Literary Landmarks

MEREDITH NICHOLSON RESIDENCE
1500 N. Delaware St.   638-1500

Formerly home to early 20th-century novelist and nonfiction writer, Meredith Nicholson, this lovely brick structure now houses the offices of the Indiana Humanities Council. As such, it's not open for public tours, but you might want to call and ask if there's a time you could come by and look around.

Literary Stars

Throughout its history, Indianapolis has had its share of literary stars. Some lived here during their youth and left to make their reputations elsewhere; others called Indianapolis home in the midst of their fame. Among the best known of the city's luminaries, past and present, are:

Sara T. Bolton (1814-1893)

Indiana's unofficial poet laureate, Bolton came to Indianapolis in 1831, having married local newspaper publisher Nathaniel Bolton. Here she raised two children, worked on political and social causes and wrote poems. Probably her best-known work was the nationally distributed "Paddle Your Own Canoe," which contained the lines:

Nothing great is lightly won
Nothing won is lost
But if you succeed you must
Paddle your own canoe.

Janet Flanner, a.k.a. Genet (1892-1978)

The daughter of a prominent Indianapolis family, Flanner got her early training in writing as an arts reporter and reviewer for *The Indianapolis Star*. When she was 26, she married and moved to New York, rarely returning. Moving once again when she was 30, this time to Paris, she finally found her voice as a writer when she began doing a column for *The New Yorker* in 1925; using the pen name Genet, she wrote a semimonthly "Letter from Paris," as well as other pieces for the magazine, for 50 years. She also wrote a number of books, including *An American in Paris* (1940) and *Paris Journals, 1944-1965* (winner of a National Book Award in 1966).

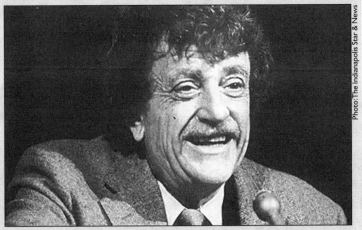

Photo:The Indianapolis Star & News

Kurt Vonnegut Jr. is one of America's leading satirists.

Etheridge Knight (1931-1991)

From his beginnings as a poet while imprisoned in the Indiana State Prison, Knight went on to become one of the country's best-known and most-respected black poets. Winner of a number of writing awards, Knight was also in demand as a reader and workshop leader at universities and prisons. Among his best known collections of poems are *Poems from Prison* (1968), *Belly Song and Other Poems* (1973), and *Born of Woman* (1980). In 1986, his book, *The Essential Etheridge Knight* won the Before Columbus American Book Award.

Meredith Nicholson (1866-1947)

The author of 29 books and scores of essays and stories, Nicholson began his writing career on the staff of *The Indianapolis News*. From there he went on to success as a businessman, but dissatisfied, he continued to write. The success of his history of Indiana, *The Hoosiers,* in 1900 led Nicholson to turn to writing full-time. Among his best-known works are the novels *House of a Thousand Candles* and *A Hoosier Chronicle* and a volume of biographical sketches entitled *Old Familiar Faces*.

Nicholson gave up writing in the 1930s, becoming at the behest of President Franklin Delano Roosevelt a diplomat, serving at posts on Paraguay, Venezuela and Nicaragua.

Booth Tarkington (1869-1946)

Son of a local circuit court judge, Tarkington turned a boyhood penchant for mischief and theatrics into a lucrative career as a fiction writer and playwright. A graduate of Princeton University where he was a star in the drama department, as well as the editor of three publications, Tarkington nearly derailed his career through his drinking. Despite his love of alcohol, he managed to capture national attention in 1899 with the publication of his novel, *The Gentleman from Indiana*.

Other books and plays followed, but meanwhile, his first marriage floundered. Finally, in 1912, he went on the wagon — his career blossomed even further as he turned out such well-received books as *Penrod*, a collection of stories about a eponymous young hero, and *The Magnificent Ambersons* (1919) and *Alice Adams* (1921), both Pulitzer Prize-winning novels. Tarkington is widely regarded as one of Indianapolis's leading early 20th-century literary lights, along with Riley and Nicholson.

Kurt Vonnegut Jr. (1922-   )

Born into a prominent family (Kurt Vonnegut, Sr. was a well-known architect), Vonnegut left Indianapolis to serve in World War II. After the war, he joined General Electric's public relations department where he remained for several years while writing stories and novels on the side. Widespread popularity of such Vonnegut books as *God Bless You Mr. Rosewater*,

Player Piano and *Slaughterhouse Five* in the 1960s and 1970s allowed him to write full-time. Since then, he has continued to be one of America's leading satirists and social critics.

Dan Wakefield (1932-)

The author of such novels as *Going All the Way* and *Starting Over*, as well as such nonfiction books as *New York in the Fifties*, Wakefield left Indianapolis for New York in 1952. There he made a name for himself as a journalist, contributing to such publications as *Atlantic Monthly* and *Esquire*. Wakefield returns frequently to his hometown for readings and speeches.

JAMES WHITCOMB RILEY HOUSE
528 Lockerbie St.   *631-5885*

Without a doubt one of the city's best-known landmarks, literary or otherwise, this two-story brick Victorian was Riley's home for the last 23 years of his life. And it looks as if he just stepped out for a minute — there's a pen on his desk and a hat on his bed — rather than for eternity (he died in 1916).

This house, with its faded, worn rugs and furniture, is a mecca of sorts for Riley fans who come from around the world to pay homage to a poet who parlayed a penchant for rustic dialect and simple rhythms into bestsellerdom. Among his best-known works are such schoolroom mainstays as "'Little Orphant Annie" and "When the Frost Is on the Punkin'.'"

The Riley House, which is listed on the National Register of Historic Places, is open Tuesday through Saturday 10 AM to 4 PM and Sunday noon to 4 PM. It's closed on major holidays. Admission is $2 for adults, $1.50 for seniors, 50¢ for children 7 to 17 and free for those 6 and younger.

JAMES WHITCOMB RILEY GRAVE
Crown Hill Cemetery, 700 W. 38th St. 925-8231

Atop the Strawberry Hill, at the highest natural point in Indianapolis, Riley's grave is one of the city's memorable memorials. It's a great place for a picnic, especially on a clear sunny day when you can gaze out on the city as it spreads out in all directions from Crown Hill.

Note the small headstone next to Riley's Greek temple that reads, "The Poet's Favorite Niece." That's her only identification — and her only legacy.

To find Riley's memorial, enter the cemetery at the 34th Street gate and follow the signs.

The near-east side neighborhood of Woodruff Place, between Michigan and 10th streets near the Indiana Women's Prison was likely the setting of Booth Tarkington's *The Magnificent Ambersons*. Many of the area's homes have been restored and are indeed magnificent.

Insiders' Tips

BOOTH TARKINGTON HOUSE
4270 N. Meridian St.

Formerly the home of Pulitzer Prize-winning novelist and playwright Booth Tarkington, this magnificent Tudor-style mansion is still a private residence and therefore not open for tours. But it's worth driving by just to catch a glimpse of the elegance in which one of the city's literary lions once lived.

Inside
Sports

Indianapolis takes its sports seriously. A quick look around at the quantity and quality of local sports facilities and events will provide evidence enough. And just try to get tickets to the Indianapolis 500 or the state high school basketball finals.

People here love sports. And they've got plenty to love. Cheer on first-tier professionals (the NBA's Indiana Pacers, the NFL's Indianapolis Colts), farm teams, the International Hockey League's Indianapolis Ice and the American Association baseball's Indianapolis Indians. Attend world-class events in track and field, swimming, diving and gymnastics; local high school competitions; international rowing and cycling; and the Hoosier State Games.

But this isn't your ordinary sports-loving place. In Indianapolis, sports aren't just entertainment — they're an integral part of local economic development efforts. So much so that they were a driving force behind the city's dramatic revitalization in the 1980s.

In Indianapolis, sports are not only good for business, they *are* good business. It was that realization that led city officials to make sports, specifically amateur sports, a linchpin in the local economy.

Amateur Sports Capital

The 1980s were a decade of rejuvenation for U.S. cities, as civic leaders throughout the nation joined forces with businesses and citizens groups to revital-

Photo: The Indianapolis Star & News

Market Square Arena opened in 1974 and is the current home of the Indiana Pacers and the Indianapolis Ice.

ize sluggish economies and revamp stagnant communities. Critical to each city's efforts was a marketing plan aimed at enhancing its image, making it attractive to public- and private-sector investors and to potential conventioneers and tourists. Of the dozens of cities engaged in image-enhancement efforts, none was more successful than Indianapolis.

Wielding a savvy marketing strategy, community leaders transformed Indianapolis from a faltering industrial center into a city that *Newsweek* dubbed "the Cinderella of the Rustbelt." However, the closest thing to a glass slipper in that transformation was an athletic shoe, an appropriate symbol for a city that used sports to turn itself into one of the most hospitable places in the country for athletes of all ages and abilities.

Today, few places in the United States can rival Indianapolis for number of amateur sports organizations and world-class training and competition facilities, or for the quantity and quality of sporting events. Presently 20 national and international sports organizations have their headquarters in Indianapolis; since 1974, the city has built or renovated more than $168 million worth of sports facilities. The availability of those facilities has resulted in Indianapolis hosting more than 330 amateur sporting events, including the 1987 Pan American Games and the 1991 NCAA Final Four. Between 1977 and 1991, the direct economic impact of amateur sports in the city was $1.05 billion.

Through deliberate and skillful planning, Indianapolis has become the self-proclaimed "Amateur Sports Capitol of the World."

In the Beginning

The roots of the city's sports focus can be traced to the implementation of Unigov,

the merger of the city of Indianapolis with surrounding Marion County to form a unified government structure. Agreed to by the Indiana Legislature in 1969, Unigov actually went into effect on January 1, 1970. Immediately the city's population nearly doubled, its geographic size quadrupled, and its tax base multiplied many times over.

That same year, the Amateur Athletic Union (AAU) moved its national headquarters to Indianapolis. At the time, the AAU was the umbrella organization for 13 amateur sports organizations. It helped with the administration of each sport's program, the marketing of its membership services and the regulation of its competitions.

Having the AAU in Indianapolis gave the city a leg up when Congress passed the Amateur Athletics Act of 1978, which directed the formation of independent governing bodies for all sports in which the United States has Olympic athletes. Suddenly the amateur sports groups operating inside AAU headquarters were free to set up separate operations wherever they liked.

Several of the fledgling national governing bodies headed for what they saw as greener pastures: Colorado Springs, home of the U.S. Olympic Committee. However, recruiters with offers of relocation funds and free office space eventually wooed several back to Indiana. Today, in addition to the AAU, Indianapolis is the home of USA Track and Field, USA Gymnastics, U.S. Diving, the U.S. Rowing Association, U.S. Synchronized Swimming, U.S. Water Polo, and the U.S. Canoe/Kayak Team.

The reason city officials wanted amateur sports organizations to establish their headquarters in Indianapolis was simple: What better way to ensure that the city would be considered a primary candidate

Bush Stadium

Bush Stadium, 1501 W. 16th Street, is one of the city's most beloved sports facilities. Built in 1931, the art-deco stadium with its ivy-covered walls and terrazzo floors is home to American Association Baseball's Indianapolis Indians. The site of the baseball competition during the 1987 Pan American games, it was also used for the baseball scenes in the movies *Eight Men Out* and *Roommates*.

However, now in need of major league repairs, the stadium's future is uncertain. The Indians will be moving to a new downtown stadium in 1996, and city officials have proposed tearing it down. But the Historic Landmarks Foundation of Indiana is hoping to rally enough public support to save it from the wrecking ball.

This is one of America's classic stadiums — and a reminder of what going to a baseball game used to be like before domed stadiums and big business supplanted the pleasures of the game.

Photo: The Indianapolis Star & News

Bush Stadium, built in 1931, is home of minor league baseball and was used for the baseball scenes in the movies, Eight Men Out *and* Roommates.

to host national and international events? But before they could sell the city as a viable place to hold events, civic leaders knew they needed high-quality facilities capable of meeting the exacting standards of athletes, coaches and trainers. In other words, expensive facilities.

Enter the Lilly Endowment. Founded in 1937 by the family of pharmaceutical corporation founder Eli Lilly, the endowment's mission in part is to provide financial help to projects aimed at improving the quality of life in Indianapolis.

Fortuitously, Congress had passed a tax act in 1969 that required foundations to give away a minimum percentage of their assets annually. Just as city officials began casting about for ways to fund the building of new sports facilities, the Endowment was looking for new areas in need of funds. As any athlete will tell you, timing is crucial to success in sports.

With financial support from the Endowment as well as from corporate and municipal coffers, Indianapolis started building athletic facilities and bidding to host national and international events. Today the city can boast having some of the finest facilities in the country and of attracting some of the finest sporting events in the world.

Since 1982, Indianapolis has hosted an array of events, including the 1982 National Sports Festival (now the U.S. Olympic Festival). Indianapolis was the first city in which the festival, traditionally plagued by red ink, made a profit.

That success led to the city being selected as the site for the 1987 Pan American Games. With only two and a half years to prepare for this international event, which is second only to the Olympic Games in terms of prestige and visibility, local planners rallied the resources needed to run it successfully. The bulk of the work that went into organizing and running the Pan American Games was done by some 37,000 volunteers. The Pan Am Games brought 4,453 athletes from 38 countries to Indianapolis and led to \$9 million worth of ticket sales.

Since then Indianapolis has been the site for Olympic trials in track and field, swimming and diving; the NCAA Final Four (1991); the 1994 World Rowing Championships; the Grand Prix of Cycling (twice); and for the 1991 World Gymnastics Championships — just to name a few. Sports is a growing enterprise.

And like any enterprise, this one owes it's success in large part to the quality of its physical facilities.

Sports Facilities

While many cities can boast of having top-notch athletic facilities, few can match Indianapolis in terms of quantity, quality or accessibility. With few exceptions, the city's major sports facilities are open for use by the public whenever they're not booked for events.

The philosophy behind this policy was simple: Since public money in one form or another helped pay for the construction of many of these facilities, the public has a right to use what it paid for beyond just attending events. (For more information, see our Fitness and Recreation chapter.)

RCA DOME
100 S. Capitol Ave.

Office	262-3410
Box office	262-3389

Like a huge marshmallow, the RCA Dome dominates the southern edge of the Mile Square. One of two domed stadiums in the country attached to a convention center, this 60,500-seat facility is not only the home of the NFL's Indianapolis Colts, it also serves as a site for a variety of amateur sporting events.

In 1984, the Dome hosted the world's largest indoor basketball game when 67,596 people showed up for the U.S. Olympic Team vs. the NBA All-Stars. In 1991, it was the site of the NCAA Final Four, an event it will host again in 1997 and 2000. Every October, it hosts the Circle City Classic, a football game featuring two of the nation's finest black college teams. And since 1979, the NCAA has held its Division I Men's and Women's Indoor Track Championships at the Dome. Call for an events calendar, as well as for information on behind-the-scenes Dome tours.

Jim Harbaugh gets set to throw the ball to a receiver in the Colts' 1995 season opener against Cincinnati at the RCA Dome.

Photo: The Indianapolis Star & News

PAN AMERICAN PLAZA

201 S. Capitol Ave.

Office	237-5794
Ice skating Information	237-5555

Home to many of the city's amateur sports organizations' headquarters, as well as to the Indiana/World Skating Academy and Research Center. There are two on-site, indoor ice skating rinks: an Olympic-size, 100-feet-by-200-feet rink that's used for training purposes by amateur and professional skaters as well as for classes and public skating; and a smaller, 85-feet-by-200-feet, 1,000-seat rink that's used for competitions. The Research Center tests skaters' physical strengths and weaknesses in comparison to their levels of fitness. The quality of the rinks and the presence of the Research Center has made Indianapolis one of the country's foremost training sites for young figure skaters and hockey players.

The 12-story Pan Am Plaza office tower houses the Indiana Sports Corporation (see our sidebar in this chapter), as well as the national governing bodies (NGBs) for six Olympic sports: rowing, diving, gymnastics, synchronized swimming, canoeing/kayaking and water polo. Other sports organizations calling Pan Am Plaza home include the International Baseball Association, the National Association of Governors' Councils on Physical Fitness and Sports, the Midwestern Collegiate Conference, the Indiana Wrestling Association, and Indiana Swimming Inc.

MARKET SQUARE ARENA

300 E. Market St.

Box office	639-2112
Ticketmaster Charge Line	239-5151

This 16,530-seat facility is the home of the NBA's Indiana Pacers and the IHL's Indianapolis Ice. Built between 1971 and 1974 at a cost of $23.5 million, it has also hosted such noteworthy amateur events as the 1980 NCAA Final Four, the 1982 National Figure Skating Championships and the 1986 Gymnastics Championships of the USA.

INDIANAPOLIS TENNIS CENTER

755 University Blvd.   *278-2100*

This facility is on the campus of Indiana University-Purdue University at Indianapolis (IUPUI). It features a 10,000-seat stadium court, as well as 18 other outdoor courts and a six-court indoor facility. The permanent site of the RCA Championships (see the "Annual Sporting Events" portion of this chapter), which brings a number of top-seeded men's professional players to town every summer, the Tennis Center is a United States Tennis Association training site. It's also used for a variety of high school and college tennis events.

When not in use for amateur or professional tournaments, the courts are available to Tennis Center members and non-members alike. (See our Parks and Recreation chapter.)

INDIANA UNIVERSITY NATATORIUM
901 W. New York St.   *274-3518*

This is the swimming and diving facility that Olympic gold medalist Greg Louganis once called "the best in the Western Hemisphere." There are three pools in the Natatorium: a main Olympic-size pool, an 18-foot-deep diving pool with five platforms and three springboards, and a practice pool with a bottom that can be raised or lowered to accommodate children and people with disabilities.

The Natatorium has hosted an array of national and international events, including the 1985 Synchronized Swimming World Cup Championships, the 1989 VI FINA World Cup Diving competition, the 1992 World Masters Swimming Championships, seven Olympic trials, and 12 NCAA championships.

While the Natatorium is in frequent use by high school, college, national and international athletes, it's also available to the general public. (See our Parks and Recreation chapter.)

INDIANA UNIVERSITY TRACK AND FIELD STADIUM
901 W. New York St.   *274-3518*

After seeing this facility, a writer for *Track and Field News* magazine raved: "If there is a better facility in the U.S. . . . we are unaware of it." Capable of seating nearly 20,000, the stadium features a nine-lane, 400-meter rubber track that is considered one of the world's fastest. The site of the 1988 U.S. Olympic trials, this facility also hosts the annual NIKE Track Classic. When not in use for competitions, the stadium is open to the public. (See our Parks and Recreation chapter.)

MAJOR TAYLOR VELODROME
3649 Cold Spring Rd.   *327-VELO*

This facility consists of a 333.3-meter banked track that consistently earns accolades from competitive cyclists. The site of the 1988 and 1989 Grand Prix of Cycling competitions, the velodrome (which is named for Marshall W. "Major" Taylor, a turn-of-the-century African-American cycling champion from Indianapolis), also hosts Saturday Night Lightening, a go-cart and motorcycle racing series that is televised nationally on ESPN2.

Next to the velodrome is the Lake Sullivan BMX Track, which is used for a variety of bicycle moto-cross events.

(For information on public riding at the velodrome or the BMX track, see our Parks and Recreation chapter.)

HINKLE FIELDHOUSE
Butler University
4600 Sunset Ave.   *283-9375*

If it were a person, Butler University's Hinkle Fieldhouse would be called a living legend. As it is, it's named for Butler's legendary coach (basketball, football and baseball) and athletic director Tony Hinkle (see our sidebar in this chapter). When the fieldhouse (then known as

The Indiana Sports Corporation

While no single individual or entity was entirely responsible for turning Indianapolis into a sports capital, the Indiana Sports Corporation certainly played a key role. Established in 1979, the ISC is a not-for-profit, privately funded organization directed at attracting national and international sporting events to Indianapolis and Indiana.

In the beginning, the only ISC employee was Sandy Knapp, the former vice president of promotions and marketing for the Indiana Pacers. In 1980, with the help of a volunteer management team assembled from the business community, Knapp went before U.S. Olympic Committee officials to bid on behalf of Indianapolis for the 1982 National Sports Festival. At the time, most of the sports facilities being touted in the proposal package were merely architectural renderings — the real structures had yet to be built. "We used a lot of smoke and mirrors," Knapp later said of the proposal, which was successful. Indianapolis got the festival. All it needed then were the facilities.

In the end, it got them — and in time. More than 3,000 athletes from around the country came to Indianapolis in the summer of 1982, and many were so impressed by the quality of the facilities and with the city's hospitality that they mentioned their impressions in press interviews. Indianapolis gained valuable national attention, the Sports Festival earned its first-ever profit, and the ISC proved it could do a lot with a little.

Since then, the ISC has continued its role as advocate for and promoter of Indianapolis and Indiana as sports-friendly sites. The organization has coordinated such events as the 1987 Pan American Games, and, under the auspices of its for-profit subsidiary Sports Marketing of Indiana, the 1991 PGA Championship and the GTE (now RCA) Tennis Championships.

One particularly noteworthy event that the ISC organizes annually is the Hoosier State Games (see our Parks and Recreation chapter). Attracting more than 21,000 athletes of all ages and skill levels to Indianapolis each summer, the Games is one of the largest such events in the country.

Through fund-raisers such as the annual Youthlinks Celebrity Golf Tournament, the ISC is also able to fund sports programs for young people throughout Indiana.

ISC offices are in Pan Am Plaza, 201 S. Capitol Avenue. For more information, call 237-5000.

Butler Fieldhouse) opened in 1928, it was the largest basketball arena in the United States, a distinction it retained for 20 years. While it has since been eclipsed in size, it hasn't yet been surpassed in atmosphere — if you're looking for a place that radiates history and charm, this is it. Long the home of the Butler Bulldogs, it has also hosted hundreds of high school contests, including numerous state championship games. Prior to the opening of Market Square Arena in 1974, Hinkle Fieldhouse (it was renamed in 1965) was the site of the annual state high school championship game — one of Hoosier Hysteria's ultimate moments.

More recently, this 10,800-seat arena played host to the volleyball events during the 1987 Pan American Games and to the 1994 Midwestern Collegiate Conference Men's and Women's Basketball Championships. Some of the exciting game scenes in the movie *Hoosiers* were shot inside Hinkle Fieldhouse.

PEPSI COLISEUM
Indiana State Fairgrounds
1202 E. 38th St.   927-7500

The former home of the Indianapolis Ice, the Coliseum is a 7,839-seat arena that's used for amateur hockey leagues, rodeos, and other sporting events. It's also open to the public for year-round ice skating. (See our Parks and Recreation chapter.)

WILLIAM KUNTZ SOCCER STADIUM
1502 W. 16th St.   327-7194

Built for the 1987 Pan American Games, the Kuntz Stadium consists of a 4,500-seat competition field and a 2,000-seat practice field. Operated by the Indy Parks and Recreation, this facility now houses youth soccer leagues and hosts a variety of amateur soccer competitions.

EAGLE CREEK PARK
7840 W. 56th St.   327-7110

The largest municipally owned park in the nation, Eagle Creek is also the home of the Eagle Creek Regatta Course, the only rowing course in the country sanctioned for international competition by the International Federation of Rowing Associations. Site of the U.S. Rowing National Championships since 1986, the Eagle Creek course also hosted the 1994 World Rowing Championships, the first time this event had ever been held in the United States.

Also at Eagle Creek is a world-class archery range with two competition fields.

Originally built for the 1987 Pan American Games, the range is now used primarily for archery classes.

The rowing course and the archery range are open for public use. (See our Parks and Recreation chapter.)

LITTLE LEAGUE BASEBALL CENTRAL REGION HEADQUARTERS
9802 Little League Dr.   897-6127

This is a summer camp and training facility serving 1,000 leagues throughout 13 Midwestern states. On its 30-acre site are five playing fields, a swimming pool, tennis and basketball courts and seating for 2,000.

HOOSIER HORSE PARK
Johnson County Park
Edinburgh   (812) 526-6809

Designed for use during the 1987 Pan American Games, the horse park is situated amidst the 611-acre Johnson County Park, south of Indianapolis. It includes a 14.5-mile cross-country course, three all-weather dressage arenas, a stadium jump arena, a rodeo arena, a flat saddle arena and 192 box stalls. Due to the quality of the facility, Hoosier Horse Park is the site of a variety of amateur equestrian competitions.

WOODFILL RANGE
Johnson County Park
Edinburgh   (812) 526-6809

A competitive shooting facility, Woodfill Range was also built for the 1987 Pan American Games. Now it's primarily used by soldiers from nearby Camp Atterbury, though it still hosts amateur marksmanship competitions.

Professional Sports

Though Indianapolis bills itself as the Amateur Sports Capital of the World, it hasn't ignored professional sports. To the

Photo: The Indianapolis Star & News

Indianapolis shortstop Pokey Reese completes a double play during the Indians' division-winning 1995 regular season.

contrary: The city is home to what might arguably be called one of the most famous professional sporting events in the world — the Indianapolis 500 Mile Race (see our Auto Racing chapter). It's also home to the Indiana Pacers, who in recent years have become one of the NBA's most exciting teams, and the Indianapolis Indians, long one of professional baseball's best minor league teams. Add to the mix the NFL's Indianapolis Colts and the

IHL's Indianapolis Ice, and it's clear that professional sports are vital factors in the city's overall sports marketing strategy — Plus there's the fact that they're a lot of fun.

INDIANA PACERS

Market Square Arena, 300 E. Market St.
Office 263-2100
MSA Box Office 239-5151

A fixture in Indianapolis since 1967 when the team was one of the earliest

American Basketball Association (ABA) franchises, the Pacers and their fans have weathered the fortunes and misfortunes that accompany a long-term relationship. It hasn't always been easy.

In 1967, the late *Indianapolis Star* sports editor Bob Collins and five other investors pooled $6,000 to buy a franchise in the ABA, which was then in the proposal stage. When the upstart basketball organization finally began operating, the Indiana team quickly established its dominance. Relying on the talents of such native sons as Rick Mount, Bill Keller, and George McGinnis, as well as those of such noteworthy acquisitions as Mel Daniels, Roger Brown, the Pacers and coach Bobby "Slick" Leonard showed America what basketball Indiana-style could be. Drawing crowds as large as 8,000 people at a time when the ABA game average was 5,000, the Pacers won three ABA titles — in 1970, 1972, and 1973 — and three most valuable player awards— Mel Daniels in 1969 and 1971, and George McGinnis in 1975. They were among the ABA's elite.

And Indianapolis officials showed their appreciation by building Market Square Arena to house the Pacers, who'd been playing their home contests in the Coliseum at the Indiana State Fairgrounds. But in 1976, the ABA went belly-up, and the Pacers became one of only four ABA teams to ante up the required $3.2 million to gain admission to the National Basketball Association. Resulting financial problems almost destroyed the Pacers. Top players, including McGinnis, left when Indiana couldn't meet their salary demands. In 1977, the team held an unprecedented telethon to meet operating expenses. While the community rallied to help the Pacers, fan support slipped: By the 1982-83 season, attendance at home games was less than 5,000. Making matters worse was the fact

that the Pacers consistently finished each season with more losses than wins.

In 1983, local real estate developers Melvin and Herbert Simon bought the Pacers from California businessman Sam Nassi, who'd owned the franchise since 1979. While the team continued to struggle to find the right combination of players and coaching staff, the Simons' hands-off management style allowed team president and general manager Donnie Walsh and his assistants to run the Pacers. Gradually things improved: By 1987, the Pacers were actually in the NBA playoffs.

In 1994, under the guidance of coach Larry Brown and fueled by the hot-handed three-point shooting of Reggie Miller, the Pacers nearly defeated the tough New York Knicks in the Eastern Conference finals. As it was, they pushed the best-of-seven series to the limit with a fired-up Miller trading courtside jibes with filmmaker/Knicks fan Spike Lee during an unbelievable 25-point rampage in the fourth quarter of Game Five at Madison Square Garden. Though the Knicks finally won that series in Game Seven, the Pacers had served notice that they were once again a force to be reckoned with. Pacer fans became fanatics.

Posters and banners emblazoned with "Pacer Pride" bedecked windows, cars, and lampposts throughout the city. The Pacer gift shop couldn't keep shirts and jerseys in stock. Residents planned their lives around game schedules.

In 1995, the Pacers squared off against the Knicks in the second round of the playoffs. Led by the shooting, rebounding and defensive play of Rik Smits, Dale Davis and Antonio Davis, Indiana prevailed this time. After beating the Knicks, the Pacers dropped a grueling seven-game series to the Orlando Magic in the Eastern Conference Championship.

Odd as it seems, despite their popularity, the Pacers aren't a money-making enterprise these days. Or more specifically, they're not a profit-making enterprise. Escalating player salaries, as well as lower-than-the-NBA-average ticket, broadcast, and arena advertising receipts, keep the team in the red. But that hasn't prevented other cities from approaching the Simons about buying the team— in 1993, Toronto investors reportedly offered to buy the Pacers for $100 million. The offer was rejected. Operating deficit or not, Indianapolis without the Pacers is unthinkable.

If you want to see what all the hoopla is about, go sit in Market Square and watch the team in action. Individual ticket prices for Pacers games range from $9 to $32. Group rates are available. For a season schedule and ticket information, contact the Market Square Arena box office.

INDIANAPOLIS COLTS
7001 W. 56th St.
Office	297-2658
Tickets	297-7000

It was a dark and stormy night. Sounds like the beginning of bad story, doesn't it? In a way, it is. It's the beginning of the story of how Indianapolis came to have an NFL franchise. And how Baltimore came to lose one.

When the rancor between owner Bob Irsay and longtime team franchise site Baltimore reached the boiling point in 1984, Irsay, blaming poor playing facilities and declining game attendance, responded to the siren call of Indianapolis. City officials had played on his desire to leave Baltimore by pointing to a newly built domed stadium and guaranteeing him $7 million in annual ticket sales for seven years. They'd also promised a site for a permanent Colts training facility.

That's how a line of Mayflower Transit trucks (Mayflower has its national headquarters in Indianapolis) happened to appear outside the Colts' Baltimore facility one rainy night in March 1994. Loaded with all of the Colts' gear, the trucks headed west toward Indianapolis. In sports lore, that event has come to be known as the midnight ride of the Colts.

Once the trucks arrived, Irsay and Indianapolis mayor William Hudnut held a press conference, announcing the team's new name — the Indianapolis Colts — and its new home field— the recently opened Hoosier (now RCA) Dome. Indianapolis had officially become an NFL franchise site.

Baltimore wasn't happy. Much howling and hand-wringing ensued, along with many cries of "Good riddance." The city of Baltimore filed a suit against the city of Indianapolis, alleging that it had stolen the franchise and could not designate the team as the Colts, a name the suit claimed for Baltimore. That argument was rejected by the court, and the Colts retained their name.

Locally, enthusiasm and optimism were high. The first season, 143,000 Colts fans applied for season tickets. But fans don't win NFL games — teams do. And as a team, the Colts weren't winners. In fact, by 1986, they were floundering; they lost the first 13 games of the season.

In 1987, Irsay decided his team needed a marquee player to turn the team's fortunes around. So in a trade with the Los Angeles Rams, the Colts acquired the services of Eric Dickerson, then the best running back in the NFL. With a talented offensive line protecting Dickerson and running back Albert Bentley backing him up, the Colts seemed poised for greatness.

Under the guidance of coach Ron Meyer, they won the AFC Eastern Division title and went to the NFL playoffs for

Photo: The Indianapolis Star & News

Antonio Davis is a key reserve for the Pacers in their quest for an NBA title.

The Man Who Put the Hinkle in Hinkle Fieldhouse

Paul Daniel "Tony" Hinkle (1898-1992) is an Indianapolis sports legend. A native of Logansport, Indiana, Hinkle earned All-American honors while playing basketball and football at the University of Chicago (1916-1920). After graduating from college, he pitched for a semi-pro baseball team in Chicago.

Photo: The Indianapolis Star & News

In 1921, Hinkle moved to Indianapolis, joining the Butler University coaching staff as an assistant football coach. Five years later, he was promoted to head coach. Over the next 44 years, Hinkle's Butler Bulldogs won nine Indiana Collegiate Conference titles, compiling a 171-100-12 record.

In addition to football, Hinkle also coached Butler's baseball and basketball teams. Under his direction, both teams did well — in both sports, he could boast of a 44-year win-loss record exceeding 500 percent. And in basketball, Hinkle in-

Paul D. "Tony" Hinkle was the legendary coach and athletic director at Butler University.

vented the "Hinkle System," a system that emphasized movement on the floor and the use of passes, picks and screens. The Hinkle System became a model for other coaches, including Indiana University's Bob Knight who adapted and modified it in the course of creating his own offensive strategies.

In 1928, Hinkle helped inaugurate the new Butler Fieldhouse, which for more than two decades was the largest gymnasium in the country. At various times over the years, Hinkle ran the fieldhouse concession stand and buffed its floor — all while continuing his coaching duties.

In honor of Hinkle's many contributions to the university, Butler officials named him athletic director in 1932. And in 1965, they renamed the fieldhouse — it officially became Hinkle Fieldhouse, which, in a manner of speaking, it always had been. That same year, he was elected to the James Naismith Basketball Hall of Fame.

Hinkle was widely respected throughout the country. He served for two terms (1937-1938 and 1942-1950) on the NCAA Basketball Rules Committee; he chaired the committee from 1948 to 1950. He was also the president of the National Association of Basketball Coaches (NABC), 1954-1955. In 1962, Hinkle was awarded the National Collegiate Basketball Coaches

Association Award, and in 1986 the NABC gave him its Golden Anniversary Award.

Though he retired from Butler in 1970, Hinkle remained active in both university and community affairs. When he died in 1992, he left behind a legacy that included his belief in honorable competition, sportsmanship and dedication as well as an insistence on respect for opponents, authorities and the rules of the game.

the first time in 10 years. Though they lost in the first game against the Cleveland Browns, the Colts revived the flagging interest of their Indianapolis fans.

But in the ensuing years, the team's fortunes have wavered. A number of missteps — poor draft choices and trade decisions, player injuries and coaching changes — have resulted in mediocre season records and team morale. Dickerson, who was injured in 1988, finally left the team in 1991 after earning a reputation as a prima donna for his frequent complaints about his teammates, his treatment and his salary.

Another disappointment came when Irsay signed quarterback Jeff George, who had been a local grid star at Warren Central High School. Undeniably talented, George made a lot of noise about his abilities in the press but didn't do much to help the team out of its slump. He, too, spent as much time complaining as playing before being traded to Atlanta in 1993.

In 1991, the Colts' win-loss record was a dismal 1-15, the worst in the league. With new coach Ted Marchibroda at the helm in 1992, the Colts tied the NFL's record for the best one-season turnaround by compiling a 9-7 season.

The Colts dropped 4-12 in 1993 but rebounded with two straight season-ending victories to go 8-8 in 1994. Running back Marshall Faulk was named the NFL's 1994 Rookie of the Year.

Fans have been loyal from the start. While home games aren't sellouts as they were in the first few seasons, it's not unusual for 50,000 or more people to show up for a game. For diehard NFL fans, the thrill of sitting in such a wonderful venue as the Dome overrides the often disappointing results. Individually the Colts players are local favorites, appearing in TV and radio commercials, taking part in charitable events, and generally making themselves available to the community. That goes a long way toward maintaining good will even during a losing season. Who wouldn't want to support such nice guys?

Individual tickets for Colts games run $15, $23, $25 and $29. Season tickets are $230, $250 and $290. Tickets are available at all Ticketmaster locations, including the RCA Dome box office, or by mail-order from the Colts. Call the Colts' ticket line for more information.

INDIANAPOLIS INDIANS

Bush Stadium
1501 W. 16th St.   269-3545

If you were going to handpick hometown heroes, you couldn't do much better than the Indians. The American Association farm team for the Cincinnati Reds, the Indians have been part of life in Indianapolis since 1887.

Known as the Indians from the beginning, the club has been affiliated with a number of Major League teams during the course of its history. Since its first working agreement with the Cincinnati Reds (1939-1941), the Indians have been a farm team for the Boston Braves (1946-1947), the Pittsburgh Pirates (1948-1951), the Cleveland Indians (1952-1956), the Chicago White Sox (1957-1959, 1962-1967), the Philadelphia Phillies (1960), and the Cincinnati Reds (1961, 1968-1983). When the Reds refused to allow the use of designated hitters in the minor league, Indianapolis general manager Max Schumacher switched the Indians' affiliation to the Montreal Expos (1984-1992). But for the 1993 season, the Indians returned to the Reds' fold where they remain.

During the past few decades, the Indians have readied a number of major leaguers for their careers, including such future stars as Roger Maris, Rocky Colavito and Harmon Killebrew. They've also created their own stars, the most notable being Razor Shines, who personified baseball for Indians fans for a decade before retiring in 1994.

Shines was a multiple-threat player—at first base or third, in the outfield or as a catcher, and as a designated hitter who was great in clutch situations. He was also a great motivator of his teammates and of himself. Shines worked hard in the off-season to stay in condition and to improve his game. "He was quite simply the working man's hero," wrote David B. Reddick and Kim M. Rogers of Shines in their 1988 book *The Magic of Indians Baseball: 1887-1987.*

As a team, the Indians have shone in their own right. From 1986 to 1989, the club won four consecutive American Association championships and two Triple-A Alliance World Series.

Of course, over the course of a century, everything hasn't always been rosy in the Indians' camp. Following the close of the 1956 season, for example, a severe financial deficit nearly killed the team. But city residents revived it by contributing $205,000 in operating capital. When the cash-strapped American Association was forced out of business in 1962, the Indians joined the International League for one season, then the Pacific Coast League for five more. Finally, in 1969 the American Association reformed, with the Indians once again in its fold.

Since 1931, the team's home field has been Bush Stadium, 1501 W. 16th Street, but that will change in 1996 when the Indians move to a new downtown stadium currently under construction. The impending move led the Indians' management to declare the 1995 season the stadium's "Sunset Season"—a bit prematurely as it turned out. Construction delays will force the Indians to play part of the 1996 season at Bush Stadium as well.

Tickets to Indianapolis Indians home games are $8 for box seats, $7 for reserved grandstand seats, and $5 for general admission. Season tickets are $300 for box seats and $275 for reserved grandstand. For a game schedule and ticket information, call the Indians office.

INDIANAPOLIS ICE

222 E. Ohio St.
Office   266-1234
Market Square Arena Box Office   239-5151

The top minor league affiliate for the National Hockey League's Chicago Blackhawks, the Ice play their home games at Market Square Arena, 300 E. Market Street. They are the latest in a line of professional hockey teams that have called Indianapolis home since 1939.

The first was the Capitols, a team affiliated with the National Hockey League's Detroit Red Wings. Playing in the newly constructed Indiana State Fair Coliseum, the Capitols won three divisional titles between 1940 and 1946, as well as two league championships (1942 and

1950). When the Red Wings and the State Fair Board couldn't reach a long-term lease agreement for the Coliseum in 1952, the Capitols disbanded.

Over the course of the next 35 years, four more minor league hockey teams called Indianapolis home: the Indianapolis Chiefs (1955-1962), another incarnation of the Indianapolis Capitols (1963), the Indianapolis Racers (1974-1978), and the Indianapolis Checkers (1979-1987).

(Future NHL superstar Wayne Gretzky began his professional career in Indianapolis, playing for the Racers for eight games during the 1978 season before moving on to the Edmonton Oilers.)

The Ice, an International Hockey League team, debuted in 1988. For the first year of its existence, the Ice had no NHL affiliation: It wasn't until the 1989-'90 season that the team became the official farm team for the Blackhawks. That proved to be good timing for Chicago because in that same season the Ice won 53 matches and the IHL's Turner Cup. Since then, the team has continued to be a strong presence on and off the ice and to attract new fans through smart marketing.

Feisty and talented, the young Ice players scrap to keep hockey in the headlines all through the October-to-April season. You don't have to know icing from frosting to enjoy the Ice.

Tickets for Ice home games, which are played at Market Square Arena are $13, $11 and $8; season tickets range from $175 to $285 for half-season to $300 to $475 for whole-season packages.

Tickets are available through all Ticketmaster locations, including the MSA box office; season tickets can be purchased by mail from the Ice— call the team office for information.

INDIANAPOLIS MOTOR SPEEDWAY
4790 W. 16th St.
Office	481-8500
Tickets	484-6700

Without a doubt, the Motor Speedway is the city's most enduring professional sports symbol. A local landmark since 1916, it's the site of the annual Indianapolis 500, which is billed as the world's largest one-day spectator event, and the newly inaugurated Brickyard 400, a NASCAR-sanctioned stock car race. (For more information, see our Auto Racing chapter.)

INDIANAPOLIS RACEWAY PARK
9901 Crawfordsville Rd. 291-4090

If you like drag racing, oval track racing or road racing, IRP is heaven. This facility is home to such big-time events as the annual NHRA U.S. Nationals, the Kroger NASCA 200 Grand National Stock Car Race and the Miller Genuine Draft Night Before the 500 midget car race. Ah, the smell of rubber, the roar of engines! (For more details, see our Auto Racing chapter.)

HOOSIER PARK
4500 Dan Patch Cir.
Anderson 642-RACE

While not actually an Indianapolis sports attraction, Hoosier Park is near enough (about 35 miles north on I-69) to take in, especially if you're a horse racing fan. Indiana's first pari-mutuel track, Hoosier Park features both thoroughbred and harness racing.

Annual Sporting Events

BRICKYARD CROSSING CHAMPIONSHIP
Brickyard Crossing Golf Resort & Inn
4400 W. 16th St. 484-6709

This Senior PGA Tour tournament is played on a course that spreads out around the Indianapolis Motor Speedway.

Photo: The Indianapolis Star & News

Hoosier Park in Anderson features both thoroughbred and harness racing.

Originally built in 1929, the course was completely redesigned by renown golf course architect (and former Indianapolis resident) Pete Dye in 1993. The following year, the tournament debuted. It was so successful with players and fans alike that the 1995 event attracted such renowned duffers as Gary Player and Arnold Palmer.

Ticket prices range from $20 for a one-day pass to $100 for a week-long badge that includes access to the course and clubhouse. Group ticket packages range from $600 to $2,100.

COCA-COLA CIRCLE CITY CLASSIC
Indiana Black Expo
3145 N. Meridian St.   237-5222

Established in 1984 as an event for alumni of black colleges, as well as a means of encouraging African-American children to attend college, the Circle City Classic has expanded into one of the country's largest African-American events. For a week each October, thousands of black college alumni (as well as black celebrities and athletes) gather in Indianapolis for a variety of activities, the culmina-

tion being the Classic itself — a football game between two of the country's historically black college teams (they vary from year to year). The sellout game (the proceeds help fund scholarships for black colleges) is played in the RCA Dome.

Tickets to the game are $10, $15 and $25 and are available at all Ticketmaster locations, including the RCA Dome box office, or by mail-order from the RCA Dome Ticket Office, 200 S. Capitol Avenue, Suite 150, Indianapolis, 46225.

THE RCA CHAMPIONSHIPS
Indianapolis Tennis Center   632-8000
755 University Blvd.   (800) 622-LOVE

Every August some of the biggest names on the men's professional tennis circuit (Jim Courier, Pete Sampras, Todd Martin) come to the city for this nine-day event. Consistently ranked as the "tournament of the year" by the players, the RCA Championships is big-time tennis at its best.

Indianapolis has a long and storied history of support for and involvement with tennis. From 1922 to 1968, it was the site of the Western Open, the oldest amateur tennis tournament in the country. From 1922 until 1965, Indianapolis hosted it every other year; in 1966, it became the tournament's permanent home. However, in 1969, the United States Tennis Association (USTA) moved the U.S. Clay Court Championships to Indianapolis — the Western Open then moved to Cincinnati. As the last tournament before the prestigious U.S. Open, the Clay Courts became an important stop for many of the world's top players eager to fine tune their games for the Open. So popular were the Clay Courts locally that city officials decided to build the Indianapolis Sports Center (now the Indianapolis Tennis Center) in 1978.

Ironically, that same year the U.S. Open switched from clay to hard courts, and players began to shun the Indianapolis tournament and play those on hard courts. By 1986, tournament officials were having a hard time getting top-seeded men's players to commit to the Clay Courts. In 1987, local tournament organizers decided to pave the Sports Center's courts, and the USTA moved the Clay Courts to South Carolina.

In 1988, a $13 million construction project began, turning the Sports Center into the Tennis Center. In addition to paving the existing clay courts, a new tennis stadium replaced the old one, and an indoor tennis complex was added. Impressed with the results, the USTA made the Indianapolis Tennis Center a regional training center and announced the creation of a new sanctioned hard court tournament— the one now known as the RCA Championships.

Other tennis highlights throughout the years have included the Indiana Loves, a member of the short-lived World Tennis Team league (1975-1978). The Loves played matches at the Indiana Convention Center and Market Square Arena. And from 1982-1992, the Indianapolis Racquet Club hosted a Virginia Slims Ginny circuit tournament (1982-1987) and a Kraft series tournament (1988-1992), both sanctioned by the Women's Tennis Association.

Individual session tickets for the RCA Championships range from $8 to $50, depending on seat locations and sessions. Season tickets range from $150 to $400. Tickets are available at the Indianapolis Tennis Center box office or by mail.

YOUTHLINKS INDIANA CELEBRITY GOLF TOURNAMENT
Indiana Sports Corporation
201 S. Capitol Ave., Ste. 1200   237-5000

A joint presentation of the Indiana Sports Corporation and Indiana Black Expo, the Youthlinks Celebrity Golf Tournament is held in late June each year. The event attracts present and former professional and Olympic athletes, coaches, broadcasters, politicians and sports executives from throughout the country to Indianapolis for a day of golf dedicated to raising money to help fund youth sports programs and scholarships.

Past Youthlinks participants have included Olympic speed skater Bonnie Blair, former Indianapolis 500 champion Tom Sneva, CBS sports announcer Billy Packer, screenwriter Angelo Pizzo (*Hoosiers* and *Rudy*), Indiana University head football coach Bill Mallory and Indiana's senior U.S. Senator Richard Lugar.

Since its inception in 1988, Youthlinks has raised more than $2.5 million for such programs as CHAMPS, a grants program that benefits local sports activities for young people; Future Olympians, a grants program that assists Olympic-caliber athletes in need of financial help to meet the costs of training, equipment, travel and medical expenses; and Indiana Evans Scholars, a scholarship program for former golf caddies who graduate in the top 25 percent of their high school class and need assistance with college expenses.

Youthlinks events take place at various area golf courses; in 1995, the courses were Brickyard Crossing, Broadmoor Country Club and Crooked Stick Golf Club. For up-to-date schedule and ticket information, contact the Indiana Sports Corporation.

Sports Organizations

In addition to the facilities, teams and events listed in this chapter, Indianapolis is home to a number of national sports organizations. While these organizations primarily represent the interests of coaches and athletes in specific sports, they're also good sources of information for spectators interested in learning more about individual sports.

AMATEUR ATHLETIC ASSOCIATION (AAU)

3400 W. 86th St. 872-2900

The A.A.U. promotes and develops amateur sports in the United States. A nonprofit, volunteer-driven organization, it represents some 1 million athletes, coaches, volunteers and officials. The AAU also hosts the annual James E. Sullivan award dinner; the award itself, which is named for a former AAU president, recognizes amateur athletes for their character, sportsmanship, leadership and ideals. Past Sullivan Award winners have included track star Carl Lewis and diving champion Greg Louganis.

NATIONAL GOVERNING BODIES (NGBs)

The following organizations regulate and sanction national competitions within their respective Olympic sports and represent those sports and their athletes in the international arena.

U.S. Canoe/Kayak Team, 201 S. Capitol Avenue, Suite 610, 237-5690

USA Gymnastics, 201 S. Capitol Avenue, Suite 300, 237-5050

Photo: The Indianapolis Star & News

Professional male tennis players, such as Jim Courier shown here, participate in the RCA Championships at the Indianapolis Tennis Center each August.

USA Track & Field, 200 S. Capitol Avenue, Suite 140, 261-0500

United States Diving Inc., 201 S. Capitol Avenue, Suite 430, 237-5252

United States Rowing Association, 201 S. Capitol Avenue, Suite 400, 237-5656

United States Synchronized Swimming, 201 S. Capitol Avenue, Suite 510, 237-5700

United States Water Polo Inc., 201 S. Capitol Avenue, Suite 520, 237-5599

Sports-Related Attractions

When you're in the mood for sports spectating of a different sort, drop by:

THE NATIONAL
TRACK AND FIELD HALL OF FAME
One RCA Dome
200 S. Capitol Ave.   261-0483

From Jim Thorpe and Jesse Owens to Wilma Rudolph and Babe Didrickson, the achievements of 150 of track and field's greatest athletes are chronicled here. It's open daily except on special event days and holidays. Admission is $3 for adults, $2 for children 5 to 17 and free for children 4 and younger.

THE INDIANAPOLIS MOTOR
SPEEDWAY HALL OF FAME MUSEUM
4790 W. 16th St.   484-6747

This facility inside the Motor Speedway contains the world's largest, most varied collections of racing, classic and antique cars, including more than 30 Indianapolis 500 winners. It's open everyday but Christmas from 9 AM to 5 PM. Admission is $2 for adults; children younger than 16 are admitted free. (For more information, see our Auto Racing chapter.)

NATIONAL ART
MUSEUM OF SPORT (NAMS)
University Place Conference Center
850 W. Michigan St.   274-2339

If you think Leroy Nieman is the last (and only) word in art depicting athletes in action, stop by NAMS. Home to what's reputed to be the largest collection of sports-related art in the nation, this museum has works ranging from 19th-century wood engravings by Winslow Homer to a silkscreen by Mr. Floats-like-a-butterfly-stings-like-a-bee himself, Muhammed Ali. Situated inside the hotel-conference center on the campus of Indiana University-Purdue University at Indianapolis, the museum is open during regular business hours. Admission is free.

THE INDIANA
BASKETBALL HALL OF FAME
One Hall of Fame Court
New Castle   529-1891

Well, OK, it's not in Indianapolis, but given the deep and meaningful relationship people all over Indiana have with basketball, this place is part of every community in the state. Videos and artifacts depict famous players and great moments in Indiana basketball history. Interactive exhibits put visitors into the locker room and on the court. This is Hoosier Hysteria at its best.

The museum is open Tuesday through Saturday 10 AM to 5 PM and Sunday noon to 5 PM. It's closed on Mondays. Admission is $3 for adults, $1 for children.

Inside
Auto Racing

Indianapolis is synonymous with auto racing. Since 1909, when automotive entrepreneur Carl Graham Fisher joined forces with three other local businessmen to develop the Indianapolis Motor Speedway, the city and the sport of auto racing have been inextricably linked.

Today, Indianapolis is not only the site of the internationally renown Indianapolis 500, but it's also home to two more of racing's most significant events— the Brickyard 400 stock car race and the International Hot Rod Association's U.S. Nationals. In addition, area tracks also host a variety of other national and regional racing events. What's more, the presence of high-quality venues and high-visibility events has led to the creation (or relocation) of some 250 racing-related businesses in Indianapolis. The city is home to businesses ranging from race car engineering and design firms to racing organizations and equipment manufacturers.

Indianapolis is a major beneficiary of this auto-racing business. For example, a recent study revealed that the 1994 Brickyard 400 resulted in $31.5 million of direct spending by 350,000 fans and another $30 million in roll-over spending. That's an economic impact of more than $61 million from a single (and admittedly large) racing event.

Add to that the international attention that hosting large-scale racing events focuses on Indianapolis, and it's clear that racing is more than just a part of the city's history. It's also a factor in its future.

Indianapolis Motor Speedway

**GETTING TO THE
INDIANAPOLIS MOTOR SPEEDWAY**
4790 W. 16th St.(offices) 481-8500
(tickets) 484-6700
From downtown: Take 16th Street west for about 4.5 miles to the front entrance, or 30th Street west for about 4.5 miles to the back entrance.
From I-465: Follow the Speedway signs to Exit 16A, then go east on Crawfordsville Road to the track.

This is it, the granddaddy of oval track racing, a mecca for serious race fans and drivers alike. This is the place that, in a manner of speaking, put Indianapolis on the map, and it's still the city's most internationally recognized landmark. Even if they don't know exactly where the city is, people all over the world know about the Indianapolis Motor Speedway, home of the Indianapolis 500.

It began with one man's idea. The man was Carl Graham Fisher, a racing pioneer

Photo: The Indianapolis Star & News

NASCAR drivers run some practice laps at the Indianapolis Motor Speedway as they gear up for the annual Brickyard 400.

and wealthy businessman (see our sidebar in this chapter). His idea was to develop a racetrack for testing locally made automobiles (in the early decades of the 20th century, Indianapolis was home to dozens of automakers), as well as for hosting races.

Fisher pitched that idea to three of his business acquaintances. The first was James A. Allison, co-owner (with Fisher) of the Prest-O-Lite Company, an auto headlight manufacturing firm. The others were industrialists Arthur Newby and Frank Wheeler. (For more information on each of these men, see the sidebar, "The Men Who Brought the Speedway Up to Speed.")

Together these four men developed a 2.5-mile-long oval race track on a 320-acre plot of ground northwest of downtown Indianapolis. Surfaced with a combination of crushed stone and asphalt, the track opened for business on August 19, 1909.

The first race on that day was a twice-around-the-oval dash won by driver Louis Schwitzer, who guided his Stoddard-Dayton to victory despite treacherous conditions: The track's surface broke up from the heat and the traffic, leading to an accident that killed one driver, two mechanics and two spectators. That disaster led the track's owners to decide to repave the racing surface with bricks— 3,200,000 of them to be exact. Hence the track's nickname, "The Brickyard." The first official race on the new surface took place on December 17, 1909.

Following a series of poorly attended races the following year, Fisher and his partners decided to limit the race schedule to one big event — a then-unheard-of 500-mile race — to be held in May. To lure top drivers and spark fan interest, they decided to offer a huge purse: $25,000 to be split by the first 12 finishers.

Indianapolis 500

The first Indianapolis 500-Mile Race was held on Memorial Day, 1911, with Carl Fisher driving the pace car in what is believed to have been the first rolling start of an auto race. Fisher led the 40-car pack for one lap around the track before exiting as the green flag dropped, signalling the official start of the race. That first race set the pace for all those that have followed. It was fraught with drama, steeped in controversy and marred by tragedy — all elements that have reappeared time and again throughout the 500's history.

The drama was supplied by race winner Ray Harroun who, in the absence of a ride-along mechanic (which the other 39 cars in the field had), mounted a mirror above the cowling of his Indianapolis-built Marmon Wasp to help him watch for traffic. Some auto historians claim that was the first use of the rearview mirror. Thanks in part to his mirror, Harroun avoided accidents for 200 laps and crossed the finish line at the head of the field, having averaged 74.59 mph during the six hours and 42 minutes it had taken him to cover 500 miles.

The controversy came about when driver Ralph Mulford claimed he hadn't been credited with a lap he completed when an accident distracted officials. Throughout his life, Mulford contended he was the true winner of the first Indianapolis 500.

And the tragedy — well, death has been part of auto racing since auto racing has been part of life. On lap 13, Arthur Greiner crashed his Amplex, killing his riding mechanic Sam Dickson.

Since that first race, a lot has changed at the Speedway.

Ownership, for instance. In 1927, the original track partners sold the Speedway to a group of Michigan investors that included World War I flying ace (and former Indianapolis 500 driver) Eddie Rickenbacker. That group held on to the track until 1945 when three-time 500 winner Wilbur Shaw arranged for Terre Haute businessman Anton "Tony" Hulman to buy it.

Buying the Speedway proved to be an astute investment for Hulman and his heirs. The family still owns the track— and they operate it as a privately run enterprise. As such, getting certain types of information about the 500, such as attendance figures and race revenues, is impossible. The family refuses to disclose how much money the race generates, though it's obviously several million dollars, with a resulting impact on the community of hundreds of millions. Today, Hulman's grandson, Tony George, is president and CEO of the Speedway.

Another change has been in the track surface itself. While the bricks gave the track its nickname, they weren't the best racing surface since they shifted whenever the ground froze and thawed, and the slightest moisture tended to make them slippery. By the 1930s, under the Rickenbacker group's ownership, asphalt was applied to stretches of the track, a process that escalated rapidly after Hulman bought the Speedway.

By 1945, the track was in rough shape. Closed for four years during World War II, it not only needed resurfacing, but the grandstands and other facilities needed to be replaced. Hulman did that and more. By 1961, all that remained of the old brick track was a three-foot section at the start-finish line (it's still there today); the rest had been covered with asphalt.

Over the years, the cars have become very specialized. At first, many of the cars in the 500 were slightly modified versions of street cars, but today's cars (which are officially known as Indy cars) are far-removed from anything you'll ever see on any street anywhere. The cars that compete in the 500 these days are mostly chassis, engine and transmission, over which is bolted a lightweight, aerodynamic body.

And the speeds have increased tremendously. By 1919, speeds had begun to top 100 mph; by 1937, 125 mph; by 1962, 150 mph. Tom Sneva crossed the 200 mph threshold in 1977, and in 1989, Emerson Fittipaldi did better than 225 mph. And recently, well, individual lap speeds have been edging up to 235 mph, though the fastest official qualifying lap speed on record is 232.618 mph.

Then there is the money. From the original $25,000 in prize money, the 1995 Indianapolis 500 purse had grown to a whopping $8.06 million. Add to that millions more in corporate sponsorships and endorsements, lap money and other 500-related events, and the Indianapolis 500 offers drivers, car owners and technical crews one of the richest paydays in motorsports.

And finally, in 1994 the Speedway ended a 77-year-long tradition of hosting only one major race a year when it added the Brickyard 400, a NASCAR (National Association of Stock Car Auto Racing) event, to its schedule. Now there are two reasons — the 500 in May and the 400 in August — to go to the track.

"The Greatest Spectacle in Racing," the 500 lives up to its name. While many races offer fans a few days of fun — some practice time and qualification runs, then the race— the 500 stretches throughout the month of May. And throughout May, people come to Indianapolis from throughout the world.

Race crews start showing up in late April, though practice for the 500 doesn't

Indianapolis Raceway Park

We're
not your
average
race track. . .

Drag Racing . . . NHRA . . . Road Racing . . . USAC . . .
Sponsorship Packages . . . Stock Car Racing . . . NASCAR .
. .Corporate Hospitalty . . . Ride & Drives . . . SCCA . . . Driving
Schools . . . WERA . . . Car Shows . . . Street Legal Drag Racing
. . . Motorcycle Racing . . . Swap Meets . . . SuperTruck Racing
. . . Open Wheel Racing . . . Jr. Drag Racing . . . and more.

For info, call (317) 293-RACE.

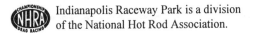 Indianapolis Raceway Park is a division
of the National Hot Rod Association.

The Men Who Brought the Speedway Up to Speed

Each of the four men who founded the Indianapolis motor Speedway — Carl Graham Fisher, James A. Allison, Arthur C. Newby and Frank Wheeler — were successful in various businesses before joining up to create the auspicious 1909 partnership that led to the development of an auto racing landmark. In fact, most of them had done business together before they formed that partnership.

Carl Graham Fisher (1874-1939), a native of Greensburg, Indiana, first tasted success when, at the age of 17, he went to work in a bicycle shop owned by his two brothers. It wasn't long before he turned his interest in cycling into a career as a championship bicycle racer and stuntman.

By nature a risk-taker, as well as a natural born promoter, Fisher turned next to automobiles, purportedly buying the first privately owned car in Indianapolis and shortly thereafter taking up auto racing. In 1902, he opened an auto showroom, selling and servicing Indianapolis-made Premiers and Wintons.

The challenges of business only stoked Graham's competitive fires, and in 1904 he set a world's record by circling a 2-mile dirt track in a car in just more than two minutes. That same year, he joined businessman James A. Allison and inventor P.C. Avery in a new business venture — the manufacture of auto headlights that operated on compressed acetylene. The resulting company, Prest-O-Lite, was a booming success.

Not only did Prest-O-Lite make Fisher wealthy, it also sparked an idea. Given the growing number of auto manufacturers in Indianapolis, he reasoned, why not build a track where they could test their products? Of course, when not in use, the track could also be used for races.

In 1908, Fisher presented his proposal for building just such a track to Allison and their mutual business acquaintances Arthur C. Newby and Frank Wheeler. It was an idea that made history — and lots of money — for each of them.

In addition to his success with Prest-O-Lite and the Indianapolis Motor Speedway, Fisher was involved in the creation of the Hoosier Motor Club, the formation of the Lincoln Highway Association and the development of Miami Beach, Florida.

James A. Allison (1872-1928) came to Indianapolis from Niles, Michigan, with his family when he was 8. Four years later, he quit school to work in his father's business, the Allison Coupon Company. When his father died in 1890, Allison and his two brothers assumed control of the company.

In addition to his partnership with Fisher in Prest-O-Lite and the Speedway, Allison set up the Allison Speedway Team Company, a machine shop, in 1913. Seven years later, he changed its name to the Allison Engineering Company— the forerunner of Allison Gas Turbine and Allison

From left, Carl Fisher, Arthur Newby, Frank Wheeler and James Allison formed a partnership in 1909 to form the Indianapolis Motor Speedway.

Transmission, which under the ownership of General Motors, became two of Indianapolis' major industrial operations. Allison also owned huge blocks of real estate in Indianapolis and in southern Florida. Locally, he developed much of the town of Speedway as it grew up around the Motor Speedway.

By nature a perfectionist, Allison must have been either an odd match or the perfect foil for his flamboyant partner Fisher.

Arthur C. Newby (1865-1933) grew up on a farm near Monrovia, Indiana, and came to Indianapolis as a 16-year-old looking for a job. Landing at Nordyke and Marmon, manufacturers of grain milling equipment (and later, of automobiles), Newby worked his way up from the mail room to a management position, all the while pursuing his true passion — bicycling. He helped found the Zig-Zag Cycling Club, which was active in Indianapolis in the 1890s.

Newby also helped found the Indianapolis Chain and Stamping Company (the forerunner of today's Diamond Chain Company), which was producing 60 percent of the nation's American-made bicycle chains by the turn of the century. Promoting bicycle racing was a natural extension of his job for Newby, and in 1896 he became a partner with Fisher and Allison in the development of a quarter-mile wooden cycling track near the intersection of Central Avenue and 30th Street. This was a trial run, of sorts, for the other racing facility they would later develop.

Following the development of the Motor Speedway in 1911, Newby went on to help establish the National Motor Vehicle Company, which built both electric and gasoline-powered vehicles. A wealthy man, Newby became a philanthropist, donating large sums of money to hospitals and universities.

Frank H. Wheeler (1864-1921) didn't arrive in Indianapolis until 1904, having first gone from his boyhood home in Manchester, Iowa, to California where he supposedly made and lost a couple of fortunes. Not long after coming to Indianapolis, Wheeler met George Schebler, an inventor who'd come up with one of the first truly workable carburetors for an internal combustion engine. It wasn't long before the Wheeler-Schebler Company was up and running, manufacturing carburetors. So successful was the company that it eventually expanded its product line to include magnetos and small electric ignition motors.

His success in the auto parts business led Wheeler to friendships and partnerships with Fisher, Allison and Newby. All three had mansions on Cold Springs Road, and Wheeler followed suit, building one adjacent to Fisher's estate. On his grounds, Wheeler grew flowers, fruits and vegetables that he gave away, primarily to children throughout Indianapolis.

officially start until the first weekend in May. It doesn't take long for things to heat up, and by mid-May the action on (and sometimes off) the track is hot and heavy as crews search for the perfect setup, the optimum engine and frame adjustment that fits both drivers and track conditions.

The second and third weekends in May are devoted to qualifications: timed laps used by track officials to determine the 33-car field for race day. The Thursday before the race is Carburetion Day, when officials from the United States Auto Club (USAC, the sanctioning organization for the 500) check each qualified car to ensure it meets USAC guidelines.

Though the high-tech engines in modern Indy cars no longer have carburetors, Carburetion Day retains its name from the time when mechanics tinkered with cars' carburetors to achieve maximum performance on race day. Now race teams adjust fuel injection setups and make other last-minute adjustments to their cars.

But as much fun as tracking track events can be, for avid people watchers it's even more fun to keep track of the characters who show up at the track. Once the Speedway opens to race crews in early May, it's also open to race fans for a nominal daily fee (depending on the day, it's usually in the $5 to $10 range). You can attend practice sessions and qualification weekends, which thousands of people do. And since practice and qualifications are all general admission, you can sit anywhere you like, except for the corporate suites, which are off-limits unless you have an invitation.

From the streets outside the Speedway to the suites overlooking the track, you're apt to see anyone from well-heeled millionaires to leather-clad bikers, from women wearing power suits to women wearing bathing suits, from mothers pushing strollers to fathers toting coolers, from young men sporting nose-rings to old men sporting straw hats. You might even catch a glimpse of some celebs, such as Paul Newman (who co-owns the Newman-Haas racing team) in the pits conferring with Mario Andretti; hometown boy-made-good David Letterman (cigar in hand) ambling down Gasoline Alley; or Tim Allen,

Photo: The Indianapolis Star & News

The pit crew plays a vital role during race day each May during the Indianapolis 500-Mile Race.

Jim Nabors or James Garner coming out of a team garage.

The parking lots are filled with gleaming Mercedes and Cadillacs, rusty Plymouths and Mercuries, large RVs and compact pickup trucks. On the streets surrounding the track, homeowners put up hand-lettered signs: "PARKING $5 ALL DAY" or "NO PARKING," depending on their entrepreneurial bent or devotion to their lawns.

Inside the track, the air is redolent with sunscreen and sweat, beer and popcorn. If the cars aren't running, you can catch some tunes or track updates from a nearby boombox. If they are running, you can't hear yourself think, at least for those few moments when they come roaring past.

Nothing can prepare you for your first up-close-and-personal experience of an Indy car doing what it does best— going extremely fast. The decibel level is way off the scale— these cars are *loud*! And at full tilt, they're more of a blur than they are recognizable vehicles.

Indianapolis in the month of May is as close as this place gets to Mardi Gras —

and the closer it gets to Race Day, the more like Mardi Gras it becomes.

May at the Speedway

Early in the month, you can go out to the track and watch as racing teams put their cars (and drivers) through shakedown runs, trying to figure how to eek every bit of speed possible out of their machines and how to adjust the cars for maximum handling and safety. If you go on a weekday, crowds are usually small, and you can sit virtually anywhere you want to watch the action.

As the month progresses, attendance grows, especially on weekends. By Carburetion Day, there are a lot of people around. Traffic outside the Speedway slows to a crawl sometimes. And race day — well, suffice it to say that the Indianapolis 500 is reputed to be the largest one-day sporting event in the world, with a crowd estimated to be as large as 500,000 people (though, as we've said, the Speedway refuses to divulge actual attendance figures).

In brief, here's May at the track:

• Practice sessions: These begin on the first Saturday of the month and run daily through Carburetion Day.

• Qualifications: These timed lap sessions take place on the second and third weekends of the month.

• Carburetion Day: This is the Thursday preceding the race.

• Race Day: This is the Sunday of Memorial Day Weekend.

Tickets

Tickets for the 500 cost $15 for general admission to the track's infield or $18 to $100 (depending on location) for reserved seats. These prices are for tickets purchased through the Speedway box office, if you can get them.

The Indianapolis 500 sells out every year, seemingly within days. Here's how it works: As soon as one year's race ends, tickets for the next year's race go on sale. Mail-order ticket order forms are accepted at the Speedway box office the day after race day and within a couple of weeks all of the next year's tickets have been sold.

Does that mean you can't get tickets? Of course not. Ticket brokers always have Indianapolis 500 tickets available. Try contacting:

TicketMaster	239-5151
Circle City Tickets	841-8056
Court Side Tickets	254-9500
Front Row Tickets	255-3220
Preferred Tickets & Tours	636-0099
Tickets Galore	247-8497
Tickets on Wheels	579-6924
Tickets Together	322-0000
Tickets Up Front	633-6400, (800) 860-INDY

Of course, if you'd rather get your tickets for free, listen to your radio. It seems that every radio station in the area has a May promotion that involves giving away race tickets.

Or you can get a job. Many area businesses use race tickets as employee incentives to improve sales and service, or they raffle off tickets for charity or have an office pool with tickets as the prize.

In other words, even though the race is perennially sold out, it doesn't mean you can't get in. Where there's a will, there's probably a ticket.

Brickyard 400

Rumors about the Speedway hosting a second major racing event had circulated for several years before Tony George announced in 1993 that NASCAR would add a race to its Winston Cup stock car series — a 400-mile event to be held at the Speedway. Christened the Brickyard 400, the first running of the new race was held on August 6, 1994, before a sellout crowd of some 350,000 fans.

Indiana native and 22-year-old NASCAR circuit phenom Jeff Gordon roared around the Speedway to victory in the first Brickyard, earning more than $613,000 for his driving prowess. (The total purse for the race was $3.2 million.) In the process, Gordon became every aspiring young driver's hero and many a young female racing fan's fantasy. Handsome, friendly and tremendously talented, he was (and still is) a public relations gold mine for NASCAR.

For the 1995 Brickyard, Gordon was back, and he was the toast of the town. Posting the fastest qualifying time earned him the pole position for the race, but handling problems cost him the race, which was delayed for several hours due to torrential rains. NASCAR veteran Dale Earnhardt won with an average speed of 155.218 mph, earning more than $500,000 in cash and prizes. The total purse for the 1995 event was $4.5 million.

Racing Festivals

In Indianapolis, an auto race isn't necessarily a stand-alone event — at least two of the major races aren't. They come complete with festivals.

THE 500 FESTIVAL

201 S. Capitol Ave., Ste. 201   636-4556

From the first running of the Indianapolis 500 in 1911, community leaders started promoting the idea of a citywide celebration to mark the event. But it took 46 years before the first 500 Festival became a reality. Since then, it has become as much a part of May as the race itself.

In fact, the month-long 500 Festival *is* May in Indianapolis.

Among its many events are:

A giant Mickey Mouse is just one of many floats on hand for the 500 Festival Parade in May.

• **The Mini-Marathon**: The Festival literally hits the ground running with the annual mini-marathon on the first Friday in May. The 13.1-mile event attracts runners from around the world.

•**The Mayor's Breakfast**: This gathering of mayors from towns and cities statewide epitomizes the term "power breakfast." In addition to politicians, it attracts a variety of Indiana's movers and shakers as well as ordinary folks willing to ante up $35 for a ticket. This event culminates with each ticketholder getting the chance to drive his/her car around the Speedway's 2.5-mile track.

•**500 Festival Kids Day**: Held on Monument Circle, this is the city's largest outdoor festival for children. It regularly attracts more than 30,000 youngsters and their families to such activities as Big Wheel races, arts and crafts, sports clinics, science demonstrations and hands-on music-making.

•**The 500 Ball**: A black-tie gala held at the Indiana Convention Center on the Friday before the race, this event brings out 2,500 of the area's well-heeled. It also attracts many of the celebrities who are in town for the race.

•**The 500 Festival Parade**: Held the day before the race, this huge parade is the Festival's *piece de resistance*. It includes elaborate floats and marching bands, celebrities and all 33 of the race's drivers, clowns and giant helium balloons — all moving past several thousand spectators lining downtown streets. How big of a deal is the parade? If you want to sit in the bleachers that line the parade route, you'll need a ticket, which you can get for $10 from 500 Festival Inc. Call 636-4556 for information. Otherwise, bring a lawn chair or be prepared to stand for the duration (which thousands of parade-goers do). Well, not only is it telecast locally, but nationally on cable TV's Nashville Network.

THE 400 FESTIVAL

201 S. Capitol Ave., Ste. 201   237-3407

Not only did the Brickyard 400 make its debut in 1994, but its companion festival did too. At present, it's a much smaller affair than the 500 Festival: The 1995 400 Festival consisted of five events (not counting track activities).

• **Do Run Run**: Sponsored by WRTV 6, this fun run isn't nearly as serious as the 500 Festival's mini-marathon. Held on the Saturday prior to the Brickyard 400, Do Run Run events — 5K competitive walk, a 5K family fitness waldk and a 10K run — follow a ciruit from the IUPUI campus around the Indianapolis Zoo to Military Park.

• **Circle Fest**: A daylong downtown festival, Circle Fest brings thousands of people to the Circle for live music and food from noon to midnight on the Saturday before the race.

• **Welcome NASCAR Rally**: Held at Pan Am Plaza from noon to 5 PM on the Tuesday prior to the race, this event welcomes NASCAR competitors to town.

• **400 Festival Kids' Day**: Hosted by the Major Taylor Velodrome and the Lake Sullivan Sports Complex, this evetn for kids between ages 6 and 12 is on the Thursday before the race from 10 AM to 3 PM. It includes a foot race, sack races, dancing and games.

• **Miller Genuine Draft Race Fest**: Combining a huge picnic/barbecue with a rock concert, this evetn is held on the Thursday prior to the race from 3 PM to midnight at the Indiana State Fairgrounds.

August at the Speedway

Given the brief history of the Brickyard 400, August at the Speedway isn't nearly as crazy as May. And the practice and qualifying rounds for the 400 are much shorter than those for the 500. Practice for the Brickyard begins just three days prior to the race, with qualifying taking place on Thursday and Friday of that week. The race is on the first Saturday of the month.

The practice and qualifying sessions are open to the public. Track admission on those days is $5 for Wednesday, $10 for Thursday and Friday.

Tickets

Like the 500, the Brickyard 400 sells out, though not as fast. And good seats aren't as hard to come by as they are for the 500. Available by mail from the Indianapolis Motor Speedway box-office, tickets are priced at $15 for general admission to the track's infield and $18 to $100 for reserved seating.

If you can't get them from the Speedway, all the major ticket brokers noted for Indy tickets have them as well.

Motor Speedway Attractions

INDIANAPOLIS MOTOR
SPEEDWAY HALL OF FAME MUSEUM
4790 W. 16th St.   *484-6747*

On the grounds of the Motor Speedway, this facility contains cars and race memorabilia that span the history of the Indianapolis 500. Including the yellow Marmon Wasp that Ray Harroun drove to victory in the first 500-mile race in 1911, paintings, photos, programs, pit passes, engines, helmets and trophies—this is the sanctum sanctorum of the 500.

It's also a repository of products from the city's glory days as a center of automobile manufacturing. Former Indianapolis-made models such as Stutz, Cole, Marmon, National and Duesenberg are all represented in the museum's collection.

The Hall of Fame, which dates to 1952, was established to commemorate the achievements of drivers and auto makers alike who've influenced racing. From Eddie Rickenbacker and Louis Chevrolet to Tony Hulman and Mario Andretti, the Hall of Fame pays homage to the greats.

The Indianapolis Motor Speedway Hall of Fame Museum is open every day except Christmas from 9 AM to 5 PM. Admission is $2 per person; children younger than 16 get in free.

BRICKYARD CROSSING
4790 W. 16th St.   *(offices) 481-8500*
                            (tickets) 484-6700

An 18-hole championship-level golf course originally built in 1929 and redesigned by legendary course architect Pete Dye in 1991, Brickyard Crossing is inside (holes 7 through 10) and adjacent to the Speedway. This is home to the Senior PGA Tour's Brickyard Crossing Championship tournament (for more information, see our Sports and Parks and Recreation chapters).

TRACK TOUR
4790 W. 16th St.   *(offices) 481-8500*
                            (tickets) 484-6700

Whenever the track isn't in use, you can tour it aboard a minibus that takes you all around the world's most famous oval. Ask about tour availability at the Hall of Fame Museum.

Indianapolis Raceway Park

GETTING TO THE
INDIANAPOLIS RACEWAY PARK
10267 E. U.S. Hwy. 136   291-4090

Indianapolis Raceway Park is just west of Clermont on U.S. 136, about 7 miles northwest of the Indianapolis Motor Speedway and 15 miles northwest of downtown Indianapolis.

Indianapolis Raceway Park (a.k.a. IRP) has certainly earned its reputation as "America's Great Race Place." IRP's facilities include a 4,400-foot drag strip, a .686-mile oval, and a 2.5-mile road course (with 15 turns). All are asphalt-paved. From drag racing to sports cars, this multitrack venue west of the city is as much a part of auto racing history as the Indianapolis Motor Speedway.

The permanent home of the National Hot Rod Association's premier event, the U.S. Nationals, IRP also hosts the Kroger NASCAR 200, the Miller Genuine Draft "Night Before the 500" midget car races and Ford Formula 2000 races, the Sports

The Race Cars

The Speedway's two races utilize different types of cars. Those in the Indianapolis 500 are specially built Indy cars, low to the ground and very high-tech in terms of their mechanical and frame components. An Indy car is 78.5 inches wide, 195 inches long, 32 inches high and has a wheelbase of between 109 and 112 inches. It weighs 1,550 pounds and runs on methanol racing fuel.

The machines racing in the Brickyard 400 are stock cars, essentially modified (very modified) versions of street cars, such as the Chevy Monte Carlos, Ford Thunderbirds and Pontiac Grand Prixes.

They're 60 inches wide, 194 inches long, 51 inches high and have a wheelbase of 110 inches. A stock car weighs 3,400 pounds and runs on ordinary gasoline — some on leaded, others unleaded.

The one thing the two types of cars have in common in noise. They both make lots of it.

Photo: the Indianapolis Star & News

Visitors to the IMS Hall of Fame check out the race cars.

Car Club of America Nationals, the Corvette Nationals, and the MOPAR Nationals. It's also the site of such events as the American Motorcycle Association's ProStar championships, the Midwest Enduro go-cart championships and the annual Sunrayce solar-powered vehicle competition.

In addition to its on-site crowds, IRP has attracted a national following among racing enthusiasts who tune into ESPN's *Thunder Series* and the Total Sports Network to watch telecasts of the venue's events.

What's more, race driver training programs such as FAST Company Racing School (see the Racing Schools portion of this chapter) and the Skip Barber Racing School use IRP's road course for classes ranging from the introductory to the professional level.

In the late 1950s, Frank Dicke

dreamed of owning a half-mile-long asphalt oval racetrack. When he approached driver Rodger Ward and USAC officials Tom Binford and Charlie Brockman, they liked what Dicke — a well-dressed businessman with plenty of experience in promoting sprint, midget and stock car races at a dirt track in his home town of New Bremen, Ohio — outlined for them. They agreed to join forces and develop Dicke's track somewhere in the Central Indiana area.

That somewhere turned out to be near Clermont, about 15 miles northwest of downtown Indianapolis. Originally envisioned as a modest $75,000 project, the track's development budget grew as the partners dreamed up additions to Dicke's simple oval. A drag strip, for instance. And a road course. By 1960, it was clear that they had a $1 million-plus project on their hands.

To raise some of the needed finances, the partners sold 50,000 shares of stock at $10 each. Indianapolis Motor Speedway owner Tony Hulman was the largest shareholder, and he continued to buy new stock as it was issued or as other shareholders sold theirs.

IRP's drag strip started hosting meets in September 1960; the 273-acre facility's other tracks followed in 1961. As the project developed, it was obvious that IRP was going to be a major racing venue, and it received a major vote of confidence when National Hot Rod Association (NHRA) officials decided to hold the prestigious U.S. Nationals at IRP in September 1961.

That was also the year that IRP's road course was the site of a 200-mile sports car race that attracted such well-known drivers as Lloyd Ruby, Ken Miles and IRP partner (and road course designer) Rodger Ward. Another sports car event in 1961 included drivers Roger Penske and Jim Hall, both of whom are now owners of successful Indy car teams.

The same oval track, which had been increased in distance from Dicke's half-mile concept to five-eighths of a mile, hosted stock and sprint car events in which Indianapolis 500 drivers Parnelli Jones and A. J. Foyt took part. In retrospect, 1961 was an auspicious beginning for IRP.

In the years since, IRP has earned a reputation as one of the country's premier racing venues. During that time it has hosted such historically significant events as the Yankee 300 (later the Yankee 250) stock car race from 1963 to 1972; the first road course race ever sanctioned by USAC in 1965; and several American Motorcycle Association races in 1962 and in 1967 to '69. One event that got away at the last minute was the 1965 Formula One Grand Prix of the United States. Behind-the-scenes politics led the American Competition Committee of the United States to yank the Grand Prix away from IRP, leaving everyone involved to speculate "What if?'

Not that there was a lot to lament. So pleased was the NHRA and its drivers with IRP that the U.S. Nationals became a permanent fixture there. And in 1979, the NHRA bought IRP outright.

Since then, IRP has become one of the best-known racing venues in the United States.

The U.S. Nationals

With a handshake under a tree outside Detroit Dragway's pit area, IRP cofounder Tom Binford and NHRA president Wally Parks agreed in 1960 to develop a national championships drag racing event in Indianapolis. On that basis, Parks and other

Speedway Speak

You'll hear a lot of Speedway-related terms bandied about in Indianapolis. Here's a primer on a few:

- **The Brickyard**: That's the Speedway's nickname, derived from the early days when the track was actually made of paving bricks.
- **Gasoline Alley**: This is the garage area inside the Speedway. Visitors are free to wander through this area, peeking inside garages where mechanics and technicians fiddle with team cars. Asking for driver autographs is OK in Gasoline Alley; pestering busy drivers or race crews is not.
- **Yellow Shirts**: These are the Speedway's security volunteers. You'll see them everywhere throughout the facility; they provide directions and prevent access to restricted areas.
- **Pit Pass**: This is the much-coveted key to getting past a Yellow Shirt into the pit area alongside the track. With a pass, you're in; without one, you're rubbernecking to see what's going on in the pits.
- **Snake Pit**: Not to be confused with the racing teams' pit areas, this is a portion of the track's infield that once was the domain of bikers, drunks and pickup trucks with lawn chairs in their beds. It was here you'd hear guys calling out lewd requests to women to reveal their body parts as they walked by, and it was here where some of the women complied. It was Woodstock and Altamont, Steppenwolf and Hank Williams, Jr., beer bellies and big belt buckles. But now it's not.

Concerned about the infield's reputation as a rough and dangerous place, Speedway officials started policing the area more closely a few years ago. While there are still some rowdies around, it's a much tamer place than it used to be.

The garage area inside the Speedway is known as Gasoline Alley.

- **Qualifications**: These are the officially timed laps that racing teams use to get their cars entered into either the Indianapolis 500 or the Brickyard 400. For the 500, only 33 cars are allowed in the race; for the 400, the number is 41.

- **Pole Position**: At the start of the race, cars are lined up according to the qualifying times; the fastest qualifier is placed in the front row, closest to the infield. That's the pole position.

- **The Turns**: There are four turns on the Speedway's 2.5-mile oval, and track regulars have their favorites (and they'll gladly debate the merits of theirs and shortcomings of the others).

Turn One offers a view of the start/finish line and lets you gauge how smoothly (or badly) the race starts.

Turn Two provides a vantage point on the first long straightaway and lets you see the jockeying for position that often happens as drivers try to pull away for a run down that straightaway.

Turn Three allows you to see the cars coming off the straightaway and heading for the crucial fourth turn.

Turn Four is the point at which drivers try to reposition themselves for the second long straightaway, the one that leads to the finish line.

Of course, there are those fans who spurn the turns for the straightaways, especially for the impossible-to-get seats by the start/finish line.

Happy racing!

NHRA officials decided to hold the U.S. Nationals at IRP in 1961. Fan response was so great (in its short existence, IRP had never had such large crowds) that the U.S. Nationals have been a permanent fixture at IRP ever since.

The U.S. Nationals are the longest-running (six days), richest-paying (the 1995 purse was $2 million), most well-attended (more than 150,000 fans) event in drag racing history. More than 1,000 racing teams, including those of such superstars as "Big Daddy" Don Garlits, Indiana's own Bob Glidden, Don "Snake" Prudhomme and Ed "Ace" McCulloch make for exciting events.

The Nationals consist of a series of races, including elimination rounds, in four categories: Top Fuel Dragster, Pro Stock, Funny Car and Sportsman Class. Depending on the day, qualifications and competitions start as early as 8 AM and run into the evening.

General admission, one-day tickets for the U.S. Nationals range from $5 to $45 for adults and from $5 to $10 for children 6 to 15; children 5 and younger are admitted free. Advance tickets are $5 off. Six-day passes are $130 in advance, $168 at the gate. All advance tickets include pit passes. Tickets are available from IRP or through area TicketMaster locations.

For information on dates and times, contact Indianapolis Raceway Park.

Other Events at IRP

In addition to the U.S. Nationals, IRP hosts a variety of other racing events during its March-to-October season. What follows are highlights form the track's calendar.

Because dates and admission costs vary, contact the IRP's box office (293-RACE) for current schedules and ticket information.

THE KROGER NASCAR 200

Since its inaugural running in 1982, the Kroger NASCAR 200 has become the largest, most prestigious short track stock car race in the Midwest. Attracting more than 30,000 fans annually, this event is credited with proving the appeal of a NASCAR event in Central Indiana, paving the way for the creation of the Brickyard 400 at the Indianapolis Motor Speedway.

The Kroger NASCAR 200 attracts such well-known drivers

as Dale Earnhardt, Darrell Waltrip, Brett Bodine and Jeff Gordon. In fact, Gordon, a graduate of nearby Tri-West High School, learned many of his racing skills at IRP.

MILLER GENUINE DRAFT "NIGHT BEFORE THE 500"

As is evident from its title, this event is held the night before the Indianapolis 500. It includes a USAC-sanctioned midget car race, as well as a Formula Ford 2000 series race. Current NASCAR vunderkind Jeff Gordon won a "Night Before the 500" midget car event while still in high school.

CORVETTE NATIONALS

This annual May event pulls in Corvette owners and fans from around the country who come to IRP for a weekend-long car show and drag race competition. At this event you'll see everything from classic "Route 66"-era 'vettes to thunderous track-ready reminders that Corvettes really are high-performance machines designed for speed. It's a chance to see hundreds of examples of an American car that is poetry in motion and at ease.

SUPER CHEVY SHOW

For Chevy enthusiasts, this July event is heaven on earth.

It's an all-Chevrolet combination of a drag race, car show and swap meet. You can gate as souped-up Camaros roar off the line, gawk at lovingly restored Bel-Airs and Malibus and shop for a new hood ornament for your '65 Impala ragtop. If it's a Chevy, it's here — or at least someone who knows how to get it is.

MOPAR NATIONALS

Held each August, this is the largest Chrysler-only car show, drag race and swap meet in the nation. Like its Chevy counterpart, the MOPAR Nationals offer Chrysler, Dodge and Plymouth fans a chance to watch their favorites in action on the track and off as well as buy, sell and trade MOPAR parts and vehicles.

IRP Performance Park

In early 1995, IRP broke ground for the construction of the first building in its new Performance Park. The building will house a 14,000-square-foot garage complex. Individual garages in the complex will be leased to racing teams and other motorsports businesses such as IRP's official racing school Fast Company (see the "Racing Schools" section of this chapter).

In 1996, the second phase of Performance Park will open $1.5 million worth of new corporate suites. Spanning two hills between the oval track from the drag strip, the suites complex will allow visitors to see events on both courses. Individual suites are expected to sell for $7,500 to $22,500.

Indianapolis 500 Winners

Year	Driver	Year	Driver
1911	Ray Harroun	1956	Pat Flaherty
1912	Jay Dawson	1957	Sam Hanks
1913	Jules Gouz	1958	Jim Bryan
1914	Rene Thomas	1959	Rodger Ward
1915	Ralph DePalma	1960	Jim Rathman
1916	Dario Resta	1961	A.J. Foyt Jr.
1917-1918 War Years: No Race		1962	Rodger Ward
1919	Howard Wilcox	1963	Parnelli Jones
1920	Gaston Chevrolet	1964	A.J. Foyt Jr.
1921	Tommy Milton	1965	Jim Clark
1922	Jimmy Murphy	1966	Graham Hill
1923	Tommy Milton	1967	A.J. Foyt Jr.
1924	Joe Boyer and L.L. Coru	1968	Bobby Unser
1925	Peter DePaolo	1969	Mario Andretti
1926	Frank Lockhart	1970	Al Unser Sr.
1927	George Souders	1971	Al Unser Sr.
1928	Louis Meyers	1972	Mark Donohue
1929	Ray Keech	1973	Gordon Johncock
1930	Billy Arnold	1974	Johnnie Rutherford
1931	Louis Schneider	1975	Bobby Unser
1932	Fred Frame	1976	Johnny Rutherford
1933	Louis Meyer	1977	A.J. Foyt
1934	Bill Cummings	1978	Al Unser Sr.
1935	Kelly Petillo	1979	Rick Mears
1936	Louis Meyer	1980	Johnny Rutherford
1937	Wilbur Shaw	1981	Bobby Unser
1938	Floyd Roberts	1982	Gordon Johncock
1939	Wilbur Shaw	1983	Tom Sneva
1940	Wilbur Shaw	1984	Rick Mears
1941	Mauri Rose and Floyd Davis	1985	Danny Sullivan
1942-1945 War Years: No Race		1986	Bobby Rahal
1946	George Robson	1987	Al Unser Sr.
1947	Mauri Rose	1988	Rick Mears
1948	Mauri Rose	1989	Emerson Fittipaldi
1949	Bill Holland	1990	Arie Luyendyk
1950	Johnnie Parson	1991	Rick Mears
1951	Lee Lallard	1992	Al Unser Jr.
1952	Troy Ruttman	1993	Emerson Fittipaldi
1953	Bill Vukovich	1994	Al Unser Jr.
1954	Bill Vukovich	1995	Jacques Villeneuve
1955	Bob Sweikert		

Other Venues

INDIANAPOLIS SPEEDROME
802 S. Kitley Ave.   *353-8206*

From April to September, this place is the home of rough-and-tumble racing, the down-home home of stock car and Figure 8 races. On a banked, fifth-mile course, drivers jockey and bump, careen and clip, rocket and smash — in short, this is where race fans go to escape the glitz and glitter that, at the Speedway and IRP, sometimes interfere with the sheer pleasure of watching drivers match speed, guts and driving abilities. Over the years, such soon-to-be-stars as A.J. Foyt, Johnny Rutherford and Darrell Waltrip have honed their skills at the Speedrome. For most events, tickets are $8 to $10 for adults and $3 for children. Contact the Speedrome for a schedule and specific ticket information.

INDIANA STATE FAIRGROUNDS
1202 E. 38th St.   *927-7500*

The Fairgrounds contain a 1-mile dirt track that hosts a variety of auto and motorcycle races every year, including the Hulman Hundred, a 100-mile dirt car event held the Friday before the Indianapolis 500; and the Hoosier Hundred, another 100-miler on Labor Day weekend. This is where you can catch future Indy Car and NASCAR kings honing their skills.

PUTNAM PARK ROAD COURSE
470 E. Northfield Dr.
Brownsburg   *852-7007*

Built in 1991, Putnam Park was designed for club racing, testing and driver schools. The long course is 1.8 miles in length and includes 10 turns and a main straightaway that's 2,275 feet long. The short course in just over a half-mile long and includes four turns. Both courses are paved with a special asphalt mix that minimizes tire wear while maximizing tire adhesion.

Putnam Park hosts a variety of races sanctioned by the Sports Car Club of America, Enduro Kart (go-carts) and the Western-Eastern Roadracers Association (motorcycles). It's also used for time trials and driver training by Corvette, BMW, Ferrari, Miata and Porsche clubs, as well as by many car and tire manufacturers. Additionally, professional racing teams use Putnam Park to test their vehicles.

For a schedule of public events, contact Putnam Park.

Racing School and Organization

FAST COMPANY
15 B. W. Franklin St.
Greencastle   *653-2532*

For motorsports fans whose need for speed has them yearning to get behind the wheel, Fast Company offers the opportunity. As Central Indiana's only racing school and as the official racing school of Indianapolis Raceway Park, Fast Company provides hands-on driving instruction to aspiring race drivers and racing buffs who want to see what it's like to sit behind the wheel.

Using actual Sports Car Club of America Spec Racers, company instructors (all of whom have racing experience ranging from Karts to Formula One) put prospective drivers through an intensive three-day program at IRP (April-October) and at other tracks in warmer climates (January-March).

Founded by driving school veteran Hank Chapman in 1991, Fast Company

Speedway Airwaves

The Indianapolis Motor Speedway not only hosts two of the world's major auto races, it also broadcasts those races on its own radio and television outlets.

The Indianapolis Motor Speedway Radio Network consists of 600 stations in the United States and Canada, plus several hundred other stations worldwide that pick up the race broadcast via Armed Forces Radio.

WNDY (INDY-TV), Channel 23, is the Speedway's official television station. Due to that status, WNDY has unparalleled access to a variety of track events and personalities— and its track-related programming is beamed out to other stations and cable channels around the country, including ESPN.

has fast become a hot ticket among racing enthusiasts and corporations (several of which award Fast Company classes to top management and sales performers). What separates Fast Company training from that offered by national racing schools is its policy of allowing participants to pass one another on the track.

As this book went to press, Fast Company was preparing to move its operations from Greencastle to new quarters under construction at IRP in the fall of 1995.

UNITED STATES AUTO CLUB, INC. (USAC)

4910 W. 16th St.   *247-5151*

This is the nonprofit sanctioning organization that oversees and regulates more than 150 auto racing events every year, including the Indianapolis 500. In addition to its role as a regulatory body, USAC is also actively involved in safety issues. Over the years, it has been responsible for a number of improvements in the structure of racing cars, the construction of tracks and the development of protective apparel for drivers and pit crew members.

Photo: The Indianapolis Star & News

The city offers several challenging public golf courses.

Inside
Parks and Recreation

Part of what makes Indianapolis such a great place to live and raise a family are the top-notch recreational opportunities in and around central Indiana. With four distinct seasons and the facilities in which to enjoy them, Hoosiers spend a lot of time enjoying the outdoors. Of course, they also play a lot of sports, and that's covered here too, in the Recreation portion of this chapter. (For spectator sports see our Sports chapter.) In the Parks section, we've highlighted our favorite places to commune with nature.

We have great city parks here in Indianapolis, including one of the largest municipal parks in the country, that offer programs ranging from traditional tennis and swimming classes to such offbeat possibilities as moonlight hikes, community flea markets and out-of-town adventures. Programs are designed for all ages; you'll find classes for children as young as 2, summer camps for school-age kids, ecological and art-related courses for teenagers and special options for seniors and those with disabilities. Some of the most interesting activities are open to all ages,

and they're all surprisingly affordable. Pick up a free copy of the Indy Parks and Recreation *Fun Guide* at family centers or community buildings within parks; a new one comes out every few months for each new season with all the time, place and price details. Contact the parks department, 327-0000, or write 1426 W. 29th Street, 46208.

Indiana also boasts an excellent state park system, and many of the parks are within easy driving distance of Indianapolis. The state also manages forests, lakes and reservoirs, fish and wildlife areas and historic sites, all of which offer outstanding opportunities for exploring nature. The Department of Natural Resources publishes tons of brochures, guides and special updates about its many properties and programs. The annual *Indiana Recreation Guide* provides details about such options as camping, hunting and fishing at state facilities, and *Outdoor Indiana*, the DNR's bimonthly magazine, features beautiful wildlife photography and nature-related writing with a statewide focus. Contact the DNR, 232-4124 or (800)

Indy Parks and Recreation offers an array of fitness and recreation programs, and the classes aren't just for kids. Adults can sign up for such options as country line dancing, bonsai or even tie-dying — at very affordable prices. To get a seasonal *Fun Guide*, call 327-0000.

Insiders' Tips

622-4931 (in Indiana only) or write 402 W. Washington Street, Indianapolis 46204.

Parks

City Parks

You can find terrific parks all across the city, some that boast pools or aquatic centers, others that regularly draw players for pickup basketball games. Each neighborhood has its favorites, but here we've spotlighted some of the city's most popular. All parks are open from dawn to dusk, and only Eagle Creek charges admission; pools and aquatic centers within parks also have admission fees. The new aquatic centers feature such water park amenities as slides, sand play areas, diving boards and water playgrounds.

EAGLE CREEK PARK
7840 W. 56th St.   327-7110

The Lilly family (of Lilly pharmaceuticals) figures prominently in the history of Indianapolis, and it was J.K. Lilly who purchased this tract of land northwest of the city as a nature preserve. The 3,100 acres of park and 1,300 acres of water were given to Purdue University in the late 1950s, but the university, unable to maintain such a large hunk of land, sold it to the City of Indianapolis. For a $2 per car fee, $3 on weekends, Eagle Creek, one of the largest municipal parks in the country, provides a wide range of recreational options and is one of the nicest things about living in Indianapolis.

Open year-round from dawn to dusk, the park includes Eagle Creek Reservoir, and the marina offers sailing, canoe, kayak and rowboat rentals, plus sailing or sailboarding lessons. It's great fun to rent a Sunfish and sail around the reservoir; little kids enjoy rowing along the shore-

line with Mom and Dad. The parks department offers evening pontoon and canoe rides throughout the summer to explore wildlife along the water's edge. The park also includes a three-acre sandy beach (with lifeguards); a one-acre ecology pond; the five-acre Lilly Lake, where you can rent a paddle boat or enjoy bank fishing; and several skating ponds for wintertime fun.

Off the water, Eagle Creek Park boasts more than 10 miles of trails ranging from easy to moderate in difficulty. Paths wind through open meadows, past the reservoir and into mature woods full of beech, maple, tulip, white ash and black cherry. Visitors often see deer, especially in the early morning, but please don't feed them. You'll probably also spot Canada geese and wood ducks on the water, as well as plenty of smaller creatures such as rabbits and groundhogs.

The Nature Center Complex, which includes a 38-acre arboretum with self-guided trails, a nearly 600-year-old Douglas fir log, native wildflowers and specialty gardens offers an educational perspective on the park and its occupants.

Additional facilities include shelters and retreat houses, a world-class archery field, a shooting range and, whenever we have at least four inches of snow, cross-country skiing. Keep in mind that hunting, trapping, camping and ground fires are prohibited, as are snowmobiling and horseback riding.

HOLLIDAY PARK
6349 Spring Mill Rd.   327-7180

This park, incredibly popular among young families, features probably the best playground in the city. Its three main play areas (one for the littlest kids is enclosed) offer varying levels of climbing difficulty, with ladders, slides, tires and poles. The

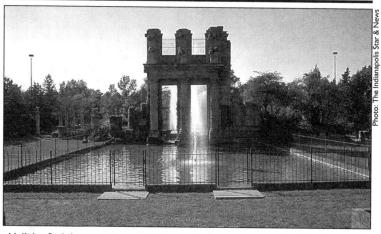

Photo: The Indianapolis Star & News

Holliday Park boasts "the ruins," statues that originally graced a New York City building and columns from a local convent.

tallest has twisty tube slides that kids can't get enough of. They're also fascinated by "that spider web thing" (see our Kidstuff chapter), a rope climbing contraption that just about defies description. The playground also includes the more traditional swings, plus ones that accommodates wheelchairs.

Holliday Park also features great trails, many recently improved, that lead down to White River, where kids can wade, fish and poke around along the riverbank. The parks department offers a summer hike series for all ages that explores the trees, flowers, geology and wildlife of Holliday Park, as well as a "parks after dark" program that features moonlight hikes, stargazing and a discussion of the nocturnal creatures that inhabit the park.

Though there has been talk of removing them, Holliday Park also boasts "the ruins," statues near the community center that originally graced a New York City building and columns from a local convent. The nearby wedding circle, a brick colonnade and walkway that leads up to a gazebo, offers an especially lovely spot

for an outdoor wedding, if you don't mind the occasional walker or jogger in the background.

ELLENBERGER PARK
5301 E. St. Clair St.   *327-7176*

Tucked in the middle of the historic Irvington neighborhood, Ellenberger Park offers that area's many young families plenty of recreation options. It's a beautiful park, with rolling terrain, a fitness trail, ball fields, a skating rink (ice skating in the fall and winter; roller and in-line skating in summer), playgrounds, a swimming pool, tennis and volleyball courts and lots of scenic picnic sites.

BROAD RIPPLE PARK
1450 Broad Ripple Ave.   *327-7161*

Also popular with young families, Broad Ripple Park features a conveniently sized play area (big enough to keep the kids occupied, yet small enough for Mom or Dad to monitor), a family center where lots of classes are held, a pool and — a real plus — a library branch. On weekday mornings you'll see lots of moms and kids head from the family center to the playground to the library.

The park also offers public boat launching into White River, bank fishing, plenty of shady picnic sites, open areas (nice for kite flying) and ball fields.

RIVERSIDE PARK

2420 E. Riverside Dr.   *327-7171*

After considerable renovation, Riverside Park reopened last year with a new aquatic center, a family center with weight equipment, a community room and banquet facilities. It also features softball and baseball diamonds where various leagues from around the city play, a basketball and tennis court and two playgrounds.

The park will also be included in the new Riverside Regional Park, a sports mecca that will stretch from Bush Stadium on 16th Street to the future Penrod Art Park at the Indianapolis Museum of Art on 38th Street and encompass the Kuntz Memorial Soccer Stadium, the Major Taylor Velodrome, three golf courses and the Wilbur Shaw Memorial Soap Box Derby Hill.

SOUTHEASTWAY PARK

5624 E. County Line Rd. S.   *861-5167*

Southeastway has been called one of the park system's best kept secrets, though it's sure to become more well-known as residents discover its fishing, hiking trails, picnic sites and, when there's at least four inches of snow, its cross-country skiing. A summer hike series that includes such programs as earth medicines, tree trivia and a "stream stomp" highlight Southeastway's natural attractions. Kids enjoy learning about creepy-crawlies during Bugfest and hiking by the light of a full moon during Moonlight Madness.

GARFIELD

2450 Shelby St.   *327-7220*

The city's oldest park, Garfield features a formal sunken gardens, a historic conservatory, an amphitheater, top-notch horseshoe pits, ball fields, tennis courts and a pool and family center. The gardens are being restored to their former grandeur, and the conservatory has been undergoing renovation and was scheduled to open in late 1995. A wonderful place to visit on a chilly winter day (see our Kidstuff chapter), the conservatory will reopen with a new look and an emphasis on the world's disappearing rainforests. But you can still count on such traditional favorites as the holiday poinsettia show and sale each December.

MAROTT PARK

7300 N. College Ave.

You won't find playgrounds, swimming pools or skating rinks at Marott Park. Even though it's one of the city largest, bigger than both Holliday and Broad Ripple parks, the emphasis here is on nature. Trails that wind through 70 acres of woods lead down to White River and offer a soothing antidote for city stress. Once you head into the woods or meadows, it's tough to remember you're still in the middle of the city, with Broad Ripple about 10 blocks south and Nora about 10 blocks north. Kids like the river access (see our Kidstuff chapter), where they can splash and explore along the bank. Throughout the summer, Marott's Saturday Morning Meanders guide visitors through the various habitats within the park, and the area offers good wildlife viewing year-round.

KRANNERT PARK

605 S. High School Rd.   *483-3250*

New amenities make Krannert even more popular with westsiders. It now features an aquatic center, a fishing pond that's a perfect place for kids to learn to wet a line, shaded picnic areas, a playground and ball fields. It also offers lots of neat classes that teach such skills as ancient methods of making fire with string, flint and steel (plan to get dirty at this one), earth and sky navigation and backyard horticulture.

LAKE SULLIVAN SPORTS COMPLEX
3601 Cold Springs Rd.   327-VELO
This sports complex includes the Major Taylor Velodrome, a BMX track, soccer fields, a sand volleyball court and, of course, Lake Sullivan, where bank fishing yields largemouth bass, bluegill, redear sunfish, green sunfish and channel catfish.

INDY ISLAND
8575 E. Raymond St.   862-6867
Billed as the state's only indoor water park, Indy Island is one of the most unique recreation options in town. Located at the new Warren Township Middle School, this water wonderland features a lap pool and therapy pool, plus such kid-pleasing attractions as the 150-foot water slide and water playground, geysers, a meandering "lazy" river, a vortex whirlpool and a water basketball/volleyball area. Local outdoor pools operate from around Memorial Day through Labor Day, but Indy Island offers plenty of wet fun year-round.

State Parks and Facilities

Indiana's state parks and recreational facilities offer plenty of outdoor options, and many are quite convenient to Indianapolis. In fact, White River State Park, still under development downtown, will eventually offer a wide range of activities. The Indianapolis Zoo is within the park boundaries, and there is much discussion as to what sort of additional development would be appropriate. In 1995, Gov. Evan Bayh signed into law the Legislature's plans for a new state park at Ft. Benjamin Harrison, a northeast-side military base slated for closing.

All state parks offer a variety of programs and service; nine employ full-time naturalists. Kids can earn Smokey's Friend patches, and older outdoor buffs can become Junior Naturalists and then participate in the Hoosier Ecologist program. The whole family can enjoy music, theater and dance performances scheduled at state parks throughout the summer.

Visitors to Indiana's parks and recreational areas should be especially vigilant about cleaning up after themselves. In 1994 the DNR initiated a carry-in/carry-out policy regarding trash. To avoid odors, scavenging animals and annoying bees that resulted from open trash barrels, state parks, reservoirs and recreation areas now require that visitors carry back out with them any trash they bring in. Gate attendants will provide the bags; tourists are responsible for the appropriate disposal of their own garbage. Note, however, that campgrounds still have trash receptacles for campers.

William Kuntz Memorial Soccer Stadium, 327-7194, which is operated by Indy Parks, has hosted a number of national and international soccer events. When not in use for competitions, it's available for league play.

Insiders' Tips

Getting Into the Great Outdoors

Plenty of other possibilities are available for the outdoor buff as well, from gardening to spelunking, and you can probably find a bunch of like-minded enthusiasts who have organized a group or club around your interest. Here are some popular nature-related organizations to help you find a little camaraderie. Peruse this list of local organizations and get personally involved with the great outdoors.

INDIANA WILDLIFE FEDERATION

950 Range Line Rd., Ste. A
Carmel 46032   571-1220

This is the parent organization for 47 conservation clubs and for individual members interested in environmental concerns. Primarily an education group, the federation's major project is the distribution of educational packets to elementary school teachers in all 92 Indiana counties. The organization is also involved in programs to create "backyard habitats" for wildlife. Individual membership is $20; members receive a magazine every other month as well as political updates on environmental issues.

NATURAL RESOURCES VOLUNTEERS

402 W. Washington St., Room W256
Indianapolis 46204   233-3854

This new group offers Hoosiers a way to conserve and protect the outdoors through volunteer efforts. Volunteers work at historic sites and the Indiana State Museum. They portray historical figures, protect our rivers as Hoosier Riverkeepers and donate their skills in all sorts of other ways. The DNR needs carpenters, typists, electricians, gardeners and other skilled volunteers to work in nature preserves, state parks, forests, historic sites and offices across the state.

THE NATURE CONSERVANCY,

Indiana Chapter
1330 W. 38th St.
Indianapolis 46208   923-7457

This is the local chapter of an international organization dedicated to protecting land, water and endangered species. Organization members work to acquire land to set aside as natural areas, and this chapter naturally focuses on preserving Indiana's wild places. An individual membership is $25; members receive a magazine every other month and a newsletter three times a year.

SIERRA CLUB, HOOSIER CHAPTER

6140 N. College Ave.
Indianapolis 46240   253-2687

Affiliated with the well-known national organization, this group works on environmental issues that have a local impact; members are concerned with development in Decatur Township and protecting the White River. The group often hosts guest speakers at its monthly meetings; a recent outing took members to Deam Lake State Recreational Area for a photography weekend. Individual dues are $35; members receive a bimonthly magazine and newsletter.

BROWN COUNTY STATE PARK

Ind. 46 between Columbus
and Nashville   *(812) 988-4418*

This is the place Indianapolis residents head when the leaves start to turn. In one of the state's most scenic counties, it draws tons of tourists year-round. Don't expect solitude; in the middle of summer and on autumn weekends lines just to get in the park can be frustratingly long, and rental cabins are often booked two years in advance.

Still, you can't beat the amenities. Only an hour or so away from Indianapolis (via I-65 south to Ind. 46 W.), it's the state's biggest park with rolling terrain, plenty of picnic spots and scenic overlooks for picture-taking, a pool, well-maintained camping facilities and lots of wildlife. In fact, managing the ever-increasing deer population has become troublesome in recent years. Tourists who toss treats out of car windows contribute to the problem, so snap all the pictures you want, but don't feed the animals.

The park offers an abundance of hiking trails, several types of camping facilities, fishing lakes and a horsemen's campground, but no hunting. The park's Abe Martin Lodge offers pleasant accommodations for those who prefer comfort over camping.

Nashville, with its many artists and artisans, is nearby, and the town offers an abundance of top-notch arts and crafts (in addition to the standard touristy merchandise). The village itself draws thousands of tourists, so traffic into the town is quite heavy on summer and fall weekends and again during the holidays. Go midweek to avoid the crowds.

YELLOWWOOD STATE FOREST

722 S. Yellowwood Rd.
Nashville   *(812) 988-7945*

For a bit more nature and somewhat smaller crowds, try Yellowwood State Forest, a beautiful area known for its fishing and boating. Not far from Brown County State Park, Yellowwood offers fewer amenities than the popular park, but you can get a little closer to nature. The forest offers camping and hiking, but it also allows hunting, so hikers must remain alert and stay within the appropriate areas.

T.C. STEEL HISTORIC SITE

4220 S. T.C. Steele Rd.
Nashville   *(812) 988-2785*

Close to both Brown County State Park and Yellowwood, this historic site includes the home, gardens and studio of Hoosier impressionist artist T.C. Steele, who helped establish Nashville as an artists' colony. The somewhat remote setting is beautiful in the fall, but in the spring, the rolling terrain blooms with hundreds of daffodils.

McCORMICK'S CREEK STATE PARK

Rt. 5, Box 282
Spencer   *(812) 829-2235*

Some would say Owen County is even more scenic than Brown County. It's certainly less traveled and less commercial. For those who don't mind driving a bit farther, McCormick's Creek State Park, about 14 miles northwest of Bloomington, offers an alternative to Brown County.

Indiana's first state park, McCormick's Creek boasts thickly wooded areas, unique limestone formations, a waterfall and even caves. It's great for hiking and offers a variety of camping facilities. The housekeeping cabins are quite popular, though, and are often booked a year in advance. The park's Canyon Inn offers comfortable accommodations and a great breakfast buffet.

TURKEY RUN STATE PARK
Rt. 1, Box 164, Marshall, 47859   597-2635

This park, situated west of Indianapolis, offers lots of recreation possibilities. Rent a bike or a horse, hike the deep sandstone ravines, splash along Sugar Creek, camp or take it easy in the Turkey Run Inn (which boasts an indoor pool).

It's also fun to rent a canoe from one of the roadside liveries and paddle through the park and beneath covered bridges on Sugar Creek. Most canoe rentals will drop you off, pick you up downstream and take you back to your car.

SHADES STATE PARK
Rt. 1, Box 72
Waveland, 47989   (812) 665-2158

This is the place to go for a little peace and quiet. Fewer amenities means fewer crowds, and sometimes that can be a big plus. Still, there's camping, hiking, reservable shelters and, oddly enough, an airstrip, where you can lean against a tree and watch a few small planes land or take off. At Shades State Park, about 17 miles southwest of Crawfordsville off Ind. 47, you can hike through some spectacular

scenery; its deep ravines were once known as "the shades of death." Hence, the name. Sugar Creek also runs through this park, and the views from a canoe can be even better than from the trails.

Nearby Pine Hills Nature Preserve offers even more scenery and even fewer crowds but fairly strenuous hiking.

MOUNDS STATE PARK
4306 Mounds Rd.
Anderson   642-6627

Just off I-69 in Madison County (less than an hour northeast of Indianapolis), Mounds State Park offers a small campground, trails, picnic sites and a swimming pool. But the main attractions are the curious earthworks, built by prehistoric Indians around 160 B.C. Archeologists believe they were used for religious ceremonies. Also of interest is the nature center, located in the Bronnenberg House, one of the oldest homes in Madison County.

MORGAN-MONROE STATE FOREST
6220 Forest Rd.
Martinsville   342-4026

About 45 minutes south of Indianapolis on Ind. 37 lies Morgan-Monroe State Forest, which has been called the gateway to southern Indiana's rolling, wooded terrain. It's certainly beautiful and includes more than 23,000 acres of virtually unspoiled forest. It offers a small campground, hiking trails, fishing and hunting. It also offers the reservable Draper's Cabin, a no-frills log cabin where you'll have a roof over your head but little else; you gather your own firewood, build your fire and carry in bedding and provisions.

Hunting is allowed in Morgan-Monroe, so hikers are advised to wear bright colors and stay within designated areas.

Photo: The Indianapolis Star & News

McCormick's Creek State Park in Owen County offers gorgeous fall colors.

LAKE MONROE
4850 Ind. 446 S.
Bloomington   *(812) 837-9546*

The water is the draw here, and Lake Monroe, not far from Bloomington and Indiana University, offers plenty of it. Its 10,750 acres offer waterskiing, beaches and fishing, while the recreational area boasts hiking trails, a nature center, picnic areas and more than 300 campsites.

BROOKVILLE LAKE
P.O. Box 100, Brookville, 47012   647-2657

Very popular among the RV crowd, Brookville Lake offers loads of amenities, including a 5,260-acre lake with two beaches and room for waterskiing, as well as more than 400 campsites. Located southeast of Indianapolis, Brookville also has hiking trails, plenty of picnic sites and shelterhouses. Naturally, the lake provides excellent fishing, and hunting is allowed as well.

WHITEWATER CANAL HISTORIC SITES
P.O. Box 88, Metamora 47030   647-6512

Not far from Brookville is the historic village of Metamora, with its Whitewater Canal and the Metamora Grist Mill. You can ride a horse-drawn boat on the canal, browse through the village's 120 antique and craft shops or hike or bike along the Whitewater Canal Trail.

Camping

Many state properties, including parks, forests and fish and wildlife areas, offer a variety of camping, ranging from primitive to electric; a few offer ultra-primitive backcountry camping (you hike in and hike out). Prices in 1995 ranged from $2.50 per night for bare-bones campsites in the winter to $13 for Class AA spots at some reservoirs. Most state parks will take reservations, usually beginning in March, for your favorite campsite; though you can call to check on availability, all reservations must be made by mail directly to the camp-ground. The DNR's free *Indiana Recreation Guide* (see chapter introduction) spells out all the details.

Another helpful publication, *The Hoosier Camper Guide*, available free from the Recreational Vehicle Council, 247-6258, lists Indiana's privately owned camp-grounds.

Recreational Activities

Are you ready to come out and play? Whether you're interested in fitness or just in fun, you'll find that Indianapolis has a lot to offer.

Enjoy yourself.

General Information

Several local organizations offer a variety of fitness and recreation programs. Among them are:

INDY PARKS AND RECREATION
1502 W. 16th St.   327-7200

Indy Parks operates an array of pro-grams for adults and children at parks, community centers and schools through-out the city. Call and ask for a copy of the most recent *Fun Guide*, a publication that lists what's going on, where and when. Then it's a matter of making some choices — from archery to wrestling, there's some-thing for everyone.

INDIANAPOLIS SPORTS CLUB
Municipal Gardens
1831 Lafayette Rd.   636-1626

Run by Indy Parks, this club provides developmentally disabled teens and adults (16 years an older) opportunities to take part in a variety of sports and recreational activities.

JEWISH COMMUNITY CENTER
6701 Hoover Rd.   251-9467

With the opening of its new indoor pool and state-of-the-art fitness center in the spring of 1996, the JCC will have one of the best fitness and recreational facilities in the city. An indoor tennis center is also un-der construction. All this in addition to cur-rent offerings— an outdoor pool, tennis courts and playing fields, as well as a roster of fitness and recreation activities. You need not be Jewish to become a member of the JCC and take advantage of its programs.

YMCA MAIN OFFICE
615 N. Alabama St.   266-YMCA

There are 11 YMCA facilities in the greater Indianapolis region. Each one of-fers various programs for children and adults. Contact individual Y's for details:

Baxter Branch YMCA (south), 7900 S. Shelby Street, 881-9347

Fall Creek Parkway Branch YMCA (central), 860 W. 10th Street, 634-2478

Intercollegiate Branch YMCA, But-ler University, 4600 Sunset Avenue, 283-9542

Arthur Jordan Branch YMCA (north), 8400 Westfield Boulevard, 253-3206

Ransberg Branch YMCA (east), 501 N. Shortridge Road, 357-8441

West District Branch YMCA (west), 7412 B Rockville Road, 271-5305, and in Lebanon, 482-0481

YMCA at the Athenaeum (down-town), 401 E. Michigan Street, 685-9705

Hamilton County Branch YMCA, 942 N. 10th Street, Noblesville, 776-3440

Barbara B. Jordan Branch YMCA, 2039 E. Morgan Street, Martinsville, 342-6688

Ruth Lilly YMCA Outdoor Center, RR 1, St. Paul, 525-6730

YWCA
4460 Guion Rd.   299-2750

Some of the activities at this northwest-side facility are for girls and/or women only, others are for families. Individual and family memberships are available.

In addition to these organizations, churches and community centers throughout the city operate a variety of fitness and recreational programs for adults and/or youth. Among them are:

BOYS & GIRLS CLUBS OF INDIANAPOLIS
5532 W. Raymond St.   241-1712

This organization operates six area clubs for young people, offering a variety of sports and fitness activities such as basketball, volleyball, swimming, soccer, martial arts, etc. Contact the club nearest you for details:

Atkins Unit, 3131 W. 16th Street, 632-5766

Concord Village Unit, 3125 Concord Court, 635-1214

Gorman Unit, 1400 English Avenue, 632-2010

Keenan-Stahl Southside Unit, 1949 E. Troy Avenue, 784-4561

LeGore Unit, 5532 W. Raymond Street, 241-0557

Wheeler Unit, 2310 E. 30th Street, 926-4222

Archery

EAGLE CREEK PARK
7840 W. 56th St.   327-7110

Eagle Creek Park boasts a world-class archery field; archery competition during the 1987 Pan Am Games was held here. The field now is primarily used for classes and competition.

FALL CREEK BAIT AND TACKLE
4215 E. Fall Creek Pkwy. N. Dr.   251-9229

Don't be mislead by the store's name; this shop also caries a complete line of arrows. It also handles repairs and boasts an indoor archery range. Call for information on target and bow hunter leagues.

J & J ARCHERY
3438 Madison Ave.   784-3632

J & J provides archery sales and service, arrow fletching and repair and a large indoor range. The staff can also set you up with an archery league.

VAN'S ARCHERY SHOP
5526 W. Stones Crossing Rd.
Greenwood   422-9315

Here you'll find the state's largest selection of bows and accessories in addition to 22 indoor shooting ranges. You can also sign up for lessons or get involved in an archery league.

Ballroom Dancing

HEARTLAND BALLROOM DANCERS
722 N. Howard Rd.
Greenwood   271-9319

This organization, a chapter of the United States Amateur Ballroom Dancers Association, hosts monthly dances, offers workshops, forms dance teams and pro-

---

McCormick's Creek State Park, southwest of Indianapolis in Owen County, offers the same gorgeous fall colors as Brown County State Park but with fewer crowds. If you do head for popular Brown County in autumn, go mid-week and avoid some traffic.

Insiders' Tips

motes ballroom dancing at local festivals. It also sponsors an outreach program for youngsters, seniors and physically challenged individuals.

Birdwatching

AUDUBON SOCIETY, AMOS W. BUTLER CHAPTER
3650 Cold Spring Rd.   *926-9456*

Contact this group for information on a variety of nature-related activities in addition to birdwatching.

INDY PARKS AND RECREATION
1426 W. 29th St.   *327-0000*

The parks department regularly schedules Saturday or Sunday morning bird hikes, often with members of the Amos Butler Audubon Society. Beginners can learn about the calls and habitats of resident and migratory birds; experienced birders can hone their skills.

Baseball and Softball

If "Take Me Out to the Ball Game" makes you yearn not for peanuts and Crackerjack, but for the thrill of snagging a grounder or hefting a bat in your hand, then here are a few options.

Softball

INDY PARKS AND RECREATION SOFTBALL OFFICE
1426 W. 29th St.   *327-7202*

Indy Parks operates a variety of softball leagues including recreational and competitive divisions for men, women and coed play. These leagues compete at three sites, all of which are also available for rental, other softball games or tournaments:

Bluff Park, 555 W. Hanna Avenue

Chuck Klein Softball Complex, 4702 Rockville Road

Riverside Park, 2420 N. Riverside E. Drive

Other sites around the city also offer softball league play and facility rentals. These include:

Indianapolis Sports Park, 6701 S. Harding Street, 784-7447

Midwest Softball, 7509 New Augusta Road, 875-8833

Mongans Sports Club, 1188 Moon Road, 839-6220

Stony Creek Softball Park, 1405 S. Post Road, 899-4733

Youth Baseball and Softball

For young people, male and female, there are a number of baseball and/or softball options:

Franklin Township Girls Softball, 4151 S. Bazil Avenue, 862-6741

Franklin Township Rookie League, 6620 Shelbyville Road, 782-3161

Indianapolis Police Athletic League, 50 N. Alabama Street, 236-3321

Little League Baseball Central Regional Headquarters, 9802 Little League Drive, 897-6127

With 16 area leagues, each with some 400 players, Little League baseball is a going enterprise in the Greater Indianapolis area. For general information, contact regional headquarters, which can put you in touch with the league nearest you. Some of the leagues in the metro area are:

Beech Grove Little League, 724 S. Ninth Avenue, Beech Grove 784-1348

Bell-East Little League, 3340 N. German Church Road, 894-0505

Carnine Little League, 1001 S. Belmont Street, 685-9411

Indiana Central Little League, 4910 S. Keystone Avenue, 783-1066

Irvington Little League, 6945 E. Raymond Street, 357-0620

Lowell Little League, 5600 E. Terrace Avenue, 359-3979

Southport Little League, 350 Anniston Drive, Southport 784-0716

Warren Little League, 11850 Brookville Road, 862-4899

Westlane Delaware Trail Little League, 1301 W. 73rd Street, 253-9933

ROUNDTRIPPER BASEBALL ACADEMY
138 W. Carmel Dr., Carmel   767-3013

For youngsters (and parents) who take baseball seriously and want to improve existing skills and develop new ones, Roundtripper may be the answer. Classes are offered for Pee Wees (6- to 8-year-olds) through teens in hitting, fielding, pitching, softball and conditioning.

Basketball

You're smack dab in the middle of hoops country, so you know there have to be plenty of places to play (besides your driveway). And there are. Try these:

Leagues

INDY PARKS AND RECREATION
1502 W. 16th St.   327-7200

Indy Parks operates a number of leagues and programs at a number of sites around town, including:

Men's "C" Basketball League: For less competitive players, 18 years old and older, who want to play for fun and exercise.

Men's 35 & Over Basketball League: The name says it all.

Men's Open Basketball League: For competitive players, 18 and older.

Men's College Basketball League: For high-energy, college-age players.

Women's Open Basketball League: For female competitive players, 18 and older.

Over 25 Half-Court Basketball: For those players who regard full-court basketball as cruel and unusual punishment.

Parent/Child Basketball: For parents and kids who want to play together for the fun of it.

Indiana Pacers Drug Free Basketball League: For youngsters 9 to 17 who want the opportunity not only to play basketball, but also to learn teamwork, cooperation and discipline in a setting that emphasizes equal play for everyone and the importance of staying drug free.

LIGHTED OUTDOOR COURTS

In addition to the preceding offerings, the parks department maintains outdoor basketball courts at 40 parks throughout the area, including lighted courts at these locations:

Belmont Park, 1300 N. Belmont Street

Bethel Park, 2945 E. Minnesota Street

Bertha Ross Park, 3700 N. Clinton Street

Pride Park, 1129 S. Vandeman Street

Watkins Park, 2360 Dr. Martin Luther King Jr. Street

JEWISH COMMUNITY CENTER
6701 Hoover Rd.   251-9467

Basketball is one of a variety of sports and fitness activities at this northwest-side complex for adults and kids.

YMCA MAIN OFFICE
615 N. Alabama St.   266-YMCA

Most of the area Y's offer a variety of basketball programs for adults and children ranging from leagues to open court time. Contact the main office above or the Y nearest you (see list in the "Organizations" portion of this chapter) for details.

COMMUNITY LEAGUES

Many area churches, schools and community centers host evening and weekend basketball leagues or programs. Contact the ones in your neighborhood for information.

Bicycling

Bicycling is a booming pastime in Central Indiana, both from a fitness and a recreational standpoint. If you're serious about cycling, or want to make contact with people who are, there are three organizations you need to know about:

INDIANA BICYCLE COALITION (IBC)
P.O. Box 20243, 46220   (800) BIKE-110

This bicycle advocacy organization acts as the hub for more than 20 cycling groups statewide, representing their concerns on issues that have an impact on cyclists. IBC also serves as a resource for cyclists, state and local government officials and members of the media in need of accurate information on bicycling in Indiana. IBC is also developing a series of maps designed specifically for cyclists, indicating safe routes throughout the state.

CENTRAL INDIANA BICYCLING ASSOCIATION (CIBA)
P.O. Box 55405, 46205   255-0559, 251-2422

With more than 1,500 members, CIBA is one of the largest bicycling organizations in the country. Members can take part in a variety of types of rides throughout the year, including the rigorous Hilly Hundred— a two-day, 100-mile ride held each October in the hills of south central Indiana. (See separate entry in the "Bicycle Tours" section of this chapter.)

TRAIL
P.O. Box 441854   783-2430

Founded in 1994, this organization represents mountain bikers' interests, especially in regards to gaining access to public lands (state park and state forest trails) for off-road riding. TRAIL also promotes off-road safety and courtesy and provides members with information on accessible trails throughout the Midwest. There is cross-membership between CIBA and TRAIL, and both are member organizations of IBC.

Where to Ride

While Indianapolis is noticeably deficient in bike paths, there are designated bike routes throughout the area. Look for roads and streets with bike route markers (signs bearing the symbol of a bicycle) alongside them. These routes tend to be less busy and more scenic than main arteries.

To help riders sort out where they should or should not ride, the Mayor's Bicycle Task Force developed a map indicating safe and unsafe routes. You can get one for free by joining the Central Indiana Bicycling Association (see entry above), or buy one for $2 from the Indiana Department of Natural Resources (DNR), 402 W. Washington Street, 232-4180. Some area bike shops stock them as well.

Other options include:

CENTRAL CANAL TOW PATH

One of the most popular trails in the city is the Central Canal tow path. The path, which runs south from Broad Ripple

Photo: The Indianapolis Star & News

The Major Taylor Velodrome hosts world-class cycling events.

and passes through residential and non-residential areas, attracts runners, walkers and bicyclists alike. Tree-lined and well-maintained, the path is a lovely alternative to busy streets. If you follow the path all the way from Broad Ripple to 30th Street, which is the most scenic portion of the path, it's about 3.5 miles.

PARK ROUTES

A number of Indianapolis parks contain bike trails and/or bike routes. These include:

Brookside Park, 3500 Brookside Parkway S. Drive, 327-7179

Douglass Park, 1425 E. 25th Street, 327-7174

Eagle Creek Park, 7840 W. 56th Street, 327-7148

Ellenberger Park, 5301 E. St. Clair Street, 327-7176

Riverside Park, 2420 E. Riverside Drive, 327-7171

TRACK RIDING

If you're looking for a safe auto-free, dog-free, pothole-free place to ride, try:

MAJOR TAYLOR VELODROME AND LAKE SULLIVAN BMX TRACK
3649 Cold Spring Rd.   *327-VELO*

Named in honor of Marshall "Major" Taylor, an Indianapolis cyclist who became the first black American to win a world championship (in 1899, he won two world bicycle racing titles), the Velodrome not only hosts world-class cycling events, it also encourages public use of the facility when no events are scheduled. Open riding — group or individual — is Monday through Friday from 10 AM to 5 PM.

Bicycle Tours

HILLY HUNDRED
Central Indiana Bicycling
Association   *251-2422*
P.O. Box 55405, 46205   *255-0559*

Generally held in early to mid-October, this annual two-day event covers a 100-mile route through the hills of south central Indiana. Not for the faint-of-heart or the out-of-shape — 50 miles a day over this undulating terrain takes its toll. Due to the Hilly Hundred's popularity, CIBA now limits participation to the first 5,000 registrants. For information, contact CIBA.

TRAILS UNLIMITED
RR 4, Box 318
Nashville 47448   (812) 988-6232

If the idea of riding through some of the wild backcountry of Brown County appeals to you, Trails Unlimited offers a 15-mile mountain bike excursion that *Bicycling Magazine* called a "high adrenaline" event. Reservations are required — rides take place on Saturday or Sunday morning.

HOOSIER BIKEWAY SYSTEM
Department of Natural Resources
402 W. Washington St.   232-4180

The 800-mile-long Hoosier Bikeway System is a series of 11 routes throughout the state that are considered safe for cyclists. The DNR sells guidebooks of the routes for $1 each.

Boating

Just because Indianapolis is situated smack in the middle of farming country, without even a navigable river, doesn't mean we don't have a lot of boating aficionados; you'll see plenty of those "I'd Rather Be Sailing" bumper stickers. And those who want to really get their feet wet will find plenty of opportunities.

EAGLE CREEK PARK MARINA
7840 W. 56th St.   327-7130

Here you can sign up for sailing or sailboarding lessons or rent a rowboat, canoe, kayak, catamaran, sailboat or pontoon.

GEIST MARINA
11695 E. Fall Creek Rd.   849-8455

Call the marina at popular Geist Reservoir for information on slip rentals or details on area fishing.

MORSE LAKE MARINA
2099 Hague Rd.
Noblesville   984-3301

Morse is just about as popular as Geist, so the water here can get crowded. Call for details on boating and fishing.

Bowling

If bowling brings to mind visions of TV's Al Bundy (or, for another generation, Archie Bunker), then you haven't kept up with this rapidly growing pastime. Around here, this family-oriented activity has become quite popular. Local leagues exist for kids, couples, singles — you name it. Several organizations can provide you with detailed information on leagues and competitive play: Central Indiana Tournament Bowlers Association, 784-3753; Greater Indianapolis Bowling Association, 578-1000; Indiana Youth Bowling Association, 357-2695; and Indianapolis Women's Bowling Association, 353-9422. Also, check out one of the many bowling alleys around town. Here are a few to get you started.

ACTION BOWL DUCKPIN BOWLING
325 S. College Ave.   632-2879
1105 S. Prospect Ave.   686-6006

Duckpins are shorter and squattier and the bowling balls smaller (making duckpin bowling easier for kids and novices), but the point is the same: Set 'em up and knock 'em down.

ALL STAR BOWL
726 N Shortridge Rd.   352-1848

Here you'll find 48 lanes, a new "accuscorer," a pro shop that offers videotaping, a lounge, a snack bar and bumper bowling.

EAGLE BOWL CENTRE

2802 Lafayette Rd.   926-2333

Billing itself as "a new adventure in bowling," this facility offers 36 lanes, league play, open bowling and lessons. You can also take advantage of the restaurant, arcade, billiards and lounge.

NORA BOWL

1300 E. 86th St.   846-2516

This bowling alley offers 36 lanes, automatic score keeping, a lounge and loads of free parking. Occasionally it runs reduced price specials.

NORTH EASTWOOD BOWL

8939 E. 38th St.   898-4333

You can sign up for league play, enjoy open bowling or take lessons at this facility. It also offers a pro shop, arcade, lounge and the popular bumper bowling.

SPORT BOWL

3900 S. U.S. 31   788-0878

You can reserve one of the 32 lanes for open bowling or sign up for lessons or league play. You'll also find a lounge, snack bar, arcade and pro shop.

WOODLAND BOWL

3421 E. 96th St.   844-4099

A big draw here is the smoke-free environment. You'll also find 80 lanes, a variety of leagues and bumper bowling.

Fencing

So you've always wanted to learn the fine art of swordsmanship (or you just want to put your rapier wit to good use)? Check out:

INDIANAPOLIS FENCING CLUB

401 E. Michigan St.   635-7477

Based downtown in the Athenaeum, this organization is an affiliate of the U.S.

Fencing Association. It offers classes for beginners (9 years old to adult) and participates in national competitions.

Fitness Training

Both Indy Parks and area YMCAs offer an array of fitness activities ranging from aerobics to weight training. For information, contact Indy Parks or the Y nearest you (see entries in the "Organizations" section of this chapter).

Other options include:

NATIONAL INSTITUTE FOR FITNESS AND SPORT

250 N. University Blvd.   274-3432

This is a state-of-the-art fitness research, education and training facility. Open to professional and amateur athletes, as well as the general public, the institute contains a 200-meter indoor track, a regulation-size basketball court, a rubberized workout floor and weight- and cardiovascular-training equipment.

Memberships here are not cheap (students pay a one-time intitiation fee of $75 plus $35 per month; others pay the initiation fee plus $500 per year or $140 per quarter), but they offer the added value of fitness testing done by well-trained staff members who also help tailor individual workout programs. This is the fitness facility of choice for a variety of area businesses, police and fire departments and serious athletes.

BALLY'S SCANDINAVIAN

5435 Pike Plaza Rd.   293-9436
517 U.S. Route 31 N.   885-0242
8831 Commerce Crossing   844-1515

Calling itself "America's Health Club" (there are 340 clubs nationwide), Bally's three Indianapolis-area sites offer aerobics classes, StairMasters, free weights and weight machines, racquetball courts, indoor

The Eagle Creek Regatta Course is the only rowing course sanctioned for international competition.

pools, indoor tracks and the much-Ballyhooed (via TV commercials) 30-minute workout program.

FAMILY FITNESS CENTERS

7126 N. Keystone Ave.	255-9751
6407 E. Washington St.	359-6938
7325 W. 10th St.	271-9544

At the three Family Fitness sites you'll find Cybex circuit training equipment, Hammer Strength equipment and free weights as well as recumbent cycles, treadmills and step aerobics classes. There's a private workout area for women and personalized instruction and nutritional guidance for all members. It's open seven days a week.

GOLD'S GYM

8736 E. 21st St.	897-7556
4041 Office Plaza Blvd.	297-5238
8481 Bash St.	598-9399

From aerobics to body-sculpting, each Gold's Gym site has the equipment and the staff to help you tone down or bulk up. At Gold's, you'll find an array of free weights and weight machines, stair climbers and treadmills, aerobics classes and trained personnel who can help make best use of them.

GREENBRIAR ATHLETIC CLUB

1275 W. 86th St.	257-3261

With 12 racquetball and handball courts, along with aerobics classes, StairMasters and Life Cycles, Greenbriar aims to get your heart pumping. And for your muscles there are free weights and Nautilus machines available, as well a staff trainer to help you make best use of them.

LIVRITE FITNESS CENTRE

51 N. Illinois St.	464-2010
6220 N. Butler Ave.	257-1004

Each of the Livrite locations has an indoor pool and track, plus treadmills, StairMasters, rowing machines and exercise bikes. There are also tons (literally) of free weights, as well as Nautilus machines, aerobics and aquacize classes, and racquetball and basketball courts. An exercise physiologist is available at each site to help you develop a personalized training program, and there's a massage therapist to help you work out the after effects of working out.

RACQUETS FOUR SPORTS CENTRE
4002 Southport Rd. 783-5411

From water aerobics to indoor tennis, swimming to basketball, racquetball to aerobics, Racquets Four offers plenty of ways to get fit. There's also an indoor track— and (for those who overdo it) whirlpools, a sauna and an on-site massage therapist.

ZIKE'S FITNESS & AEROBIC CO.
6450 W. 10th St. 248-2326

Consistently rated on of the city's best health clubs by the readers of *Indianapolis Monthly* magazine, Zike's specializes in programs for people who are new to fitness training. On the club's roster are fat-burning classes, aerobics classes, StairMasters, Nautilus and other weight equipment and a world-class body building program.

FITNESS TRAILS
Usually a half-mile to 1 mile in length, these trails include fitness stations that offer runners or walkers a chance to perform stretches and strength-enhancing exercises designed to increase personal fitness levels. You'll find trails at:

Broad Ripple Park, 1450 Broad Ripple Avenue

Christian Park, 4125 English Avenue

Garfield Park, 2450 Shelby Street

Municipal Gardens, 1831 Lafayette Road

Sahm Park, 6800 E. 91st Street

Football
If your idea of a great afternoon of football includes actually laying your hands on a ball and running like mad for the end zone, then check into the football programs offered by:

INDY PARKS AND RECREATION
1502 W. 16th St. 327-7200

Men-only and coed teams play in Indy Parks' flag football program. Additionally, the parks department can probably hook you up with some of the football teams and leagues that use park facilities for their games.

INDIANAPOLIS SPORTS PARK
6701 S. Harding St. 784-7447

This multi-sports complex on the south side of town is used by a number of teams.

Go-carts and Minigolf
Load up the family or grab a date and head to one of these recreation centers for some good clean fun.

GREATIMES
5341 Elmwood Ave. 780-0300

You can enjoy 36 holes of miniature golf plus go-carts and arcade games at this family fun park.

POST ROAD RECREATION CENTER
4700 N. Post Rd. 897-7908

This 15-acre facility offers four go-cart tracks that operate year round, plus a golf driving range, 18-hole miniature golf and bank shot basketball.

PUTT-PUTT GOLF & GAMES
10499 E. Washington St. 899-4536
6320 W. 34th St. 291-7437
1936 E. Southport Rd. 787-4852

You'll find the traditionally kitschy mini golf courses, plus go-carts and game rooms at these facilities; call about group rates for parties.

RUSTIC GARDENS GOLF DRIVING RANGE
1500 S. Arlington Ave.   *359-8183*

This location offers a lighted driving range and putting green as well as 27 holes of miniature golf on real grass.

Golf

Public Courses

"Golf course building is an art," Pete Dye, renowned course designer and former Indianapolis resident, said in a 1995 interview with the *Indianapolis Business Journal*. "I design (courses) with a challenge for golfers of all levels." Indianapolis has three Dye-designed public courses where you can pit your skill level against his artfulness.

BRICKYARD CROSSING
4790 West 16th St.   *484-6572*

This 18-hole, championship-caliber course on the grounds of the Indianapolis Motor Speedway includes three lakes, 72 sand traps and 650 trees. The site of the annual Brickyard Crossing Championship, a Senior PGA Tour event, it's not a course for the fainthearted.

EAGLE CREEK
8802 W. 56th St.   *297-3366*

Golf Digest rated this 27-hole complex inside Eagle Creek Park as one of the top 50 public courses in the nation. Built in 1971 and renovated in 1988, the facilities include an amateur golf training center and driving range in addition to nine- and 18-hole courses.

WILLIAM SAHM GOLF COURSE
6880 E. 91st St.   *849-0036*

This is the course that Dye himself rates among his best local efforts; it was also one of his first. It's an open, flat course

of moderate length. A creek and lake offer additional challenges and considerable scenic beauty.

COFFIN
2401 Cold Springs Rd.   *327-7845*

Inside Riverside Park, this course recently underwent major renovation. You'll find tree-lined fairways, rolling terrain and plenty of water hazards.

DOUGLASS
2801 Dr. Andrew J. Brown Ave.   *924-0018*

Relatively short with few hazards and compact, well-trapped greens, this nine-hole, par 34 course appeals to beginners and seniors.

PLEASANT RUN
601 N. Arlington Ave.   *357-0829*

This 18-hole course comes with seven water hazards and tree-lined fairways. A winding creek makes it quite scenic.

RIVERSIDE
3600 White River Pkwy. W. Dr. N.   *923-0841*

The oldest course in the city, Riverside has small greens, mature trees, and relatively flat terrain with few hazards. This is a course that appeals to a wide range of players.

SARAH SHANK GOLF COURSE
2901 S. Keystone Ave.   *784-0631*

This is a beautiful course with open fairways and two creeks. The terrain rolls slightly and includes some wooded areas.

CARL E. SMOCK GOLF COURSE
3910 S. County Line Rd. E.   *888-0036*

This is one of the longest courses in the city, with large greens, open fairways and multiple sand traps. You'll also find two creeks, two ponds, and hills — all adding to the excitement.

A. J. THATCHER GOLF COURSE

4501 W. Vermont St.   244-0713

A short course with narrow tree-lined fairways and three water holes, this is a challenging course for the average golfer.

WHISPERING HILLS

10751 Brookville Rd.   862-9000

The newest municipal course in the city, Whispering Hills offers rolling hills, lakes and woods — in other words, all the obstacles you could ask for.

WINDING RIVER

8400 S. Mann Rd.   856-7257

The longest nine-hole course in the city, Winding River consists of wide fairways and rolling terrain with few hazards.

Hunting and Fishing

Unless you own a good-size stand of woods, or have permission from someone who does, it may be best to stick to state-owned lands that are managed for hunting. State forests, recreation areas and reservoirs all allow various types of hunting, but Indiana's 16 fish and wildlife areas may offer the best option: they're maintained primarily for hunting and fishing. Most allow deer, dove, squirrel, upland game and waterfowl hunting.

Indiana hunters must have a license, available from some sporting goods stores, bait shops and, of course, from the DNR. Contact the Division of Fish and Wildlife, 402 W. Washington Street, Room W273, 46204, or call 232-4080 for more information.

Hunter education programs are now required for all first-time hunters born after 1986 and teach youngsters about firearm safety and responsible hunting. For class schedules, contact the DNR's Division of Law Enforcement at 232-4010.

Fishing enthusiasts ages 17 to 64 need a license to fish in Indiana; these are generally available where hunting licenses are sold. Good fishing holes around Indianapolis include park lakes, especially Eagle Creek, city property along the west side of Fall Creek from 30th to 38th streets and along Fall Creek Parkway from 38th Street to Geist Reservoir. Bank fishing is also allowed along White River in Holliday, Marott and Broad Ripple parks. Stocked species include largemouth bass, smallmouth bass, channel catfish, bluegill and crappie.

Atterbury Fish & Wildlife Area, south of Indianapolis near Edinburgh, offers plenty of nearby fishing and hunting opportunities. Call 232-7535 for information.

Geist Reservoir, north of the city in the Lawrence area, and **Morse Reservoir** near Noblesville, both of which feature incredibly pricey on-the-water homes, also offer public access for fishing (and, of course, boating), as does **Eagle Creek Park**.

Ice Skating

Facilities

CARMEL ICE SKADIUM

1040 Third Ave. SW, Carmel   844-8888

This is a year-round ice facility open for figure skating and hockey. Open to the

---

Rent a pontoon boat at the marina and cruise around Eagle Creek Reservoir. Each boat seats up to 10 people and comes complete with a grill.

Insiders' Tips

public, this "skadium" is also available for private rentals.

PEPSI COLISEUM

1202 E. 38th St.   *927-7536*

Open from October to April for public skating, this rink also offers lessons and league hockey.

INDIANA/WORLD SKATING ACADEMY

201 S. Capitol Ave.   *237-5555*

Public skating year round — whenever skating or hockey events or practices are not going on. This is your chance to skate in a place designed to bring out the best in world-class skaters.

INDY PARKS AND RECREATION

1426 W. 29th St.   *327-0000*

Indy Parks operates two indoor rinks that are open for ice-skating from October to April: Ellenberger Ice Rink, 5301 E. St. Clair Street, 327-7176; and Perry Ice Rink, 541 E. Stop 11 Road, Greenwood, 888-0070.

Organizations

INDIANAPOLIS SKATING CLUB

c/o Carmel Ice Skadium   *844-8888*
1040 3rd Ave., SW, Carmel   *844-3574*

This organization, which is a member club of the United States Figure Skating Association, provides its members (adults and children) opportunities to practice figure skating, free style and ice dancing. It also offers learn-to-skate classes. The club skates three nights a week, September through April, at the Carmel Ice Skadium.

INDY SPEED SKATING CLUB

c/o Indiana/World
Skating Academy   *237-5555, 848-9410*

If whizzing across the ice as a blur of blades, is your dream, this organization

can help you realize it. The club meets twice a week at the Indiana/World Skating Academy to practice.

SYCAMORE CLUB

c/o Perry Ice Rink
415 E. Stop 11 Rd.   *888-0070*
Greenwood   *888-2957*

Whether you're a competitive skater or just like gliding around for fun, this group offers you a chance to do so with like-minded skaters during the Perry Ice Rink's October-to-April season.

WINTER CLUB

c/o Pepsi Coliseum   *927-7536*
1202 E. 38th St.   *888-5543*

From kids to grandparents, this club provides ice time for its members at the Coliseum, October through April. The club offers individual and group lessons, and helps train competition-level skaters as well as recreational ones.

In-Line Skating

While you'll see a lot of in-line skaters on streets and sidewalks in certain areas of the city — downtown, Meridian Kessler, Butler Tarkington, Broad Ripple — there are other options. Some of the parks — most notably Eagle Creek, Garfield, Krannert and Holliday — have ample roadways for skating. Or you can go to:

ELLENBERGER PARK

5301 E. St. Clair St.   *327-7176*

PERRY PARK

451 E. Stop 11 Rd.   *888-0070*

From June to August, the skating rinks at these two parks are open for in-line skating. Learn-to-skate classes for children and adults are also available.

MAJOR TAYLOR VELODROME

3649 Cold Spring Rd.   *327-VELO*

As long as there are no cycling events

Indiana State Park Inns.

Naturally Comfortable.

Where we cover all your needs, from family visits to business conferences.

Abe Martin Lodge • Brown County State Park
P.O. Box 547 • Nashville, IN 47448
812-988-4418

Canyon Inn • McCormick's Creek State Park
P.O. Box 71 • Spencer, IN 47460
812-829-4881

Clifty Inn • Clifty Falls State Park
P.O. Box 387 • Madison, IN 47250
812-265-4135

Turkey Run Inn • Turkey Run State Park
R.R. 1, Box 444 • Marshall, IN 47859
317-597-2211

Spring Mill Inn • Spring Mill State Park
Box 68 • Mitchell, IN 47446
812-849-4081

Potawatomi Inn • Pokagon State Park
6 Lane 100 A Lake James • Angola, IN 46703
219-833-1077

INDIANA STATE PARK INNS

THE GARRISON
formerly Officers and Civilians Club

– Sunday Brunch –
10 a.m. - 1:30 p.m.

Baked Salmon
Carved Roast Beef & Ham
Omelet & Waffle Bar
Eggs, Bacon, Sausage,
French Toast and Much More.

$9.50 including beverage

Children under 12 – ½ price

Special Meetings
for reservations call (317) 543-9592

- All of your Holiday occasions
- Large Ballroom (holds 200 +)
- Service Clubs

6002 North Post Road
I-465 to 56th Street, East to Post Road,
North on Post Road approximately four blocks

Breakaway to BLOOMINGTON
INDIANA

W hether it's the excitement of an Indiana University sporting event or the relaxation of a day lounging at the lake, Bloomington/Monroe County is your perfect vacation destination.

✤ World class musical performances ✤ International restaurants ✤ Wineries ✤ Wilderness areas ✤ Three lakes for water adventure ✤ Shopping and antiques in downtown Bloomington

Make the Visitors Center your first stop for information on things to see and do while in the area. You'll find maps, brochures, and other local information. Call us for area hotel availability and help with your travel plans.

800/800-0037

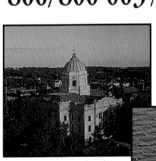

Come out and play.

MONROE COUNTY CONVENTION & VISITORS BUREAU
2855 N. WALNUT STREET, BLOOMINGTON, IN 47404 812-334-8900 FAX 812-334-2344

Escape from the City

OLIVER WINERY

35 miles south of Indpls. on St. Rd. 37
"Open Year-Round"

(800) 25-TASTE ◆ (812) 876-5800

Picture Yourself at

The Pointe

Get away to it all at Indiana's finest restort on the shores of 11,000 acre Lake Monroe in the scenic hills of Southern Indiana.

Fully Equipped Condominiums
• 18 Hole PGA Championship
Golf Course • Five Tennis
Courts • Olympic Size
Outdoor Pool • Bicycle
Rentals • Beach
Volleyball Playground
• Fine Dining
• Lounge

THE POINTE
Golf & Tennis Resort

**2250 E. Pointe Road
Bloomington, Indiana 47401
812-824-4040 or 1-800-860-8604**

The IU Natatorium is a great place to swim or enjoy watching others during major events.

scheduled, you can skate on the Velodrome's banked track Monday to Friday, 10 AM to 5 PM. A modest fee buys you two hours of skating time. During the summer, you can also take skating classes.

RCA DOME

100 S. Capitol Ave.   *262-3410*

During the winter, the Dome's concourse is open for in-line skating. Call for a schedule and fee information.

Martial Arts

Indy Parks offers classes in various martial arts disciplines at various parks' activity centers. Call 327-0000 for information. Several YMCA branches also offer martial arts instruction. Contact your nearest Y for details.

With more than three dozen commercial martial arts studios to choose from, you're bound to find one that's right for you. Some of the choices include:

A-1 MASTERS MARTIAL ARTS

6957 Madison Ave.	*783-7000*
5999 Crawfordsville Rd.	*244-3600*
8859 Pendleton Pike	*898-0704*
1744 E. 86th St.	*571-1400*
2989 W. 71st St.	*328-1400*

The focus at all five A-1 centers is on building confidence, teaching self-defense and self-discipline and enhancing fitness. A-1 instructors teach traditional Korean martial arts; classes are open to men and women.

STEVE ANDERSON'S AOK KARATE STUDIO

8402 E. Washington St.	*895-0195*
2501 S. Madison Ave.	*788-7050*
3820 N. High School Rd.	*299-1580*
3815 N. Shadeland Ave.	*542-0025*

Owned and operated by World Martial Arts Hall of Famer Steve Anderson, the four A.O.K. studios teach karate, kung fu, judo, jiu jitsu and taekwondo. Classes for men, women and children are available.

CHOI BROTHERS' ORIENTAL MARTIAL ARTS COLLEGE & FITNESS CLUB

5404 W. 38th St.   297-1000
7275 N. Keystone Ave.   257-4458

Youn Pyo Choi and Joon Pyo Choi (the latter was a U.S. Olympic coach in 1988) offer instruction in taekwondo and other martial arts, including the use of weaponry. They strive to instill confidence, patience and respect in their students while teaching self-defense and improving coordination. Classes are open to men, women and children.

HERB JOHNSON'S KARATEWORLD CHAMPION KARATE USA

9423 E. Washington St.   898-4444
5060 E. 62nd St.   255-6872

Three-time world karate champion and trainer of 14 other world champions, Herb Johnson runs a karate program that stresses self-discipline and self-confidence. Personalized instruction for men, women and children includes group and private lessons, as well as training for women in self-defense and rape protection.

RAY SARKINE'S MARTIAL ARTS SCHOOL

6324 W. Washington St.   241-5425

With more than 20 years experience in martial arts, Ray Sarkine teaches aikido, kick boxing and weaponry use to men and women in private and group settings. He also offers classes for kids.

JERRY SMITH'S SELF DEFENSE SYSTEMS INC.

7624 S. Meridian St.   887-5425

Under the direction of fifth-degree black belt Jerry Smith, this facility offers instruction in street combat techniques, knife and stick fighting, close-range gun and knife defense and kick boxing. Private lessons are available for men and women.

Roller Skating

When was the last time you strapped on a pair of roller skates and wobbled out to skate the night away with your friends? Well, here's your chance.

ELLENBERGER PARK

5301 E. St. Clair St.   327-7176
Perry Park, 451 E. Stop 11 Rd.   888-0070

Operated by Indy Parks, these two rinks offer both roller and in-line skating from June through August.

UNITED SKATES OF AMERICA

3902 Glen Arm Rd.   291-6794

These two sites are the local outlets of the largest chain of roller rinks in the Midwest. They offer state-of-the-art audio and lighting systems, clean-with-a-sheen hardwood skating floors and contemporary decor. In addition to public skating, they host private birthday parties and other special events and offer group skating rates.

Rowing

EAGLE CREEK REGATTA COURSE

Eagle Creek Park
7350 Eagle Beach Dr.   327-7110

The only rowing course in the United States that's sanctioned for international competition by the International Federation of Rowing Associations, the Eagle Creek regatta Course is open for use by trained and certified rowers. Instruction and certification for rowers from high school age to adult is available through Community Rowing of Indianapolis (CRI). Call 297-7185 for information.

Running

INDY RUNNERS INC.
290-RUNR

For serious runners, this is the organization to belong to. An affiliate of the Roadrunners Club of America, Indy Runners provides training information and racing opportunities for both recreational and competitive runners. It also hosts a variety of events, ranging from weekly runs to races, throughout the year.

INDIANA UNIVERSITY TRACK AND FIELD STADIUM
901 W. New York St.   274-3518

The premier outdoor running facility in the city, this Olympic-caliber stadium has a nine-lane, 400-meter rubber track that is considered one of the fastest in the world. When not in use for competitions, the stadium is open for public use. Contact the IU Natatorium, which is adjacent to the stadium and connected to it by a tunnel, about guidelines and fees.

There are other outdoor tracks at various schools throughout the city, most of which are available for public use. If you like to run outdoors, but not around an oval, there are a number of other good places. Try these parks:

Lake Sullivan Sports Complex, 3601 Cold Springs Road

Riverside Park, 2420 E. Riverside Drive

Garfield Park, 2450 Shelby Street

Holliday Park, 6349 Spring Mill Road

Other good running options include the **Central Canal** towpath south from Broad Ripple; **Fall Creek Parkway**, north of 46th Street; and **Washington Street** west of Circle Centre, past the Indianapolis Zoo and back through the IUPUI campus.

Snow Skiing

Cross-Country

With four inches of snow on the ground, you can ski the trails at:

EAGLE CREEK PARK
7840 W. 56th St.   327-7110

Ten miles of trails wind through this park. Some trails require experience; all guarantee a good workout. You can rent equipment at the park if you don't have your own.

SOUTHEASTWAY PARK
5624 E. County Line Rd. S.   861-5167

With 188 acres of woods and open land, this park is a good place to practice your skills. You can rent skis, boots and poles here, but you'll have to bring your own motor control.

Downhill

OK, Aspen this isn't. And slopes there aren't — at least not in the immediate metropolitan area. But if you don't mind driving an hour or two, you can get to some Indiana hills that are tall enough to allow you to gather a little speed before reaching the bottom.

SKI PAOLI PEAKS
Paoli   (812) 723-4696

Whether you're a beginning skier or a flashy snowboarder, this facility 100 miles south of Indianapolis has something for you. Giant snow-making machines keep the 15 slopes and trails ski-ready even when Mother Nature hasn't any snow to spare. The longest run here is 3,300 feet; the vertical drop is 300 feet. There are package deals available ranging from learn-to-ski excursions to midnight madness and holiday specials.

SKI WORLD

Nashville   *(812) 988-6638*

This downhill complex in Brown County, about 45 miles southwest of Indianapolis, has a vertical drop of 310 feet. The longest run is 2,500 feet, but if you're a beginner you can practice your moves on the bunny slope. You'll also find chair lifts and rope tows to get you up the slopes and a lodge and restaurant once you've come back down. You can rent your equipment or buy it from the on-site ski shop.

Soccer

Both Indy Parks and YMCA branches offer soccer instruction and team play. Contact Indy Parks, 327-0000, or the Y nearest you for information.

Another good way to find out what's going on locally is to contact the largest soccer equipment supplier in the area:

SOCCER UNLIMITED

622 S. Range Line Rd., Carmel   *848-4797*
916 E. Main St., Greenwood   *888-0640*

At either of these locations, you can locate teams and leagues throughout Central Indiana. One organization you're likely to hear about is the Metropolitan Soccer Club, which represents a number of soccer teams around the state. For information, call 253-8816 or 786-3557.

Other area soccer organizations are:
Central Indiana Youth Soccer League, 5954 N. College Avenue, 726-0009

Indiana Youth Soccer Association, 5954 N. College Avenue, 255-0499

Northeast Youth Soccer League, 7045 Hampstead Lane, 842-6975

There are several good soccer fields in the area, including:
William Kuntz Memorial Soccer Stadium, 1502 W. 16th Street, 327-7194

German Park, 8600 S. Meridian Street, 881-0053

Juan Soloman Park, 64th Street and Grand View Drive, no phone

Zionsville Soccer Park, Bloor Road, 873-3491

INDY INDOOR SOCCER & SPORTS

6382 W. 34th St.   *291-2729*

INDY INDOOR SOCCER & SPORTS

6382 W. 34th St.   *291-2729*

Despite its name, this is a soccer-only facility. During the winter, it hosts amateur teams (kids' teams and adult teams) from throughout central Indiana; in the summer, it organizes in-house teams and holds kids' soccer camps.

INDY SPORTS & FITNESS INC.

4002 N. Franklin Rd.   *898-2285*

The wind may be howling outside, but inside this northeast-side facility soccer balls are flying. In addition to indoor soccer leagues for kids and adults, Indy Sports also offers arena football (flag only, no tackle), basketball and volleyball. In the spring, play moves outdoors where there are five softball diamonds and two sandpit volleyball courts.

Swimming

INDIANA UNIVERSITY NATATORIUM

900 W. New York St.   *274-3518*

On a daily basis, except when a major event is scheduled, the Natatorium's main pool is open for lap swimming. There are also learn-to-swim classes, scuba-diving classes, and water safety classes available.

If you're looking for more than a place to swim, the Natatorium has Polaris weight machines, aerobic classes, and other fitness activities available.

INDY PARKS AND RECREATION
1426 W. 29th St.   *327-0000*

In addition to the Natatorium, other public swimming facilities include the following park pools. Unless otherwise noted, these are all outdoor pools, open between Memorial Day weekend and Labor Day weekend. Those with adult lap swimming schedules or lap pools are noted. Call individual sites for specific information.

Bethel Pool, 1634 Golay Street, 327-7324

Broad Ripple Pool, 1450 E. Broad Ripple Avenue, 327-7333

Brookside Aquatic Center, 3500 Brookside Parkway S. Drive, 327-7331

Douglass Pool, 2759 Dr. Andrew J. Brown Avenue, 327-7325

Ellenberger Pool, (offers separate adult lap swimming times), 5301 E. St. Clair Street, 327-7326

Garfield Pool, 2450 Shelby Street, 327-7327

Gustafson Pool, 3110 Moller Road, 327-7334

Indy Island Aquatic Center, (indoor water park, including a separate lap pool), 8575 E. Raymond Street, 862-6867

Krannert Aquatic Center, (has a separate lap pool) 605 S. High School Road, 484-3252

Martin Luther King Pool, 1701 Broadway Avenue, 327-7332

Perry Aquatic Center, 451 Stop 11 Road, 889-0825

Rhodius Pool, 1001 S. Belmont Avenue, 327-7328

Riverside Aquatic Center, 420 E. Riverside Drive, 327-7171

Sahm Aquatic Center, 6800 E. 91st Street, 849-2227

Thatcher Pool (indoor), 4649 W. Vermont Street, 484-3270

Wes Montgomery Pool, 3501 N. Hawthorne Street, 327-7329

Willard Pool, 1700 E. Washington Street, 327-7330

Public Beaches

Absent either a large lake front or sea shore, Indianapolis is lacking in large public beach facilities. Still, there is:

EAGLE CREEK BEACH
7602 Eagle Beach Dr.   *327-7132*

Part of Eagle Creek Park, the beach abuts Eagle Creek Reservoir, and offers a wide stretch of sand, as well as shade trees and picnic sites. Swimming is permitted. Lifeguards are on duty during the Memorial Day to Labor Day beach season.

Tennis

INDIANAPOLIS TENNIS CENTER
755 University Blvd.   *278-2100*

As the site of the annual RCA Championships, one of the favorite tournaments for players on the Men's Professional Tennis tour, the Tennis Center is the crown jewel of the local tennis scene. There are 18 outdoor courts and six in the companion indoor facility. When not in use for competitions, the courts are available to Tennis center members and nonmembers alike. Membership entitles you to court reservations, lessons and other amenities not available to nonmembers.

INDY PARKS AND RECREATION
1426 W. 29th St.   *327-0000*

In addition to maintaining public tennis facilities, Indy Parks also provides court time to two significant tennis programs — the National Junior Tennis

League, which provides young people ages 7 to 18 with tennis instruction, and the Indiana Recreational Tennis Foundation, which offers adult lessons, clinics and league play. Indy Parks maintains public tennis facilities at a number of sites, including:

Broad Ripple Park, 1450 Broad Ripple Avenue, 327-7161, six lighted courts

Christian Park, 4200 English Avenue, 327-7163, three courts

Douglass Park, 1425 E. 25th Street, 327-7174, four lighted courts

Ellenberger Park, 5301 E. St. Clair Street, 327-7176, 12 lighted courts

Garfield Park, 2450 Shelby Street, 327-7220, six lighted courts

Fall Creek & 16th Park, Fall Creek Parkway and 16th Street, 267-0532, 10 courts

Oxford Terrace Park, Rural Avenue and 30th Street, 267-0532, 10 courts

Perry Park, 451 E. Stop 11 Road, 888-0070, four courts

Rhodius Park, 1001 S. Belmont Street, 327-7165

Riverside Park, 2420 E. Riverside Drive, 327-7171, 12 lighted courts

Sahm Tennis Center, 6801 E. 91st Street, 327-7203, five lighted courts

Tarkington Tennis Center, 45 W. 40th Street, 327-7178, eight lighted courts

Watkins Park, 2360 Dr. Martin Luther King Jr., 923-9818, four lighted courts

INDIANAPOLIS RACQUET CLUB

8249 Dean Rd.   *849-2531*

This facility has indoor and outdoor tennis courts available for use by members and nonmembers.

Volleyball

Indy Parks maintains sand volleyball courts at the following sites:

Ellenberger Park, 5301 E. St. Clair Street, 327-7176

Lake Sullivan Sports Complex, 3601 Cold Springs Road, 327-VELO

Post Road Community Building, 1313 S. Post Road, 327-7214

Thatcher Park, 4649 W. Vermont Street, 484-3270

Additionally, a number of the YMCA branches offer indoor volleyball. Contact the branch nearest you for details.

Inside
Daytrips and
Weekend Getaways

While Indianapolis and surrounding environs offer ample recreational, cultural and historical sites and activities, sometimes it's nice to get away for awhile. Thanks to the foresight of Indiana's forefathers, that's easy to do.

Situated as it is in the center of the state, Indianapolis offers easy access to places of interest throughout Indiana. Whether for a day or a weekend, you owe it to yourself to explore what the state has to offer. Here are some suggestions. (As throughout the book, all telephone numbers are in the 317 area code unless otherwise noted.)

Daytrips

U.S. Highway 40 E. Corridor

The Old National Road, which was the first to link Indianapolis with the East Coast, is now U.S. Highway 40. Its eastern segment between Indianapolis and Richmond is rich with things to do, especially for history buffs and antique lovers.

GREENFIELD

Just a 35-mile jaunt east of Indianapolis, Greenfield was the boyhood home of famed Hoosier poet James Whitcomb Riley, author of such enduring schoolroom classics as "Little Orphant Annie" and "When the Frost Is on the Punkin'." His family home at 250 W. Main Street (U.S. Highway 40), 462-8539, has been preserved and is open to visitors.

To see the swimming hole where Riley and his childhood chums passed many a hot summer afternoon, stop by **Riley Memorial Park** at the intersection of U.S. 40 and Apple Street. You'll also find the **Old Log Jail Museum** in this park, a testimony to the ingenuity of pioneer jailers who embedded nails in the log walls to prevent prisoners from sawing their way out.

Woodworking of another sort provides the historical backdrop for **BarnaBe's Cafe, Sodas, & Spirits**, 462-2883, in downtown Greenfield. Once a lumber mill, this old-fashioned soda fountain is an inviting stop, complete with stained-glass windows, a tin ceiling and antiques.

For more daytrip tips, look for Channel 13 weatherman Bob Gregory's "one-tank trips," quick commercial-length spots highlighting notable destinations within easy driving distance.

Insiders' Tips

Photo: The Indianapolis Star & News

Indoor and outdoor pools flank an entrance to French Lick Springs Resort in Southern Indiana.

KNIGHTSTOWN

This town, just minutes east of Greenfield, is one of several antique centers along U.S. 40. The **Knightstown Antique Mall**, which houses 75 dealers, is a treasure trove of furniture and collectibles. For information about this mall and other area dealers, call (800) 676-4302.

There are more than 700 antique dealers positioned on or near U.S. 40 between Knightstown and Richmond, which has led to the highway's designation as "Antique Alley." (For more details, see our Shopping chapter.)

Also in Knightstown, at 112 W. Carey Street, you'll find the **Carthage, Knightstown & Shirley Railroad**, (800) 676-4302, which offers an excursion train trip through the surrounding countryside. The 10-mile route crosses the Big Blue River, recapturing the scenic pleasures of rail travel. (See our Kidstuff chapter for more information.)

NEW CASTLE

Let's start with the obvious: You're in the heart of basketball country. Hoosier Hysteria, that affliction that hits fans on every level from high school hoops to the NBA playoffs, isn't hyperbole. It's a fact of life in Indiana, and nowhere will you find its history chronicled better than in the Indiana Basketball Hall of Fame, 408 Trojan Lane, New Castle, 529-1891.

Utilizing multimedia and computers, artifacts and interactive displays (try hitting the winning shot as the clock ticks off the final five seconds of a game), the Hall of Fame celebrates the role that basketball has played in Indiana over the past century. Appropriately enough, right next door is New Castle High School, home of the world's largest high school gymnasium.

To get to the Indiana Basketball Hall of Fame, take U.S. 40 E. to the Ind. Highway 3 Exit. Follow Ind. Highway 3 into New Castle.

CAMBRIDGE CITY

At one time, Overbeck Pottery was one of this country's best-known producers of stoneware, and Cambridge City's own Overbeck sisters (there were six of them) were responsible for the artistry of that pottery. The **Museum of Overbeck Pottery**, 33 W. Main Street, 478-3335, chronicles the Overbecks' achievements and their contributions to American art history.

Indiana history is the focus of the **Huddleston Farmhouse Inn Museum**, U.S. 40 W., 478-3172. This restored farm focuses on life as it was lived by a 19th-century family and the pioneers who stopped here on their way west along the National Road.

RICHMOND

In 1966, a gas main explosion ripped through downtown Richmond, killing and injuring scores of people. But out of that tragedy, the city created something special: a nationally acclaimed pedestrians-only district that combines historic buildings, brick walkways, green spaces and flowing fountains. The result, which is known as the **Promenade**, is a wonderful place to while away a couple of hours shopping or merely sitting under a shade tree.

If you time your visit correctly (spring or summer), you can also catch the splendor of the **E.G. Hill Memorial Rose Garden** and the **All American Rose Garden**, both in Glen Miller Park, 2500 National Road E. (U.S. 40), 962-1511. The former is a memorial garden planted in honor of Richmond's famed rose specialist, Gurney Hill, who developed a number of popular roses; the latter is an award-winning garden containing 1,600 roses as well as hundreds of other flowers.

At the **Indiana Football Hall of Fame**, 815 N. A Street, 966-2235, you'll find displays of football history from Indiana high school, college and professional players. For pigskin lovers, this place makes clear the fact that there's more to sports in Indiana than hoops.

For more information about the Richmond area, contact the Richmond-Wayne County Convention and Tourism Bureau, 600 Promenade, 935-8687 or (800) 828-8414.

The I-65 S. Corridor

I-65 S. connects Indianapolis with Louisville, Kentucky. However, you don't have to take that two-hour trip to find something to do — in fact, all it takes is a 45-mile drive down to the Edinburgh-Columbus area. That's a daytrip worth taking.

EDINBURGH

At the intersection of I-65 and U.S. 31, on the outskirts of this small farming community, you'll find the **Horizon Outlet Center**, (812) 526-9764, home of 65 factory outlet stores, including Eddie Bauer, Spiegel, Levi Strauss and Corning/Revere.

COLUMBUS

Without a doubt, one of the most architecturally significant communities in the world, this town of some 31,000 people contains buildings and sculptures by some of the 20th century's most renowned architects and artists, including such luminaries as I.M. Pei and Henry Moore. The best way to get oriented and educated is to drop by the **Columbus Visitors Center**, 506 Fifth Street, (812) 372-1954. There you'll find maps and audio tapes you can use for self-guided tours of the town's architectural landmarks; you can also call ahead and reserve a place on a guided tour. For advance information, contact Columbus Area Visitor Information, (812) 378-2622.

If wandering around town makes you hungry, drop by **Zaharako's Confectionery**, 329 Washington Street, (812) 379-9329. In this turn-of-the-century landmark, you'll find onyx soda fountains, a genuine Tiffany lamp and a 1908 German pipe organ. And don't forget the homemade ice cream, candy and sandwiches.

Also in the turn-of-the-century vein is the **Columbus Inn**, 445 Fifth Street, (812) 378-4289. Formerly the town's city hall, it's now one of the Midwest's most elegant bed and breakfasts. It contains 30 rooms and five suites, all with cherry furniture (including custom-made beds from France). There are also three daily tea times: morning, afternoon and high.

If you're a mall aficionado, make sure you check out The **Commons on Washington Street** in downtown Columbus. Designed by famed architect Cesar Pelli, The Commons not only contains a variety of stores, but it also houses a wonderful play area for children and a fascinating scrap metal, kinetic sculpture by Jean Tinguely called *Chaos I*.

BROWN COUNTY

For rugged, natural beauty, you can't beat Brown County. Less than an hour's drive south of Indianapolis (I-65 south to State Road 46 west), this is hill country.

Sugar Grove
Vineyard and Winery
(317) 839-9886
611 Newlin Rd. Mooresville

Mon. - Fri. 5-9
Sat. 10-7 Sun. 12-7
Bottle & Case
Sales on Sundays!

Free Wine Tasting   Free Winery Tours
Wines by the glass, bottle or case
Picnic Area, bring a basket!

Like a herd of shaggy humped prehistoric creatures, the heavily wooded hills of Brown County spread across the landscape for miles, a feast for the eyes and the heart. It's easy to fall in love with this place.

A lot of people have. And some of them have stayed. Professionals, mostly, from Indianapolis, Columbus and Bloomington. People who can afford to build or buy the lovely log houses in or near Nashville commute to their jobs, but there's not enough of them to make much of a crowd. Brown County is still sparsely populated. There's no real industry here, and the land rolls too much to support large farms. Tourism is the largest single source of income for many of the county's residents who are painters, potters, silversmiths, antique dealers and restaurant and hotel employees. People live here because they love it, not because they expect to get rich off what amounts to seasonal work. Summer and fall are the busy times, but that doesn't mean that the pace escalates too much. Brown County isn't the fast track, and the folks here like it that way. It's somewhere you can go to slow down, take a walk in the woods, browse through art galleries or sit and contemplate your place in the universe.

On weekends in October, at the height of leaf season, the hills are ablaze in gorgeous colors and people pour in from around the state (and from surrounding states). On peak color weekends expect crowds standing in line at restaurants, jostling through the Nashville streets and jamming the entrance to Brown County State Park.

But even then, if you venture off the main byways onto lesser-traveled county roads, you can enjoy the splendor of the landscape far from the maddening crowds. Brown County is a place you owe it to yourself to discover and explore.

Some favorite Brown County spots are:

Nashville: Fifteen miles west of Columbus on State Road 46, you'll find Nashville, home of some 700 residents and 250 restaurants, art galleries and craft and antique shops. The county seat, it's also the surrounding county's cultural and tourism center.

Brown County's reputation as a haven for artists and craftspeople is well deserved and evident in the fact that throughout Nashville you'll find galleries and shops selling pottery, jewelry, quilts, wood carvings, hand-blown glassware, handmade musical instruments and metal sculptures. In fact, many such shops are housed in a downtown facility known as the **Artists Colony Shops**, 125 S. Van Buren, (812) 988-0600.

If you're wandering the streets looking for a change of pace, stop by the **John Dillinger Historical Museum**, 90 W. Washington Street, (812) 988-1933. Inside you'll find about 95 percent of all the known artifacts from Indiana bad boy Dillinger's life and reign as one of America's most wanted criminals.

For a museum of another sort, try the **Brown County International Blacksmith Museum**, 98 W. Washington Street, (812) 988-8811. The only museum in the world dedicated to the history of blacksmithing, it contains examples of items made by blacksmiths in 20 countries over the past 4,400 years.

If you're hungry, the **Nashville House** at the corner of Main and Van Buren streets, (812) 988-4554, is in order. Here you'll find baked ham and roast turkey, fried chicken and barbecue ribs, sassafras tea and fried biscuits with baked apple butter — food guaranteed to make you clean your plate, all served up in a room filled with antiques. It's country cookin' at its finest.

The **Brown County Playhouse** on S. Van Buren Street, (812) 988-2123, is the state's longest-running professional stock theater. It produces comedies, musicals and mysteries during the summer and fall, using performers from Indiana University's theater and drama department.

Other theaters in the area include the **Nashville Follies Theatre**, 63 E. Washington Street, (812) 988-9007 or (800) 449-SHOW; the **Pine Box Theater**, 168 Jefferson Street, (812) 988-6827; and the **Melchior Marionette Theatre** on the west side of S. Van Buren Street, 535-4853.

Like its larger namesake in Tennessee, Nashville is home to a popular Country music venue. The **Little Nashville Opry**, a mile west on S.R. 46, plays host to a variety of local, regional and national musicians during a season that runs from March through November. For information, call (812) 988-2235.

Brown County State Park, Indiana's largest, is right outside of Nashville on SR 46. With 15,000 acres, this park is a splendid place to spend a day hiking (there are 27 miles of roads, hiking and horse trails) and picnicking — unless you're trying to do it in October, during the height of leaf season. The wooded hills ignite in glorious color in the fall, and that attracts throngs of sightseers; estimates range up to 100,000 visitors on some autumn weekends. If you go during that time, expect to wait to get through the gate to the park. But the rest of the year, this area is a wonderful place to visit.

When the snow flies in Brown County, skiers head for **Ski World** on S.R. 46 southwest of Nashville, (812) 988-6638. With eight slopes and trails, a ski shop and a lodge, this place is as close as you can get to Aspen in Indiana. It's also the site of the annual Brown County Winter Festival in February. Open year round, Ski World's warm weather activities include water slides, bumper boats, go-carts, and batting cages.

One of the earliest and best-known artists to live and work in Brown County was T.C. Steele (1847-1926) whose landscapes and other paintings earned him an international reputation. You can visit his home, gardens and studio at the **T.C.**

Steele State Historical Site, 1.5 miles south of S.R. 46, near Belmont.

Bean Blossom: This tiny community north of Nashville on S.R. 135 has long been the home of the annual Bean Blossom Festival, a summer celebration of bluegrass music organized and hosted by the father of bluegrass, Bill Monroe. You'll also find the Bill Monroe Bluegrass Hall of Fame right on S.R. 135. For more information, call (812) 988-6422.

Gnaw Bone: If you've got a taste for the sweeter things in life, stop by this burg 4 miles east of Nashville on S.R. 46 in the fall. That's when sugarcane from area fields is turned into molasses at the **Brown County Sorghum Mill**, which uses a process involving a horse-powered press. Not only does this place sell sorghum but also other Brown County specialities such as persimmon pudding, apple butter and black walnut fudge. The only caveat is that the mill is only open September through November.

For more information on the preceding and other Brown County attractions, contact the Brown County Convention & Visitors Bureau at the corner of Main and Van Buren streets in Nashville, (800) 753-3255 or (812) 988-7303.

BLOOMINGTON

Less than an hour south of Indianapolis via S.R. 37 (or if you're in Brown County, a few minutes west of Nashville on S.R. 46), you'll find Bloomington. As the home of Indiana University, Bloomington is the cultural heart of south central Indiana. The setting for the movie *Breaking Away*, it's a place where the arts, sciences, sports and humanities intermingle in the classrooms and on the streets. It's a town of blue-collar laborers and white-collar academics. It's busy and bustling yet comfortable and unpretentious. It's a place where pedestrians and bicyclists are as prevalent as drivers.

The place to start, if you're new to town, is the university campus, which was rated one of the five most beautiful in the country by author Thomas Gaines in his book, *The Campus as a Work of Art*. Set amidst 1,860 acres of rolling, wooded land, the university includes numerous buildings constructed from Indiana limestone mined from area quarries. Among the campus' many attractions are the I.M. Pei-designed **Indiana University Art Museum** on E. Seventh Street, (812) 855-5445, which is home to some 30,000 artifacts and works of art, including examples from Greek and Roman, African and Pre-Columbian, Native American and Asian cultures.

Murals by Thomas Hart Benton grace the lobby of the **I.U. Auditorium**, across from the Art Museum on E. Seventh Street, (812) 855-1103. The auditorium plays host to concerts, Broadway shows, dance performances and theatrical productions during its fall-to-spring season.

Also on E. Seventh Street, next to the Auditorium, is the **Lilly Library**, internationally acclaimed for its collection of rare books, manuscripts and musical composition sheets. On permanent display are such rarities as a Gutenberg Bible (printed be-

For a real change of scenery, look into local airline American Trans Air's one-day trips. You're on the beach in the Bahamas before noon but back home in time for the 11 o'clock news.

Insiders' Tips

fore 1456), the Coverdale Bible (the first in English, c. 1535) and the original printing plates for John James Audubon's *Birds of America* series. For information about the library's hours and services, call (812) 855-2452.

If you're on campus some Friday night during the school year and suddenly have a ringing sensation in your ears, don't fret. It's just the bells in the **Metz Carillon Tower**, at the intersection of 17th Street and Jordan Avenue, that you're hearing. There are regular Friday evening carillon concerts.

Speaking of music, the **I.U. School of Music** consistently ranks with Julliard in terms of quality and prestige. The importance that the university places on its music program is evident in the **Musical Arts Center** on Jordan Avenue, (812) 855-7433. Inside is a 1,460-seat opera theater, home of the longest opera production season in the western hemisphere. In front of the building, you'll find one of Alexander Calder's sculptures.

Art of another sort — the fine art of basketball — is evident every fall and winter in **Assembly Hall** on 17th Street, (800) 447-4648. Home of the Hoosiers basketball team coached by Bob Knight, Assembly Hall also houses the university's department of intercollegiate athletics and its Athletic Hall of Fame. Next door to Assembly Hall is Memorial Stadium where I.U.'s football team does battle every season.

But the I.U. campus isn't all there is to Bloomington. In the downtown district alone you'll find a variety of art galleries, crafts and collectibles shops, bookstores, clothing stores and restaurants. In the center of the 11-block downtown district, surrounded by shady trees and well-kept lawns, is the limestone courthouse, c. 1908. The courthouse grounds are often the site of community events, including lunchtime concerts by local performers.

Just south of the courthouse is **Fountain Square**, an enclosed mall that houses a number of art galleries and speciality shops. Two blocks north, you'll find the Antique Mall, a renovated grocery store that is now home to some 100 antique dealers.

But there's more to life than sightseeing and shopping — like food, for instance. And in Bloomington, which attracts students and instructors from around the world, there's something to please every palate.

Feel like Greek food? Try the **Trojan Horse**, 100 E. Kirkwood, (812) 332-1101, for great gyros. Prefer Yugoslavian? Then head for **Janko's Little Zagreb**, 223 W. Sixth Street, (812) 332-0694. How about some sushi? You'll find it at **Ekimae Japanese Restaurant**, 12th and Walnut streets, (812) 334-1661. For fresh fish, oysters and lobster, **Fisherman's Dock** at 4501 E. Third Street is the place. If it's wood-fired oven pizza you're craving, the only place to go is the **Malibu Grill**, 106 N. Walnut Street, (812) 332-4334.

But without a doubt, the most unexpected restaurant in town is the **Snow Lion**, 113 S. Grant Street, (812) 336-0835. It's one of the only restaurants in the country to specialize in Tibetan food. Owned by Jigme K. Norbu, the nephew of the Dali Lama, the Snow Lion serves up dishes that make use of traditional Tibetan spices and herbs while playing down the Tibetan preference for dishes that utilize such things as liver and fat.

The restaurant is not Bloomington's only link to Tibet. The city is also home to the **Tibetan Cultural Center**, Indiana University Memorial Hall, (mailing address: P.O. Box 2581, Bloomington 47402), (812) 855-8222. The TCC owns 20 acres

Photo: The Indianapolis Star & News

The most impressive home in Madison may be that of J.F.D. Lanier, whose loans to the state equipped Union troops during the Civil War.

south of town, on which you'll find the only Tibetan *chorten* in this country. The chorten is a 35-foot-tall concrete monument that pays tribute to the thousands of Tibetans who have died during the decades of Chinese control of Tibet. The chorten is at 3655 Snoddy Road, and visitors can stop by free of charge.

If you're ready for a break, there's plenty of outdoor recreational opportunities in the area. For swimming, fishing and sailing in a beautiful setting, head for **Lake Monroe**, a 10,750-acre manmade lake about 10 miles south of Bloomington. While there are fancy resorts offering tennis, golf and accommodations, you don't have to be guest at one of them to enjoy the lake. Take S.R. 37 to the Harrodsburg Exit, then take Strain Ridge Road east and follow the signs.

If you prefer staying closer to town, check out Griffy Lake, a 109-acre, manmade lake that's open only to non-motor-ized boats. Fishing (with the proper Indiana license) is permitted: Griffy contains largemouth bass, bluegill, redear sunfish and channel catfish. Two hiking trails and a nature trail wind through the 1,200-acre nature preserve that surround the lake. To get to Griffy Lake, take the 45/46 Bypass to Matlock Road, then turn north and follow the road to the lake.

If your idea of a day in the country includes wine, a trip to the **Oliver Winery**, 7 miles north of Bloomington on S.R. 37 (the address is 8024 N. State Road 37), is in order. Indiana's oldest and largest winery, this place is as friendly as it is successful. Tours are free, as is wine tasting. Since its founding in 1971, Oliver Winery has created several award-winning wines and made many friends by holding free concerts and hosting an annual summer festival on its lovely, rolling acres. To learn more, call (812) 876-5800.

If you prefer grain to grapes, drop by the Brewpub in **Lennie's**, 1795 E. Tenth Street, (812) 323-2112, home of The Bloomington Brewing Company, for a taste of hometown brews. Tours are free every Saturday.

Anyone familiar with the resorts in Bloomington will want to turn their daytrip into a weekend getaway. **The Point Golf and Tennis Resort**, 2250 E. Pointe Road, (800) 824-4040, is a private 400-acre resort that includes golf, tennis, water sports and luxurious condominiums. The PGA Championship golf course, five tennis courts, an Olympic-size pool, a playground and bike rentals offer plenty of recreational possibilities.

FourWinds Resort and Marina, 9301 Fairfax Road, (800) 538-1187, on the shores of Lake Monroe provides a peaceful retreat amid beautiful scenery. You can sail, swim, enjoy PGA Championship golf, tennis, fitness trails and planned activities for kids.

For more information about Bloomington and surrounding Monroe County, contact the Monroe County Convention & Visitors Bureau, 2855 N. Walnut Street, (800) 800-0037.

The I-69 Corridor

I-69 starts (or ends, depending on your perspective) at Indianapolis and extends north to Lansing, Michigan. But for daytrip purposes, we'll venture no more than an hour's drive up the road, starting at Anderson.

ANDERSON

About 30 miles north of Indianapolis, this town is home to several interesting attractions, starting with **Mound State Park**, 4306 Mounds Road, 642-6627. This park offers a glimpse into Indiana's distant past through a number of earthen mounds built by the prehistoric Adena-Hopewell Indians. The largest mound, the Great Mound, is thought to date from 160 B.C. There's also an on-site nature center as well as hiking trails.

History of another kind is evident at the **Historical Military Armor Museum**, 2330 N. Crystal Street, 649-8265. This facility is home to the most complete collection of light tanks (from WWI to the present) in the country, all of which have been restored to fully operational condition. (And you were ready to settle for a Hummer!)

Speaking of armored vehicles, Anderson is also the site of the **Indianapolis Colts Training Camp**, on the campus of Anderson University, every July and August. For a modest admission fee, you can watch NFL players up close as they prepare for a new season. For information, call 643-5633 or (800) 533-6569.

Also on the university's campus is the **Reardon Auditorium**, 1100 E. Fifth Street, 641-4140, home of the Anderson Symphony Orchestra. The performance hall is known for its excellent acoustics as well as for its marvelous architecture.

For knockout performance halls, check out the **Paramount Theatre Center**, 1124 Meridian Street, 642-1234. Harkening back to the glories of big movie houses, this c. 1920 facility contains both a theatre for classic movies and stage productions and a lavish ballroom for special events.

For centuries, Bavarian artisans have handcrafted wax art figures and ornaments. Now, at **Alpine Acres**, 5080 W. S.R. 32, 649-4342, you can watch the craft being done and buy the end results. This is one of the few places in the United States where traditional wax art techniques are in use.

1994 Indiana VISTA Award for Excellence In Tourism

BILLIE CREEK
V·I·L·L·A·G·E

Home to three Covered Bridges, 30 Historic
Buildings, General Store, Craft Demonstrations
and Year Round Special Events.

52 Miles West of Indianapolis on U.S. 36
R.R. 2 Box 27, Rockville, Indiana 47872   317-569-3430

Hoosier Park, 4500 Dan Patch Circle, 642-RACE, is Indiana's first pari-mutuel harness and thoroughbred racing track. Even if you're not the wagering type, it's fun to watch the horses run and hard not to get caught up in the excitement.

For more information about the Anderson area, contact the Anderson/Madison County Visitors & Convention Bureau, 6335 Scatterfield Road, 643-5633 or (800) 53-ENJOY.

FAIRMOUNT

By dying young and becoming a legend, rebel without a cause James Dean put this small farming community, his hometown, on the map. It's the site both of his grave, which is in Park cemetery on County Road 150E, 948-4040, and of the **James Dean Gallery and Gift Shop**, 425 W. Main Street, (800) 748-3326, which contains the world's largest collection of Dean memorabilia. Fairmount, which incidentally was also the childhood home of cartoonist Jim Davis, the creator of "Garfield" who now lives and works in nearby Muncie, is also the site of an annual James Dean festival every September. For information, contact the Fairmount Historical Museum, 203 E. Washington Street, 948-4555. To get to Fairmount, take I-69 N. to S.R. 26.

MUNCIE

Central Indiana isn't a place you'd expect to find tropical splendor, but find it you will in Ball State University's greenhouse, home of the **Wheeler Orchid Collection**. With 7,000 plants, this collection contains more varieties of orchids than any other in the world. You'll find the greenhouse amid a 17-acre botanical wonderland known as Christy Woods, which houses an arboretum, gardens and a nature center. For information, contact the university's biology department, 285-8820.

As the home of the Ball Corporation, internationally known for its glass canning jars and other containers, Muncie is a glass lover's gold mine. The **Ball Corporation's Glass Collection**, which is on exhibit in the company's headquarters, 345 S. High Street, 747-6100, features examples of glass work from canning jars to aerospace items. And **Indiana Glass Outlet**, 1300 Batavia at S.R. 32, 284-7046, is a warehouse-size outlet for all sorts of glassware.

The **Minnetrista Cultural Center,** 1200 N. Minnetrista Parkway, 282-4848, is a multifaceted facility in which galleries showcase exhibitions devoted to history, art, science and industry. It also hosts concerts and various theme festivals.

For more information on the Muncie area, contact the Muncie Visitors Bureau, 425 N. High Street, 284-2700 or (800) 568-6862.

Weekend Getaways

While our Daytrips suggestions will get you started exploring central Indiana, if you've got a whole weekend, you can wander farther afield. The state abounds with historic, scenic and intriguing destinations. Some require a two- or three-hour drive, but if you have a couple of days — even in the middle of the week — then gas up the car, throw in an overnight bag and set out to see the state.

Of course, you can always head to Chicago, St. Louis or Cincinnati, three traditional out-of-state getaways, but here we'll direct you to some of our best in-state destinations. We do suggest, of course, that you always call ahead or make reservations; after a day of shopping or sightseeing, no one wants to face a no-vacancy sign.

We've tried to spread out across the state, and if you manage to get away to all eight of our weekend wonders, then you really will have "wandered Indiana." (Wander Indiana was a license plate slogan and state tourism theme some years back.) And while you're wandering, don't hesitate to stop along the way and check out some of our previously mentioned Daytrip destinations.

Send us a postcard.

Amish Country

One of the country's largest Amish settlements is in northern Indiana. Concentrated in Elkhart and LaGrange counties, this area, called the Crystal Valley, is home to a thriving, growing Amish community that eschews many of today's modern conveniences in favor of a simple life built around God, family and community.

The Amish came to the area in the 1800s, and settlements grew around the towns of Napanee, Middlebury and Shipshewana. The small towns and cities in the area have become well-known for shops that showcase the many Amish-made products: fine furniture, quilts, woven rugs and, perhaps most tempting, delicious food items. In the rural areas, you'll drive past farms still plowed with draft horses; notice how many houses aren't connected to electric lines or telephone poles.

You'll also soon notice the many horse-drawn buggies that travel the roads of Elkhart and LaGrange counties. The LaGrange courthouse still boasts operational hitching posts, and you'll even see buggies hitched outside fast food restaurants. Snap a photo of the buggy if you're so inclined, but don't photograph the Amish people; being photographed violates their religious code and can make them very uncomfortable.

To learn about the Amish lifestyle and see the countryside at the same time, plan to begin in **Elkhart** (be sure to allow several hours to get there). For the most direct route from Indianapolis, take U.S. Highway 31 north to U.S. 6, then take U.S. 6 about 15 miles to Napanee; travel north on Ind. 19 into Elkhart. At the Elkhart County Visitors Center, just off Ind.

19 near I-80/90, you can pick up the **Heritage Trail**, a tour route that extends 90 miles through northern Indiana's Amish country.

At the visitors center, a refundable deposit gets you a guidebook, map and cassette tape that lead you off the beaten path and into the countryside via the Heritage Trail. Though the trail can be driven without stops in just more than two hours, you'll want to poke along at your own pace, stopping here and there to browse, shop and dine at some of the finest establishments in the Midwest (keep in mind that some shops and establishments close on Sunday). You'll discover the historic **Bonneyville Mill**, the oldest continuously operating grist mill in Indiana, where daily from May through October water power still grinds corn, wheat, buckwheat and rye; flours and meals are available for purchase. The grist mill is in **Bonneyville Mill County Park**, 2.5 miles southeast of Bristol on County Road 131, south of Ind. 120.

In **Middlebury**, you can park the car and explore the town on foot, stopping in at quilt shops and antique stores before driving out to **Das Dutchman Essenhaus**, 240 U.S. Highway 20, (219) 825-9471. This huge operation serves up some of the area's best food in its warm, comfortable Country Kitchen. Served family style or à la carte, the hearty country fare proves excellent — comfort food at its best. Essenhaus offers delicious broasted chicken, roast beef, homemade noodles, real mashed potatoes — and for goodness sake, don't forget the pies. Before or after dinner, browse through the nearby shops surrounding the Country Kitchen and the adjacent Country Inn, where you'll find baked goods, homemade candies, housewares, crafts and clothing.

The Heritage Trail continues farther east to **Shipshewana**, where you can easily spend a whole day. The small town, called Ship-she by the locals, offers shops full of antiques, gifts and handmade crafts as well as inviting restaurants and cafes. But on Tuesdays and Wednesdays from May through October, the town hosts thousands of visitors at the Shipshewana Auction and Flea Market. More than 1,000 outdoor vendors sell everything from antique china to designer sunglasses. At the **Antique and Miscellaneous Auction Barn**, visitors bid on one-of-a-kind treasures, and at the livestock auction next door, you can watch as dealers from across the country buy and sell cattle, hogs and the highly regarded Amish draft horses. Across the street from the flea market, the **Menno-Hof Visitors Center**, (219) 768-4117, presents an in-depth look at Amish and Mennonite cultures. The **Morton Street Bed and Breakfast Homes**, (800) 447-6475, three stately homes in the middle of Shipshewana, offer charming accommodations — and breakfast at the well-known **Buggy Wheel Restaurant**, which serves up tasty soups and sandwiches. Call (800) 447-6475 for more information.

Back on the Heritage Trail, you'll hit **Goshen**, which offers excellent shopping. **The Old Bag Factory**, a restored 1890s manufacturing complex, includes 17 shops showcasing local artists and artisans. Then in **Napanee**, known for top-quality cabinetry, you'll find **Amish Acres**, 1600 W. Market Street, Napanee, (800) 800-4942, an 80-acre farm listed on the National Register of Historic Places. Interpreters explain the Amish way of life, and craft demonstrations showcase such traditional skills as quilting, weaving, broom making and baking with an outdoor brick oven. But the place is likely most famous for its threshers' dinners in the Restaurant Barn, meals that begin with thick, hearty bean soup and end with fresh shoofly pie; the 650-seat restaurant earns high ratings. Visitors can also watch a performance of the Broadway musical *Plain and Fancy*, a comedy about Amish life and love, in the **Round Barn Theatre** from late April through mid-November. Lodging is available at the adjacent Inn at Amish Acres.

From Napanee, the Heritage Trail heads back north to **Wakarusa**, host of the annual **Maple Syrup Festival** in early spring, before leading travelers back to Elkhart.

Lodging is available all across Elkhart and LaGrange counties, and you'll find everything from cozy bed and breakfasts to modern motel chains. Some of the most well-known inns include the **Checkerberry Inn**, (219) 642-4445, whose award-winning restaurant was featured in *Gourmet* magazine; **Coneygar Bed and Breakfast**, (219) 825-5707, a 40-acre horse farm with beautiful views and rolling countryside; the **Patchwork Quilt Country Inn**, (219) 825-2417, situated on a quiet farm outside Middlebury very close to the Michigan state line; and the **Victorian Guest House**, (219) 773-4383, an elegant 1887 historic home in Napanee.

For more information on Northern Indiana's Amish country, contact the Elkhart County Convention and Visitors Bureau, 219 Caravan Drive, Elkhart, 46514, or call (800) 262-8161.

Fort Wayne

While Indiana's Amish country offers excellent shopping, browsing and antiquing, in nearby Fort Wayne visitors will find loads of family-related activities. A two-hour drive up I-69 from Indianapolis brings you to Fort Wayne, Indiana's second-largest city and home to more than 190,000 residents.

Here you'll find plenty of activities to build a weekend around. Arrive early on a Saturday and head to **Fort Wayne's Children's Zoo**, 3411 Sherman Boulevard, (219) 427-6800, a facility ranked among the top 10 in the country and host to more than a half-million visitors each year. Of special note is the world's only endangered species carousel, the African Veldt, the Australian Adventure and the new Indonesian Rain Forest Exhibit; Orangutan Valley, phase II of the exhibit, opened in June 1995. The well-maintained zoo features easily accessible, paved walkways, beautiful landscaping and enough variety to keep youngsters tugging Mom and Dad along to the next exhibit. The zoo opens from late April through mid-October.

Kids will also dig **Science Central**, 1950 N. Clinton Street, (219) 424-2413, a brand-new hands-on interactive science center that was scheduled to open in the fall of 1995. Designed to make math, science and technology enjoyable and accessible for everyone, Science Central allows kids of all ages the opportunity to create their own earthquake, bend a rainbow, dance across a giant keyboard, walk like an astronaut across a moonscape and peer out from inside a giant bubble. And Kids Central is a special exhibit area designed for youngsters ages 2 through 7.

Another new Fort Wayne attraction is the **Lincoln Museum**, 200 E. Berry Street, (219) 455-3864, which houses the world's largest private Lincoln collection. The new 30,000-square-foot downtown facility, scheduled to open in September 1995, includes 11 galleries, four theaters and computerized and hands-on exhibits for all age groups. Call for details.

Sports fans can cheer on the **Class A Wizards** baseball team, the **Fury CBA** basketball team or the **Komets IHL** hockey

Photo: The Indianapolis Star & News

"Garfield" comic strip creator Jim Davis is a native of Fairmount and currently resides in Muncie.

team. Call (219) 483-1111 for details on sports schedules and ticket information.

Those who want to strap on some skates themselves should head out to **Glenbrook Square Mall**, which in addition to more than 170 stores features an indoor ice skating rink. For a more pastoral afternoon, check out the **Lakeside Rose Garden**, 1400 Lake Avenue, (219) 427-6000, where visitors can enjoy more than 2,000 rose bushes representing more than 150 varieties in one of the country's largest rose gardens. Explore a tropical paradise as well as a desert environment at the **Foellinger-Freimann Botanical Conservatory**, 1100 S. Calhoun Street, (219) 427-1267. **The Allen County Public Library**, 900 Webster Street, (219) 424-7241, offers the country's second-largest genealogy department with professional on-site counselors to help you begin or continue a search for your family's roots.

If you visit Fort Wayne in mid-July, plan to attend the **Three Rivers Festival**, a nine-day extravaganza of music, art, sports and entertainment. Call (219) 745-5556 or (219) 424-3900 for details.

But if you're in the area in the winter, you owe it to the kids to head north to **Pokagon State Park**, (219) 833-2012; it's in Steuben County near Angola off I-69. The beautiful area is a natural for outdoor activities year round, but the most exciting attraction is the .25-mile toboggan track. Yes, you have to tote your rented toboggan uphill, but the trip down on the well-maintained track is one thrilling ride. Pile on the toboggan with the kids, and let it take your breath away. The park and its newly renovated Potawatomi Inn (which features an indoor pool, sauna and whirlpool — tempting after all that tobogganing) is open year round, but the toboggan track only operates from Thanksgiving through February.

On the way to or from Pokagon, stop in

Auburn, the DeKalb County seat, and visit the **Auburn Cord Duesenberg Museum**, 1600 S. Wayne Street, (219) 925-1444. Listed on the National Register of Historic Places, the art deco building, once the 1930 factory headquarters of the Auburn Automobile Company, now houses more than 100 vehicles, from the early "horseless carriage" to luxurious Duesenbergs of the 1930s to sports cars of today. The museum opens every day except Thanksgiving, Christmas and New Year's Day; call for admission fees and group and family rates.

You'll find all the major motel chains in the Fort Wayne area as well as charming bed and breakfast inns. Popular restaurants include the more than a dozen Don Hall's restaurants; try the prime rib at **Don Hall's Factory**, 5811 Coldwater Road, (219) 484-8693, or the steaks, seafood and Cajun cooking at **Don Hall's Old Gas House**, 305 E. Superior Street, (219) 426-3411. Or you can splurge at the highly regarded **Cafe Johnell**, 2529 S. Calhoun Street, (219) 456-1939. Don't miss the fresh fish, duck and prime filets.

For more information, contact the Fort Wayne Convention and Visitors Bureau, 1021 S. Calhoun Street, Fort Wayne, (800) 767-7752.

French Lick

There is really no quick and easy way to reach Orange County, home of basketball legend Larry Bird, from Indianapolis. To get to **French Lick Springs Resort**, 8670 W. State Road 56, (800) 457-4042, a grand old 485-room hotel, you just have to take your time. And maybe that's part of the allure of the place that once hosted the movers and shakers (and, some say, gamblers and gangsters) of the 1920s and '30s.

The scenic route through Brown

County and the Hoosier National Forest requires driving the curvy Ind. 135 south from Indianapolis to Salem, then taking Ind. 56 west to Paoli. There you'll pick up U.S. 150 for a while before getting back on 56 for a few miles to French Lick. Or you can head south from Indianapolis on Ind. 37, travel through Bloomington, Bedford, Mitchell and Orleans before hitting Paoli and continue on from there, which will likely prove quicker. Still, set aside several hours for the drive. Regardless of route, the trip through southern Indiana offers beautiful scenery, especially in the fall.

Once in the tiny town of French Lick, it's easy to find the resort. The elegant old hotel dominates the town. Once inside the elegant lobby, it feels as if you've stepped back in time. You can easily imagine the resort in its heyday when people came to relax in the soothing mineral baths the resort was famous for. The "Pluto Water" that bubbled up from a natural spring was thought to have healing properties; you can still relax in a Pluto mineral bath in the hotel's well-known spa. Though the hotel offers a number of spa packages, the treatments, which include massages, a salt rub, a sea mud wrap, facials, manicures and pedicures, can be purchased à la carte as well. They don't come cheap, though. A 60-minute facial will set you back nearly $50; you can be wrapped in sea mud for about $40. But a 30-minute Pluto mineral bath only costs around $12.

If being plastered with mud isn't your idea of a good time, the resort also offers golf just about year round, and golf packages generally include 36 holes of golf (per night's stay) on the 18-hole **Valley Golf Links** or, for an extra fee, on the Donald Ross-designed **Country Club Course**. Tennis and ski packages are available (Paoli Peaks is only about 9 miles away), and the resort also schedules holiday weekend packages throughout the year. Prices in 1995 (based on double occupancy with meals included) vary from $69.50 per person for a basic room to fall and winter golf getaways at $99 per person to a two-day spa sampler for $299 per person.

While you're in the area, check out the former **West Baden Springs Hotel** in nearby West Baden. There's been considerable interest in restoring the once-magnificent domed building that, until the Houston Astrodome was built, was the largest freestanding domed structure in the country.

Also nearby is the huge **Patoka Lake** and the adjacent **Tillery Hill State Recreation Area**, which offers camping, boating, hunting, fishing, a swimming beach — even a Frisbee golf course. For more information, contact the Department of Natural Resources Office of Reservoir Management, 402 W. Washington Street, Room W282, Indianapolis 46204, or call 232-4060. Contact the Patoka Lake office directly at Route 1, Box 290, Birdseye, 47513, or call (812) 685-2464.

Indiana Dunes

You don't expect surf and sand in Indiana, but just head northwest to Lake Michigan and you'll find both — though it will take you several hours to get there. The Indiana Dunes National Lakeshore stretches across Porter and LaPorte counties, and the area offers visitors from Central Indiana a definite change of scenery. Indeed, the unique area ranks fourth among the entire National Park System for plant diversity, and the land offers considerable diversity as well. Here you can explore bogs, marshes, beaches, an oak forest, the state's largest tract of ancient prairie and the park's largest living sand dune. Bring your camera or sketchbook if you want to capture a bit of the park to take home; all plants, natural and historic features are protected by law — do not disturb them.

Begin your visit at the **Dorothy Buell Memorial Visitors Center**, on Kemil Road at U.S. Highway 12, 3 miles from Ind. 49, (219) 926-7561; the facility was named for an early crusader who worked to save the dunes from encroaching industrialization. Here you'll find plenty of information about the area, a bookstore and an accessible trail amid wooded dunes. Pick up a map and you can head either east or west along the lake, go for a swim or just walk along the beach. There's nothing like a beach at sunset to make you forget the road construction and rush-hour gridlock back home. (Keep in mind, however, that some areas within the park are private property; you'll see plenty of posh lakeside homes in the ritzy Beverly Shores area.)

The **Mt. Baldy** area on the eastern end of the National Lakeshore, which features the parks' largest living sand dune, offers climbing — on marked trails — with the payoff of beautiful vistas; other climbing dunes are located at West Beach at the opposite end of the lakeshore. But don't be too disappointed if nearby steel mills or the Northern Indiana Public Service Company facilities mar your view. Northwest Indiana is simply an industrialized area. Still, the protected dune areas really are beautiful. Central Beach, Kemil Beach and West Beach are watched by life guards in the summer, and these popular areas hosts thousands of visitors each year.

You'll find campgrounds and picnic sites all along the **National Lakeshore**, 1100 N. Mineral Springs Road, Porter, (219) 926-7561, and in the **Indiana Dunes State Park**, 1600 N. 25 E., Chesterton, (219) 926-1952. The lakeshore area is also home to two historic farms: the **Baily Homestead**, a newly restored home and historic cemetery with hiking, tours and activities; and the **Chellberg Farm**, a turn-of-the-century active farm with tours, demonstrations and animals. For more information about either homestead, call (219) 926-7561.

Those who prefer shopping bags to sunscreen also head to northwest Indiana, but they have **Michigan City** in mind, home of **Lighthouse Place Outlet Center**, 601 Wabash Street, (219) 879-6506. Shoppers come to hunt for bargains in such outlets as **Bennetton**, **Reebok**, **Speigel**, **Florsheim**, **Corning Revere**, **Pepperidge Farms** and **London Fog**. The many shops in this unique downtown mall are open from 9 AM to 8 PM Monday through Saturday and from 10 AM to 6 PM Sunday.

Also in Michigan City is the **Old Lighthouse Museum**, (219) 872-6133, the state's first lighthouse, built in 1858 and enlarged in 1904. Keepers lived here until 1940 when the U.S. Coast Guard assumed control of the light. Restored by the Michigan City Historical Society, the lighthouse now houses a museum that showcases the history of lighthouses as well as special exhibits and changing displays. To reach the museum, take I-94 east to U.S. 421; follow that north all the way to Ninth Street. Turn right then immediately left onto Pine Street. Follow Pine as it curves into Washington Park, and watch for signs. The museum is open Tuesday through Sunday from 1 to 4 PM; it closes on Mondays, holidays and for the month of February.

Other area attractions include the **Wizard of Oz Museum** in Chesterton, where you'll find collector dolls, accessories and memorabilia from the movie. The mid-September **Wizard of Oz Festival** has featured some of the original MGM munchkins as well as other Oz-related celebrities. Call (219) 926-7048 for museum and festival information.

For a bit more thrill, consider parasailing. You take off and land from the boat that pulls the parachute; you don't even get wet. Take along a camera or binoculars and enjoy the view as you rise skyward and sail above Lake Michigan. No special skills are required, and just about anyone can parasail: young, old, physically challenged (the minimum weight is 70 pounds; the maximum is 300). If it sounds appealing, contact **Up, Up & Away Parasail**, (800) 655-3880, a business based in nearby New Buffalo, Michigan. You can parasail from mid-May through September every day except Tuesday and on weekends in October — weather permitting, of course.

After a day at the beach, you'll need a rest, and you'll find major motel chains and cozy bed and breakfast inns throughout the area. Try The **Brickstone Bed and Breakfast**, 215 Sixth Street, in Michigan City, (219) 878-1819, an historic dwelling built in 1880 by the First Congrega-

tional Church as its parson's home. Or check out **The Inn at Union Pier**, 9708 Berrien Street in Union Pier. Only 200 steps from the beach, this relaxing hostel was selected as one of the area's best small inns by *Chicago Magazine*. For more information on the Dunes region, contact the Porter County Convention, Recreation and Visitor Commission, 800 Indian Boundary Road, Chesterton 46304, or call (219) 926-2255.

Lafayette/West Lafayette

It only takes about an hour to get to Lafayette from Indianapolis, making this western Indiana city a perfect quick getaway. For a terrific Lafayette-area getaway, plan for mid-October and hit the Feast of the Hunters' Moon, visit Wolf Park and take in a Purdue Boilermakers football game.

One of the best festivals in the area (see sidebar in our Events and Festivals chapter) is the **Feast of the Hunters' Moon**, a recreation of an 18th-century gathering of French and Native Americans. Scheduled for October 12 and 13 in 1996 at Fort

Photo: The Indianapolis Star & News

Visitors to Pokagon State Park in northeastern Indiana enjoy the toboggan run.

Ouiatenon Historic Park, the festival features lots of costumed participants who recreate 18th-century life with everything including food, military drills and Native American dances. For more information, contact the Tippecanoe County Historical Association, 909 South Street, Lafayette, 47901, or call 742-8411.

Wolf Park, on Jefferson Street (call 567-2265 for directions), a unique education and research wildlife park, features several packs of wolves and a herd of bison as well as coyotes and foxes. On Wolf Howl Night, held year round on Friday evenings, visitors can watch the wolves when they're most active, learn how the wolves communicate and even join in on some howling themselves. On Sunday afternoons from May through November, the wolves are allowed to test a small herd of healthy bison. Though the wolves are not allowed to injure the bison, visitors can watch as the wolves test their prey and as the bison protect themselves and their young against predators. The park opens daily from May through November from 1 to 5 PM; it's closed on holidays. Guided tours are offered on weekends.

A fall weekend in the Lafayette area just wouldn't be complete without some Boilermaker football. For some real rivalry, plan to attend a game against Indiana University, Notre Dame or the University of Michigan. Get ready for some energetic cheering; Purdue fans take their football seriously. For ticket information and other details, call the Purdue University Athletic Ticket Office, 494-3194.

If you don't care to spend Saturday or Sunday in the bleachers, then head downtown and explore Lafayette's historic architecture: the renovated **1882 Tippecanoe County Courthouse** on the town square, 423-9326; the **Fowler House** county historical museum, 909 South Street, 742-841-

8411; and the **Greater Lafayette Museum of Art**, 101 S. Ninth Street, 742-1128. You'll also find numerous specialty shops, antique stores and the usual bookstores and clothing shops indigenous to college towns as well as a wide variety of restaurants, including everything from pizza joints to prime rib.

Though the area abounds with chain motels, check out the **Purdue University Union Club** at the corner of State and Grant streets, (800) 320-6291, to get a real feel for the campus. **University Inn and Conference Center**, 3001 Northwestern Avenue, (800) 777-9808, is another comfortable near-campus option.

For more information on events and lodging, contact the **Greater Lafayette Convention and Visitors Bureau**, 301 Frontage Road, Lafayette 47905, or call (800) 872-6648.

Madison

This charming river town prospered in the early 1800s as the area's main river port, railway center and supply town for pioneers moving into the Old Northwest Territory. And today, thanks to plenty of preservation work, Madison offers visitors a beautiful downtown, historic architecture and an inviting atmosphere.

Except for the July 4th weekend, when the town hosts the Madison Regatta and the Governor's Cup hydroplane race, when unlimited hydroplanes zoom along the water at 200 mph, Madison is a quiet community. Visitors enjoy walking along the riverfront, prowling through antique shops and exploring the town's 133 blocks that are listed on the National Register of Historic Places.

Start at the **Visitors Center**, open daily at 301 E. Main Street, (800) 559-2956, and watch a video presentation and pick up a map of the area. On a walking tour, you can stop in at the **Early American Trades Museum**, 313 E. First Street, (812) 273-6568, and watch demonstrations by such 19th-century craftsmen as wheelwrights, blacksmiths and carpenters. The museum opens weekends from late April through Thanksgiving and on weekdays by appointment.

Madison's downtown area features several restored homes, including the **1849 Shrewsbury-Windle House**, 301 W. First Street, (812) 265-4481, a National Historic Landmark; the **Jeremiah Sullivan House**, 304 W. Second Street, (812) 265-2484, an 1818 mansion that features the only known restored Federal serving kitchen in the country; the **Francis Costigan House**, 408 W. Third Street, (812) 265-2967, home of one of the area's famed architects; and **Dr. William D. Hutchings Office**, 120 W. Third Street, (812) 265-2967, a 19th century doctor's office preserved exactly as used by Dr. Hutchings, a local physician, until his death in 1903. Most homes open daily from April through November.

The most impressive Madison home may be that of **J.F.D. Lanier**, whose loans to the state equipped Union troops during the Civil War. His 1844 home, 511 W. First Street, (812) 265-3526, a Greek Revival mansion and National Historic Landmark, is open daily (except Mondays) year round. The mansion grounds also include a restored 1850s cutting and vegetable garden.

Though you'll find few chain motels in Madison, the town boasts a variety of charming bed and breakfast inns, including the well-known **Cliff House**, 122 Fairmont Street, (812) 265-5272; the antique-filled **Federal Inn**, 710 E. Main Street, (812) 265-4501; the cozy **Old Madison Bed and Breakfast**, 517 Mulberry Street, (812) 265-6874; and the comfortable **Schussler House Bed and Breakfast**, 514 Jefferson Street, (800) 392-1931. The city also offers lots of cozy cafes and restaurants to choose from clustered in the downtown historic district. You'll find delicious light fare at the **Cinnamon Tea Room**, 302 West Street, (812) 273-2367; and hearty sandwiches and dinners at the **Historic Broadway Hotel and Tavern**, 313 Broadway Street, (812) 265-2346.

For more information about Madison, contact the Madison Area Convention and Visitors Bureau, 301 E. Main Street, Madison 47250, or call (800) 559-2956.

Saint Mary-of-the-Woods

Not all getaways need be focused on shopping and sightseeing. Those looking for a more spiritual experience will appreciate the serenity of Saint Mary-of-the-Woods, the mother house of the **Sisters of Providence**, a Roman Catholic order of women religious, and home to **Saint Mary-of-the-Woods College**.

To reach this spiritual oasis, take I-70 west to Terre Haute; take Exit 3, and travel north on Darwin Road. Turn right on U.S. Highway 40, left onto U.S. Highway 150, then left again onto Saint Mary's Road. Begin your visit at the Providence Center, the welcome center for all visitors to Saint Mary-of-the-Woods that includes the **National Shrine of Our Lady of Providence,** a candlelit area that holds the portrait of Our Lady of Providence; the **Heritage Museum** and the **Hall of Memories**, which tells the history of the site through exhibits and photographs; and the **Gift Shop**, where you'll find unusual gifts, religious items and "sister-made" crafts.

More than 300 sisters live at Saint Mary-of-the-Woods, and visitors are welcome to celebrate Mass with the sisters in the **Church of the Immaculate Conception** on Monday through Saturday at 11:30 AM and on Sunday at 10 AM. Visitors can also explore the grounds and visit other sacred places: the **Blessed Sacrament Chapel**; the tiny, outdoor **Saint Anne Shell Chapel**; and the **Our Lady of Lourdes Grotto**, a replica of the Lourdes Shrine in France. Other grottoes and shrines can be discovered along wooded paths that crisscross the grounds on guided or self-guided walking tours.

Families are invited to visit the center, and events throughout the year allow parents to share a spiritual experience with their children. Among the 1995 events were the outdoor family **Stations of the Cross** during Lent; **Vespers** in the Church of the Immaculate Conception each Sunday during Lent at 4 PM; an **environmental walk** in September that includes readings, leaf rubbing and picnicking; and a special **Children's Sabbath** in October at the 10 AM liturgy in the Church of the Immaculate Conception that includes a special reception honoring children.

Another favorite event is the **Sisters of Providence Annual Christmas Bazaar and Bake Sale** held each fall in mid-November. Items sell quickly, and you'll have to arrive early to purchase the sister-made quilts, needlework, paintings, wall hangings, Christmas ornaments, candy and baked goods at this popular sale.

Breakfast, lunch and dinner are available daily in the **O'Shaughnessy Dining Room**; a bountiful Sunday Brunch at the Woods, including Belgian waffles, hearty entrees and an extensive dessert selection, is available on Sundays from 10:30 AM until 1:30 PM. Overnight lodging is available at Saint Mary-of-the-Woods College, (812) 535-4141, or at a number of motels located at the intersection of I-70 and U.S. Highway 41.

For more details on tours, pilgrimages and special events, contact the Providence Center, Sisters of Providence, Saint Mary-of-the-Woods 47876, or call (812) 535-3131. For additional lodging information, contact the Terre Haute Convention and Visitor Bureau at (812) 234-5555.

Vincennes and New Harmony

Southwestern Indiana abounds with historical sights, so get ready for a history tour when you plan a getaway here. Begin at **Vincennes**, Indiana's oldest city. It'll take you more than two hours to get here from Indianapolis. Though it doesn't look like a direct route, the quickest way is likely I-70 west to Terre Haute, then U.S. Highway 41 south to Vincennes; Ind. 67 also leads from Indianapolis to Vincennes, though you'll be traveling on a two-lane state road and going through lots of small towns along the way.

Vincennes, the former territorial capital was founded in 1732. Situated right on the banks of the Wabash River, it played a pivotal role in the American Revolution. The George Rogers Clark Memorial commemorates a little-known but extremely important battle that took place on February 25, 1779 — the only Revolutionary War battle fought in Indiana. Clark and a small band of men marched more than 180 miles through often-flooded plains to surprise the British Lt. Gov. Henry Hamilton and capture Fort Sackville — and gain control of the Northwest Territory.

A massive granite and marble memorial now marks the location of **Fort**

Photo: The Indianapolis Star & News

The Amish in Shipshewana travel by horse and buggy.

Sackville. Inside murals depict the fort's capture; listen to the story via headphones as you look around the rotunda, which also boasts a larger-than-life statue of Clark. A bench runs along the wall of the rotunda; sit at one end of it and have a friend sit at the opposite end and whisper to you. Thanks to the room's architecture, you'll hear the whisper as though it were right in your ear.

Near the memorial, other historic sites offer a glimpse into life in the Indiana Territory. Indiana's first church, the **Old Cathedral** (St. Francis Xavier Catholic Church), boasts parish records dating from 1749; a cemetery includes graves of early settlers and Native Americans. **Grouseland**, the mansion home of Territorial Gov. William Henry Harrison, later the country's ninth president, is furnished with some period pieces. The home, at 3 W. Scott Street, can be toured daily except for Thanksgiving, Christmas and New Year's Day; an admission fee is charged. A few blocks away is **Vincennes**

University, an early Indiana college, as well as the **Elihu Stout Print Shop**, a reproduction of an early print shop, and the **Old Indiana Territory Capitol** building.

For a real taste of Vincennes' historic past, plan a visit during Memorial Day weekend, when the **Spirit of Vincennes Rendezvous** takes place. Offering Revolutionary battle recreations, authentic arts and crafts of the era and plenty of Colonial-style meals to sample, the rendezvous draws more than 30,000 visitors each year. And 1996 will mark the 20th anniversary of the festival.

Many motels serve Vincennes, which is home to comedian Red Skelton, and if you arrive Friday evening, you can spend Saturday morning soaking up the history. Try the **Executive Inn Hotel and Convention Center**, a complete travel and entertainment center with a pool, bakery, gift shop and **Dillon's Country Dance Hall**, (800) 457-9154. If camping is your thing, try Kimmell or Wabash Trails parks; call (800) 886-6443 for parks information. For more information on the Rendezvous, lodging or Vincennes in general, contact the Vincennes/Knox County Tourism Commission at 27, N. Third Street, Vincennes, or call (800) 886-6443.

Unless you're visiting during the Rendezvous, most historic sites in Vincennes can be seen in a morning. Hit the highway after lunch and head south on U.S. 41, then take I-64 west to Ind. 68 at Poseyville. This curvy road will lead you west to New Harmony, one of Indiana's most unique villages.

The site of two utopian communities, the tiny town boasts a rich historic legacy. Led by George Rapp, a group of Lutheran Separatists came to the area from Wurttemberg, Germany, in 1804, to create a model community while awaiting the millennium. By 1824, the group had built more than 150 structures. The village was later sold to Robert Owen, a Welsh-born industrialist who hoped to fulfill his own utopian dream of educational and social equality. Joined by a number of creative thinkers of the day, their contributions to education, trade schools and women's suffrage had far-reaching influence.

Today, many of the historic buildings are open for touring; the whole village can be easily explored on foot. Begin a visit at the **Atheneum/Visitors Center** at North and Arthur streets, (812) 682-4474, a surprisingly modern building designed by Richard Meier that includes an auditorium, exhibits and gift shop; tours begin here.

Wander through the town on your own if you prefer. Don't miss the **Roofless Church** on North Street, an interdenominational church, walled but indeed roofless, which was dedicated in 1960 to honor New Harmony's religious heritage. In the **Harmonist Cemetery**, off West Street, are buried in unmarked graves 230 members of George Rapp's Harmonie Society. Woodland Indian burial mounds dating from c. 800 A.D. are also within cemetery walls. The **Labyrinth**, a restored maze of hedges that symbolized the Harmonist's difficult journey toward perfection, can be found about eight blocks south of the stoplight on Ind. 69. See if you can find your way to the middle and back out again. (Don't worry; the hedges are only about shoulder high, and you can easily keep a friend in view.)

The downtown area of New Harmony includes plenty of interesting shops; a number are open on both Saturday and Sunday. The **New Harmony Inn**, 506 N. Street, (812) 682-4491, provides beautiful accommodations furnished with a Shaker-like style and simplicity. Eighteen of the 90 rooms feature fireplaces; many have balconies overlooking the beautiful gardens. Pleasant lodging can also be found at the **Old Rooming House**, 916 Church Street, (812) 682-4724; or the **Raintree Bed and Breakfast**, 503 West Street, (812) 682-5625. While in town, don't miss dinner — and the Shaker lemon pie — at the well-known **Red Geranium Restaurant**, 508 N. Street, (812) 682-4431.

Camping is available at the nearby **Harmonie State Park**. For information, write Route 1, Box 5A, New Harmony 47631, or call (812) 682-4821.

For more information on the area contact Historic New Harmony, P.O. Box 579, New Harmony 47631, or call (812) 682-4488.

Inside
Business and Industry

Chicago newspaper columnist Mike Royko once dismissed Indianapolis as a racetrack in a cornfield.

To give Royko his due, there is an element of truth to that stereotype. Indianapolis is the home of not one but four racetracks, the best known of which hosts one of the world's most prestigious auto races. The Indianapolis Motor Speedway is a significant presence in the city. So are the other tracks — Indianapolis Raceway Park, home of the National Hot Rod Association's U.S. Nationals and of Sports Car Club of America races; the Indiana State Fairgrounds' track, home of such events as the Hoosier Hundred; and the Speedrome, home of numerous midget and sprint car races.

Then there are all the other racing-related businesses. More than 250 Indianapolis-area companies are involved in motorsports activities, the largest concentration of such businesses outside of southern California. There are car designers, car graphics, component makers, safety equipment manufacturers, engineering firms and a number of racing teams — IndyCar teams, National Hot Rod Association teams and Sports Car Club of America TransAm teams.

Clearly, Indianapolis is a town that understands the business value of racing.

And, yes, there are cornfields all around Indianapolis. As it has been since the city's founding, farming is an important component in the local economy. According to

Photo: The Indianapolis Star & News

Eli Lilly is a multinational pharmaceutical manufacturing giant.

the Indianapolis Chamber of Commerce, there are more than 600 agribusiness firms in the Indianapolis area.

Still, important as they are, auto racing and agriculture are only a part of the economic scene in Indianapolis. To see the vitality and diversity of business and industry in Indianapolis, you have to look beyond Royko's stereotype.

From Naptown to Stardom

Over the past decade and a half, Indianapolis has enjoyed tremendous growth as a business center, fueled in part by its bootstrap approach to economic development. Faced with the decline of traditional heavy industries and the subsequent loss of several major factories in the late 1970s and early '80s, local business and government leaders worked hard to develop new business initiatives and foster entrepreneurial endeavors.

The first step was the consolidation of city and county government. Known as Unigov, this 1970 state legislative act expanded the boundaries of Indianapolis, enabling it to encompass almost all of Marion County. The city's geographic area jumped from 84 to 388 square miles, and both the population and the tax base nearly doubled. This laid the groundwork for subsequent construction projects and business development efforts.

The results have been dramatic. From a long period of sluggishness that had earned the city the nickname "Naptown," Indianapolis emerged as one of the success stories of the 1980s. Focusing their devel-

opment efforts on sports, city leaders forged innovative public-private partnerships to fund the renovation of existing amateur and professional sports facilities and the construction of new ones, investing more than $168 million in such projects.

It was a gamble, but one that paid off handsomely. With world-class facilities in place, the city attracted world-class events — and lured a number of amateur sports organizations to relocate their headquarters here. Aggressive promotion of the city and its sports capabilities raised its profile nationally and internationally and led to the self-proclaimed title of "Amateur Sports Capital of the World."

That focus improved the Indianapolis economy. Between 1977 and 1991, sports organizations and events added more than $1 billion to local coffers.

Naptown had awakened. Dubbed the "Star of the Snow Belt" by the *Wall Street Journal*, Indianapolis suddenly became an attractive site for companies looking to relocate or for entrepreneurs looking for a friendly environment for start-up businesses.

And what could be friendlier than a place that can claim easy access as one of its selling points?

Location, Location, Location

One of Indianapolis's oldest assets — its central geographic location— is also one of its strongest. According to a study done by the Chicago Association of Commerce and Industry, Indianapolis is the most cen-

Insiders' Tips

In offices across town, the *Indianapolis Business Journal* is required reading every Monday morning (although subscribers receive it Saturday and get the jump on everyone else).

In Indianapolis, one key fits all.

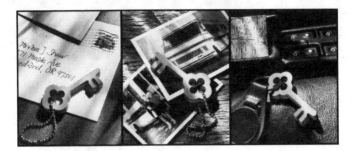

You don't have to go knocking on doors all over town to find the financial services you need. In Indianapolis, Society Bank is your key to both personal and business products and services.

Just make one stop. We'll help you with everything from your savings and checking accounts to loans and trust services. Plus, we have the resources to meet virtually any financial need of your business.

For more information on our products, or to find out the location of a Society Bank near you, call 1-800-KEY2YOU. Once you come through our door, you'll see how easily other doors will open, too.

EQUAL HOUSING LENDER

A KeyCorp Bank
Member FDIC

Society®

America's First Choice

Photo: The Indianapolis Star & News

Thomson Consumer Electronics is a center for RCA products.

trally located city to the top 100 U.S. markets. More than 65 percent of the people in the United States live within a 700-mile radius of Indianapolis.

What's more, four major interstate highways and five major railway routes connect in Indianapolis. And 17 airlines provide direct and nonstop services to 90 destinations from Indianapolis International Airport. Ease of access for passenger and freight transport alike makes Indianapolis attractive to companies looking for production and distribution sites.

Quality of Life

With an eight-county metropolitan statistical area (MSA) of 3,080 square miles and an MSA population of approximately 1.25 million people, Indianapolis is the 12th-largest U.S. city. Consistently ranked as one of the cleanest, safest places to live, it's a comfortable place to run a business and raise a family.

The authors of the 1994 edition of *The Places Rated Almanac* ranked Indianapolis eighth among 43 North America cities surveyed, citing favorable job prospects

as one of the city's attractions. In fact, Indianapolis has one of the highest job growth rates in the nation. At the same time, a low cost of living coupled with an effective buying income that's higher than the national average make Indianapolis an affordable place to live.

What's more, tax rates in Indianapolis are significantly lower than those in many other metropolitan regions — though Indiana's auto excise tax, which is based on the age and value of a vehicle, is a shock to many out-of-staters accustomed to paying a flat fee for their license plates. However, the excise tax will be reduced approximately $70 per car when a tax relief package passed by the state Legislature takes effect in 1996.

Economic Development Alliance

In 1992, a number of local organizations banded together to attract new businesses to Indianapolis and to help existing ones maintain and expand their operations. Known as the Indianapolis Economic Development Alliance, this coalition includes

GIFTZ

Everyone likes getting gifts — and for Indianapolis area companies, there's no better gift than having easy access to goods they've bought overseas. That's what GIFTZ gives them.

The Greater Indianapolis Foreign Trade Zone (GIFTZ), a nonprofit subsidiary of the Indianapolis Airport Authority, provides local companies a quick, cost-effective entry point for imports. Like islands unto themselves, foreign trade zones exist outside of the purview of U.S. Customs; anything that's shipped to a foreign trade zone is held there duty-free. Only upon release from the zone into a U.S. Customs territory are imports subject to duties.

But at Indianapolis International Airport, even that process is relatively painless since, in addition to the foreign trade zone facilities, there is a U.S. Customs Port of Entry onsite. When a company is ready for merchandise stored at GIFTZ, it is sent through Customs inspection, duties are assessed and the company has what it needs in a timely manner.

GIFTZ consists of a 62,000-square-foot warehouse, a 174,000-square-foot parking area and a 2,600-square-foot office complex. All that space allows the trade zone to store a variety of imported items, which it releases to area manufacturers and other businesses on an as-needed basis.

GIFTZ is one of the largest foreign trade zones in the United States, and it's poised to get bigger, at least in terms of the companies it serves. With the passage of the North American Free Trade Agreement, GIFTZ's central location proved attractive to a number of European firms looking for distribution channels to serve customers throughout the United States, Canada and Mexico.

The presence of GIFTZ is a gift that looks likely to keep on giving.

For more information, contact GIFTZ, 487-7200.

representatives from the City of Indianapolis, the Indianapolis Economic Development Corporation, Indianapolis Power & Light Company, Citizens Gas & Coke Utility, Indianapolis Water Company, the Indianapolis Airport Authority, the Indianapolis Network for Employment and Training, Indianapolis Downtown, Inc., and the Indianapolis Regional Small Business Development Center.

By coordinating their efforts and sharing their resources, alliance members work cooperatively rather than at cross purposes when courting new businesses to locate in Indianapolis and to help existing ones remain or expand here. In its first two years, the alliance was responsible for helping 47 new businesses open here, as well as for helping 110 existing businesses expand.

As a result, the alliance's efforts led to Indianapolis setting three annual job-creation records: in 1992, more than 3,600 new jobs were added to the local employment ranks; in 1993, almost 3,800; in 1994, the figure was nearly 5,000.

For more information on the alliance,

contact the Indianapolis Economic Development Corporation, 236-6262.

Division of Workforce Development

More jobs mean a greater need for qualified workers. To ensure that companies can find qualified employees, the Division of Workforce Development (DWD) was established in May 1994. Working in conjunction with the Office of Economic Development and the Indianapolis Network for Employment and Training, the DWD links companies in need of workers with people in need of jobs.

To learn more, contact the DWD, 232-7670.

Removing Regulatory Roadblocks

Regulatory guidelines can be both a blessing and a curse: The best of them protect consumers and businesses alike; the worst of them prevent innovation and throw up bureaucratic barriers. Enter the Regulatory Study Commission.

Formed by Mayor Stephen Goldsmith in 1992, the RSC is charged with enhancing local business productivity, encouraging entrepreneurial activities, streamlining the process of getting business permits and licenses, and helping consumers get the lowest possible prices on local products and services. To achieve those aims, the commission reviews existing and proposed regulations and eliminates those that seem unnecessary or burdensome.

So far, the commission's work has led to the deregulation of taxicab licenses, a simplified process of getting construction permits, and an easing of restrictions on sidewalk vendors. Commissioners have also examined the fairness and flexibility of zoning ordinances. The RCS depends on input from local businesses to identify regulations in need of its particular brand of TLC. For more information, contact the Mayor's Action Center, 327-4622.

Global Initiatives

Though demographically not as cosmopolitan as Chicago, Indianapolis is home to some 500 companies that do business internationally. Exports of Indianapolis-produced goods and services total some $1.5

Photo: The Indianapolis Star & News

USA Group is a nationwide guarantor of federally sponsored student loans.

billion annually, while global investments in local manufacturing, warehousing and distribution facilities are directly responsible for 17,000 jobs.

Over the past few years, Indianapolis has developed sister-city relationships with Taipei, Taiwan; Cologne, Germany; and Monza, Italy. In addition, it shares a cultural and business exchange program with Scarborough, in the Canadian province of Ontario.

But that's just the beginning. Since 1992, efforts have been afoot to increase opportunities for local companies to do business globally. Toward that end, the Global Initiatives Task Force, which consists of local government and business leaders, has spent the past few years looking for ways to identify new international business prospects throughout Europe, Canada, Mexico, South America, Asia, Africa and the Middle East.

These efforts are bound to escalate even further as the global marketplace continues to encompass more and more goods and services. Traditionally the Crossroads of America, Indianapolis is making inroads around the world in hopes of becoming if not *the* Crossroads of World Trade, at least a vital way station.

Where Business Is Done

There isn't really a central business core in Indianapolis. You'll find businesses large and small spread throughout the city. However, there are key pockets of activity, most notably in the following areas:

•Downtown: In the office towers and commercial buildings throughout the Mile

INDIANAPOLIS
ECONOMIC DEVELOPMENT ALLIANCE

The Indianapolis Economic Development Alliance is an evolving group of Indianapolis organizations focused on common economic development goals.

- Indianapolis Economic Development Corporation
- City of Indianapolis
- Indianapolis Airport Authority
- Indianapolis Power & Light Company
- Citizens Gas & Coke Utility
- Indianapolis Water Company
- Indianapolis Private Industry Council
- Indianapolis Downtown, Inc.
- Indianapolis Project, Inc.
- Small Business Development Center

320 NORTH MERIDIAN ST.
SUITE 900
INDIANAPOLIS, IN 46204-1727
317•236•6262
FAX 317•236•6275

Square, you'll find some of the city's biggest law firms, financial institutions, stock brokerages, insurance companies and state agencies.

•North: Meridian Street, north of 82nd Street, is a hotbed of business activity with a number of commercial buildings and office parks housing large mortgage and real estate firms, banks and investment companies, data management operations, insurance companies, marketing and advertising firms, and publishing companies.

•Northeast: Office parks in the Keystone Crossing, Castleton, Westfield and Fishers areas offer modern amenities to insurance and financial services companies, accounting and law firms, telecommunications and software companies and real estate and advertising agencies. This is also the area of upscale retail malls and strip centers as well as of high-volume, upscale auto dealerships.

•Northwest: Office parks in the Michigan Road and 86th Street region, as well as along West 71st Street, house a variety of small- and medium-size businesses in such diverse fields as information management, computer sales and service, cellular communications, insurance, human resources and publishing.

•West: Factories and warehouses share space with small office parks and retail strip centers. This area of town is also home to a number of the city's auto-racing enterprises.

•East: Once home to the city's industrial corridor, this area still contains some factories as well as warehouse and distribution centers. It's also home to Washington Square Mall, one of the city's largest retail centers.

•South: Manufacturing is alive and well on the south side, which is home to factories large and small in addition to machine shops, medical labs, small office parks

and one of Indiana's largest shopping malls — Greenwood Park Mall.

Major Players

Indianapolis has long maintained a diverse economic base, which has helped the city as a whole weather recessions and business closings. A lively mix of manufacturing, insurance, transportation, financial operations, agriculture, communications, data processing, publishing, software development, real estate development and management, federal/state/local government agencies, legal firms and retail companies accounts for many of the 32,000-plus employers in the Indianapolis metropolitan area.

According to figures published by the Indianapolis Chamber of Commerce, the city's employment leaders are:

•Eli Lilly and Company, a multinational pharmaceutical manufacturing giant and one of the city's oldest continually operating companies: 8,750 employees

•Allison Engine Company, manufacturer of gas turbine engines: 5,700 employees

•Marsh Supermarkets, Inc./Village Pantry Markets, a locally owned retail grocery chain: 5,100 employees

•Allison Transmission, manufacturer of heavy-duty transmissions: 4,700 employees

•Ameritech, the Indiana headquarters of the Chicago-based telecommunications holding company: 3,134 employees

•The Associated Group, an insurance and healthcare services company: 3,000 employees

•Thomson Consumer Electronics, a research, design and marketing center for RCA products: 2,186 employees

•USA Group, Inc., a nationwide

United We Stand

United Airlines is in the process of building one of the world's largest aircraft maintenance facilities on the grounds of Indianapolis International Airport. The $800 million project, known as the Indianapolis Maintenance Center, will cover 2.9 million square feet when completed. Phase I is done and operating now, but the final portion of the five-phase project isn't scheduled for completion until 2004.

Maintenance centers completely overhaul and repair aircraft, in effect taking an entire plane apart and reassembling it. When the United facility is fully operational, it will consist of 11 hangars and will operate 24 hours a day, seven days a week. Projected employment is at least 6,300 workers.

To land the contract for this facility, Indianapolis competed with 92 other cities around the country. In the end, it was the airport's strong infrastructure and the amount of on-site land available (300 acres), as well as the quality of the city's workforce, low construction costs, central location and $297 million in incentive payments that convinced United officials Indianapolis was the right place.

But while providing financial incentives to lure United here, city and state officials insisted on the company agreeing to repay those incentives if it reneges on promises it made regarding employment and corporate investment. This unprecedented stipulation took urban development experts around the country by surprise and led to predictions that other cities will follow suit when negotiating development deals with businesses.

Photo: The Indianapolis Star & News

United Airlines is building one of the world's largest aircraft maintenance facilities at the Indianapolis International Airport.

guarantor of federally sponsored student loans: 1,958 employees

• American Trans Air, the nation's largest charter airline: 1,800 employees

• Federal Express, which has a regional hub for its express mail services at Indianapolis International Airport: 1,800 employees

• Boehringer Mannheim Corp., manufacturer of medical devices and diagnostic products: 1,793 employees

• Conseco, Inc., a locally founded and owned insurance holding company: 1,000 employees

Resources

If you're looking for more information about the business climate and/or employment opportunities in the Indianapolis area, contact the following agencies.

THE INDIANAPOLIS CHAMBER OF COMMERCE
320 N. Meridian St.   464-2222

For more than a century, this nonprofit organization has been working on behalf of local businesses on such issues as infrastructure, taxes and workforce development. The Chamber provides its 3,200 member businesses (and others, upon request) with up-to-date research on area demographics and market trends as well as with networking opportunities, executive consultation services, leadership training and information on international trade concerns.

THE DEPARTMENT OF METROPOLITAN DEVELOPMENT
Directors Office
2041 City County Building   327-4141
Mayor's Action Center   327-4622

This city-county department, which administers the city's tax abatement and industrial revenue bond programs, is charged with helping businesses apply for assistance through these programs as well helping individuals and businesses contend with issues related to zoning, construction and development permits.

THE INDIANAPOLIS ECONOMIC DEVELOPMENT CORPORATION
320 N. Meridian St.   236-6262

A nonprofit organization, the IEDC provides businesses with an array of resources, including access to information about the local business community and climate, business contacts, potential sites and financial and operational assistance.

THE INDIANAPOLIS NETWORK FOR EMPLOYMENT AND TRAINING
17 W. Market St.   684-2400

A private, nonprofit organization, iNET provides corporate clients with information about the local labor market as well as with employee recruitment services and training funds.

THE INDIANAPOLIS REGIONAL SMALL BUSINESS DEVELOPMENT CENTER
342 N. Senate Ave.   261-3030

One of 14 business assistance programs in Indiana, the center provides management and technical assistance, business training, and special programming to small businesses.

THE ENTREPRENEUR BUSINESS CENTER
55 S. State Ave.   236-0143

The first city-assisted small business incubator, the Center opened in 1993. Since then it has helped nearly 50 small businesses with such services as business counseling, affordable space, financing and training.

So successful has the Center been that

INSIDERS' GUIDE®
Showcase

WASHINGTON Square   10202 E. Washington St.

3919 Lafayette Rd.   LAFAYETTE SQUARE

6020 East 82nd St.

CASTLETON SQUARE

BUTLER UNIVERSITY

4600 Sunset Avenue,
Indianapolis, IN

(317) 940-8000

"Locally owned and operated
for over two decades"

(317) 780-8800

8901 S. Meridian St.
(317) 888-3303

Marian College

3200 Cold Springs Road
(317) 929-0123

CASTLETON
8600 Allisonville Rd.
(317) 849-5300

GREENWOOD
665 U.S. 31 North
(317) 888-1301

GRAHAM'S CRACKERS
5981 E. 86th
(317) 842-5727

THE FASHION MALL
KEYSTONE AT THE CROSSING

North Keystone at
86th Street

a second city-assisted incubator is now under development.

INDIANAPOLIS DOWNTOWN, INC.
201 N. Illinois St.   237-2222

Established in 1993, IDI is a nonprofit agency focused on developing, marketing and managing the downtown district. It works with both established and new businesses on such issues as transportation, parking, space leasing, beautification and crime control; at the same time, it promotes downtown as a viable place to live and play.

Inside
Real Estate

If you're looking for a comfortable place to live, you've found it. According to *U. S. News & World Report*, Indianapolis ranks 12th among the top-100 most desirable housing markets in the country.

For home buyers, one of the local real estate market's most desirable traits is affordability. According to the Indiana Association of Realtors, during the first quarter of 1995, the median price for a single-family house in Indianapolis was $89,900 — compared to a national median price of $107,000.

Of course, as in any metropolitan area, actual prices are all over the map. Depending on location, features and condition, local housing prices can range from the low thousands for a fixer-upper to a few million for a country estate. New homes generally start around $70,000 and escalate to some ten times that; if money's no object, you can pay even more and get what you pay for.

For renters, there are literally thousands of choices — inexpensive efficiencies, luxurious penthouses, downtown lofts and suburban townhouses. Whether you want to live in a renovated factory, a restored Victorian or a contemporary apartment community, chances are you'll find what you want at prices that are often a real value compared to rates in other regions of the country.

Because you'll find information on specific neighborhoods in our Neighborhoods chapter, this chapter concentrates on in-

Photo: The Indianapolis Star & News

Beautiful homes, like this one on the city's south side, can be found throughout the metropolitan area.

formation helpful to those readers in need of housing-related services such as real estate companies, home builders, apartment finders and management services and movers.

It won't take you long to find that Hoosier hospitality isn't just a phrase — it actually exists. Welcome home.

Real Estate Companies

The following is a sampling of area real estate companies. While not comprehensive by any means, it does give a fair representation of the types of services available locally.

A.M. RELOCATION
12774 N. Old Meridian St.
Carmel   *848-1588*

Founded in 1980, A.M. Relocation focuses its efforts on corporate relocation. The local affiliate of the international RELO network, which consists of 800 independent relocation firms, A.M. Relocation provides residential sales and rental services, including area tours for newcomers, temporary lodging and transportation and home previews.

CARPENTER REALTORS/ BETTER HOMES & GARDENS
8722 N. Meridian St.   *844-4400*
                            (800) 635-4043

Carpenter REALTORS specializes in residential brokerage, family relocation and corporate transfers. Founded in 1970, the firm has 17 branch offices and 380 licensed sales associates throughout India-

napolis and Marion County as well as surrounding counties. It's the city's exclusive representative for Better Home & Gardens' real estate subsidiary.

CENTURY 21
250 E. 96th St.   *574-7421*

With 38 independently owned and operated offices and some 660 sales associates in the metro area, Century 21 is a major force in the local real estate market. While dealing primarily in residential resales, about a third of Century 21's area offices also offer building and development services either directly or through affiliated builders and developers. Among the other products and services available through select offices are corporate transfer guides, house and apartment rentals, mortgage brokerage and title insurance.

ERA REAL ESTATE ADVANTAGE
6338 N. College Ave.   *580-1263*
                            (800) 886-ERA1

With more than 20 years experience and 14 offices in central Indiana, Electronic Realty Associates Ltd. provides buyers and sellers throughout the country with electronic access to area housing information (including pictures) via Prodigy and Internet. Its services include buyer or seller representation, home warranties and relocation assistance.

A.H.M. GRAVES CO. INC.
1119 Keystone Way, Carmel   *844-4545*

Founded in 1924, A.H.M. Graves has seven offices throughout the greater In-

---

Insiders' Tips

Locals and visitors alike enjoy Sunday drives, with the *Star's* real estate section in hand, through the lavish neighborhoods of Carmel and Geist and around Eagle Creek and Morse reservoirs.

Relocating to Indianapolis?

We'll help you find new points of interest.

Before you can select a neighborhood – or a new home – you need to know the facts about your new community.

By calling our professional Family Relocation Service Center, we'll acquaint you with those points of interest that are important to you and your family. And, we'll send you our exclusive Newcomers Welcome Package that contains valuable, up-to-date information on area home prices, schools, recreation, shopping and much more.

So when you're ready to relocate to Indianapolis – give us a call. With 17 sales offices and two Mall Marketing Centers in the area, we know metropolitan Indianapolis.

SOLD
Carpenter
REALTORS®

Better Homes and Gardens®

800-635-4043

Nobody Knows
Homes Better™

dianapolis area. Among the services that Graves offers are residential sales, relocation, and mortgage qualification and financing.

PENNINGTON-LINE REALTORS
941 E. 86th St., Ste. 115   *251-1574*

This small but prestigious firm specializes in high-end residential real estate such as that found in the pricier portions of the Meridan-Kessler and Butler-Tarkington neighborhoods.

RE/MAX OF INDIANA
8888 Keystone Crossing, Ste. 1550   574-3355

Since entering the marketplace in 1988, RE/MAX of Indiana has grown from four offices and 37 sales associates to its present 54 offices and 750 associates statewide. Focusing specifically on residential real estate, RE/MAX offers regional and international referrals, sales information and advertising services as well as a corporate relocation program.

F.C. TUCKER
Residential Real Estate Services Division
9279 N. Meridian St.   571-2200

With 11 residential sales offices and more than 400 sales associates, Tucker has become one of the city's leading real estate firms. Founded by the late Fred C. Tucker in 1923, the company has a full-time relocation staff to help newcomers get acquainted with the city and local real estate options. Tucker also prides itself on its up-to-date understanding of the real estate market and the trends affecting it, an understanding that's based on ongoing research efforts. A full-service company, Tucker also offers mortgage and construction services through its ancillary operations.

Home Builders

If you'd prefer to build instead of buy an existing home, the following list is a representative sampling of local builders.

BILTMORE HOMES INC.
25 W. Ninth St.   *756-7777*

With the tagline "Quality Homes — Affordable Prices," Biltmore focuses on making home ownership available to people who can't necessarily swing six-figure mortgages. With houses in areas around the city, Biltmore offers a variety of models in prices that start around $70,000.

BRENWICK
12722 Hamilton Crossing Blvd.
Carmel   *574-3400*

Specializing in what it calls "the art of creating neighborhoods," Brenwick develops residential communities with homes ranging from $130,000 to $1 million plus.

DAVIS HOMES
3755 E. 82nd St.   *595-2836*

With more than 40 years experience in the Indianapolis market, Davis Homes builds homes in the $90,000-to-$250,000 range in communities throughout the greater metropolitan area.

DELUXE HOMES/TRIMARK HOMES
9202 N. Meridian St., Ste. 300   843-9514

North to south, east to west, you'll find Deluxe Homes and Trimark Homes throughout Marion County. Prices range from the mid-$70s to the low $100s.

DURA-BUILDERS
745 Beachway Dr.   *487-1800*
                (800) OWN-DURA

Locally owned and operated since 1971, Dura-Builders offers a variety of models and styles in developments throughout central Indiana. Prices range from $80,000 on up.

THE ESTRIDGE GROUP
1041 W. Main St., Carmel   846-7311

With housing communities throughout the area, the Estridge Group is one of several building and development operations under the Estridge Companies banner; others include custom home design and building services. Prices for Estridge homes range from the low $100,000s to $450,000.

HANSEN & HORN GROUP INC.
7275 N. Shadeland Ave.   849-8136

For more than 17 years, Hansen & Horn have been building homes in and around Indianapolis; prices range from $90,000 to $130,000 plus.

M/I HOMES & M/I SCHOTTENSTEIN HOMES INC.
8465 Keystone Crossing, Ste. 145   254-0336

From its Horizon Series of moderately priced homes to its more expensive models, M/I offers a variety of housing options throughout the area. Prices range from around $80,000 to $160,000 and up.

MELODY HOMES
P.O. Box 116, N. Front St.
Whiteland 46184   535-5311

With a focus on making home ownership affordable, Melody Homes offers homes from the $70,000-to-$95,000 range in housing developments throughout the Greater Indianapolis region.

C.P. MORGAN CO. INC.
301 E. Carmel Dr., Ste. E-300
Carmel   848-4040

Specializing in the development of its own communities (marketing angle: "The only builder in the neighborhood"), C.P. Morgan offers homes from $70,000 to more than $210,000, with a heavy concentration on the northeast and northwest sides of town.

RYLAND HOMES
7400 N. Shadeland Ave.   845-0674

This national builder has been constructing homes locally since 1978. Ryland homes, which range from $90,00 to more than $160,000, are available in housing developments throughout the area.

TRINITY HOMES INC.
3713 Turfway Ct.   293-3690

Touting attention to detail and commitment to quality, Trinity Homes offers a variety of homes in a number of central Indiana communities.

Mortgage Companies

The mortgage business is a big business, as anyone who has ever financed a home knows. And as in any other business transaction, it pays to shop around. Here are some places to start locally:

AAMI-American Acceptance Mortgage, 5610 Crawfordsville Road, 243-3007

ACC-American Capital Mortgage Corporation, 8250 Haverstick Road, Suite 250, 475-4160, (800) 401-4160

AccuBanc Mortgage Corporation, 9333 N. Meridian Street, Suite 320, 844-0834, (800) 477-5542

American Construction Funding/American National Mortgage, 9000 Keystone Crossing, No. 120, 571-5590, 879-5711

Approved Mortgage Corporation, 2650 Fairview Place, Suite Q, Greenwood, 882-2255, 846-4480

Countrywide, 3435 E. 86th Street, 253-7627, 481-0062

Custom Mortgage, 1408 N. Pennsylvania Street, 687-1400

Federal Home Mortgage Services, 5435 Emerson Way, Suite 200, 562-4900

Greenbriar Mortgage, 690 Royal St. George, Greenwood, 881-6082, (800) 388-5487

1-800-OWN-DURA

Indianapolis's First 24-hour Community Information Line

Dura-Builders announces Indianapolis's first and only **24-HOUR COMMUNITY INFORMATION**  **LINE**, which provides the latest information on Dura-Builders locations, directions, availability, pricing and much more. This is a free service available to you 24 hours a day.

Simply call **1-800-OWN-DURA** from any Touch-Tone phone. The **COMMUNITY INFORMATION LINE** is **THE SOURCE** for the latest information that will save you time and money when determining your house-hunting needs. It's that easy. The latest on Indy's  best communities is at your fingertips 24 hours every day at **1-800-OWN-DURA**. Call us today!

"Locally owned and operated for over two decades"

Home Mortgage Corporation, 8445 Keystone Crossing, Suite 165, 882-7334, 254-4488

MetroBank, 10333 N. Meridian Street, 573-0274

Mortgage Guarantee Inc., 8383 Craig Street, 598-0000

Society National Bank, Indiana, 10 W. Market Street, (800) 769-LOAN

Winterwood Mortgage, 3195 W. Fairview Road, Suite B, Greenwood, 888-1135, (800) 421-1135

Publications

For more information about the local real estate market, check the real estate section in *The Indianapolis Star* on Sunday or pick up the following free publications at area grocery stores, banks and drugstores.

New Homes Directory, Zart Publications Inc., 7301 E. 90th Street, Suite 102, 842-0288

Homes & Land, Holloway Publications Inc., 1132 S. Range Line Road, Suite 102, 846-2898

IBJ's Executive Homes, Indianapolis Business Journal, 431 N. Pennsylvania Street, 634-6200

Indianapolis Homes Illustrated, Great Lakes Photojournal Press, 1717 W. 86th Street, Suite 480, 879-1717

Apartments

There are too many apartments in the Indianapolis area — as well as too great a variety of prices, locations and amenities — to create a useful list in this chapter. But there are some resources, such as free publications, apartment finders (including *The Indianapolis Star* and *The Indianapolis News*) and management companies, that you can turn to for help.

Publications

As with the real estate publications listed, the following publications are available free at area grocery stores, banks, and drugstores.

GREATER INDIANAPOLIS APARTMENT GUIDE
Haas Publishing Companies Inc.
7202 E. 87th St., No. 115   849-8884

Published monthly, this guide provides information about prices, locations and features, as well as photos, maps and telephone numbers. It's also available at area libraries and colleges and at the airport.

APARTMENT TOUR GUIDE
Linder Publishing Inc.
6866 Hillsdale Ct.   579-2099

Organized by geographic location, this monthly provides information about prices and features for a number of area apartment communities.

RENTER'S GUIDEBOOK
Zart Publications Inc.
7301 E. 90th St., Ste. 102   842-0288

A bimonthly, this publication provides a breakdown of prices, lease stipulations and features for apartment complexes throughout the metropolitan area.

Apartment Finders

The following are companies that specialize in helping apartment seekers find apartments with the right amenities, in the right areas for the right prices, or as close as is humanly possible.

Apartment Locator Consultants, 99 E. Carmel Drive, Suite. L, Carmel, 844-7708, (800) 637-1472

Photo: The Indianapolis Star & News

Homes in the Indianapolis area come in a variety of shapes and sizes.

Apartment Locators, 7301 E. 90th Street, 842-0311, (800) 876-0288

Apartment Finders, 5660 Caito Drive, 542-7291; 1 W. Main Street, Greenwood 888-4807

Metro Apartment Locators, 5369 E. 82nd Street, 577-1447, (800) 999-7942

Apartment Showplace, 5858 E. 82nd Street, 841-2787, (800) 847-3733

Ready to Call Indiana Home?

CALL ERA®

We put service first

✔ Computer-assisted Home Finding Network
✔ Guaranteed Sale and Equity Advance Program
✔ First Time Buyer Services
✔ Home Warranty Plan
✔ Complimentary 80 page ANSWERS™ Book to Help You Plan Your Move

Call the ERA Regional Office
317/580-1263 or 800/886-ERA1

Management Companies

In a city the size of Indianapolis, there are scores of apartment management companies, representing everything from multiple complexes to small four-apartment buildings. The following list is a selection of some of the management companies in the area.

Barrett & Stokely Inc., 3755 E. 82nd Street, 845-4171

Borns Management, 200 S. Meridian Street, Suite 440, 635-9020

The Bryant Company, 8515 Cedar Place Drive, Suite 104, 253-7500

Dearborn Group Management, 4900 Edinborough Lane, 241-4103

The Gene B. Glick Management Company, 8330 Woodfield Crossing Boulevard, 469-0400

Harcourt Management Company Inc., 3901 W. 86th Street, 872-0044

The J. C. Hart Company, 10401 N. Meridian Street, 573-4800

Insignia Management Group Inc., 8760 Lemode Court, 875-5733

NHP Management Company, 8606 Allisonville Road, 849-8090

Pedcor Management Corporation, 6150 E. 75th Street, 579-7262

The Regency-Windsor Company, 8500 Keystone Crossing, 257-4944

Revel Real Estate Services Inc., 101 W. Ohio Street, Suite 850, 684-3333

Edward Rose of Indiana, 7901 Crawfordsville Road, 297-3060

Sentinel Real Estate Corporation, 6370 W. 37th Street, 297-1244

The Sexton Companies, 9001 N. Meridian Street, 846-4444

Stallard & Associates, 3540 N. Meridian Street 924-6256

Stenz Management Company Inc., 429 N. Pennsylvania Street, Suite 10, 262-4999

Van Rooy Properties, 1030 N. College Avenue, 684-7300

Zender Property, Management Company, 1321 N. Meridian Street, Suite 211, 488-8800

Moving Companies

AMERICAN RED BALL WORLD WIDE MOVERS

1335 Sadlier Cir., E. Dr. 353-8331

One of the largest household goods transport companies in the country, American Red Ball has its international headquarters in Indianapolis.

BIG RON'S MOVING & STORAGE INC.

105 S. Denny St. 357-0494

Designated the best deal in moving by *Indianapolis Monthly* magazine, Big Ron's will move you or help you move yourself.

J. J. CARTER & SON OF INDIANA INC.

4219 S. High School Rd. 923-1548

This is the local agent for Allied Van Lines.

ROBERT CARTER VAN LINES

9750 Zionsville Rd., Zionsville 873-3144

Family owned and operated for nearly 70 years, this firm provides moving and storage services to 39 states.

CROWN MOVING & STORAGE INC.

8040 Castleton Rd. 842-8111

This is the local agent for Wheaton Interstate Moving.

HOOSIER LOGISTICS

3331 Raton Ct. 899-7700

This is the local agent for Bekins.

JONES MOVERS INC.

1426 Sadlier Cir., W. Dr. 353-9217

A family-owned operation for 30 years, Jones Movers offers local and long-distance carrier and storage services.

JOYCE MOVING & STORAGE

1012 E. Sumner Ave. 788-9210
(800) 356-6562

This is the local agent for Joyce Van Lines.

MAYFLOWER TRANSIT INC.

9998 N. Michigan Rd. 875-1967

A giant in the truck transport business, Mayflower was the moving company that packed up the Baltimore Colts and moved them west to Indianapolis one night in 1984.

PERKINS VAN & STORAGE INC.

5034 Lafayette Rd. 297-3100

This is one of the local agents for United Van Lines.

PLANES MOVING & STORAGE

2521 Planes Dr. 895-1444, (800) 242-0057

This is another local agent for United Van Lines.

SAFEWAY MOVING SYSTEM

2828 N. Emerson Ave. 545-7533

This is the third local agent for United Van Lines.

STUART'S MOVING & STORAGE INC.

2058 Dr. Martin Luther King Jr. St. 924-0505

Stuart's provides packing, crating and transport of household goods to and from the 48 contiguous states.

Inside
Neighborhoods

Indianapolis is often called a city of neighborhoods. On all sides of town are tree-lined streets, well-kept homes and a community spirit to keep them that way. A renewed appreciation for our central city neighborhoods began in the late 1960s, when the first urban homesteaders started eyeing the Victorian cottages in Lockerbie Square, the mansions of Woodruff Place and the grand old homes of the Old Northside and Herron-Morton. This revitalization continued into less well-known areas, and now places such as Cottage Home and Fletcher Place have become havens for renovators as well.

We have so many old, established neighborhoods — not to mention new developments — that discussing them all proves nearly impossible. Here we've tried to spotlight our city's most well-known neighborhoods, as well as up-and-coming districts and to take a look at new developments and exclusive addresses. We'll start downtown and work our way out into the residential areas, then on to the suburbs for an inside look at where Indianapolis lives.

Lockerbie Square

Considered one of the best examples of Victorian renovation in the country, Lockerbie Square exudes charm. This downtown neighborhood of cobblestone streets, restored Victorians, wrought-iron fences and tiny flower gardens was once home to Hoosier poet James Whitcomb

Photo: The Indianapolis Star & News

Platted in 1872, Woodruff Place was an exclusive out-of-the-city getaway featuring fountains and grassy esplanades.

Riley; his home has been restored and is open for touring (see our Attractions chapter). Bounded by Michigan, New York, Davidson and East streets, Lockerbie Square attracts professionals who work downtown, members of the arts community and historic preservationists who belong to its active neighborhood association.

Midtown

This area is seeing considerable redevelopment, and includes the Canal District, Indiana Avenue and Lockefield Gardens. As recently as the early '80s, the downtown portion of the Central Canal was little more than a weed- and trash-filled ditch. It's now a watery oasis in the middle of the city, with walkways, fountains, bridges and nearby residential and business development such as Canal Overlook and Canal Commons. However, there has been some opposition from longtime residents, some of whom were forced to move to make way for development.

Nearby Indiana Avenue, famous in its heyday for its celebrated jazz joints, has also undergone significant change in recent years. Though still dominated by the Madame Walker Urban Life Center, an excellent example of African- and Egyptian-inspired architecture and a focal point for the African-American community, much of the neighborhood housing stock has been cleared over the years to make room for the growth of IUPUI (the Indianapolis campus of Indiana and Purdue universities). Still, some of the remaining historic retail space is being converted into apartments, as is a former church building, and construction on a new apartment complex and a nearby restaurant and retail development continues.

Renovation is complete on Lockefield Gardens, one of the nation's first public housing complexes. Built in 1936, Lockefield Gardens was a model community of tidy brick buildings and beautiful grounds. As the inner city deteriorated after World War II, however, so did Lockefield Gardens, and it languished as a boarded-up eyesore for years. The 1980s saw renewed interest in living downtown, and Lockefield Gardens was renovated as apartments.

Chatham Arch

Between Lockerbie and the Old Northside, Chatham Arch has seen a great deal of renovation in the past five years. Anyone who bought in the mid- to late '80s, when the neighborhood was just being rediscovered, is sitting pretty now. Downtown professionals and young families love the housing stock, which ranges from two-bedroom cottages to larger Italianate homes. The nearby Real Silk factory lofts, with East Coast-style exposed brick and wood floors, also attract professionals as well as empty-nesters to this popular neighborhood.

Cottage Home

East of Chatham Arch lies the Cottage Home neighborhood, where renovation is less concentrated and where bargains can still be found. The late-19th century workmen cottages, small two- or three-bedroom frame houses built for early laborers and factory workers, that make up the bulk of this neighborhood's housing stock can prove less daunting for do-it-yourselfers than the more sprawling homes of, say Herron-Morton. Expect to see continued interest in this area over the long haul.

Fletcher Place

Platted in 1835, Fletcher Place is one

of the city's oldest neighborhoods and was home to many recent immigrants. The neighborhood still holds onto its German, Irish and Italian heritage; Holy Rosary Catholic Church, with its annual Italian Festival, has been a neighborhood mainstay over the years, and Klemm's German Sausage and Meat Market is nearby. This near-south side neighborhood achieved historic designation in the mid-1980s and began to see a corresponding rise in the number of rehabs and renovations of its 19th and early 20th century cottages. It's bounded by I-70 and Lord and East streets and is near Fountain Square, another historic area.

Fountain Square

South of Fletcher Place, Fountain Square is bounded by Shelby Street, English and Keystone avenues and Pleasant Run Parkway. Its historic business district is home to the Indianapolis Downtown Antique Mall and the Fountain Square Antique Mall. The neighborhood association remains concerned with both historic preservation of its business district and the area's characteristic 19th-century workmen cottages as well as the rehabbing of low-income housing.

The Old Northside

In the late 1800s, the Old Northside was home to many prominent local residents, and the neighborhood is being rehabbed according to rigorous historical guidelines. Bounded by I-65, Pennsylvania, Bellfontaine and 16th streets, the area boasts a wide variety of housing stock, from Italianate and Queen Anne mansions to small carpenter cottages. Though the area has been plagued by crime in the past, an active neighborhood association and a renewed emphasis on community policing has helped curb such problems. The Old Northside attracts a variety of residents, including Lt. Gov. (and gubernatorial hopeful) Frank O'Bannon and his wife, Judy. The neighborhood also includes a number of low- to middle-income apartment buildings and a string of attached townhomes and condominiums.

Herron-Morton Place

More and more young families are moving into such near-downtown neighborhoods as Herron-Morton, an area bounded by 16th, Pennsylvania and 22nd streets and by Central Avenue. Home to the John Herron School of Art (at least until it moves to the former law school building on the main IUPUI campus) and the annual Talbott Street Art Fair, the neighborhood attracts an eclectic mix of residents who enjoy its artistic atmosphere and offbeat reputation. As with the Old Northside, vigilant neighbors and an increased police presence have worked to reduce crime and prostitution in the area. Despite such realities of urban life, many people can't resist Herron-Morton's grand Victorians, Italianates and Queen Annes, and renovation continues.

Neighborhood home tours, such as those in Meridian-Kessler, Irvington and Woodruff Place, offer great ways to get an inside look into these popular areas.

Insiders' Tips

Photo: The Indianapolis Star & News

Lockerbie Square is considered one of the best examples of Victorian renovation in the country.

Woodruff Place

Platted by James Woodruff in 1872 as an exclusive out-of-the-city getaway, the neighborhood was inspired by the residential parks of Italy and France and may be the setting for Booth Tarkington's *The Magnificent Ambersons*. The self-contained area features statuary, grassy esplanades and water fountains, which the neighborhood association has worked hard over the years to restore. Though some remain split up into apartments, many of the grand old mansions have been restored. Unfortunately, the surrounding area isn't nearly as grand. Woodruff Place is bounded by 10th, Michigan and Tecumseh streets and by West Drive; the Indiana Women's Prison is a nearby neighbor.

Irvington

This historic east-side neighborhood was once home to Butler University and retains something of a literary ambiance; it's home to one of the city's oldest and most active book study groups. The large neighborhood boasts a wide variety of housing styles, from 1800s mansions to bungalows and farm houses. Residents count the resulting mix of socioeconomic levels and ethnic backgrounds a plus; they enjoy Irvington's diversity. Still, they wish for more new business development along the Washington Street, where the artsy Irving theater is located, corridor and wonder how the closing of Howe High School will affect the area that is bordered by 10th Street, Brookville Road and Edmondson and Kitley avenues.

Little Flower

As neighborhoods gain in popularity, naturally they go up in price. Irvington, for example, has long been seen as a more affordable alternative to Meridian-Kessler. But with Irvington's increasing popularity, those who like its style but can't afford its price tag have turned to the Little Flower area. Named for Little Flower Catholic Church and bounded by 10th and 16th streets and Emerson and Shadeland avenues, the area is a transitional neighborhood — young couples and families are buying from older residents.

Chapel Hill

On the west side, the Chapel Hill area is also home to plenty of young families. They like the traditional homes and subdivisions in this large area that centers around 10th Street from I-465 to Girls School Road. Residents enjoy plenty of shopping and easy interstate access.

University Heights

The area around the University of Indianapolis, around the 1400 block of E. Hanna Avenue, boasts the same appeal as Little Flower: It's a more affordable alternative to such neighborhoods as Irvington and Broad Ripple, areas that are becoming increasingly more expensive. Savvy buyers can discover tidy bungalows, similar in style to those in ever-popular Broad Ripple, for much less money.

Meridian-Kessler

This large and diverse neighborhood, bounded by 38th and Meridian streets, Winthrop Avenue and Kessler Boulevard, includes lavishly restored Meridian Street mansions and beautiful Tudors and colonials as well as modest two-story homes in need of a lot of work. But this range in housing stock means diversity in neighbors; there's a mix of socioeconomic levels and ethnic backgrounds similar to that of Irvington and Butler-

Tarkington. A small retail district at 49th and Pennsylvania offers a drugstore, coffee shop, a vegetarian cafe and antique shops. Young families who like Meridian-Kessler's unique shops and restaurants — but who can't afford the more established areas — are moving into the southeast section of this neighborhood and rehabbing. The active neighborhood association is putting a lot of effort into revitalizing the College Avenue corridor (see the entry on South Broad Ripple).

Butler-Tarkington

A lot of people with their hearts set on brick Tudors with leaded glass windows start here — and often find what they're looking for. The neighborhood, bordered by 38th and Meridian streets and by Westfield Boulevard and the Central Canal, offers beautifully restored homes in the Butler University area as well as some in the southwest area still in need of renovation. Butler remains one of this diverse neighborhood's strongest selling points; Clowes Hall provides superb cultural entertainment within walking distance. And a small but vibrant shopping district at 56th and Illinois, with restaurants, a grocery store, meat market, ice cream shop and upscale specialty stores, adds convenience.

Meridian Street

Historic North Meridian Street, listed on the National Register of Historic Places, stretches from 38th to 56th street and is lined with mansions built by the local movers and shakers of the early 1900s. Federal-, colonial- and Tudor-style homes boast meticulously landscaped yards; the street is especially beautiful in the spring, and St. Margaret's Hospital Guild often chooses a Meridian Street

mansion for its May Decorators' Show House. The governor's residence is here as is the former home of Pulitzer Prize-winner Booth Tarkington. Sightseers enjoy walking through the area and admiring the 1920s-era architecture. Though it does perhaps lack privacy (one resident notes that you can't really use those beautiful front yards), Meridian Street remains one of the city's most highly prized addresses.

Broad Ripple

One of the city's favorite neighborhoods, Broad Ripple — where cars stop as the many ducks and geese waddle through traffic — is active, vibrant and probably the most interesting. The streets are lined with the much-coveted Broad Ripple bungalows, and residents tend to keep the neighborhood spiffy. That's not always an easy task when thousands of people walk through the area every weekend on their way to the many bars, restaurants, art galleries and specialty shops. Teenagers, many of whom are especially fond of zooming about on skateboards, like to hang out here too. Still, you can't beat the amenities: In addition to its many specialty shops, Broad Ripple boasts a convenient drug store, grocery, hardware store, natural foods store, a superb used book shop and enough restaurants to please just about any taste. No wonder it's so popular.

South Broad Ripple

Actually the southeastern corner of Meridian-Kessler, this area, dubbed "SoBro" by those in the real estate biz, has become increasingly popular as prices rise in ultra-trendy Broad Ripple. The SoBro area includes Modern Times bookstore, Atlas Supermarket (one of the city's

Photo: The Indianapolis Star & News

Ducks abound in the canal at Broad Ripple.

best gourmet groceries), the well-known Red Key and Bulldog taverns and two coffee shops. Those who want to be near the shopping and nightlife, but who can't afford Broad Ripple's prices, look here and find well-made homes with the same amenities — hardwood floors, fireplaces, nice yards with lots of trees — for considerably less. Many do, however, require considerably more work. The area, loosely bounded by 42nd and 54th streets and College and Winthrop avenues, has seen significant redevelopment along the College corridor, where a new police precinct and fire station — and a proposed YMCA — have spurred residential renovation.

Meridian Hills

Situated north of Broad Ripple, the separate town of Meridian Hills (an "included" town under Unigov), where a three-member town board handles neighborhood concerns, boasts more wooded terrain than you'd expect in the city plus the convenient shopping and amenities of Broad Ripple and Nora. Home to more than 1,800 residents, Meridian Hills re-

mains very stable, with little new development — and residents like it that way.

Williams Creek

Some real estate professionals peg Williams Creek (another separate "included" town) as one of the most prestigious addresses within the city, much more private than historic Meridian Street, for example, but with similar cachet. The homes are situated on large lots with beautiful rolling, wooded terrain, and the neighborhood proves so popular that it's not unusual for homes to stay in the same family for generations.

Nora

This area along 86th Street between Meridian Street and Keystone Avenue, offers plenty of shopping and dining options. Still the nearby residential areas boast lots of ranch and traditional-style brick homes. Neighbors also appreciate the convenience of a branch library.

Sunset Lane

Often referred to as the city's second

Meridian Street, Sunset Lane was once home to members of the Eli Lilly family and so earned its nickname, "Pill Hill." A private drive that extends south of Kessler Boulevard toward White River, Sunset Lane boasts homes similar to the Meridian Street mansions with the privacy that Meridian Street lacks. But you won't see the "for sale" signs that are common along Meridian; homes here rarely change hands.

"Excluded" Towns

Many people who live in Greater Indianapolis make their home in our surrounding communities that lie geographically within the county but remain curiously separate. When Unigov consolidated Indianapolis and Marion County, four towns chose not to be included and earned the designation "excluded towns." It may be tough to tell where Indianapolis ends and Speedway, Lawrence, Southport or Beech Grove begin, but these towns are separate entities, each with its own personality. Those who live on S. Emerson Avenue will likely think of themselves as Beech Grove — rather than Indianapolis — residents; someone whose child plays basketball for the Speedway Spark Plugs may feel more involved in that west-side community than with greater Indianapolis. In general, these communities retain a small-town look and feel, and residents prize this atmosphere.

Speedway has the look of a small town with blocks of brick bungalows and Cape Cods, but it's only about 6 miles from downtown. It's bounded by 10th and 30th streets and by I-465 and the Indianapolis Motor Speedway. There are considerable shopping and dining possibilities nearby, but the neighborhoods remain rather quiet. Except, of course, in May when

traffic becomes heavy all over the west side, and especially in Speedway. The track now hosts the Brickyard 400 in August as well.

Fort Benjamin Harrison once dominated the **Lawrence** area, but the Army base is now slated for closing. The closure will certainly affect Lawrence, but there is a proposal to create a new state park in the base area. Within the large community you'll find traditional well-established neighborhoods (Old Lawrence) and new subdivisions and planned developments (new Lawrence), as well as plenty of shopping. Lawrence stretches from the base on Post Road to the southern edge of the Geist Reservoir area within Lawrence Township.

Southeast of downtown lies the community of **Beech Grove**. Dominated by the Conrail railyard, where down-at-the-heel passenger cars come to get refurbished, the town also boasts plenty of comfortable neighborhoods full of tidy bungalows. Beech Grove is bordered by I-465 and the Conrail line and by Southern and Perkins avenues. A major facility is the Indianapolis regional Heart Center at St. Francis Hospital.

Southport has seen considerable residential development. You find new housing subdivisions as well as traditional homes and bungalows in the older areas. Easy highway access make this community popular among commuters who work downtown or in Greenwood. The town is situated between Indianapolis and Greenwood east of Madison Avenue along Southport Road, and it boasts plenty of nearby shopping.

Around Town

Development continues all around Indianapolis, and some of the hottest ar-

Photo: The Indianapolis Star & News

Building better neighborhoods throughout the city.

eas lie just north of the central city. **Washington Township** remains so popular — but so established — that people often buy the more modest ranch-style houses scattered through the area, knock them down and build more elaborate homes. Developments such as **Cedar Knolls, Old Pickwick, Williamshire** and **Somerset Hills**, situated along or around Spring Mill and Ditch roads from 82nd to about 96th streets, offer convenience coupled with privacy — but for a price. Townships farther out, such as **Pike**, on the northwest side, see an incredible amount of new construction. With fewer traffic hassles than the north side and beautiful wooded terrain, Pike is attracting more and more upscale homeowners to such communities as **West 86th**.

Hamilton County's **Clay Township** and the city of **Carmel** continue to expand, with much of the growth concentrated in the high-end communities west of Meridian Street along Spring Mill Road. With such names as **Bridelbourne, Coppergate, Laurelwood** and

Winterwood, these developments have some of the highest price tags in the city.

Homes at **Geist Reservoir,** northeast of Indianapolis, also come with hefty mortgages. Some of the most exclusive include **Admiral's Point, Diamond Point** and **Feather Cove**, beautiful developments that have many professionals longing for an address on the water.

On the northwest side, **Eagle Creek Reservoir** offers beautiful terrain and waterfront views. **Morse Reservoir**, near Noblesville, also provides enticing waterfront homes, with the accompanying price tags.

Northern Johnson County also boasts its share of high-end custom housing and executive homes, especially in the **Greenwood** area, though prices run a bit lower than in comparable north-side communities. The convenience of the south side, with its abundant shopping and somewhat more relaxed ambience, remains a strong draw.

Par for the Course

A new twist on luxury living has been the development of golf course communities. A mainstay of Sun Belt areas, golf course housing developments have become increasingly popular across the Midwest in recent years, and Indianapolis is seeing more and more interest in these specialized communities. Some home buyers especially like the "master plan" concept, in which future growth is completely mapped out from the start. The golf course at **Valle Vista** in Greenwood, one of the city's oldest, was designed in the early 1970s by the late Bob Simmons, who also designed the course at **Prestwick**. The legendary Pete Dye created the course at Morse Reservoir's **North Harbour** as well as the one at **Maple Creek**. One of the city's newest courses (and likely the state's largest golf course development), **Hamilton Proper** incorporates some of Hamilton County's federally protected wetlands into the Arthur Hills-designed course.

Inside
Education

Learning can be a lifelong pursuit, and Indianapolis residents will find educational opportunities for all age levels, from preschool through continuing adult education. The city is home to the state's largest school district (Indianapolis Public Schools), a strong system of religious and private schools and an impressive array of colleges and universities.

Improving our schools remains a priority, and just about everyone has an opinion on current educational issues. To really find out about individual schools, our school systems or universities, talk to parents and students, visit classrooms, ask questions and get involved. But here's a quick primer to get you started.

Public Schools

Although Unigov legislation merged many city and county services and governmental bodies in 1970, public schools were not included in the merger. There just wasn't enough support for the idea. So today there are 11 school districts in Marion County. Indianapolis Public Schools serves students within the old city boundaries, with much of its enrollment coming from Center Township. Beech Grove and Speedway, as excluded towns under the Unigov system, maintain their own districts. And the remaining townships — Franklin, Decatur, Lawrence, Perry, Pike, Warren, Washington and Wayne — serve the rest of the county.

Photo: The Indianapolis Star & News

Butler University draws about 4,000 students to its 290-acre campus 4 miles north of downtown.

A university on the move.

The University of Indianapolis is distinctive private university emphasizing a challenging academic environment, a flourishing campus community of international diversity, and students and faculty responsive to societal needs. For information, write the Office of the President at 1400 E. Hanna Avenue, Indianapolis IN 46227, or call 1-800-232-8634.

University of
Indianapolis

INDIANAPOLIS PUBLIC SCHOOLS

120 E. Walnut St.   266-4411

IPS, which serves about 50,000 students, is a system in transition. The state's largest school system has struggled in recent years to deal with such urban problems as decreasing enrollment, increasing violence and an overall dissatisfaction with court-ordered busing.

That's the big picture. But the system is full of small success stories, places where people are making a difference and working to improve our schools. Local teachers participate in National Writing Project workshops. Parents volunteer in their children's classrooms. Business leaders adopt high schools. Innovative ideas are being explored in IPS magnet options across the city. These special programs highlight a variety of educational theories and approaches stressing such varying focuses at the elementary level as traditional reading, writing and arithmetic; Montessori methods; critical thinking; arts and sciences; and language arts and communication. In fact the Key School, an elementary magnet based on the idea of multiple intelligences, such as linguistic, musical or mathematical, has gained national recognition from *The New York Times* and *Life* magazine for its innovative approach.

Middle schools expand on these areas and further develop specific skills. The Key Renaissance Middle School builds on the well-regarded elementary program. Shortridge offers a program in the arts and humanities, Harshman has developed the Center for Math/Science/Technology, and Coleman offers the Center for Foreign Language and Global Studies. John Marshall has developed a Pre-International Baccalaureate program, and Crispus Attucks offers its Academic Academy, a program specially designed to be especially challenging.

High school magnets offer more extensive study in such areas as the performing and visual arts at Broad Ripple, foreign language, math and science and vocational careers at Arsenal Tech, agricultural technology at Emmerich Manual and business and finance at Northwest. And the Arlington College Preparatory Academy at Arlington High School is modeled on the International Baccalaureate, a program of study similar to those required for admittance to many universities around the world.

In 1992 then-superintendent Shirl Gilbert instituted Select Schools, a program that allowed parents some choice as to what school their child attended, limited, of course, by the requirements of U.S. District Judge S. Hugh Dillin's 1971 desegregation ruling, which resulted in some African-American students being bused to predominantly white township schools. Beginning in the fall of 1993, parents have listed up to five school choices, and their child is assigned to the highest available selection. Though there have been some administrative glitches, many educators have high hopes for the limited-choice program.

Butler University was the first college in Indiana and the third in the nation to admit women on an equal basis with men. It was the first in Indiana to allow students — with parental consent — to choose electives.

Insiders' Tips

School Districts

INDIANAPOLIS PUBLIC SCHOOLS
120 E. Walnut St., Indianapolis   266-4411

BEECH GROVE CITY SCHOOLS
5334 Hornet Ave., Beech Grove   788-4481

METROPOLITAN SCHOOL DISTRICT OF DECATUR TOWNSHIP
7523 Mooresville Rd., West Newton   856-5263

FRANKLIN TOWNSHIP COMMUNITY SCHOOL CORP.
6141 S. Franklin Rd., Indianapolis   862-2411

METROPOLITAN SCHOOL DISTRICT OF LAWRENCE TOWNSHIP
7601 E. 56th St., Indianapolis   546-4921

METROPOLITAN SCHOOL DISTRICT OF PERRY TOWNSHIP
1130 Epler Ave., Indianapolis   787-7266

METROPOLITAN SCHOOL DISTRICT OF PIKE TOWNSHIP
6901 Zionsville Rd., Indianapolis   293-0393

SPEEDWAY CITY SCHOOLS
5335 W. 25th St., Speedway   244-0236

METROPOLITAN SCHOOL DISTRICT OF WARREN TOWNSHIP
9301 W. 18th St., Indianapolis   898-5935

METROPOLITAN SCHOOL DISTRICT OF WASHINGTON TOWNSHIP
3801 E. 79th St., Indianapolis   845-9400

METROPOLITAN SCHOOL DISTRICT OF WAYNE TOWNSHIP
1220 S. High School Rd., Indianapolis   243-8251

Voters within most of these areas select their own school boards; the town or city councils in Beech Grove and Speedway appoint theirs. All have five members, except for IPS and Warren and Wayne townships, which have seven.

Who says you can't give your kids the world?

Perhaps the greatest gift you can give your children is the ability to compete in an increasingly interdependent world. By enrolling your children in the International School of Indiana, you're doing just that. ISI is a non-profit, independent school, offering a curriculum of academic excellence in the elementary grades, and is one of only a few in the country that features multi-lingual curricula. To find out how you can bring the world to your children, call (317) 926-1951 or write to ISI, 612 West 42nd Street, Indianapolis, Indiana 46208.

INTERNATIONAL SCHOOL OF INDIANA

Dropping enrollment within the system, however, has forced a number of school closings. Two high schools, George Washington on the west side and Thomas Carr Howe on the east side, closed at the end of the 1994-'95 school year, despite considerable student and neighborhood protest. Budgetary shortfalls and fewer students may mean more schools will face closing in the future.

Another current issue within IPS is the creation of middle schools — buildings that incorporate 6th, 7th and 8th grades — to replace the traditional 7th- and 8th-grade junior highs. A few years ago IPS adopted a middle school approach, which emphasizes smaller classes, team teaching and tough discipline, and quickly converted its junior highs. Some schools were left with little time to train staffs in the new philosophy, and progress, such as improvement in attendance and national test scores, has been slow.

These issues received a great deal of attention as the school board searched in early 1995 for a new superintendent to replace Gilbert. Though hired before school ended in the spring of 1995, the 1995-'96 school year is the first for new

IPS superintendent Dr. Esperanza Zendejas, who in her previous job boosted test scores, improved facilities and elevated the reputation of the troubled Brownsville, Texas, school system. She has taken a wait-and-see attitude toward the middle schools, giving them a year to show improvement, though she has mentioned the possibility of establishing traditional primary schools encompassing kindergarten through eighth grade. Zendejas has also placed schools across the system on probation, instituting accountability programs that hold schools to strict standards of academic achievement.

The city's school system will likely see even more improvement and innovation as teachers and administrators rise to the challenge and continue to wrestle with the demands of an urban school district.

Though facing their own concerns with test scores, violence and enrollment, the township schools nonetheless enjoy perhaps a less-tarnished public image. Still, a major source of controversy remains over the township schools' role in desegregation. Since 1981, African-American students have been bused from IPS to schools in

BUTLER UNIVERSITY

The University of Choice Since 1855!

For information, please call 1-800-368-6852 or 940-9351

4600 Sunset Avenue, Indianapolis, IN 46208

Who's in Charge?

Here's a quick introduction to the new Indianapolis Public School superintendent, Dr. Esperanza Zendejas, culled from *The Indianapolis Star* and *The Indianapolis News* reports.

• The youngest of nine children, Zendejas was born in Michoacan, Mexico; her father was a migrant worker and illegal alien. Zendejas became a U.S. citizen in 1973.

• As a youngster, Zendejas played baseball and ran track. Today, the former cheerleader enjoys watching basketball and football and is looking forward to experiencing Hoosier Hysteria.

• Zendejas worked as a teacher and coach while her husband went to school. They later divorced, and she raised her daughter, Baleria, alone while earning a master's degree and school administration credentials. Zendejas also has a son, Xchel.

Photo: The Indianapolis Star & News

Esperanza Zendejas is in her first year as superintendent of Indianapolis Public Schools.

• A dozen years ago, she was a single mother struggling to finish her doctorate at Stanford University. Zendejas taught tennis lessons, cleaned houses and received food stamps to help make ends meet.

• Zendejas' daughter is now in college and her elementary school-age son lives for the time being with his father in Arizona.

• On the job, Zendejas stresses accountability and though former employees call her a tough, demanding boss, they also say she's very fair.

• In her former Brownsville, Texas, post, she implemented nontraditional programs such as Saturday classes and has promised to find the money for such programs here.

• Zendejas, who earned $105,000 in Brownsville, will make $135,000 at IPS.

Perry, Wayne, Franklin, Decatur, Lawrence and Warren townships to maintain the mandated racial balance. However, no township students have been bused to IPS. In 1984, Judge Dillin ruled that parents of children bused to townships can run and vote in township school board elections, facilitating more parental involvement.

Still, opinions as to the success of busing as a means to desegregation remain mixed. Before the 1995-'96 school year began, the IPS school board approached Judge Dillin about relaxing the strict racial-balance guidelines that require more than 5,000 African-American students to be bused from IPS out to the townships. And Indianapolis Mayor Stephen Goldsmith has made no secret of his desire to push the issue back into court in an effort to end forced busing. Many residents would like to see all students allowed to attend neighborhood schools, and locals continue to speculate as to the feasibility of a countywide metropolitan school district.

Private and Parochial Schools

Those looking for an alternative to public schools will find a number of excellent options in Indianapolis. All are day schools; interest in local boarding schools waned in the 1960s. Some local schools can prove quite expensive. Tuition can run as much as $8,000 a year; still, many have waiting lists of interested students. And parents often begin gathering information on schools while Junior is still in diapers.

Most private schools maintain entrance requirements, usually a combination of exam and interview, and hold high expectations for their students. Some administer ISTEP or similar achievement tests, which allow parents to see how the schools stack up; most private schools that administer such tests surpass public school performance.

Area parochial schools remain committed to serving their parish or congregation and may accept students without the entrance exams often associated with some private schools, though these schools also expect high levels of achievement. Though generally open to all interested students, many church-affiliated schools offer reduced tuition to parishioners or church members.

Choosing the right school for your child requires plenty of research — and a lot of legwork — but the following information should get you going.

ARCHDIOCESE OF INDIANAPOLIS
Office of Catholic Education
1400 N. Meridian St.   236-1430

The Catholic Church maintains the largest system of religious education in the city, with a history that extends back to 1859. Though most began as parish schools that served a distinct population, the Archdiocese of Indianapolis now administers four high schools and 33 elementary or primary (K-8) schools in the four Indianapolis deaneries, covering Marion, Hendricks and Hancock counties and parts of Morgan and Johnson counties.

A 1989 media blitz and additional advertising in 1991 to increase awareness of Catholic schools as an alternative to public education seems to have worked; enrollment was up more than 5 percent in 1991-92. Currently, nearly 15,000 students attend Roman Catholic schools in Marion County.

But religion isn't necessarily the draw. Between 12 and 14 percent of students are not Catholic. As for curriculum and textbook selection and teacher certification, Catholic schools remain in accordance with Indiana Department of Education standards, though they outperform Indianapolis Public Schools across the board on standardized tests. In addition, more than 90 percent of students who enter Catholic high schools as freshman graduate in four years.

Tuition for the 1995-'96 school year at the inter-parochial high schools averaged about $2,500 for the first student in a Catholic family. Tuition at the 33 elementary schools, located in neighborhoods across the

Marian College

A Small College with Big Advantages.

Rosie (Wilson) Albright '69

Executive Vice President and General Manager, Beauty Care Division Revlon Consumer Products Worldwide

---

Karl Hertz, Ed.D. '61

Superintendent Mequon-Thiensville, WI School District

To find out more about Marian College, call the Office of Admissions at
toll free
1-800-772-7264
or fax us at
(317)929-0287.

Marian College
"The College that Mentors"
3200 Cold Spring Road
Indianapolis, Indiana
46222-1997

"Marian was a wonderful part of my life where I was able to develop a belief in my academic capability while gaining a true understanding of the beliefs of St. Francis."

"I have very positive memories of Marian. The education I received was excellent. The sense of values and integrity that are integral parts of a Marian College education have been absolutely critical to me in my career. "

Daycare Dilemmas

As anyone with children knows, choosing a daycare provider can prove difficult, especially if you're new to town and haven't built up that all-important list of baby-sitters. Though Indianapolis offers a variety of options — from private homes to national chains — many parents find themselves at a loss as to how to launch a search for appropriate care. Though a few employers offer on-site facilities, most notably USA Group, which has been lauded by *Working Mother* magazine, in most cases parents must seek out child care without their employer's assistance. If you find yourself in this situation, here are a few places to turn for help.

Offering a computer database of child care providers, **Parent Solutions**, 924-2312, provides members with referrals, a parenting handbook, first aid and CPR training, workshops, newsletters and telephone support.

Day Nursery sponsors **Child Care Answers**, 631-4643, which offers licensing and subsidy information, a child-care checklist and quality indicators.

Indiana Licensed Child Care Association, 925-8785, also offers information on day care provider licensing, as does **YWCA Child Care Resource and Referrals**, (800) 598-5688.

Those looking for a '90s-style Mary Poppins can contact: **Indy Nannies Plus**, 842-7711; or **Nanny Connection Inc.**, 546-2669. These businesses interview clients and screen potential nannies, taking much of the hassle out of finding child care. You can expect to pay a placement fee as well as a retainer. Wages for a full-time live-out nanny may run from $300 to $400 a week.

Many families who have hired an au pair have enjoyed the cultural exchange. Similar to a nanny, these young Europeans, about ages 18 to 25, generally stay in this country for a year and live with a family, experiencing family life while looking after the children. For information on au pairs, contact **Au Pair America**, (800) 928-7247; **AuPairCare**, (800) 4-AU-PAIR; or the **Au Pair Homestay Program**, (815) 385-4423.

Other day-care options include **Unique "7" Academy**, 733 S. Missouri Street, 637-1529, a 24-hour, seven-day-a-week child development center. Unique "7" offers before- and after-school programs, a preschool and kindergarten and other educational programs. It accepts drop-ins, offers Saturday-night sleepovers and can accommodate infants through age 13.

Sanders Diversified Home Services, 2575 E. 55th Place, Suite D, 254-1851, provides nannies as well as sick child care, a backup service for when you get caught without child care.

city, as well as in Beech Grove, Greenwood, Brownsburg, Plainfield and Greenfield, runs about $1,500 for the first Catholic child. Rates are lower for additional students in the same family. Contact your local parish or the Office of Catholic Education at the above number and see the following write-ups for more information.

BREBEUF

PREPARATORY SCHOOL

PREPARATION

At Brebeuf, a Jesuit College Preparatory School, students focus on attaining the knowledge and skills necessary for meeting the challenges of adulthood as well as entrance to, and success in, the most demanding universities. In all programs, young men and women are encouraged to develop to their highest potential.

Brebeuf, an interfaith high school, serves the entire Indianapolis area. Faculty, staff and students are committed to the goals of Jesuit education.

To learn more about Brebeuf, about a financial assistance program available to academically qualified students, and about the preparation that lasts a lifetime, call 872-7050.

BISHOP CHATARD HIGH SCHOOL

5885 Crittenden Ave.   *251-1451*

Enrolling approximately 550 students in grades 9 through 12, Chatard, located in a Broad Ripple-area neighborhood, boasts a student-teacher ratio of 16-to-1. Like all local Catholic high schools, Chatard holds a first-class commission from the Indiana Department of Education and offers art, music, drama, sports programs and plenty of extracurricular activities. About 12 to 14 percent of the student body is not Roman Catholic, though all students participate in religion class and activities. Tuition for Catholic students is about $2,400; $4,200 for non-Catholics.

CARDINAL RITTER JR./
SR. HIGH SCHOOL

3360 W. 30th St.   *924-4333*

Ritter serves about 450 students in grades 6 through 12 at its west-side location. It boasts a student-teacher ratio of about 15-to-1, holds a first-class commission from the Indiana Department of Education and offers art, music and drama as well as plenty of sports and extracurricular activities. All students participate in religion class and activities, though approximately 12 to 14 percent of students are not Roman Catholic. Tuition for parishioners is approximately $2,440; about $4,450 for nonparishioners.

BREBEUF PREPARATORY SCHOOL

2801 W. 86th St.   *872-7050*

Though affiliated with the Roman Catholic Church, Brebeuf is a Jesuit school founded in 1962 by the Chicago Province of the Society of Jesus. Brebeuf serves as an interfaith high school with students from a variety of religious backgrounds. About 50 percent are Roman Catholic, 40 percent Protestant and 10 percent Jewish and other

Parents of children new to Indianapolis Public Schools must submit a Select Schools application; contact IPS at 226-4000.

Insiders' Tips

faiths. The rigorous college prep curriculum is quite well-regarded; 99 percent of graduates gain admittance to college. Brebeuf enrolls approximately 670 students in grades 9 through 12, and tuition stands at about $6,000.

BUREAU OF JEWISH EDUCATION
6711 Hoover Rd. 255-3124

With recently expanded facilities, the Bureau of Jewish Education, or BJE, provides preschool programs for students from as young as 2½ through kindergarten. Though it enrolls students from a variety of religious backgrounds, students celebrate traditional Jewish holidays and observe the Shabbat (Sabbath) on Fridays.

CATHEDRAL HIGH SCHOOL
5225 E. 56th St. 542-1481

Administered as a private rather than parish-affiliated school since 1973, Cathedral High School was originally downtown across from St. Peter and Paul Cathedral; hence, the name. The former all-boys school purchased the former Ladywood campus on the northeast side after the Sisters of Providence closed their girls school in 1976; Cathedral then moved from downtown and became co-ed. By the early '90s the school's enrollment was about 57 percent male and 43 percent female; approximately 75 percent of students are Roman Catholic. The school enrolls about 900 students, and at least 96 percent of them continue on to college after graduation. Tuition is about $4,500.

THE CHILDREN'S HOUSE
810 E. 64th St. 253-3033

Though most local Montessori programs concentrate on preschool through about age 9, The Children's House, a nonprofit facility founded in 1972, offers an ungraded elementary school enrolling students from age 5 through 14; an all-day Montessori preschool serves children from age 2 through 4. The school offers open classrooms, a traditional curriculum, and Spanish, Latin, art and ballet classes at its new north-side address. Tuition is about $3,000.

COLONIAL CHRISTIAN SCHOOL
8140 Union Chapel Rd. 253-0649

Offering prekindergarten through high school, Colonial Christian provides a traditional Christian atmosphere as well as college prep courses in a Bob Jones University curriculum. The approximately 350 students score among the top 10 percent of schools nationwide in national Iowa testing. Tuition runs about $2,300.

HEBREW ACADEMY
6602 Hoover Rd. 251-1261

Since 1971, the Hebrew Academy of Indianapolis has offered a traditional Jewish education. Enrolling about 275 students in pre-K through 8th grade, the academy offers a curriculum that parallels state requirements in addition to providing students with in-depth instruction in Hebrew, and students consistently perform as well as or better than public school students on standardized tests. Tuition is approximately $5,000.

HERITAGE CHRISTIAN SCHOOLS
6401 E. 75th St. 849-3441

An interfaith school serving children in kindergarten through 12th grade, Heritage Christian enrolls more than 1,000 students. The school offers a traditional curriculum and college prep courses and holds high academic standards. Tuition runs about $3,500.

INTERNATIONAL SCHOOL OF INDIANA
612 W. 42nd St. 926-1951

Currently offering preschool through 5th grade, the International School stresses

What do we produce?
An educated workforce.

Ivy Tech State College is the link between you and
a valuable workforce. Which is good for everyone,
including the state. In Central Indiana call 921-4800.

academic excellence and is one of only a few in the country that features multilingual curricula. Even preschoolers experience immersion in a foreign language; the school currently offers a French-American and a Spanish-American track. A recent addition to the Indianapolis educational scene, International School opened in September 1994 after a Lilly Endowment-funded study by the Indiana International Issues Task Force recommended the development of an international school. The school, which has received considerable support from the business community, parents and other volunteers, is near the Butler University campus and enrolls about 45 students (though the school eventually plans to expand through the 12th grade). Tuition is approximately $6,000 a year; some financial aid is available.

LUTHERAN HIGH SCHOOL OF INDIANAPOLIS
5555 S. Arlington Ave.   787-5474

Indianapolis Lutheran High School began in 1976 with 17 students. By the early '90s, a growing enrollment necessitated a new school, and Lutheran High School of Indianapolis opened at its current location in September 1991. Affiliated with the Missouri Synod of the Lutheran Church, Lutheran High School holds a first-class commission from the Indiana Department of Education. It enrolls approximately 250 students in grades 9 through 12, and tuition for church-associated members is about $2,500 (about $4,200 for non-associated students).

MERIDIAN ACADEMY OF THE ARTS
1640 Fry Rd.   885-9222

Indiana's only fine arts elementary school, Meridian Academy of the Arts enrolls approximately 100 students in kindergarten through 6th grade and hopes to expand its offerings through the 8th grade (the facility's Creative Learning Center offers preschool and prekindergarten programs as well). Students participate in hands-on art-related activities in visual arts, dance, drama, music and language. Even the youngest study violin, piano, French, Spanish, braille and sign language; learn puppetry; put on plays and present their talents in monthly performances. Academic subjects are stressed as well, but within a holistic philosophy that incorporates the arts into math, science, social studies and other traditional courses. Tuition is about $4,000 a year.

ORCHARD COUNTRY DAY SCHOOL
615 W. 63rd St.   251-9253

Established in 1922 when it opened in a N. Meridian Street home with an enrollment of 20 students, Orchard Country Day School has offered a progressive curriculum emphasizing individual educational goals for each child. With an 8-to-1 student-teacher ratio, the school's enrollment now stands at just under 600 in prekindergarten through 8th grade at its 50-acre site on the northwest side of the city. Tuition stands at about $6,000; some financial aid is available.

PARK TUDOR
7200 N. College Ave.   254-2700

Created in 1970 when Park School for boys and Tudor Hall for girls merged, Park Tudor offers prekindergarten through 12th grade instruction in an academically challenging college-prep environment. The school, which enrolls more than 800 students, is divided into Lower School, Middle School and Upper School, and stresses English composition, laboratory sciences, mathematics, foreign languages and the arts. The student-teacher ratio in the Upper School is approximately 9-to-1. The 74

SAINT RICHARD'S SCHOOL

1960

St. Richard's School.
An independent Episcopal day school.
Challenging academics. Standards of excellence. Sound learning rooted in Christian faith, worship and ethics.

3243 N. Meridian St., Indianapolis, Indiana 46208
(317) 926-0425   Fax (317) 921-3367
"Knowledge and Values for a Lifetime"

Saint Richard's School welcomes students of any race, religion, color and national or ethnic origin.
Financial aid information and several payment options are available upon request.

---

graduates in 1994 were accepted at schools across the country. An emphasis on academics plus top-notch facilities, a beautiful 55-acre campus, a wide variety of athletics and extracurricular activities and a great deal of parent participation characterize this well-regarded school. Tuition ranges from about $4,500 in the lower grades to more than $8,000 at the high school level; approximately one student in seven receives financial aid.

RONCALLI HIGH SCHOOL
3300 Prague Rd.   *787-8277*

This south-side school, a consolidation of two former Catholic high schools, enrolls about 800 students in grades 9 through 12. Like all local Catholic high schools, Roncalli holds a first-class commission from the Indiana Department of Education and offers such classes as music, art and drama in addition to academic and religion classes; it has strong sports and extracurricular activity programs as well. Tuition runs about $2,600. About 12 to 14 percent of students are not Roman Catholic.

SCECINA MEMORIAL HIGH SCHOOL
5000 Nowland Ave.   *356-6377*

Named for Father John Scecina, the only priest from the local diocese to be killed in action in World War II, Scecina High School enrolls about 520 students in grades 9 through 12. Holding a first-class commission from the Indiana Department of Education, Scecina offers the standard academic and religion classes in addition to art, music and drama; it also boasts a strong sports program and plenty of extracurricular activities. The student-teacher ratio stands at about 17-to-1. Tuition for Catholic students is approximately $2,300, $4,200 for non-Catholics, who make up about 12 to 14 percent of the student body.

ST. RICHARD'S
3243 N. Meridian St.   *926-0425*

Modeled on the traditional English country day school, St. Richard's is an independent Episcopal school; the parish of Trinity Episcopal Church, though located next door, has no control over the school. Stressing rigorous academics and high expectations, St. Richard's enrolls about 300 students from numerous eth-

Photo: The Indianapolis Star & News

*Runners, whether getting ready for competition or just staying in shape,
have lots of room to roam.*

nic and religious backgrounds in prekindergarten through 8th grade. The school is based on Christian ethics and requires chapel attendance; students wear uniforms. Annual tuition is about $5,000; financial aid and several payment options are available.

SYCAMORE SCHOOL
1750 W. 64th St.   *253-5288*

Established in 1985 by parents who wanted an advanced curriculum for their children, Sycamore School offers an environment in which academically talented students can reach their potential while studying in a challenging environment. Learning is individualized, and the approximately 400 students in preschool through 8th grade explore a wide range of subjects. Tuition ranges from about $1,800 to about $5,400, and limited financial aid is available.

Colleges and Universities

BUTLER UNIVERSITY
4600 Sunset Ave.   *283-9255*

Emphasizing the traditional arts and sciences, Butler University draws approximately 4,000 students to its 290-acre campus 4 miles north of Monument Circle. The beautiful campus is situated in a residential area along the east bank of White River and the Central Canal, a location that places it near downtown and the popular Broad Ripple area yet provides a definite campus feel. The traditional frat row features houses for some of the 14 national fraternities and sororities that serve Butler students.

The university includes five colleges from which students earn bachelor's and master's degrees: Liberal Arts and Sciences, Education, Business Administration, Pharmacy and the Jordan College

of Fine Arts. The campus features 20 buildings, a formal botanical garden and a nature preserve. The university's newest structure, the Residential College, opened in 1990. It houses 480 students in a learning-living center with faculty in residence. A $4 million addition to the Atherton Student Union was completed in 1993.

The acoustically perfect Clowes Memorial Hall brings a wide range of cultural programs, concerts and Broadway productions to Indianapolis, and the Hinkle Fieldhouse, named for Butler's legendary coach Paul D. "Tony" Hinkle, still packs in fans for college basketball and high school sectional, regional and semi-state games.

Tuition is approximately $14,000, with room and board at $4,200.

FRANKLIN COLLEGE
501 E. Monroe St.
Franklin   *738-800*

This small school, which has ranked as one of the top-15 Midwest college values and as one of the 10-best Midwest liberal arts and science colleges, offers associate's and bachelor's degrees in 25 areas of study. It enrolls about 900 students, most of whom live on or around the handsome campus, which boasts attractive collegiate-looking red brick buildings. The college, south of Indianapolis in Franklin, the Johnson County seat, serves as a cultural focal point for the area bringing a variety of performances and lecture series to the community.

Tuition is about $11,000, and room and board is approximately $4,300.

INDIANA WESLEYAN UNIVERSITY
3520 Commerce Crossing   *574-3971*

Though the main campus is in Marion, a community northeast of Indianapolis, Indiana Wesleyan has a presence here due to its unique LEAP program (leadership education for adult professionals) that leads to a master's degree in business administration. The 26-month MBA program is designed to fit into the schedule of a working professional; indeed, three years work experience is required, in addition to a bachelor's degree, for admittance to the program. Concentrating on one subject at a time, students meet locally one night a week for the four-hour classes.

IUPUI

425 University Blvd.   *274-4591*

The bulky acronym stands for an equally lengthy name (Indiana University-Purdue University at Indianapolis), but the extra-long moniker may be appropriate for the city's largest university. Created in 1969, the campus has grown since the two universities came together to expand their regional programs and now enrolls nearly 28,000 students. Indeed, only IU-Bloomington beats IUPUI in size, dispelling the myth that this downtown campus is just a commuter college.

With more than 170 degree programs, from associate through doctoral levels, this urban campus on the west side of downtown offers the widest array of educational options in the state. It boasts Indiana's largest law school, the state's only medical and dental schools, the country's largest nursing school and its oldest physical education school.

Other innovative aspects include Learn and Shop, an award-winning program that offers college classes in shopping malls across the city, and Weekend College, the country's largest program of weekend teaching; in fact, five degree programs can be completed entirely on weekends. These programs serve IUPUI's large enrollment of nontraditional students, many of whom are returning to school or are juggling ca-

reers and family in addition to college. A program called SPAN serves academically advanced students in grade 6 through 12 who want to earn college credit while still in high school or middle school.

The IUPUI campus, which includes such top-notch facilities as the IU Natatorium, continues to expand; a $32 million state-of-the-art library was completed in 1993, a new law school building is on the agenda, and the John Herron School of Art will eventually move to the main campus from its 16th Street location into the old law school building.

In-state tuition for undergraduates is about $93 per credit hour, about $126 per credit hour for graduate students.

IVY TECH STATE COLLEGE

1 W. 26th St.   *921-4800*

Created by the Indiana General Assembly to provide "occupational training of a practical, technical and semi-technical nature," Ivy Tech, formerly known as Indiana Vocational Technical College (hence, the initials "I.V." through which the college came by its name Ivy Tech) offers a wide range of courses in 13 regions throughout the state. The Central Indiana Region enrolls approximately 6,000 students in 36 areas of study. Students earn associate's degrees and technical certificates in such fields as nursing, computer informational systems, electronic technology and culinary arts. Ivy Tech is fully accredited by the North Central Association of Colleges and Schools.

Tuition for Indiana residents is approximately $58 per credit hour.

MARIAN COLLEGE

3200 Cold Spring Rd.   *929-0321*

This progressive liberal arts college has been ranked by *Money* magazine as one of the best private college values based on

KEEPING THE PROMISE

• The Franklin College Leadership Program: Molding today's students into tomorrow's leaders.

• The Professional Development Program: Opportunities for professional growth in preparation for a changing future in the new Dietz Center for Professional Development.

• National recognition:
Classified by the Carnegie Foundation for the Advancement of Teaching as Baccalaureate I – the nation's highest level and including only 4.5 percent of the nation's colleges and universities.
The John Templeton Foundation 1993 Honor Roll for promotion of integrity and education.

• The presenter of national speakers through lectures by the Roger D. Branigin, Chair in History, the Maurice V. and Rose S. Johnson, Chair in the Humanities, the Edna B. Lacy Endowed, Chair in Business and Entrepreneurship, the E. Don and Joyce Tull, Chair in Business and Management and the Elmon and Lucile Williams, Chair in the Law and Public Service

• The home of the Pulliam School of Journalism and Indiana High School Press Association

Franklin College

501 East Monroe Street
Franklin, Indiana 46131-2598
317-738-8187

academic performance and actual cost. Known for its "ethically sensitive" approach to education, this Catholic institution enrolls students from a wide range of religious and ethnic backgrounds. The school prides itself on its mentoring approach to education and boasts a student-teacher ratio of 13-to-1.

The college's 1,400 students earn bachelor's or associate's degrees in such programs as education, liberal arts, nursing, business and other professional studies. Approximately 15 percent of the student population are minorities, and nearly 40 percent are older, nontraditional students who commute from Indianapolis or nearby areas. Still, nearly 40 percent live in residence halls on the 114-acre campus.

The park-like campus on the city's northwest side includes the Allison and Stokely mansions, two grand historic homes — available for public use — built by developers of the Indianapolis Motor Speedway. And the college's Kaufman Stadium serves as the city's official amateur baseball field.

Tuition for 12 to 20 credit hours is about $5,000.

MARTIN UNIVERSITY

2171 Avondale Pl.   543-3235

One of the city's most unique educational resources, Martin University was founded by a Benedictine priest, the Rev. Fr. Boniface Hardin, to serve minority and low-income college students. Only seven students attended then-Martin Center College in its first year in 1977. But by 1990, when the school achieved its university designation, it enrolled 1,100 students and boasted a 72-member faculty, of whom 45 percent held doctoral degrees.

Students earn undergraduate degrees in 26 fields of study. In 1992, the North Central Association of Colleges and Schools, this area's accrediting body, authorized Martin University to grant master's degrees, and it offers graduate degrees in community psychology and urban ministry studies.

The private, liberal arts school, which focuses on student-centered learning, takes a multicultural, multiracial approach to education and continues its original mission of serving the nontraditional student; indeed, the average age of a Martin University student is 40. A program called Prior Learning Assessment awards college credit for life experience and skills gained on the job or in community work.

Tuition runs about $200 per credit hour.

UNIVERSITY OF INDIANAPOLIS

1400 E. Hanna Ave.   788-3216

This 60-acre south-side residential campus, which enrolls approximately 4,000 students offers more than 65 undergraduate majors, as well as 12 graduate programs, including the state's first executive MBA program. The university is known for an emphasis on academics and boasts a highly regarded nursing school as well as the Krannert School of Physical Therapy, which ranks as one of the nation's best.

But the school, firmly grounded in the liberal arts, also places a high priority on communicating with its students. Every class is taught by a professor — not a graduate assistant — and classes are kept at a modest size to encourage student involvement and retain the emphasis on teaching.

The private institution attracts students from across the United States and from nearly 40 countries, though plenty of students come from the Indianapolis and central Indiana area. One of the draws is the new Christel DeHaan Fine Arts Center, a $10.2 million facility that includes a two-tiered Viennese-style performance hall, practice rooms, art studios, a gallery and lecture hall.

Tuition is about $11,000, with room and board at about $4,000.

Bible Colleges and Religious Institutions

AENON BIBLE COLLEGE
3939 Meadows Dr.   *547-9541*

This institution, affiliated with the Pentecostal Assemblies of the World, enrolls about 100 students who earn degrees in missions, Christian education, music and religious studies. Tuition is about $65 per credit hour.

BAPTIST BIBLE COLLEGE
2305 N. Kitley Ave.   *352-8736*

Offering bachelor's degrees in religious education and pastoral studies, this independent Baptist school that enrolls about 140 students also grants associate's degrees and certifications in Bible studies. Tuition is about $55 per credit hour.

CHRISTIAN THEOLOGICAL SEMINARY
1000 W. 42nd St.   *924-1331*

Though affiliated with the Disciples of Christ, this seminary takes an ecumenical approach to education. The seminary's approximately 325 students come from dozens of religious backgrounds to study for the master's degrees in divinity, theology, marriage and family therapy and counseling; students can also earn a doctorate in ministry. The Edvyean Repertory

Theatre at CTS concentrates on "theater with a purpose." Tuition stands at about $182 per credit hour.

HERITAGE BAPTIST UNIVERSITY
1301 W. South County Line Rd.   *882-2327*

Established in 1955, this independent Baptist school enrolls approximately 100 students who earn bachelor's and master's degrees in pastoral studies and education; it also offers secretarial studies. Tuition for full-time students is about $70 per credit hour.

INDIANA BIBLE COLLEGE
3350 Carson Ave.   *784-8069*

Approximately 200 students come to Indiana Bible College, affiliated with the United Pentecostal Church, to study Bible theology, music, religious education and missions. Tuition is about $925 per semester, with room and board between $312 and $372 a month.

Business and Technical Schools

ARISTOTLE COLLEGE
5425 S. U.S. Hwy. 31   *784-5400*

The approximately 100 students at the Indianapolis location of Aristotle College receive training in medical assisting and healthcare administration and can earn certificates and associate's degrees in health management. Tuition is about $5,000 for medical and dental assisting, about $10,000 for the health management associate's program.

At a loss as to what to do with kids during summer vacation? Check out Indy Parks and Recreation and YMCA summer day camps. They can keep youngsters occupied all summer with a wide range of age-appropriate activities.

Insiders' Tips

Photo: The Indianapolis Star & News

Students arrive for the start of the 1995-96 school year.

ITT TECHNICAL INSTITUTE
9511 Angola Ct.   *875-8640*

Offering training to nearly 1,000 students in business, technology and skilled trades, ITT Tech grants degrees in a variety of fields including electronics engineering technology, automated manufacturing technology, computer-aided drafting and hospitality management. Tuition ranges from about $2,000 to $2,500 per quarter.

INDIANA BUSINESS COLLEGE
802 N. Meridian St.   *264-5656*

More than 700 students enroll in the business-related courses offered at Indiana Business College and can earn associate's degrees in such areas as accounting; and secretarial and office, hotel, fashion or travel management. Tuition is about $80 per credit hour.

INTERNATIONAL BUSINESS COLLEGE
7205 Shadeland Station   *841-6400*

This school offers training or associate's degrees in such fields as accounting, computer programming, graphic design and medical and dental assisting.

LINCOLN TECHNICAL INSTITUTE
1201 Stadium Dr.   *632-5553*

Students at Lincoln Tech study in such fields as automotive and diesel service management and architectural drafting and can earn diplomas and associate's degrees in applied science. Tuition runs between $200 and $250 per credit hour.

MIDWEST CAREER COLLEGE
5881 E. 82nd St.   *594-0090*

Focusing on medical careers, Midwest Career College provides students with the training necessary to become medical assistants.

PROFESSIONAL CAREERS INSTITUTE
2611 Waterfront Pkwy. E. Dr.
299-6001, 298-4971

This school offers students training in medical or dental technology and business or computer sciences as well as a new paralegal program.

Inside
Healthcare

No one likes to get sick. But it happens. And should it happen to you in Indianapolis, you're in luck. Not the getting sick part, but the being in Indianapolis part. That's because Indianapolis is home to some of the finest healthcare facilities and practitioners in the country.

For the record there are 25 hospitals (including those with more than one site) in the greater Indianapolis area. Among them are such renowned institutions as the Indiana University Medical Center,

home not only to one the nation's most respected pediatric hospitals but also to the largest nursing school and the second-largest medical school in the United States. Methodist Hospital, the largest hospital in Indiana, operates a number of widely admired programs including an orthopaedic unit that has repaired the bones and joints of some of the world's elite athletes — professional race car drivers, NBA and NFL players. And St. Vincent Hospital's cardiac care unit attracts physicians and surgeons

COSMETIC ✦ PLASTIC
Reconstructive and Hand Surgery

- ✦ Breast Enlargement/Reduction
- ✦ Face, Eye or Neck Lift
- ✦ Chin Remodeling
- ✦ Nasal Surgery
- ✦ Dermabrasion/Chemical Peeling
- ✦ Scar Revision
- ✦ Tummy Tuck
- ✦ Liposuction
- ✦ Hair Transplant
- ✦ Spider Vein Therapy
- ✦ Permanent Eye Liner
- ° Consultation fee waived if surgery scheduled

Dr. Qazi has been practicing plastic, reconstructive, cosmetic and hand surgery for over 22 years. Dr. Qazi is board certified by the American Board of Plastic Surgeons, and has extensive experience in all of the above procedures

Plastic Surgery Center of Indiana P.C.
Dr. Haroon M. Qazi, M.D.
(317) 923-4822 or 1-800-762-4150
1935 N. CAPITOL AVENUE, INDIANAPOLIS

from around the world who come to learn new techniques. There are also numerous specialized hospitals and clinics, community health centers and immediate care facilities. And an array of national and regional medical organizations have their headquarters here.

From a business perspective, healthcare plays a significant role in Indianapolis. In addition to a medical bag full of healthcare providers, the city counts pharmaceutical manufacturer Eli Lilly and Company, medical diagnostic equipment manufacturer Boehinger Mannheim Corporation, and insurance and health services company The Associated Group among its largest employers.

So, if you're going to get sick, this isn't a bad place to do it. You'll be taken care of quite well.

Metropolitan Hospitals

COMMUNITY HOSPITALS INDIANAPOLIS
1500 N. Ritter Ave.   *355-1411*

Originating in 1956 as a single hospital on the city's east side, Community Hospitals Indianapolis has expanded to the point of operating hospitals at three sites around Indianapolis as well as several immediate-care centers and specialized clinics.

In 1994, Community Hospitals Indianapolis joined forces with St. Vincent Hospitals and Health Services (see separate entry in this chapter) to form the St. Vincent-Community Health Network, the largest health services network in Indiana. Under this arrangement, the two organizations combine their resources and function as a unified entity for planning, budgeting and operating purposes, yet each retains its name and assets and continues to operate as a separate corporation. And as this book went to press, Community and St. Francis Hospital and

Health Centers (see separate entry in this chapter) were exploring the possibility of the latter also joining the network.

The three Community Hospitals Indianapolis sites and their services are:

Community Hospital East
1500 N. Ritter Ave.   *355-1411*

This 739-bed facility contains a full-service, 24-hour emergency room, orthopaedic and neurology services, a cardiovascular program that includes diagnostic and rehabilitation services, a cardiac catheterization lab, a maternity center, a chest-pain emergency unit, a same-day surgery center, a rehabilitation center for stroke and brain injury victims, a sleep/wake disorders center and an occupational health center.

Also on-site is the Regional Cancer Center East Pavilion.

Community Hospital North
7150 Clearvista Dr.   *849-6262*

With 290 beds, this facility includes a women's unit, a single-room maternity care program, a stress care center and comprehensive medical and surgical services (including a full-service emergency room). Also on-site are the Indiana Surgery Center and the Regional Cancer Center North Pavilion.

Community Hospital South
1402 E. County Line Rd.   *887-7000*

Containing 150 beds, this facility offers complete medical and surgical services, a full-service emergency room, diagnostic imaging, a breast disease diagnosis and treatment program, fertility services, a cardiac rehabilitation program, cardiopulmonary testing, a cardiac catheterization lab and single-room maternity care.

Community Hospitals Indianapolis also operates five MedCheck Immediate

Care Centers throughout the city. (See the "Immediate Care Facilities" section of this chapter.)

INDIANA UNIVERSITY MEDICAL CENTER
1100 W. Michigan St.   274-8682

On the downtown campus of Indiana University-Purdue University at Indianapolis (IUPUI), the Indiana University Medical Center consists not only of two well-respected healthcare facilities — University Hospital & Outpatient Center), a specialized adult hospital, and the James Whitcomb Riley Hospital for Children, Indiana's only comprehensive pediatric hospital — but also of the Indiana University School of Medicine (the second-largest medical school in the country), the Indiana University School of Nursing (the largest nursing school in the country), the Indiana University School of Dentistry, and the Indiana School of Allied Health.

In fact, the I.U. Med Center's various training programs educate the majority of Indiana's healthcare workers. Approximately two-thirds of the physicians presently practicing in Indiana received all or part of their medical training at the Med Center.

In addition to training healthcare workers, the Center also conducts research and testing on a wide array of fronts. In fact, given their affiliation with the Schools of Medicine and Nursing, one of the Med Center hospitals' primary focal points (aside from patient care) is research. And its drug testing laboratory is one of only two in the United States accredited by the International Olympic Committee.

The Med Center is also a regional center for organ and tissue transplantation. It was the site for a number of Indiana firsts in that arena: the first kidney transplant, liver transplant, cornea transplant, bone marrow transplant, pancreas transplant, and infant and newborn heart transplants.

In 1994, a national study of hospitals resulted in the I.U. Medical Center, which was examined as a single entity, being designated one of the nation's 100 top-performing hospitals.

The Med Center's on-site facilities include:

University Hospital & Outpatient Center
550 University Blvd.   274-5000

Since opening its doors in 1971, University Hospital has become a national leader in patient care for cardiovascular, neural and rheumatic diseases as well as for cancer, hypertension and liver and endocrine diseases. The hospital is also a major center for heart, bone marrow, kidney, liver, and pancreas transplantations. Its radiation therapy facility houses two of the world's most powerful pieces of radiation treatment equipment: a 40-million electron volt linear accelerator and the Scanditronix Medical Microtron.

Adjacent to University Hospital, the Robert W. Long Hospital serves as the Med Center's outpatient and family practice facility. It also houses the Elks Cancer Research Center, the Multipurpose Arthritis Center and the Specialized Center for Research into Hypertension.

James Whitcomb Riley Hospital for Children
702 Barnhill Dr.   274-2273

Known simply as Riley Hospital, this facility specializes in pediatric care. Half of the hospitals patients are younger than the age of 2, a quarter are less than 2 months old. The seventh-largest hospital of its type in the country, Riley cares for children with cancer (only three other U.S. hospitals see more young cancer pa-

Photo: The Indianapolis Star & News

University Hospital & Outpatient Center are two well-respected healthcare facilities at the IU Medical Center.

tients), heart problems and pulmonary disorders.

It's also home to Indiana's only hemodialysis center for children with kidney failure as well as to the state's only center for severely burned children. In addition, the hospital offers bone marrow, heart and liver transplantation programs, and specialized diagnostic and care services for rare and debilitating diseases.

As this book went to press, Riley was in the process of building a multimillion-dollar pediatric research center that will significantly expand the I.U. Med center's pediatric disease research capabilities.

METHODIST HOSPITAL OF INDIANA
1701 N. Senate Blvd.   *929-2000*

The largest single-site hospital in Indiana, Methodist, which contains 1,140 beds, was established as a ministry of the Methodist Church in 1908. It quickly became a leader in the use of medical technology, installing one of the city's first x-ray machines in 1909. Working in concert with local pharmaceutical company

Eli Lilly and Company, Methodist was also one of the country's major centers of research into the use of insulin in treating diabetes (1922). More recently, it was the first hospital in the country to use an extracorporeal shock wave lithotripter to pulverize kidney stones (1984).

Today, in addition to an array of medical and surgical services (including a full-service emergency room), Methodist offers a number of specialized care services: an arthritis center, a breast health program, a cancer center, a center for geriatric medicine, a diabetes clinic, a kidney stone institute, a heart and lung institute, an eye institute and a behavioral care center. A Level 1 Trauma Care Center, Methodist also has Life Line helicopter services to airlift critically injured patients to the hospital for immediate care. Also on-site is Methodist Children's Hospital, which specializes in pediatric medicine.

In a move to decentralize delivery of services, Methodist has begun establishing healthcare complexes around the I-465 beltway that encircles Indianapolis. These complexes offer such services as family practice, immediate care, pediatrics, obstetrics and gynecology, gastroenterology, orthopaedics and sports medicine. They provide a variety of outpatient services: surgery, magnetic resonance imaging, mammography, ultrasound, x-ray, lab services and family life/public education. The complexes open presently are:

Eagle Highlands Outpatient Center, 6850 Parkdale Place, 329-7222

Methodist Medical Plaza South, 8820 S. Meridian Street, 865-7424

Methodist/Witham Medical Clinic at Zionsville, 1650 W. Oak Street, Zionsville, 873-8800

Other Methodist-affiliated outpatient complexes are being developed on the city's east side, as well as in Carmel and Greenwood.

RICHARD L. ROUDEBUSH VA MEDICAL CENTER

1481 W. 10th St.	635-7401
2601 Cold Spring Rd.	635-7401

Named for former Indiana Congressman and Veterans Administration director Richard L. Roudebush, the VA Medical Center is a 440-bed, two-division operation open to American military veterans. Providing primary and specialized medical, surgical, psychiatric and neurological care, the center serves as a referral hospital for Veterans Administration medical centers throughout Indiana and central Illinois.

Among the center's specialized services and programs are cardiothoracic surgery, electrophysiology, radiation oncology, dialysis, diagnostic imaging, neuropsychiatry and treatment for chemical dependency. There is also an active research and development division with ongoing projects in diabetes, alcoholism, chronic ischemic heart disease, immunology, liver disease, cancer chemotherapy and endocrine bone diseases.

In operation since 1952, the W. 10th Street division is near the Indiana University Medical Center, and as such it serves as a teaching site for Indiana Medical School students. Its primary patient care areas are medicine, surgery and neurology.

The city's original (1932) VA hospital, the Cold Spring Road division now focuses on mental health and behavioral sciences. This division also includes a 60-bed on-site nursing home.

ST. FRANCIS HOSPITAL & HEALTH CENTERS

1600 Albany St., Beech Grove   787-3311

Founded in 1912 by two members of the order Poor Sisters of St. Francis Seraph of the Perpetual Adoration, this is one of Indiana's largest Catholic healthcare organizations. In addition to its main Beech Grove campus, St. Francis was scheduled to open its South Campus facilities at the intersection of S. Emerson Avenue and Stop 11 Road in late 1995.

Among the services available at the 441-bed Beech Grove site are 24-hour emergency care; cardiac testing, care and rehabilitation; radiology; a breast center; occupational and physical therapies; women's health services; a sleep disorders center; wellness programs; and inpatient and outpatient mental health services.

Slated to open on the South Campus as this book went to press were an emergency/inpatient care center (emergency room services, maternity care, gynecology, pediatrics, diagnostics); an ambulatory care center (radiology, pharmacy, surgery and recovery rooms, lab services); a cancer care center; a family health center;

and a medical office building for physician specialty groups.

St. Francis also operates PromptCare, a center for minor emergency care. (See the "Immediate Care Facilities" section of this chapter.)

ST. VINCENT HOSPITALS
AND HEALTH SERVICES

2001 W. 86th St.   338-2345
13500 N. Meridian St., Carmel   582-7000

St. Vincent is operated by the Daughters of Charity of St. Vincent de Paul, a Catholic order dedicated to serving those in need. Founded in 1881 by four Daughters, St. Vincent has grown both in size and in the scope of its services. Originally housed in a former seminary, St. Vincent now includes two hospitals (one in Indianapolis, one in Carmel) as well as ancillary facilities for counseling, mental and physical therapies and cardiac care. The organization also operates three occupational health centers and five outpatient care centers.

A leader in cardiac care, St. Vincent also offers comprehensive services in orthopaedics, cancer care, pain management, obstetrics, sports medicine, stress management and alcohol and drug rehabilitation. The hospital's Institute on Aging provides specialized services to seniors, while its hospice program focuses on caring for people with limited life expectancies.

In 1994, St. Vincent joined forces with Community Hospitals Indianapolis (see separate entry in this chapter) to form the St. Vincent-Community Health Network, creating in the process the largest healthcare network in Indiana. The network combines the resources of the two organizations while allowing each to retain its individual identity and to operate as separate corporations.

WESTVIEW HOSPITAL

3630 Guion Rd.   924-6661

Westview is central Indiana's only osteopathic hospital. Osteopathic medicine is based on the concept that the body's various systems work together to maintain good health. What other healthcare providers now call "wellness," osteopathic physicians have championed for more than a century — and Westview has provided to Indianapolis residents for two decades.

With 191 physicians and 95 RNs on staff, Westview is a full-service medical and surgical facility. This 120-bed hospital offers a variety of traditional medical services such as cadiopulmonary, radiology, neurology, surgery, a 24-hour emergency room, a laboratory, intensive and extended care units and physical, speech and occupational therapies — all with an osteopathic emphasis on building good health.

WINONA MEMORIAL HOSPITAL

3232 N. Meridian St.   924-3392

Since 1956, this 250-bed, acute-care facility has been offering Indianapolis residents a variety of primary and specialty care services. With a medical staff of 300 physicians, Winona provides 24-hour emergency care, cardiovascular services, gynecological services, surgery (inpatient and outpatient), radiology, orthopaedic services, cosmetic surgery, neurology and neurosurgery, urology, cancer care, dermatological services and physical, occupational and speech therapies. The hospital's specialty care services include a diabetes center, foot and ankle centers, laser surgery, a sleep/wake disorders center, a bloodless surgery and medicine program, senior citizen health centers, a wound care center, a weight re-

It's a big city. You're new in it. And you need a doctor.

Now what?

Now us.

We're The Women's Hospital of Indianapolis. And our Women's Health Resource Center is designed for women just *like you.* Because we can help find the right doctor just *for you.*

We specialize in women's care.

We have hundreds of physicians, obstetricians, gynecologists and other specialists. We'll locate the ones convenient for you, tell you about their practices, and even help schedule your first appointment if you'd like.

Call 872-1821.

Call us today. And you'll see it's not such a big city after all. Not when you have *friends* like us.

The Women's Hospital–Indianapolis

8111 Township Line Road, Indianapolis, IN 46260

duction program and psychiatric and chemical dependency centers.

WISHARD MEMORIAL HOSPITAL
1001 W. 10th St.   *639-6671*

The oldest hospital in Indianapolis, Wishard was originally known as Indianapolis City Hospital when it opened in 1866. From the beginning, its primary mission has been to provide healthcare to the city's poor and uninsured. Since 1975, it has functioned as an autonomous component of the Indiana University School of Medicine. Wishard was the state's first hospital to attain the status of being a Level 1 Trauma center, and it also is home to one of the state's foremost burn treatment units.

In addition, there is a special on-site tuberculosis treatment unit as well as a critical care unit that provides surgical, medical and cardiac intensive care. Wishard also houses a 40-bed inpatient mental health unit in conjunction with the Midtown Community Mental Health Center.

Wishard and the IU School of Medicine jointly operate the Regenstrief Health Center, an outpatient unit that provides primary and acute care for some 3,500 to 4,000 patients a week.

THE WOMEN'S HOSPITAL-INDIANAPOLIS
8111 Township Line Rd.   *875-5994*

Since its inception in 1983, The Women's Hospital-Indianapolis has specialized in providing obstetrical, gynecological and reproductive care services to women in the Greater Indianapolis area. Additionally, this facility offers women general medical and surgical services, reconstructive and cosmetic procedures, comprehensive infertility treatment, radiology services and psychiatric services for children, adolescents and seniors.

REGIONAL HOSPITALS
Hancock Memorial Hospital
801 N. State St., Greenfield   *462-5544*

This 91-bed facility in Greenfield, east of Indianapolis, provides a variety of inpatient and outpatient services including emergency care, critical care, cardiology, a cardiac catheterization lab, maternity care, radiology, surgery, respiratory therapy, radiation oncology, physical rehabilitation (physical, occupational and speech therapies) and home healthcare. There's also an on-site women's health resource center and a transitional care unit.

HENDRICKS COMMUNITY HOSPITAL
1000 E. Main St., Danville   *745-4451*

Serving the needs of Hendricks County residents, this facility offers 24-hour emergency care, same-day surgery, laser and laparoscopic surgery, mammography, sports medicine, advanced diagnostic imaging and home health services. There's also an on-site private-room birth center. Additionally, the hospital conducts a number of community programs including health screenings, safe sitter training, sign language classes and diabetes education.

JOHNSON MEMORIAL HOSPITAL
1125 W. Jefferson St., Franklin   *736-3300*

In business since 1947, Johnson Memorial Hospital is a 165-bed facility providing primary care services to the residents of Johnson County. The hospital's medical staff includes 58 primary care physicians and specialists as well as 125 consulting specialists who also practice at other Central Indiana hospitals.

Johnson Memorial's services consist of acute medical and surgical care for adults and children (including critical care), 24-hour emergency care, maternity care, re-

Photo: The Indianapolis Star & News

Methodist Hospital is the largest single-site hospital in the state.

habilitation therapies, occupational health and outpatient diagnostics, treatment and surgery. There is also a long-term care center and an on-site child-care center for children between the ages of 6 weeks and 6 years.

KENDRICK MEMORIAL HOSPITAL/
KENDRICK HEALTHCARE CENTER

1201 Hadley Rd., Mooresville   831-1160

Established in 1881, this facility south of Indianapolis consists of a variety of specialized medical and surgical centers. On-site centers include:

Kendrick Family Physicians: This group of physicians provides families with primary healthcare such as physical exams, allergy treatments, well-baby care, children's preventative care, chronic care, lab/x-ray/diagnostic services and referrals to specialists. For information, call 831-9340.

The Regional Center for Colon and Rectal Care: This center specializes in the diagnosis and treatment of colon and rectal problems ranging from hemorrhoids to cancer. For information, call 834-2020 or (800) 601-2323.

The Kendrick Prostate Tumor Center: This center specializes in the treatment of prostate cancer through the use of radioactive seed implantation. Other Kendrick centers include:

The Kendrick Center for Women
1203 Hadley Rd.   831-9345

This facility provides health screening, diagnostics and treatment for women in a variety of areas including breast health, gynecology, fertility, contraception, prenatal care, menopause management, urinary incontinence and sexually transmitted diseases.

The Center for Hip & Knee Surgery/
The Sports Medicine Clinic
1199 Hadley Rd.   831-2273

With internationally renowned orthopaedic surgeons Merrill Ritter, M.D. and E. Michael Keating, M.D. on staff, the Center for Hip & Knee Surgery is a leader in joint replacement techniques and technologies. The Sports Medicine Clinic treats physically active people of all ages, with special emphasis on high school, college and recreational athletes.

Acute-Care Hospitals

The following three facilities specialize in serving patients whose healthcare needs require extended hospital stays, serving people with complex medical conditions who are stable but who need long-term medical care.

AMERICAN TRANSITIONAL HOSPITAL-INDIANAPOLIS
3232 N. Meridian St.   *931-1676*

This is a 40-bed facility on the third floor of Winona Memorial Hospital.

THC-INDIANAPOLIS
898 E. Main St., Greenwood   888-8155

This 38-bed facility is inside CPC Valle Vista Hospital (see entry in the "Special Needs Hospitals and Programs" section of this chapter).

VENCOR HOSPITAL OF INDIANAPOLIS
1700 W. 10th St.   636-4400

This is a 59-bed facility inside a renovated factory near Indiana University Medical Center.

Rehabilitation Hospitals

LIFELINES CHILDREN'S REHABILITATION HOSPITAL
1707 W. 86th St.   872-0555

The only pediatric rehabilitation hospital in Indiana, this 35-bed facility specializes in helping infants, children and teens recover from or adjust to the effects of prematurity, head or spinal cord injuries, neuromuscular diseases, aneurysms, brain tumors, multiple bone fractures, amputations, burns or genetic or chromosomal anomalies. Patients are usually referred to Lifelines by their physicians.

In addition to working with the young patients, the hospital staff, which includes physicians and nurses trained in a variety of pediatric specialties as well as therapists and social workers, provides family education and training.

REHABILITATION HOSPITAL OF INDIANA
4141 Shore Dr.   329-2000, (800) 933-0123

A joint effort of Seton Health Corporations, a subsidiary of St. Vincent Hospitals and Health Centers, and MH Healthcare, a subsidiary of Methodist Hospital of Indiana, this 80-bed facility specializes in providing inpatient and outpatient services for adults affected by spinal cord injuries, brain injuries, strokes, amputations, orthopaedic problems, neuromuscular disease, burns and disabilities related to any of the preceding. Patients come to Rehabilitation Hospital via referrals from physicians, nursing homes, insurance companies or families or on their own.

Among the services offered are occupational and physical therapies, respiratory therapy, psychological testing and counseling, speech therapy and social and educational assistance.

Special Needs and Services

CHARTER HOSPITAL OF INDIANAPOLIS
5602 Caito Dr.   545-2111, (800) 843-9299
CHARTER INDIANAPOLIS BEHAVIORAL HEALTH SYSTEM NORTH
11075 N. Pennsylvania St.   575-1000
(800) 999-6555

These two facilities provide special programs for individuals dealing with drug and alcohol abuse, sexual orientation issues, eating disorders, depression, anxiety, phobias and emotional dependency. The Caito Drive facility provides both inpatient and outpatient services to adults and young people, while the Pennsylvania Avenue facility is a residential treatment site for children and adolescents.

CPC VALLE VISTA HOSPITAL
898 E. Main St., Greenwood   887-1348

A full-service, 96-bed, private psychiatric facility, CPC Valle Vista Hospital provides a range of services to children, teens and adults with emotional, behavioral and addiction problems. Among the hospital's services are outpatient, partial hospitalization, inpatient, continuing care and residential treatment programs, along with a 24-hour mobile psychiatric assessment team, a speakers bureau, seminars and support groups.

CROSSROADS
REHABILITATION CENTER INC.
4740 Kingsway Dr.   466-1000

This is central Indiana's largest provider of rehabilitation services and training programs for children, adolescents and adults with mental and/or physical disabilities. Among the organization's services are child development, speech and audiology, physical and occupational therapies, training and placement, vocational evaluation and work adjustment.

DAMIEN CENTER INC.
1350 N. Pennsylvania St.   632-0123

Established in 1987 by Christ Church Cathedral and SS. Peter and Paul Cathedral, the Damien Center provides counseling and support services to people with HIV-AIDS and their families. Among its services are medical and dental referral, financial and legal assistance, housing and transportation arrangements and counseling and education programs.

FAIRBANKS HOSPITAL INC.
8102 Clearvista Pkwy.   849-8222
FAIRBANKS
GREENWOOD COUNSELING CENTER
1000 N. Madison Ave., Ste. W-5   888-2801

Founded in 1945, Fairbanks Hospital was Indiana's first full-service chemical dependency treatment facility. Today, it spe-cializes in providing services for chemically dependent adolescents and adults and their families. Using a multidisciplinary team approach, Fairbanks' physicians, nurses, counselors, psychiatrists, psychologists, clinical social workers, family therapists and dieticians provide detoxification, inpatient, day-treatment, outpatient and aftercare services.

The Greenwood Counseling Center offers outpatient services for clients who live on the south side of Indianapolis.

KOALA HOSPITAL OF INDIANAPOLIS
1404 S. State Ave. 783-4084, (800) 562-5212
KOALA COUNSELING CENTER
532 Turtle Creek N., Ste. H-2   782-3190

Since 1978, Koala has been providing mental health services to adolescents and adults in the Indianapolis area. Included among those services are outpatient counseling (individual, family and group), inpatient assistance with substance abuse and emotional problems, outpatient help for chemical dependency and alcohol and drug education programs. In addition to the main hospital site, Koala also operates a counseling center on the city's south side.

PLANNED PARENTHOOD
OF CENTRAL INDIANA
3219 N. Meridian St.   925-6747

For more than 60 years, Planned Parenthood of central Indiana has been providing family planning and reproductive health services to Indianapolis area residents. In addition to its Meridian Street facility, the organization operates clinics at these locations:

Castleton, 8121 Center Run Drive, 849-9304

South side, 4024 Madison Avenue, Ste. A, 788-0396

Northwest side, 8847 Commerce Park Place, 876-1774

East side, 9385 E. Washington Street, 899-4731

Westfield, 17902 U.S. 31 N., Westfield, 896-2594.

Community Health Centers

In Indianapolis, community health centers (CHCs) are situated in medically underserved neighborhoods. While their fundamental mission is to provide primary healthcare to individuals and families whose circumstances (lack of insurance, poverty, homelessness) would otherwise prevent access to care, CHCs are available to anyone living in their services areas.

The services available through not-for-profit CHCs are identical to (and in some cases, more extensive than) those available through for-profit clinics and private physicians' offices. From physical exams and prenatal care to pediatrics and gerontology, CHCs offer high-quality, low-cost healthcare.

Indianapolis CHCs include:

Barrington Health Center, 3401 E. Raymond Avenue, 788-4719

Citizens Health Center, 1650 N. College Avenue, 924-6351

Blackburn Community Health Center, 2700 Dr. Martin Luther King Jr. Street, 921-6580

Forest Manor Community Health Center, 3840 N. Sherman Drive, 541-3400

Fountain Square Community Health Center, 1435 Shelby Street, 686-5379

Northeast Community Health Center, 6042 E. 21st Street, 357-2794

Northwest Community Health Center, 7440 N. Michigan Road, 921-6580

People's Health Center, 2340 E. 10th Street, 633-7360

Southeast Health Center, 901 S. Shelby Street, 488-2040

Southwest Health Center, 2202 W. Morris Street, 488-2020

Immediate-Care Facilities

While offering fewer and less sophisticated medical services than those available through hospital emergency rooms, immediate care facilities are convenient and less costly alternatives for treatment of minor injuries or illnesses. Area immediate care sites include the following.

Broad Ripple MedCheck*, 1091 Broad Ripple Avenue, 355-3400

Carmel MedCheck*, 313 E. Carmel Drive, Carmel, 575-0655

Castleton MedCheck*, 82nd Street and Shadeland Avenue, 588-7800

Doctors Immediate MedCenter, 9598 Allisonville Road, 842-7750

Emergency Medical Care South, 534 Turtle Creek N. Drive, 788-5573

Fast Care, (Inside Winona Memorial Hospital), 3232 N. Meridian Street, 927-2273

First Care, 1350 E. County Line Road, 865-2169

Fishers Crossing Immediate Care, 11979 Fishers Crossing Drive, Fishers, 842-0202

Immediate Care Center (west), 650 N. Girls School Road, 271-5080

Immediate Care Center (east), 992 N. Mitthoeffer Road, 899-5546

Immediate Care Center (northwest), 7363 N. Michigan Road, 293-8223

Immediate Care Center (north), 860 E. 86th Street, 580-3200

Immediate Care Center (south), 1278 N. Madison Avenue, Greenwood, 888-3508

Lawrence MedCheck*, 10840 Pendleton Pike, 823-8121

FAIRBANKS HOSPITAL

Chemical dependency treatment programs for men, women, adolescents, and their families.

- Free Assessments
- Inpatient/Outpatient Programs
- Family Program
- Adult/Adolescent Education
- Free Aftercare
- Training Workshops/Seminars

(317) 849-8222 • (800) 225-HOPE

8102 Clearvista Parkway • Indianapolis, IN 46256

Library Park Family Health & Immediate Care, 1664 W. Smith Valley Road, Greenwood, 888-8112

MedCheck East*, 1703 N. Post Road, 355-3200

PromptCare**, 4770 S. Emerson Avenue, 782-3009

Plainfield Medical Care, 1620 E. Main Street, Plainfield, 839-8484

Zionsville Immediate Care, 1650 W. Oak Street, Zionsville, 873-8888

*All MedCheck centers are operated by Community Hospitals Indianapolis.

**PromptCare is operated by St. Francis Hospital & Health Centers.

Mental Health Services

In addition to the mental health services available through the facilities listed in the Special Needs Hospitals and Programs section of this chapter, the following organizations provide help to people with mental and emotional problems.

For help in finding a therapist, call Indianapolis Referral Service, 844-1546.

MARION COUNTY
MENTAL HEALTH ASSOCIATIONS
2506 Willowbrook Pkwy., Ste. 100
251-0005, (800) 901-1133

As the local chapter of the National Mental Health Association, the Marion County Mental Health Association provides support groups for people affected by mental and emotional disorders as well as for their families and for teachers who work with them. It also provides residential services for mentally ill men and women, offers mental health education programs, serves as an advocate for the mentally ill on matters of public policy and operates telephone hotlines for crisis and suicide intervention (see separate listing below).

SUICIDE & CRISIS PHONE LINE
2506 Willowbrook Pkwy., Ste. 100   251-7575

Twenty-four hours a day, 365 days a year, this phone line, a service of the Marion County Mental Health Association, will put you in touch with a trained volunteer who will listen to you, talk with you and help you find the help you need to cope with depression, suicidal thoughts and other life crises (rape, child abuse, family violence, homelessness, relationship problems).

MIDTOWN COMMUNITY
MENTAL HEALTH CENTER
964 N. Pennsylvania St.   630-7791

One of the largest providers of mental health services in the city, Midtown's Pennsylvania Street offices house its child and adolescent services, the family growth center, community and homeless mobile teams, and the community support center. Midtown also operates adult outpatient clinics at these sites:

Meridian Center, 3637 N. Meridian Street, 924-7906

People's Health Center, 2340 E. 10th Street, 685-5375

Fountain Square Center, 1308 Prospect Street, 633-4666

Westside Center, 5610 Crawfordsville Road, 244-2243

TRI-COUNTY CENTER INC.
8945 N. Meridian St.
Carmel   574-0055

This multi-site organization provides outpatient counseling services for children, adolescents, adults, seniors, and people with substance abuse problems. In addition to its Carmel facilities, Tri-County

has facilities at: 6100 N. Keystone Avenue, Suite 360, Indianapolis, 257-3903; 651 Westfield Road, Noblesville, 257-3903; 602 Ransdell Road, Lebanon, 773-6864.

Healthcare Associations

Indianapolis is home to a number of regional and national healthcare associations, many of which can be valuable sources of information for consumers.

Alzheimer's Disease Association, 5155 N. Shadeland Avenue, 542-8888

American Academy of Osteopathy, 3500 DePauw Boulevard, Suite 1080, 879-1881

American Cancer Society, (Central Indiana Area Office), 8730 Commerce Park Place, 879-4100

American College of Sports Medicine, 401 W. Michigan Street, 634-7817

American Diabetes Association, 7363 E. 21st Street, 352-9226

American Heart Association of Indiana, 8645 Guion Road, 876-4850

American Lung Association of Indiana, 9410 Priority Way W. Drive, 573-3900

Arthritis Foundation, 8646 Guion Road, 879-0321

Central Indiana Regional Blood Center, 3450 N. Meridian Street, 926-2381

Cerebral Palsy, United of Central Indiana Inc., 615 N. Alabama Street, 632-3561

Indiana Academy of Family Physicians, 4847 S. High School Road, 856-3757

Indiana Association of Osteopathic Physicians & Surgeons, 3520 Guion Road, Suite 202, 926-3009

Indiana Dental Association, 401 W. Michigan Street, 634-2610

Indiana Department of Mental

Physician Referral Services

When you're trying to find the right physician, referral services are indispensable. In the Indianapolis area, you can get help in finding a physician or specialist by contacting:

Ask-a-Nurse	351-7800, (800) 777-7775
Indianapolis Medical Society	639-3406
Speciality Physician Access Network	488-2338, (800) 575-SPAN

Most area hospitals have referral services as well. You can contact:

Community Hospitals Indianapolis	351-7800
Hendricks Community Hospital Danville	745-3759
Johnson Memorial Hospital Franklin	736-3425
Methodist Hospital of Indiana	929-2222
Riley Hospital for Children	274-4862
St. Francis Hospitals & Health Centers	782-6699
St. Vincent Hospitals & Health Services	338-2273
University Hospital & Outpatient Center	274-4862
Winona Memorial Hospital	927-2727
Wishard Memorial Hospital	634-2273
The Women's Hospital-Indianapolis	872-1804

Health, 402 W. Washington Street, 232-7800

Indiana Easter Seal Society, 8425 Keystone Crossing, 254-8382

Indiana Health Care Association, One North Capitol Street, Suite 115, 636-6406

Indiana Hospital Association, One American Square, Suite 1100, 633-4870

Indiana Lupus Foundation, 2701 E. Southport Road, 783-6033

Indiana Optometric Association, 201 N. Illinois Street, 237-3560

Indiana Pharmacists Association, 729 N. Pennsylvania Street, 634-4968

Indiana Podiatric Medical Association, 201 N. Illinois Street, 237-3569

Indiana Primary Health Care Association, 1006 E. Washington Street, Ste. 200, 630-0845

Indiana Society to Prevent Blindness, 911 E. 86th Street, 257-2020

Indiana State Medical Association, 322 Canal Walk, 261-2060

Indiana State Nurses Association, 2915 N. High School Road, 299-4575

Leukemia Society of America — Indiana Chapter, 921 E. 86th Street, Suite 205, 726-2270

Marion County Association for Retarded Citizens, 2400 N. Tibbs Avenue, 264-1422

Multiple Sclerosis Society, 615 N. Alabama Street, 634-8796

Muscular Dystrophy Association, 9102 N. Meridian Street, 571-0275

National Kidney Foundation of Indiana Inc., 850 N. Meridian Street, 693-6534

Parkinson Awareness Association of Central Indiana Inc., 721 Sherwood Drive, 255-1993

Sickle Cell Program, 3549 N. College Avenue, 927-5158

Spina Bifida Association of Central Indiana, 4648 Bluffwood Drive N., 293-3664

Inside
Retirement and Senior Services

As is true in other metropolitan areas throughout the country, Indianapolis has a rapidly expanding senior population. And a large percentage of those seniors are choosing to stay here after retirement rather than move to Florida or Arizona as so many retirees did in the past.

With an increase in the number of seniors in the community has come an increase in the number and variety of senior services. From retirement communities and elder-law attorneys, geriatric healthcare programs to job referral services, insurance counselors and transportation providers, area agencies and organizations are offering more (and more sophisticated) services for older adults than ever before.

Where to Start

CIOCA THE ACCESS NETWORK
(Senior Information and Assistance Center)
4755 Kingsway Dr., Ste. 333   254-3660
(800) 432-2422, TTY 254-5497

Formerly known as the Central Indiana Council on Aging, CIOCA The Access Network is *the* central clearinghouse for information about and access to senior services. The largest of Indiana's agencies on aging, CIOCA offers services to residents of Marion, Boone, Hamilton, Hancock, Hendricks, Johnson, Morgan and Shelby counties.

The organization's network of services includes adult day care, legislative advocacy on issues affecting older adults, in-

These seniors do water aerobics at a local YMCA.

Photo: The Indianapolis Star & News

home care, benefits counseling, care management, community education, congregate and home-delivered meals, employment, health promotion, home maintenance and modification, legal assistance, personal emergency response, transportation and volunteer development and opportunities, and, of course, information about these and other matters of interest to seniors.

If you're looking for help or information, CIOCA's Senior Information and Assistance Center is the place to start. For a handy reference, ask for the organization's free resource guide *Take Care of Yourself*, which includes a thorough listing of services and programs throughout the community.

OLDER ADULT SERVICE AND INFORMATION SYSTEM (OASIS)

L.S. Ayres, Washington Square Mall
10202 E. Washington St.   *895-9976*

Sponsored by L.S. Ayres and Methodist Hospital, OASIS offers a variety of programs designed to give adults 55 and older opportunities to go on learning, stay active and healthy, travel and volunteer throughout the community.

UNITED SENIOR ACTION

1211 S. Hiatt St.   *634-0872*

In operation since 1979, United Senior Action (USA) is an advocacy group that focuses its efforts on legislative and non-legislative matters that affect seniors. Among USA's concerns are promoting home care rather than nursing home care for the elderly, attaining fair utility rates for seniors, limiting prescription drug prices, combatting abuse and neglect of seniors, and protecting and expanding consumer rights in such areas as healthcare and health insurance. USA memberships cost $8 a year for one person, $10 for a couple.

For information on senior services in surrounding counties, contact:

Boone County Senior Service, 403 N. Lebanon Street, Lebanon, 482-5220;

Hamilton County Senior Services, 1051 N. 10th Street, Noblesville, 773-4322;

Hancock County Senior Services, 120 W. McKenzie Road, Ste. D, Greenfield, 462-3758;

Hendricks County Senior Services, 970 E. Main Street, Danville, 745-4303;

Johnson County Senior Services, 399 S. Main Street, Franklin, 736-7736;

Morgan County Coordinated Aging Services, 1139 E. Morgan Street, Martinsville, 342-3007;

Shelby County Senior Services, 120 W. Washington Street, Shelbyville, 398-0127.

Senior Centers

Offering a range of activities and services, senior centers provide older adults with access to educational opportunities, health and fitness programs, social and cultural events, and assistance negotiating the sometimes baffling array of senior-oriented legal, medical and financial programs and issues. With some 30 senior centers in Indianapolis proper as well as dozens of others throughout central Indiana, providing a comprehensive list isn't feasible. What follows are profiles of a few centers. For information on others, contact CIOCA The Access Network.

CHRISTAMORE HOUSE

502 N. Tremont Ave.   *635-7211*

This is one of the city's oldest African-American community centers, long known for its activism and advocacy efforts on behalf of its west-side neighborhood. The senior program at Christamore is open to people 55 and older and includes a multitude of activities including daily fitness classes, a hot lunch program, arts and crafts, sewing and quilting classes, Bible study classes, and shopping trips. There's also a seniors club that meets on a monthly basis; dues are $5/year.

INDIANAPOLIS SENIOR CITIZENS CENTER
708 E. Michigan St.   *263-6272*

The largest senior center in the city, the Indianapolis Senior Citizens Center (ISCC) provides its members access to such services and programs as daily meals, health education, fitness activities (swimming, yoga, walking, etc.), educational classes (nature study, Indiana history, Bible study, dance lessons, foreign language instruction, etc.), social activities (bridge, dances, concerts, holiday parties, etc.), assistance with legal, tax and insurance matters, and volunteer opportunities. Membership is open to anyone older than 60; dues are $12 per year.

JEWISH SENIOR SERVICES
Jewish Community Center
6701 Hoover Rd.   *251-9467*

Jewish Senior Services provides an array of programs for seniors including counseling, home visits, escorted transportation, assistance with insurance matters, information about and referral to other senior service providers and a national referral network for elder caregivers. In addition, the Jewish Community Center's roster of programs is open to seniors. Senior can enjoy fitness activities (for more on these, see our Parks and Recreation chapter), cultural and social activities and volunteer opportunities. Membership to the Center is open to Jewish and non-Jewish individuals and families. Call for information.

JOHN H. BONER COMMUNITY CENTER
2236 E. 10th St.   *633-8220*

At this near east-side center, area residents 60 and older can take part in a variety of activities including a wellness program, which offers weekly blood pressure screenings, exercise classes, a hot lunch program, regular social security and Medicare updates and discussions on current events. There are also twice-monthly trips to the grocery store (transportation is provided free of charge), as well as monthly trips to restaurants. Recreational activities include games (bingo and euchre), ceramics classes and choral music performances by the resident troupe the Jolly Off-Notes. The center also has an on-site adult daycare program.

LAWRENCE SENIOR ACTIVITIES
5301 N. Franklin Rd.   *549-4815*

Operated by the Lawrence Parks Department, this program is open to Lawrence area residents 55 and older. Among the activities available are ceramics classes, exercise classes, line dancing and a wellness program. There are also occasional shopping trips as well as trips to community events. Dining out is also a popular group activity.

All the museums in the Indianapolis not only welcome, but actively recruit, older adult volunteers.

Insiders' Tips

SALVATION ARMY SENIOR CENTER
234 E. Michigan St.   637-2764

This family-style center, which is open to anyone 60 or older, offers both hot breakfast and lunch programs daily, as well as a variety of classes including exercise, ceramics, church history, current events and poetry. There are also weekly grocery shopping trips, monthly blood pressure and cancer screenings and quarterly eye exams. Guest speakers are featured regularly, talking about issues such as crime, healthcare and Social Security.

Retirement Communities

For older adults who want to live on their own yet want the security of knowing that help is close by if they need it, a retirement community may be a good choice. Many retirement communities offer older adults three types of living options: independent, assisted and nursing care. Residents choose one option or another as their needs change.

Of course, such security comes at a price. While some retirement communities operate much like apartment communities, offering rental contracts, others require a hefty front-end payment to guarantee lifetime care. The following list of some area retirement communities offers you a place to start if you're interested in learning more, but as with any decision having legal and financial ramifications, make sure you understand all the terms and conditions before signing anything (especially a check).

THE ALTENHEIM COMMUNITY
3525 E. Hanna Ave.   788-4261

This nonprofit community offers residential and assisted living options, as well as an on-site, licensed healthcare facility. Living quarters include studio or one-

bedroom apartments; the monthly rental fee includes utilities, laundry services, housekeeping, an emergency call system, three meals a day and transportation services.

AMERICAN VILLAGE: JEFFERSON PLAZA
5549 Liberty Blvd.   251-5580

Set on 47 acres with a lake, this community offers independent-living cottages and apartments, assisted-living apartments, and an on-site licensed healthcare center. Among the amenities are transportation services, cleaning and laundry services, meals, utilities, cable TV and garage/carports.

ATRIUM VILLAGE
2636 N. Mitthoeffer Rd.   899-8050

This is an independent-living community, consisting of two-bedroom apartments. While utilities are included in the monthly rental fee, other amenities, such as cleaning, laundry, transportation, cable TV, cost extra.

CLEARWATER COMMONS
4519 E. 82nd St.   849-2244

This north-side community offers both independent and assisted living options in either studio or one-bedroom apartments. All utilities and meals are provided, as are cleaning, laundry, cable TV and an emergency call system.

COVENTRY VILLAGE
8400 Clearvista Pl.   845-0464

The services here ranges from independent living to on-site, licensed intermediate and skilled nursing facilities.

All meals are provided, as well as utilities and cable TV. Transportation services are provided, as is an emergency call system.

CRESTWOOD VILLAGE APARTMENTS

North: 9191 Garrison Dr.	844-9994
South: 8801 Madison Ave.	888-7973
East: 1423 N. Edmondson Ave.	356-4173
West: 215 Welcome Way Blvd.	271-6475

These four apartment communities, which are limited to people 55 and older, offer studio, one- and two-bedroom units for active, independent seniors. The monthly rent includes all utilities, as well as transportation services and recreational opportunities. Other services, such as laundry, housekeeping, telephone, cable TV, are available for an extra fee.

THE FORUM AT THE CROSSING
8505 Woodfield Crossing Blvd.   257-7406

This upscale, north-side community offers the full range of service levels, independent and assisted living, as well as on-site, licensed healthcare. Among the amenities are housekeeping and laundry services, restaurant-style dining, and social, cultural and recreational programs.

HARRISON AT EAGLE VALLEY
3060 Valley Farms Rd.   291-1112

Primarily for individuals capable of independent living, this community does offer assisted-living services. There are studio, one- and two-bedroom apartments available on a yearly lease or a month-to-month basis, with utilities and cable TV included in the deal. Housekeeping and laundry services, 24-hour security, transportation and restaurant-style dining are among the amenities.

THE HOME PLACE
6734 Millside Dr.   856-3295

This apartment community is independent-living only, with studio, one- or two-bedroom units available on a yearly lease basis. Utilities and cable TV are included in the monthly fee, as is an emergency call system and garage facilities.

HOOSIER VILLAGE RETIREMENT CENTER
533 W. 96th St.   873-3349

This community set on 150 wooded acres on the far north side is designed for independent living in cottages, duplexes or apartments, assisted living in apartments or on-site care in licensed healthcare facilities. Residents have the option of paying for a continuing care contract up front or choosing a monthly payment plan. Among the services provided are all meals, cleaning and laundry services, transportation, and cable TV.

INDIANAPOLIS RETIREMENT HOME
1731 N. Capitol Ave.   924-5839

This facility, which is across the street from Methodist Hospital, offers three levels of service: independent living, supportive assistance, and healthcare. Studio apartments are rented on a monthly basis, and the fee includes all meals, utilities, telephone, cleaning, laundry, and cable TV.

MARQUETTE MANOR
8140 Township Line Rd.   875-9700

In this northwest-side community residents have a choice of independent living facilities: studio, one- or two-bedroom apartments or an on-site, license healthcare center. The only entry option is a life contract, but once admitted almost everything is included— meals, cleaning and laundry, utilities, cable TV, an emergency call system, and transportation.

MORNINGSIDE AT COLLEGE PARK
8810 Colby Blvd.   872-4567

At this independent-living community just west of St. Vincent Hospital, residents can choose among studio, one- or two-bedroom apartments on a yearly lease basis. Rent includes all utilities, telephone and cable TV as well as cleaning and laundry services, transportation and an emergency call system.

OAKLEAF VILLAGE
8480 Craig St.   *842-6564*

In the Castleton area, not far from Community Hospital North, this independent- and supportive-living community leases studio, one- and two-bedroom apartments on a yearly basis. Included in the monthly fee are all utilities and cleaning services as well as an emergency call system. There's a flexible meal plan available, as well as transportation services.

ROBIN RUN
5354 W. 62nd St.   *293-5500*

Situated on a 70-acre campus on the northwest side, this community offers garden homes and apartments on a continuing care contract basis. Primarily an independent-living community, it does have a skilled nursing center on site. Among the services provided are all meals, utilities, cleaning and laundry.

ROLAND'S RETIREMENT CLUB
6038 W. 25th St.   *291-5228*

This independent- and assisted-living apartment community in Speedway offers studio and one-bedroom units on a monthly basis.

Included in the rental fee are all utilities, cleaning and laundry services and meals. Also on-site are a beauty and barber shop; transportation is provided for weekly shopping excursions.

WESTMINSTER VILLAGE NORTH
11050 Presbyterian Dr.   *823-6841*

Set on 57 acres on the far northeast side, this community offers both cottages and apartments for independent and assisted living. There is also Medicare-certified intermediate and skilled nursing care available. Payment options range from a life contract to a month-by-month plan. In addition to three meals a day and an emergency call system, residents enjoy paid utilities and telephone, cleaning and laundry services, transportation and cable TV.

WESTSIDE RETIREMENT VILLAGE, INC.
8616 W. 10th St.   *271-1020*

Offering independent- and assisted-living in studio, one- or two-bedroom apartments, this community also has a licensed healthcare facility on site. Included in the month-to-month rental arrangement are all utilities, as well as cleaning and laundry services. Residents' safety is protected by an emergency call system. Among the amenities are transportation and recreational activities.

Nursing Homes

For individuals in need of routine, ongoing care, an alternative to retirement community living is a nursing home. In Indiana, anyone seeking entry to a nursing home must first undergo a pre-admission screening process to evaluate his/her physical condition and to verify the need for nursing-home care. Those who can afford to pay for all their own nursing-home care can opt not to go through the screening process, but by opting out of pre-admission screening, a person risks being declared ineligible for Medicaid coverage of their nursing-home expenses for the first year after admission.

While there is no consumer organization that currently surveys and rates nursing home facilities, the following organizations do compile lists of licensed facilities and provide guidelines for choosing a nursing home:

Indiana State Department of Health, 1330 W. Michigan Street, 633-8442;

Indiana Association of Homes for the Aging, 9011 N. Meridian Street, 581-1115;

Indiana Health Care Association, One N. Capitol Avenue, Ste. 1115, 636-6406.

With more than 125 nursing homes in the Greater Indianapolis area, space prevents a complete listing. What follows is a sampling of facilities.

ALPHA HOME

2640 Cold Spring Rd.   *923-1518*

Situated on a wooded site on the near-west side, Alpha Home offers intermediate and skilled nursing care, as well as a comprehensive therapies program. Residents are offered on- and off-site recreational opportunities ranging from stretching and other fitness activities to shopping trips and cultural programs.

AMERICANA HEALTHCARE CENTERS

8350 Naab Rd. (north)   *872-4051*
8549 S. Madison Ave. (south)   *881-9164*

Both of these facilities offer inpatient and outpatient therapy programs as well as respite care. Additionally, the Naab Road facility has a subacute rehabilitation unit and a specialized Alzheimer's unit with adult daycare services. The Madison Avenue facility has a specially designed care program for terminally ill patients.

BEST AMERICAN HEALTH CARE CENTERS

Barton House (downtown)
505 N. Delaware St.   *634-9382*
Highland Manor Healthcare
2926 N. Capitol Ave. (near-north side) *926-0254*

These two Best American facilities provide residents with skilled and intermediate care services delivered by certified staff experienced in meeting a variety of healthcare needs and concerns. Both facilities are convenient to downtown shopping, cultural attractions and area churches. They offer full-time activity programs (from arts and crafts to dances) that are designed to meet the physical, mental and social needs of residents. Both are on bus routes, as well.

HEARTLAND HEALTH CARE CENTER

445 S. County Rd. 525 E.
Plainfield   *745-2522*

Set in the bucolic countryside west of Indianapolis, this beautiful new facility offers short-term respite stays, a homeward bound program and hospice care. Among its on-site programs are extensive physical, occupational, speech and respiratory therapies as well as a roster of activities designed to stimulate, improve and/or maintain residents' mental alertness and physical health.

INTEGRATED HEALTH SERVICES OF INDIANAPOLIS AT CAMBRIDGE

8530 Township Line Rd.   *876-9955*

On the northwest side near St. Vincent Hospital, this facility provides complex care for all ages. Among its programs are 24-hour registered nursing care, physician ser-

By calling 254-3660, the Senior Information and Assistance Center, you can find out anything you need to know about the programs and services available to older adults in Central Indiana.

Insiders' Tips

vices, social services, recreational therapy and specialized dietary services.

KEYSTONE HEALTH CARE CENTER
2630 S. Keystone Ave.   787-8951

This skilled and intermediate care facility across the street from Indy Parks' Sarah Shank Golf Course offers residents a choice of private or semiprivate rooms as well as adult daycare services. Keystone's therapy programs include physical, speech, respiratory and occupational.

NATIONWIDE CARE INC.
Regency Place of Castleton
5226 E. 82nd St.   842-6668
Wildwood
7301 E. 16th St.   353-1290
Regency Place of Greenwood
377 Westridge Blvd., Greenwood   888-4948

These three Nationwide Care facilities offer a continuum of healthcare services including short- and long-term care, subacute services, Alzheimers care, and physical, occupational, speech, and respiratory therapies. Each facility is close to shopping and entertainment options, as well as to churches.

SPRINGFIELD HEALTH CARE CENTER
6130 Michigan Rd. N.W.   253-3486

Offering skilled and intermediate care, this northwest side facility provides both around-the-clock and short-term care.

Its programs include physical, respiratory and speech therapies and special care for Alzheimers patients. In addition to residents' rooms, the one-story center contains a chapel and a beauty shop; outside courtyards offer residents a place to socialize.

UNIVERSITY HEIGHTS CONVALESCENT CENTER
1380 E. County Line Rd. S.   885-7050

On the campus of Community Hospital South, this facility offers a broad range of services including skilled nursing management of intravenous and pain control therapies, a special care unit for dementia patients, social service counseling and state-of-the-art physical, occupational, speech and respiratory therapies. In place of the bland meals sometimes associated with healthcare facilities, University Heights offers "home-cooked" meals.

Transportation

Unfortunately, there is not currently any transportation system in place to serve seniors who need a means of going shopping, doing their banking or going out socially. For such cases, the best that's available are discounts for the Metro bus system and for taxis.

METRO TRANSIT HALF-FARE PROGRAM
Metro Customer Service Office
36 N. Delaware St.   632-1900

Metro offers seniors 65 and older half off usual fares. To be eligible, you have to visit the downtown customer service office, show proof of your age and get an ID card.

DISCOUNT TAXI PROGRAM
Indianapolis Senior Citizens Center
708 E. Michigan St.   263-6279

On a monthly basis, anyone 60 or older can stop by the ISCC and buy a coupon book containing $10 worth of taxi fare coupons for $5.

Medical Transportation

While transportation for ordinary trips is hard to come by, there are services available for people in need of transportation to non-emergency medical appointments. Be aware that reservations are needed, and that some programs have geographic and/or income restrictions.

AMERICAN RED CROSS, INDIANAPOLIS CHAPTER

441 E. 10th St.   *684-1441*

The Red Cross provides free medical transportation from 7 AM to 2:30 PM, Monday through Friday. Call two weeks in advance.

INDIANAPOLIS SENIOR CITIZENS CENTER

708 E. Michigan St.   *263-6279*

Members of the ISCC are eligible for free transportation to and from appointments at their physicians' offices, health clinics and hospitals. Assistance is available both to mobile individuals and to those in wheelchairs.

JEWISH SENIOR SERVICES

Jewish Community Center
6701 Hoover Rd.   *251-9467*

Seniors who are JCC members are eligible for escorted transportation to medical appointments.

METRO OPEN DOOR

1501 W. Washington St.   *635-2100*

All Indianapolis residents who are confined to wheelchairs are eligible for transportation to and from medical appointments via Metro Bus's specially equipped vans. Call ahead to schedule; the cost is $1.50 one way.

Insurance Help

In the baffling world of insurance, it's sometimes hard to know who to turn to for straight answers. These organizations can help:

Acordia Senior Benefits: Ambassador Program, 6720 Parkdale Place, 290-2800, (800) 227-6219;

Indiana Department of Insurance: Senior Health Insurance Information Program, 311 W. Washington Street, Suite 300, 232-5299.

Legal Help

Finding an attorney who knows the ins and outs of elder law can be a daunting task. For help, contact one of the following.

LEGAL SERVICES ORGANIZATION OF INDIANA: SENIOR LAW PROJECT

151 N. Delaware St.   *631-9424*

Long an advocate for the legally underserved, Legal Services provides free legal advice and representation for seniors through its senior law project.

INDIANAPOLIS BAR ASSOCIATION: LAWYER/MEDIATOR REFERRAL SERVICE

10 W. Market St., Ste. 440   *269-2222*

As the representative body for Indianapolis attorneys, the IBA maintains a list of attorneys by legal specialities (including those whose expertise is in elder law) and by geographic area. The referral service is free.

Employment

Retiring from one job doesn't necessarily mean you're ready, willing or able to quit working. If that's the case, the following organizations offer job counseling, training and placement for seniors. They also act as bridges between employers seeking older workers and seniors seeking jobs. But be aware that some employment programs have age and income restrictions:

AARP Employment Program, 155 E. Market Street, Room 705, 634-6416;

CICOA The Access Network, 4755 Kingsway Drive, Suite 200, 254-5478;

Indianapolis Network for Employ-

ment and Training (iNET), 17 W. Market Street, 684-2400;

Senior Job Referral Program Indianapolis Senior Citizens Center, 708 E. Michigan Street, 237-9793.

Volunteer Opportunities

If you prefer not to work but still want to do something to occupy yourself, volunteerism is a good way to feel connected to your community and enjoy the company of variety of people from teens to other retirees. The following organizations can help you locate volunteer opportunities that are right for you.

CICOA The Access Network
4755 Kingsway Dr., Ste. 200   254-5464

In its role as central Indiana's center of information about senior organizations and programs, CICOA not only recruits volunteers for its day-to-day operational needs, it also refers people looking for specific volunteer opportunities to other agencies around the area.

Community Action
of Greater Indianapolis:
Foster Grandparent Program
2445 N. Meridian St.   927-5713

This program gives seniors who love children an opportunity to volunteer in daycare centers, community centers and after-school programs where children will benefit from the attention and compassion of older adults.

Retired Senior Volunteer Program
1400 N. Meridian St.   236-1558

This is a clearinghouse for information about a variety of volunteer opportunities throughout the metropolitan area, including opportunities in social service organizations, arts organizations, hospitals and special events.

Small Business Administration:
Service Corps of Retired Executives
575 N. Pennsylvania St.   226-7264

An ancillary operation of the SBA, the Service Corps teams up retired executives with start-up and struggling small businesses in need of expertise in areas such as finances, personnel development and marketing. Working as volunteer consultants, the Service Corps' executives help business owners and their staffs develop workable solutions to their problems, or (in the case of start-ups) create realistic business plans and implementation strategies.

Fitness and Recreation Programs

In addition to programs available through many of the senior centers listed earlier in this chapter, as well as those through the organizations and programs in the Parks and Recreation chapter, the following organizations offer senior-specific fitness and recreational opportunities:

Indy Parks & Recreation
1426 W. 29th St.   924-7059

Among this agency's offerings are "Active Older Adult Programs 50+" and the Indy Senior Olympics.

Marion County Health Department
Bureau of Health Promotion
3838 N. Rural St.   541-2092

Among its many health promotional efforts, this agency has a Silver Striders program for older adults that stresses the benefits of a walking program and offers opportunities to take part in regular organized walks.

YMCA
615 N. Alabama St.   266-9622

With nine branch facilities throughout

the greater Indianapolis area, the YMCA has a number of programs that are either geared specifically for older adults or are open to them, from the Active Older Adults program to classes in yoga and tai chi chuan. Contact Y headquarters above for information.

MALL WALKING PROGRAMS

Most of the area malls have mall walking programs, which are open to people of all ages. You can register at the mall information desks at the following sites:

Castleton Square, 6020 E. 82nd Street, 849-9993;

Glendale Shopping Center, 6101 N. Keystone Avenue, 251-9281;

Greenwood Park Mall, 1251 U.S. 31 N., Greenwood 881-6758;

Lafayette Square Mall, 3919 Lafayette Road, 291-6390;

Washington Square, 10202 E. Washington Street, 899-4567.

Associations and Support Groups

Whether you're trying to cope with a change in your own physical or mental health, or with a change in (or a loss of) a loved one, chances are you can find an association or a support group to turn to for help. While there are too many for a comprehensive list, you can contact CICOA if you're looking for a specific type of group not included among the following.

Alzheimer's Disease and Related Disorders Association, 9135 N. Meridian Street, Suite B-4, 575-9620;

Arthritis Foundation, Indiana Chapter, 8646 Guion Road, 879-0321;

Bereavement Sharing Group, Methodist Hospital of Indiana, 1701 N. Senate Boulevard, 929-8611;

Bereavement Support Group, St. Vincent Stress Center, 2142 W. 86th Street, 338-4040;

Caregivers Support Group, Heritage Place, 4550 N. Illinois Street, 283-6662;

Catholic Widowed Organization, Catholic Archdiocese of Indianapolis, 1400 N. Meridian Street, 236-1586;

Diabetes Association, East Central Region, 5501 E. 71st Street, 255-5132;

Families and Friends of Aging Persons, Jewish Community Outreach Services, 6701 Hoover Road, 251-9467;

Heart Association, Metropolitan Region, 8645 Guion Road, 876-4850;

Kidney Foundation of Indiana, 850 N. Meridian Street, 693-6530;

Lung Association, 9410 Priority Way, W. Drive, 573-3900;

Mutual Support Groups for Friends and Family of Aging Persons, Community Hospital East, 1500 N. Ritter Avenue, 355-5941;

Self-Help for the Hard of Hearing, St. Luke's United Methodist Church, 100 W. 86th Street, 244-1076;

Senior Silent Hoosiers, Indianapolis Senior Citizens Center, 708 E. Michigan Street, 263-6272 or TTY: 263-6278;

Stroke Club, Crossroads Rehabilitation Center, 4740 Kingsway Drive, 466-2010.

Senior Publications

As the senior population grows, so do the number of publications designed specifically for older adults. Locally, these publications provide information about senior concerns, as well as about area events and opportunities for seniors.

THE UNITED SENIOR ADVOCATE
UNITED SENIOR ACTION
1211 S. Hiatt St.   634-0872
The Advocate is a monthly newspaper

published by United Senior Action (see separate entry in the "Where to Start" section of this chapter). It covers the legislative and non-legislative issues that USA addresses on behalf of its members — utility rates, prescription drug prices, home care versus nursing home care, abuse and neglect of seniors, and consumer rights. *The Advocate* is available as part of a USA membership, as well as through a number of senior groups throughout Indiana.

LIFE TIMES
CICOA THE ACCESS NETWORK
4755 Kingsway Dr., Ste. 333   254-3660

A quarterly magazine available free of charge from CICOA, *Life Times* focuses on such topics as retirement communities, senior finances, aging and health, and senior-friendly travel destinations.

SENIOR BEACON QUEST
COMMUNICATIONS INC.
8935 N. Meridian St., Ste. 106   571-0101

A monthly newspaper, *Senior Beacon* covers such subjects as financial concerns, legal and legislative matters, healthcare, fitness, volunteer opportunities and travel. It's available free of charge at area libraries, grocery stores and drug stores, or by subscription ($10 per year).

Inside
Media

Indianapolis has never been recognized as a newspaper town, unlike such regional cities as Louisville, Chicago, Detroit or Cincinnati. However, it certainly has had its share of newspapers. Six months after the city was founded it could claim its own newspaper, the *Indianapolis Gazette*, which took a politically neutral position. A year later the *Western Censor* and *Emigrants Guide* began publishing and took a strong partisan stand against Andrew Jackson.

Since then Indianapolis has seen an abundance of papers come and go: lots of Sentinels, Gazettes, Leaders and Heralds. Given the city's proximity to government, local papers have traditionally been strong on political coverage, a trend that continues today.

The first radio stations went on the air in the early '20s, but Indianapolis didn't secure its own permanent station until 1924 when WFBM (now WNDE) hit the airwaves. By the early 1940s, only two other stations had signed on: WIBC and WISH. But residents weren't going without radio; many local listeners tuned in to Cincinnati's WLW.

Network television began broadcasting locally in 1950. One of the longest-running local shows was Channel 13's *Kindergarten College*, which ran from 1957 to '73. Many area youngsters watched the program, wishing they, too, could go to school

Bob and Tom are popular local personalities who now have their morning radio show syndicated in other markets throughout the country.

on TV. WFYI, the local public TV station, launched its programming in 1970 after a door-to-door fund-raising campaign by a dedicated cadre of volunteers. Following is a quick look at the major players in Indianapolis' vital media scene.

Newspapers

INDIANAPOLIS NEWS
307 N. Pennsylvania St.   633-9070
THE INDIANAPOLIS STAR
307 N. Pennsylvania St.   633-9273

When *The Indianapolis Star* made its debut in 1903, Indianapolis had three major morning newspapers and a couple of afternoon dailies, including the city's largest circulation paper, *The Indianapolis News*.

In four years *The Star* absorbed its morning competitors, while *The News* continued to grow in stature, becoming known as the "Great Hoosier Daily" and ranking as the state's most widely read and influential newspaper.

A series on wasteful government spending won *The News* the coveted Pulitzer Prize in 1932.

While *The News* was in its heyday, *The Star* began developing a reputation as "the businessmen's paper" and became recognized as well for its coverage of state government.

Purchased by Eugene C. Pulliam in 1944, *The Star* beefed up its sports pages, a women's section and launched a Sunday magazine in its attempt to overtake the two afternoon dailies — *The News* and *The Indianapolis Times*.

In 1948, with *The Star* having become the state's largest circulation paper, Pulliam purchased *The News* from the Fairbanks family and immediately began to consolidate and streamline business, circulation, production and advertising

functions of the two newspapers. He moved *The News* into quarters adjacent to *The Star* on Pennsylvania Street (its current home) to save money.

The Times, a Scripps-Howard publication, folded in 1965, leaving the city with two major dailies.

Since 1948, *The Star's* circulation has steadily climbed to a current level of 237,367 papers sold daily (413,903 on Sunday) while the paper has received numerous honors including two Pulitzer Prize awards — one in 1975 for a series on police corruption and the other in 1991 for articles on medical malpractice.

The News, which celebrated its 125th anniversary in 1994, continues to battle declining circulation figures, reaching a low of 77,630 this year.

Despite the drop in circulation, the company has kept its pledge to publish an afternoon edition. However, the newsrooms of the two dailies are no longer separate. A merger was announced in May 1995 and was implemented in September. In spite of the merger, the look of each newspaper is to remain distinct, and each maintains its own separate editorial pages as well as columnists, crossword puzzles and comic strips. No layoffs resulted from the merger, and the newspaper remains a major employer in Indianapolis with 1,400 full-time workers and 500 part-timers. Also, there are 2,965 carriers.

In addition to publishing the two dailies, the newspaper prints a weekly zoned entertainment section called *US Express* that is delivered to more than a half-million households throughout the city and surrounding seven counties.

INDIANAPOLIS BUSINESS JOURNAL
431 N. Pennsylvania St.   634-6200

The *IBJ*, as this business weekly is

called, is a must-read in offices all across town. More than 15 years old, this publication has found its niche by offering well-written, insightful business news. Owned by local businessman Michael Maurer, the tabloid-size paper can claim a circulation of approximately 17,000. The same company that publishes the *IBJ* also publishes two other business-related papers: the *Court & Commercial Record*, a daily begun in 1895 as the *Indianapolis Commerical* that is devoted to detailed listings of law suits, building permits, bankruptcies and sheriff sales as well as related articles; and the *Indiana Lawyer*, a weekly tabloid focusing on the Indiana bar.

NBC's Jane Pauley is an Indianapolis native.

THE RECORDER
2901 N. Tacoma Ave.   924-5143

The city's oldest continuously operating African-American newspaper was established in 1895 by George Pheldon Stewart and Will Porter; Stewart bought out his partner in 1899, and the paper remained in the Stewart family until the late 1980s. Local journalist Eunice Trotter bought the paper in 1988 and sold it to businessman William Mays in 1990. In the early '90s, the award-winning paper's weekly circulation stood at 15,000, and the paper continued to serve the African-American community with its news stories, issues analysis and religion section as well as arts, entertainment, sports and business coverage. Nationally syndicated columnist William Raspberry is a former *Recorder* employee.

INDIANA HERALD
2170 N. Illinois St.   923-8291

One of only two African-American newspapers that continue to publish in Indianapolis, the *Herald* was established in 1949 as the *Hoosier Herald* and was known in the late '50s as the *Indiana Herald-Times*. Despite its name changes, the weekly paper continues to serve the city's African-American community.

TOPICS NEWSPAPERS
9615 N. College Ave.   844-3311

This string of 12 weeklies and one daily — including the *Noblesville Daily Ledger*, the *Fishers Sun-Herald*, the *Castleton Banner* and the *Carmel News-Tribune* — serves the northern Indianapolis suburbs.

NUVO NEWSWEEKLY
811 E. Westfield Blvd.   254-2400

The city's only alternative newspaper, NUVO covers politics, social issues, music, film, arts and entertainment. Regular columns focus on visual arts, theater, jazz and dining. Launched in 1990, NUVO has developed a reputation for its investigative reporting on such topics as homelessness and police brutality. It also features comprehensive movie listings, restaurant reviews and racy "adult services" ads. It's available free every Thursday from numerous street-corner boxes, restaurants and businesses.

Magazines

INDIANAPOLIS MONTHLY
950 N. Meridian St.   237-9288

An award-winning general interest magazine that spotlights local personalities, trends and issues, *Indianapolis Monthly* boasts lively writing, beautiful photos and a circulation approaching 50,000. Readers look forward to the magazine's annual Best & Worst of Indianapolis each December as well as the People's Choice Restaurant Awards in May.

INDIANAPOLIS C.E.O.
911 E. 86th St.   257-8000

This monthly magazine spotlights local business movers and shakers in addition to exploring business trends and issues from a feature perspective.

INDIANAPOLIS WOMAN
9000 Keystone Crossing   580-0939

This publication has seen a lot of changes in its short lifespan. Originally called *Indy's Woman*, it was launched by *Indy's Child* (see specialty publications) in early 1994. It was sold a year later to the Weiss family, who changed its name to *Indianapolis Woman*. The monthly magazine, available free at numerous locations around town and also by subscription, covers business, health and lifestyle trends and spotlights local women in its cover stories. (Interestingly, an earlier publication called *Indianapolis Woman* — known as *IW* — which began publishing in September 1984 and later linked up with *City* magazine, ceased publication in August 1989 when *Indianapolis Monthly* owner Emmis Broadcasting bought and folded *City*.)

INDIANA BUSINESS MAGAZINE
1200 Waterway Blvd.   692-1200

Established in 1957, *Indiana Business* can claim a statewide circulation of 35,000.

Though sold on the newsstand for $2.50, most readers subscribe to the magazine for its focus on business features — the companies, people and issues behind the news. The magazine publishes monthly and also puts out two special issues: April's travel and meeting guide and August's corporate directory.

HOOSIER BASKETBALL MAGAZINE
3750 N. Guion Rd.   925-8200

In a state like Indiana, you've got to expect a magazine devoted to basketball. This massive annual, which began publishing more than 25 years ago, is *the* comprehensive guide to high school and college hoops, with an article on every high school and college team in the state, boys and girls, men and women. It also includes a page on the Indiana Pacers. The 256-page book comes out in November and is available on the newsstand for $4.50; by mail the hefty publication costs an extra $1.50 for postage and handling.

Specialty Publications

ARTS INDIANA
47 S. Pennsylvania St.   632-7894

With a circulation of about 12,000, this monthly publication covers a wide variety of arts-related news and features, spotlighting current issues and personalities in the visual, performing and literary arts throughout the state.

INDY'S CHILD
8900 Keystone Crossing   843-1494

This award-winning monthly parenting tabloid, established in 1984, covers issues related to children and families. It features a detailed monthly calendar as well as articles, regular columns, school and camp directories and special sections. The publication underwent a redesign and premiered its new "adult" look in May 1995. It's available free in libraries, bookstores, businesses and medical offices across town.

THE INDIANAPOLIS REGISTER
931 E. 86th St.   253-7461

Names and faces are the focus of this monthly tabloid that recognizes people who make a difference in Indianapolis. Anybody who is anybody — well, any woman who is anybody — will likely find herself in the pages of this publication, especially if she is involved in any sort of charity or volunteer work. The *Register* includes a variety of special sections, including ones covering entertainment and business, and is available at libraries, bookstores and businesses around town.

THE CRITERION
1400 N. Meridian St.   236-1570

Founded in 1960, *Criterion*, a successor to the *Indiana Catholic and Record*, serves the Indiana Catholic community, focusing on events, advice and scripture. In 1993, circulation exceeded 50,000. The weekly tabloid receives no financial support from the archdiocese, but it does generally express the official Catholic position on Church issues.

JEWISH POST & OPINION
2120 N. Meridian St.   927-7800

Published weekly by the Spokesman Company, this approximately 5,000-circulation paper covers local Jewish events and organizations. The *National Jewish*

Post & Opinion, published by the same company, reports on national and international events; the national paper is included with the local edition.

THE SENIOR BEACON
8935 N. Meridian St.   571-0101

Dedicated to serving senior citizens of greater Indianapolis, the Senior Beacon includes a variety of short news stories, longer features and columns on such topics as finance, fitness and travel. The monthly tabloid is available free at locations around town.

BRANCHES
P.O. Box 30348   255-5594

This bimonthly tabloid features a wide variety of articles on just about every aspect of whole-life living: spirituality, personal growth, health and the environment. The guide to services proves interesting as well; here you can find people who practice all sorts of body work, from Rolfing to acupuncture. Branches is available free at numerous locations, including coffeehouses and libraries.

KIDS' NEWSLINE
3409 W. Bando Ct.   255-7466

Children and educators from around the city write and edit this monthly newspaper covering issues, ideas and activities relevant to students in grades kindergarten through 8. Distributed free to elementary and middle schoolers, the paper is also available at Indianapolis/Marion County libraries.

Turn to the *Hoosier Basketball Magazine* for a comprehensive guide to every — and we mean every — high school or college basketball team in the state.

Insiders' Tips

Photo: The Indianapolis Star & News

Howard Caldwell, who retired in 1994, spent 35 years covering news for WRTV.

Public Programming

In 1970, Indianapolis ranked as the largest city in the country without a public television station. To change that and bring educational programming to central Indiana, a group of 3,000 women hit the streets in the summer of 1970 and waged an effective door-to-door fund-raising campaign.

Led by community leader Ardath Y. Burkhart, "Ardath's Army" raised more than $300,000. On October 4 of that same year, working from a temporary studio at the Indianapolis Museum of Art, WFYI TV20 went on the air, beginning an educational and cultural mission that continues today.

October 1995 marked the station's 25th anniversary, and since going on the air with such PBS staples as "Sesame Street," WFYI has also encouraged local programming. Its signature program, "Across Indiana," hosted by Michael Atwood, has won regional Emmy Awards for best magazine format program for three straight years. The show, which profiles people and places across the state, was also recognized in the documentary category by the Indiana Film Society. You can see other local faces during the political panel discussions of "Indiana Week in Review" and, during the legislative session, "Indiana Lawmakers."

In addition to television, WFYI FM 90.1 serves the listening community. More than 60 percent of FM 90's programming is locally produced, including Sunday afternoon's "Nothin' But the Blues."

Local support of WFYI runs strong. Though viewers and listeners long for even more local programming and complain about the telethon-like on-air fund-raising, viewer support provides nearly 40 percent of WFYI's operating budget. In 1994, more than 1,000 volunteers provided more than 8,000 hours of service.

If you'd like to get involved with public television or radio in Indianapolis, call the station at 636-2020 and volunteer your services.

TEEN TRACK

115 N. Pennsylvania St.   *638-0209*

Written by local high school students, this hefty monthly tabloid focuses on issues, opinion, entertainment and sports. The not-for-profit publication (which relies on corporate, business and individual contributions) pays more than 60 teens from 32 area high schools for their work in putting out the paper.

Radio

Though radio stations are notoriously changeable, these were the call letters and formats as this book was written. Note that phone numbers listed are for request lines.

FM Radio Stations

WICR (88.7)
788-3280

This University of Indianapolis station provides a variety of arts and information programming as well as an eclectic mix of music not available elsewhere on the dial. You can also tune for University of Indianapolis sports.

WFYI (90.1)
636-2020

The place to tune in *National Public Radio*, WFYI also programs Garrison Keillor's "A Prairie Home Companion," Michael Feldman's "Whaddya Know" and Click and Clack's "Car Talk." The station is also strong on jazz and classical music.

WTTS (92.3)
(800) 923-9887

This Bloomington station also targets Indianapolis with its mix of alternative, cutting edge and traditional rock. Naturally, it plays a lot of John Mellencamp, but it also spotlights other local and regional artists and is strong on blues programming as well. Tune in Sundays at 10 PM for Dan "Elwood Blues" Ackroyd's "House of Blues" show.

WNAP (93.1)
239-9393

The buzzard flies again on WNAP, a '70s powerhouse that has recently rejuvenated its former mascot as well as its former playlist. This is where you'll find the Eagles, Aerosmith, Styx and just about every other classic '70s group. Diehard fans tune in at 8 PM to catch *Dr. Buzzard's Original '70s Saturday Night*.

WXTZ (93.9)
233-9390

This station advertises its "sophisticated" music and plays a wide variety of easy listening tunes but has to combat its elevator music image — left over from a previous format.

WFBQ (94.7)
239-1095

This station's nationally recognized morning show features a raucous and irreverent duo known as Bob and Tom, a pair of often funny, sometimes offensive DJs who have developed an entire cast of characters and sidekicks for their 5 to 10:30 AM slot. The show is so popular, other stations around the state run it too (it can also be heard locally on WNDE-AM as well). Be sure to catch "Live Day," when the studio fills with musicians playing some great stuff. Goofiness abounds at Q-95, as it's called, but the station consistently wins high ratings for its strong mix of traditional rock and popular personalities.

WFMS (95.5)
255-9367

Modern country plays on WFMS, the area's No. 1 country station, which often goes head to head with Q-95 for top ratings. Jim and Charlie's morning show begins at 5 AM, beating most other stations by an hour. This is also the place to catch the "American Country Countdown" on Sunday mornings.

WPZZ (95.9)
736-4040

WPZZ, known as Joy 96, plays gospel music.

WHHH (96.3)
293-9600

The hits of top-40 radio are on WHHH.

WENS (97.1)
239-9797

Lite rock, which means no rap or heavy metal, is the specialty of WENS, where office workers across the city tune for music that wears a suit and tie.

WXIR (98.3)
257-8477

WXIR focuses on contemporary Christian programming.

Photo: The Indianapolis Star & News

WISH-TV news anchor Mike Ahern has been reporting on local news since the 1960s.

WZPL (99.5)
239-1099

WZPL cranks out the contemporary hits.

WQFE (101.9)
852-9119

WQFE concentrates on oldies, news and sports.

WRZX (103.3)
239-9103

"Solid rock" music with more of a cutting edge can be heard on WRZX.

WGRL (104.5)
921-1045

"The Bear" plays new hit country.

WTLC (105.7)
239-1057

This station, long an influence in the African-American community, focuses on urban contemporary music.

WGGR (106.7)
293-9600

WGGR spotlights urban adult contemporary music.

WSYW (107.1)
237-1500

Providing classical music remains the mission at WSYW.

WTPI (107.9)
239-1079

Take it easy with WTPI, a popular at-work station that programs soft hits.

AM Radio Stations

WXLW (950)
293-9600

WXLW plays traditional Christian music from 6 AM to midnight.

WIBC (1070)
239-1070

Though this station has undergone ownership and format changes in recent years, it is once again the station listeners turn to for news. When bad weather threatens, tune to 1070. Listeners also tune in for the station's morning team, with traffic reports from Big John Gillis in the WIBC helicopter. The station also programs abundant talk shows, including Rush Limbaugh's afternoon tirade.

WNDE (1260)
239-1260

Though WNDE broadcasts its sister station's mega-popular "Bob & Tom Show," the focus here is on talk and sports.

WTLC (1310)
351-1310

Still a strong voice in the African-American community, WTLC puts together a combination of black gospel music, oldies and news.

WMYS (1430)
925-1079

WMYS plays a variety from the '40s, '50s and '60s in addition to news and sports programming.

WBRI (1500)
255-5484

Religious programs are broadcast from sunrise to sunset.

WNTS (1590)
359-5591

WNTS offers religious programs from 5:30 AM to midnight.

Television

WFYI Channel 20
PBS station
1401 N. Meridian St.   *636-2020*

This station went on the air in 1970 after an incredibly successful fund-raising campaign aimed at bringing public television to Indianapolis (see sidebar). Here's where you'll find such gems as "Sesame Street" and "Reading Rainbow." In fact, more than 30 percent of the station's schedule is devoted to kids' programming. But this is also the place for the popular "This Old House" and "The New Yankee Workshop" as well as "The Frugal Gourmet." And don't miss WFYI's signature program "Across Indiana."

WISH-TV Channel 8
CBS affiliate
1950 N. Meridian St.   *923-8888*

This station features the popular anchor team of Mike Ahern and Debby Knox. Ahern has been reporting locally for nearly 30 years, the longest tenure of any current newsperson. During that time, the station as won plenty of broadcasting awards, including a CASPER award (for community service) for its reporting during the blizzard of 1978. Famous alumni include CBS correspondent John Stehr and former Today show co-host Jane Pauley.

WNDY Channel 23
Warner Bros. affiliate
4555 W. 16th St.   *241-2388*

Formerly WMCC, this station, owned by the Hulman family (of the Indianapolis Motor Speedway), has become steadily stronger in sports programming in the last year or so; IU coach Bobby Knight's basketball program now airs on Channel 23. Popular TV personality Reid Duffy, who developed the long-running segments "Duffy's World" and "Duffy's Diner" for Channel 6, signed on with Channel 23 after leaving WRTV. And there is talk that the station will develop a local newscast as well.

WRTV Channel 6
ABC affiliate
1330 N. Meridian St.   *635-9788*

Longtime anchor Howard Caldwell retired in 1994 after 35 years with this station; for years he epitomized local TV news. During that time, news programming at the station grew from 10-minute broadcasts to 90-minute news shows. The station has earned its share of awards, including a 1989 CASPER for a documentary on police-community relations. It also produces the award-winning program "At the Zoo," a show that goes behind the scenes at the Indianapolis Zoo.

WTHR CHANNEL 13
NBC affiliate
1000 N. Meridian St. 639-6397

Once deemed lackluster, this station saw considerable upgrading of its facilities and programming in the late 1970s. An increased emphasis on news resulted in numerous local awards, and former anchor Tom Cochrun won a national Emmy award for a 1982 documentary on the Ku Klux Klan. It switched network affiliates in 1979 and joined NBC (WRTV then became the local ABC affiliate).

WTTV CHANNEL 4
Independent
3490 Bluff Rd. 782-4444

This station first went on the air in 1949 and was located for a time in Bloomington (which made that south-ern Indiana city the smallest in the world to have a TV station). Though in its early days WTTV broadcast programs from all networks, it became an independent in 1957. It remains independent today, broadcasting a variety of syndicated shows and very popular college and high school sporting events, notably basketball. A whole generation of kids grew up watching its kiddie shows such as "Popeye and Janie." After a childhood of writing in to win its various contests, some of us still know its address by heart.

WXIN CHANNEL 59
Fox affiliate
1440 N. Meridian St. 632-5900

Only about 10 years old, this station went on the air (as WPDS) in 1984; new owners changed the original call letters due to viewers confusing them with PBS and WTBS. In 1986, the station became the local Fox affiliate. It offers a local 10 PM newscast that garnered notice due to its MTV-style visuals and efforts to reach a younger audience than traditional news shows.

Photo: The Indianapolis Star & News

St. John Catholic Church, the first Roman Catholic parish in the city, is a familiar part of Indianapolis' historic architecture.

Inside
Places of Worship

From its earliest days, Indianapolis has been an ecumenical kind of place. As settlers made their way here, first from surrounding states, then gradually from the East Coast and Europe, they brought with them a potpourri of religious beliefs and practices. Those beliefs and practices, in turn, gave rise to discussion and debate during interdenominational meetings and revivals conducted by itinerant preachers. (One meeting spot favored by residents was a wooded knoll in the center of town — the precursor of today's Monument Circle.)

In 1823, settlers organized a Sunday school that attracted students from a variety of denominations. Two years later, the first religious group with a congregation large enough to require its own building— the Methodists— erected a log church just south of Washington Street, the tiny town's first official house of worship.

As transportation routes improved and more people made their way to Indianapolis, religious pluralism increased. Baptists, Catholics, Lutherans, Quakers, Presbyterians, Mormons, Episcopalians, Disciples of Christ, Unitarians, Jews — all settled here during the city's first few decades. Today, the Greater Indianapolis area is home to some 1,100 congregations, spanning more than 100 denominations from African Methodist Episcopal to Zen Buddhism. While Protestantism and Catholicism predominate, there are an array of other religions and sects represented throughout central Indiana.

This region is also home to a number of religious organizations, including the Church Federation of Indianapolis, the Islamic Society of North America and the Christian Theological Seminary. (For more on each of these groups, see the "Religious Organizations" section of this chapter.)

Religion has long played a significant role in the community life of Indianapolis and as evidenced by the number and variety of churches and religious groups in the area, it still does. What follows is an overview of religious life and worship options in the area. By no means is it comprehensive, but we hope it will give you a sense of what's available here. Think of it as a spiritual snapshot of sorts.

Places of Worship

BETHEL AFRICAN METHODIST EPISCOPAL (AME) CHURCH

414 W. Vermont St.   634-7002

Organized in 1836, Bethel AME is the oldest continually operating African-American church in the city. And as it has been from the beginning, the church is active in social and racial issues. Once a station on the Underground Railroad, later the founding place of the Indianapolis chapter of the NAACP, Bethel today continues to serve those in need: the poor, the elderly, the young, both within and outside of its congregation.

Bethel AME's downtown building, constructed in the 1870s, is the only African-American church structure in Indianapolis currently listed on the National Register of Historic Places.

CENTRAL CHRISTIAN CHURCH
(DISCIPLES OF CHRIST)

701 N. Delaware St.   635-6397

Since 1833, Central Christian (which calls itself "the Church of Christ in Indianapolis") has been ministering to the spiritual and social needs of city residents. Today, in addition to its Sunday morning services and church school session, it maintains an active community outreach program that serves those in need throughout the downtown area, especially the elderly and the disadvantaged. The church's motto is "Thinking, Accepting, Acting," and its congregation and pastoral staff takes those words to heart.

CHRIST CHURCH CATHEDRAL

125 Monument Circle   636-4577

At one time in the mid-19th century there were five churches on the Circle downtown. But by 1884, Christ Church was the only one left: The others moved to new locations as the city expanded and their congregations left downtown's Mile Square district.

Today, the lovely little Gothic church on the Circle, once the subject of a book (*The Little Church on the Circle*) by pharmaceutical magnate and benefactor Eli Lilly, is one of the city's treasures. In addition to serving as the cathedral for the local Episcopal diocese and as parish church for its 750-member congregation, Christ Church also conducts two well-respected music programs: the Christ Church Cathedral Choir of Men and

Boys, which holds an annual concert series at the church; and an ongoing (though occasional) lunchtime organ music series. Christ Church's Cathedral Women host the Annual Strawberry Festival in June, serving up homemade shortcake, ice cream, strawberries and whip cream to raise money for charities.

The church structure is listed on the National Register of Historic Places. Weekday visitors are welcome, either on an informal drop-in basis or on a call-ahead formal tour basis. There are also tours available following Sunday services.

EAST 91ST STREET CHRISTIAN CHURCH

6049 E. 91st St.   849-1261

This 71-year-old church has been under the leadership of senior minister Dr. Russell Blowers since 1951. During Dr. Blowers' tenure the church has expanded: Average Sunday attendance is about 2,500, while the congregation itself numbers more than 3,000.

In addition to three Sunday morning worship services (two traditional and one contemporary) and Bible school classes for all ages, East 91st Street Christian Church offers its members a variety of other programs including home Bible study groups, a weekday preschool program and ministerial counseling. The church also hosts a number of support groups: There are groups for singles, for people recovering from divorces, for infertile couples and for battered and abused women.

Additionally, it sponsors outreach programs such as ministries for seniors and hospital-bound people as well as local missions that undertake such projects as building Habitat for Humanity houses. The church's growth and success have spawned nine daughter churches throughout the Indianapolis area.

ENGLEWOOD CHRISTIAN CHURCH
57 N. Rural Ave.   639-1541

This east-side church focuses on service both to God and to humankind. Through their Englewood Neighborhood Christian Ministries program, the church's staff and congregation operate food and clothing pantries that benefit needy individuals and families in the surrounding low-income neighborhood. They also operate an outreach program for area children, providing them a safe alternative to the streets, positive recreational activities and compassionate adults to talk to.

FIRST BAPTIST
CHURCH OF INDIANAPOLIS
8600 N. College Ave.   846-5821

Established in 1822 by 15 of Indianapolis's early settlers who met in a log schoolhouse, First Baptist Church today has a congregation of some 650 members. The church's north-side complex includes a sanctuary for 600-plus, a fellowship hall and 18 classrooms. There's also an on-site gym and shelter house, as well as baseball diamonds and tennis courts — symbols of First Baptist's popular youth athletics program that serves some 2,000 youngsters.

FIRST LUTHERAN CHURCH
701 N. Pennsylvania St.   635-9505

As its name states, this church was first Lutheran institution established in Indianapolis. Organized in 1837 by 20 local families, First Lutheran's first pastor was Abraham Reck, an advocate of a more liberal form of Lutheranism than that practiced in Europe: He believed that other denominations and religious practices had spiritual values as valid as those of the Lutheranism. He also believed in himself — in addition to First Lutheran,

Reck organized and led five other area congregations.

Given its origins, First Lutheran has long been associated with interdenominational efforts and social welfare concerns. From its Romanesque Revival-style (c.1887) structure downtown, the church's congregation operates programs for youth and the elderly. Belying the stereotype of Lutherans as prim and staid, First Lutheran advertises its vitality with the line: "157 Years Old and Still Kicking."

GRACE APOSTOLIC CHURCH
649 E. 22nd St.   925-8103

Gracing the southwest corner of the 22nd Street and College Avenue intersection is the stunning white building that houses Grace Apostolic. Designed by Walter Blackburn, a local African-American architect whose work has earned him national acclaim, the contemporary structure is an intriguing combination of angles and glass, at once formal and friendly.

Grace Apostolic is home to a variety of worship opportunities, including a number of prayer meetings and Bible study sessions throughout the week, as well as Sunday morning and evening services and church school. One Sunday service is broadcast on local FM radio station WTLC. Grace Apostolic is affiliated with the "oneness" branch of the Pentecostal Church.

GREEK ORTHODOX
CHURCH OF THE HOLY TRINITY
4011 N. Pennsylvania St.   283-3816

One of six Eastern Orthodox churches in the Indianapolis area, this facility is the only one serving Orthodox followers of Greek descent. With approximately 1,000 families on its membership rolls, Holy

Trinity is the largest Orthodox church in the city.

While it takes part in local efforts to diminish the importance of the ethnic and political differences that separate Eastern Orthodox congregations, Holy Trinity also celebrates its Greek heritage by hosting the annual Greek Festival, a week-end-long event that brings thousands of people from throughout the city to the church's Meridian Kessler location to eat Greek food and dance to Greek music.

INDIANAPOLIS BAPTIST TEMPLE

2711 S. East St.   *269-2000*

Under the leadership of the Rev. Greg Dixon, this south-side church has grown from a small group of founders in 1950 to its present status as one of the city's largest congregations, numbering more than 5,000 members. Its services have been broadcast nationwide.

A controversial figure locally and nationally, Rev. Dixon has garnered a lot of press for his involvement in the Moral Majority (he was a founding member) and Right-to-Life movements. He is also a leader in the fight to achieve absolute separation of church and state; Rev. Dixon refuses to recognize or abide by any local, state or federal regulations regarding the operation of a church or any of its related operations — schools, daycare centers, etc. As such, the Indianapolis Baptist Temple is an unincorporated entity — and one of the city's best-known churches.

INDIANAPOLIS HEBREW CONGREGATION

6501 N. Meridian St.   *255-6647*

Organized in 1856, the Indianapolis Hebrew Congregation was the first Jewish congregation in Indianapolis. Since the beginning, the IHC (an adherent to the liberal beliefs and practices of Reform Judaism) has been involved with community and social concerns. Through the years, the congregation has played an active role in the creation of the local Red Cross chapter and the Humane Society, opposed the Ku Klux Klan, participated in the Civil Rights movement and developed programs for both young people and the elderly.

Today, the IHC continues to be active beyond the walls of its N. Meridian Street synagogue, most recently as one of the founding members of the Interfaith Alliance, an ecumenical organization directed at establishing communication and cooperation among area denominations.

LIGHT OF THE WORLD CHRISTIAN CHURCH

5640 E. 38th St.   *547-2273*

Founded in 1866 as a missionary project of an existing Christian Church (Disciples of Christ) congregation, Light of the World was originally known as Second Christian Church. Focused specifically on serving the black community, by the turn of the century the church had become one of the most prestigious in the city. In 1984, the church changed its name to Light of the World Christian Church.

Today, Light of the World has a congregation is excess of 3,000 as well as a cable television ministry with a nationwide broadcast audience of some 35 million. While it remains primarily an African-American institution, the church also joins with white churches periodically to host interracial services aimed at breaking down racial barriers and establishing common ground through worship.

MASJID AL-FAJR MOSQUE AND ISLAMIC CENTER OF GREATER INDIANAPOLIS

2860 Cold Spring Rd.   *923-2847*

This small, elegant mosque is home to one of the city's independent African-American Muslim groups. In addition to

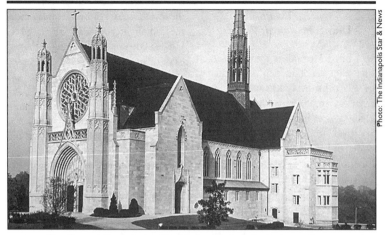

The Second Presbyterian Church is as impressive today as it was in this 1965 photo.

ministering to the needs of its members, al-Fajr also provides educational and informational materials to those who want to learn about Islam and takes an active role in issues and concerns affecting the black community.

ROBERTS PARK
UNITED METHODIST CHURCH
401 N. Delaware St.   *635-1636*

Named for Indiana's first Methodist bishop Robert R. Roberts, Roberts Park United Methodist Church was established in 1842. Twenty-seven years later the church moved from its original chapel to its present downtown building, a Romanesque structure based on the Temple of London. Now on the National Register of Historic Places, the church was built from Indiana limestone and black walnut — the latter milled from trees cut to make room for the church.

Throughout its history, Roberts Park has been active in civic affairs, including setting up the city's first public library, sponsoring the city's first religious radio broadcasts and using its facilities as a USO site during World War II. Though the years have taken its toll on membership (from a high of 1,700 members in the 1940s, the congregation today numbers some 425 who are mostly commuters from the suburbs), Roberts Park remains a vital presence in the religious and community life of the downtown area with programs focused on serving downtown workers, young people and the elderly.

ST. JOHN CATHOLIC CHURCH
126 W. Georgia St.   *637-3941*

Across the street from Pan Am Plaza, in the shadow of the Indiana Convention Center and RCA Dome, St. John is the city's oldest Catholic parish. Founded in 1840 as the Church of the Holy Cross, the church was given its present name in 1850. While its congregation has dwindled over the years, attendance benefits from St. John's location as conventioneers and tourists boost daily and weekend Mass totals.

The present double-spired brick building was constructed between 1867 and 1871, and is now listed on the National Register of Historic Places.

St. Luke's United Methodist Church
100 W. 86th St.   846-3404

United Methodists form the largest Protestant denomination in Indianapolis, a fact that St. Luke's physical layout seems to emphasize. The church and grounds spread out across acres of prime north-side real estate, a testament to the power and affluence of its congregation. But the church is also big on compassion and commitment to the multitude of needs that exist in the community. Aside from its Sunday worship services and Sunday school sessions, it hosts a variety of special interest groups for singles, widows and widowers, teens, the deaf and people with HIV-AIDS.

As evidenced by the playing fields scattered around the grounds, St. Luke's sponsors a number of youth and adult sports programs. It also provides meeting space to Boy Scout and Girl Scout troops, drama clubs and health workshops. And the church is active in outreach missionary work throughout the city and abroad.

St. Paul's Episcopal Church
10 W. 61st St.   253-1277

Situated as it is on a prominent bend in Meridian Street at 61st Street, St. Paul's is hard to miss — so is the large, round stained-glass window that dominates one wall overlooking Meridian. In addition to three Sunday morning services, St. Paul's offers a Montessori-style Sunday school program for children, a youth ministry for adolescents, a health ministry (there's an R.N. on staff), and a music program complete with individualized instruction for children and adults.

SS. Peter and Paul Cathedral
1347 N. Meridian St.   634-4519

This regal structure on the northern edge of the downtown district is center of the Indianapolis archdiocese and home of the Catholic archbishop. With a facade of Indiana limestone and an interior that includes marble statuary, mosaics and stained glass, the cathedral combines stateliness and spirituality.

In addition to serving as the parish for a small downtown congregation, the cathedral also hosts special Masses, Confirmations and Holy Order ceremonies.

Second Presbyterian Church
7700 N. Meridian St.   253-6461

One of the oldest churches in the city, Second Presbyterian also has one of the city's largest congregations — more than 3,200 members — and one of its most prominent church buildings on one of its most prominent streets. And then there's the history.

Second Prez, as the church is informally known, was founded in 1838, and its first pastor (1839-1849) was Henry Ward Beecher who went on to a pastoral post in Brooklyn, New York, where he became one of 19th-century America's most outspoken opponents of slavery and one of its best known orators. During his years in Indianapolis, Beecher not only introduced many of the ideas that later earned him national attention — ideas on slavery, morality and education — but he also took an active role in civic affairs.

Taking a cue from Beecher, another of the church's pastors, William Hudnut III, went on to regional and national prominence on the basis of his involvement in the community. After nearly a decade (1964-1973) at the helm of Second Presbyterian, Hudnut was elected mayor of Indianapolis, a post he held for an unprecedented 16 years (1976-1992). It was Hudnut who helped guide the city out of the doldrums of the 1970s and into the spotlight as one of the country's revitalized cities in the 1980s.

The church's huge French Gothic structure is magnificent with its gorgeous stained-glass windows and its glorious pipe organ. And in its magnificence, it symbolizes the power and status that has long been associated with its congregation.

Yet for all its wealth and influence, Second Prez retains compassion, reaching out to people in need through a variety of social programs and urban ministries.

TABERNACLE PRESBYTERIAN CHURCH
418 E. 34th St.   923-5458

Housed in a stately limestone structure at the corner of 34th Street and Central Avenue, Tabernacle calls itself "an urban, evangelical church with a metropolitan mission." That mission manifests itself in a variety of ways through programs designed to meet the spiritual, social and emotional needs of the congregation and the community-at-large. Tabernacle hosts support groups, offers counseling sessions and operates a large-scale youth sports program that provides some 1,500 young people, ages 6 to 14, opportunities to participate in basketball, football, softball and soccer activities.

Tabernacle holds three Sunday morning services and two church school sessions. There are on-site facilities to assist hearing-impaired and physically disabled individuals take part in worship services.

Religious Organizations

CHRISTIAN
THEOLOGICAL SEMINARY (CTS)
1000 W. 42nd St.   924-1331

Formerly affiliated with the Disciples of Christ and Butler University, CTS is now an independent school of graduate studies for individuals preparing for the ministry. Calling itself an "ecumenical seminary," CTS not only offers a preordination Master of Divinity program, but also masters-level programs in church music, religious education, religious studies and pastoral counseling. See our Education chapter for more information.

THE CHURCH FEDERATION
OF GREATER INDIANAPOLIS
1100 W. 42nd St.   926-5371

Since its creation in 1912, the Church Federation, which today consists of clergy and laypersons from Protestant and Catholic congregations throughout central Indiana, has addressed not only religious concerns but also social and community issues. Included among the Federation's areas of ongoing involvement are race relations, police-community relations, religious education, youth activities, and chaplaincies in hospitals and other public institutions.

CHURCH WOMEN UNITED
(800) 298-5551

Founded in 1898 as the Missionary Social Union of Indianapolis, this organization has a history of supporting a number of religious and social programs in the city. With a current membership of some 500 women from 300 churches and 15 denominations, CWU supports such local projects as Wheeler Mission Ministries (see entry in this section) and takes part in such annual events as World Day of Prayer and May Fellowship Day.

DAMIEN CENTER
1350 N. Pennsylvania St.   632-0123

A joint project of an Episcopal institution (Christ Church Cathedral) and a Roman Catholic one (SS. Peter and Paul Cathedral), the Damien Center provides education, counseling and psycho-social services to individuals with the HIV virus and to their friends and families.

DAYSPRING CENTER

1537 Central Ave.   635-6780

Established by the Indianapolis Episcopal Metropolitan Council in 1989, the Dayspring Center provides food, temporary housing and other forms of assistance to homeless families. It's the only family shelter in Indiana that has an on-site Head Start program. With a staff of fewer than 20 people, Dayspring relies on more than 250 volunteers to help provide its services and on financial aid from government agencies, churches and individuals to help underwrite its expenses.

DISCIPLES OF CHRIST

222 S. Downey Ave.   353-1491

This is the international headquarters for the Disciples of Christ, a branch of the Christian Church that claims some 17,000 members in the Indianapolis area. From these offices, the Disciples organization oversees a number of operations, including domestic and overseas ministries, finances, church services, a council on Christian unity and a foundation.

INDIANA CATHOLIC CONFERENCE (ICC)

1400 N. Meridian St.   236-1455

This is the lobbying arm of the Catholic Church in Indiana. The ICC repesents the state's five archdioceses in the halls and chambers of the State Capitol, talking with legislators about the Church's stance on such legislative issues as abortion, capital punishment, school choice and private school vouchers. ICC also sends periodic updates on state and national legislative matters to Catholics throughout the state.

INDIANA INTERRELIGIOUS COMMISSION ON HUMAN EQUALITY (IICHE)

1100 W. 42nd St.   924-4226

Founded in 1968 to promote interracial and interreligious communication, the IICHE is made up of 21 members from various religious organizations. Over the course of its history, the commission has dealt with such issues as school desegregation, human rights abuses and discrimination among social service providers. It has also established interracial and interreligious discussion groups, and it sponsors the annual Dr. Martin Luther King Jr. Essay Contest, which is open to schoolchildren around the state.

ISLAMIC SOCIETY OF NORTH AMERICA (ISNA)

Old State Rd. 267, Plainfield   839-8157

An Orthodox Muslim organization, the ISNA provides Muslim immigrants in the United States and Canada with the support and information they need to establish themselves in their new homes. From its Plainfield compound, which includes the mosque where boxer Mike Tyson stopped to pray after being released from the nearby Indiana Boys' School, as well as offices for the Muslim Students Association and the North American Islamic Trust, the ISNA provides educational materials to Muslims and others interested in learning about Islam.

LIGHTHOUSE MINISTRIES

520 E. Market St.   636-0209

A nonprofit, nondenominational, inner-city mission for indigent men, Lighthouse was established in 1952 by Rev. Charles Oldham. The mission provides food, lodging and clothing to homeless males, as well as healthcare and job training services. All of Lighthouse's $1 million-plus budget comes from private donations.

WHEELER MISSION MINISTRIES
222 E. Ohio St.   *635-3575*

Named in honor of its founder William V. Wheeler, who opened the Rescue Mission and Home of Indianapolis in 1893, Wheeler Mission Ministries provides a variety of services to those in need. In addition to its downtown shelter for homeless men, which includes free meals and medical care, the organization operates a camp for families and young people, a home for abused teenage girls and a mothers' club. Wheeler Mission relies primarily on contributions from individuals to meet its financial needs, though it also receives some funding from area churches and businesses.

Religious Publications

THE CRITERION
1400 N. Meridian St.   *236-1570*

A weekly newspaper, *The Criterion* focuses on issues and concerns of interest to area Catholics. See our Media chapter for more information.

JEWISH POST AND OPINION
2120 N. Meridian St.   *927-7800*

This weekly newspaper is actually two publications in one. The first, the *Indiana Jewish Post and Opinion*, focuses on matters of interest to members of Jewish communities around the state. The second, the *National Jewish Post and Opinion*, includes articles and columns of national interest; it's included in the Indiana edition. See our Media chapter for more information.

RELIGIOUS BROADCASTING COMPANIES
WKOG TV 31
1400 N. Meridian St.   *931-0310*

Operated by Kingdom of God Broadcasting, this cable TV station broadcasts Catholic religious programming 24 hours a day, though as this book went to press, none of the local cable outlets carried WKOG.

Photo: The Indianapolis Star & News

U.S. Sen. Richard Lugar is credited with helping implement Unigov during his term
as mayor of Indianapolis. He is currently seeking the Republican
party nomination for president in 1996.

Inside
Government

When Indianapolis and Marion County residents awoke on New Year's Day 1970, they had become citizens of the 11th-largest city in the country. The night before, they had been ranked 26th.

What had changed overnight is that legislation enacted by the 1969 General Assembly to merge city and county government had taken effect. Dubbed Unigov, the plan expanded the city's boundaries to encompass the whole of Marion County. It increased the population by 50 percent and created a countywide government structure.

Most accounts of Unigov's creation credit now-U.S. Sen. (and current presidential hopeful) Richard Lugar, elected mayor of Indianapolis in 1967, for much of its implementation. But an informal group of civic leaders met throughout 1968 to hash out a strategy for city-county consolidation.

By 1968 the Republicans held the mayor's office, majorities on both the city and county councils, both houses of the Legislature and the governor's office. Politically, the time was right. Lugar announced the consolidation proposal, which was called Unigov, for "unified government."

Despite the Republican stronghold on city and county government in the late '60s, there was considerable opposition to the Unigov proposal. Democrats called it "Unigrab," referring to the advantage the Republicans would gain by shifting the electoral base from the city to the county and diluting the traditionally Democratic inner city's political influence. Objections were also raised about the lack of a voter referendum, not required under Indiana law, and about the status of several separate communities within the county. Others worried that a consolidated city would expand even further to gobble up small communities beyond the county as well.

Some of these concerns were addressed by excluding four Marion County communities and by prohibiting the annexation of areas outside the county, but still the proposal did not breeze through the Legislature. Though the bill passed the Senate with a solid majority, Democrats in the House attempted to add a referendum requirement to put the proposal to the voters. But though the Republican Speaker of the

So many Hoosiers — nearly a dozen — have been nominated for or have been elected to the country's second-highest office (most recently, of course, Dan Quayle), that Indiana has been dubbed "the mother of vice presidents."

Insiders' Tips

House indicated he might not hand down the bill without an assurance that a majority of Marion County residents approved, it was handed down for a third reading on March 5, 1969, the last day legislation could pass. The legislation was signed by Gov. Ed Whitcomb on March 13, 1969, to become effective on January 1, 1970.

Though Unigov extended many services and merged some government offices throughout the county, it did not combine school districts or police and fire protection. Though proposed, the consolidation met with public disapproval and was dropped from the Unigov plan.

City/County Government

Under the Unigov plan, Indianapolis elects a mayor and a 29-member city-county council, all for four-year terms with no limits to the number of terms they may serve. Twenty-nine members make up the city-county council; 25 are elected by voters in their districts; four are elected at large. All serve four-year terms and were up for election in November 1995. For more information concerning the council, call 327-4242.

Although Unigov merged much of Indianapolis and Marion County government, four cities or towns were excluded from that reorganization: Beech Grove, Lawrence, Speedway and Southport. Their officials are elected to four-year terms that currently expire January 1, 1996.

A 1983 amendment to the Unigov legislation removed term limits from the office of mayor of Indianapolis. The change was often referred to as the "Hudnut Forever" amendment in reference to popular former mayor William Hudnut III, a Republican who succeeded Lugar and served for 16 years with a focus on economic development, downtown revitalization, environmental issues and the promotion of Indianapolis as a "sports capital."

Another Republican, former county prosecutor Stephen Goldsmith, was elected mayor in 1991 when Hudnut declined to run for a fifth term. Goldsmith has stirred up controversy, even in his own party, and gained national attention for changes he has made in how the city is run. With an emphasis on privatization, cost cutting and efficiency, he trimmed city payrolls, reduced the number of workers by more than 1,000 and lowered the budget by $10 million. Focusing on inner-city issues, Goldsmith spearheaded a community policing policy and a neighborhood revitalization program.

Mayor Goldsmith can be contacted at 2501 City-County Building, Indianapolis 46202 or by calling 327-4622.

The mayor was up for re-election in November 1995. If successful, he will begin his second term and may consider a shot at the governor's office in 1996.

State Government

Gov. Evan Bayh, a Democrat, was elected to the state's top spot in 1988 at the age of 34 and won re-election in 1992. Bayh is prohibited from another run; Indiana governors may serve only two consecutive terms. Look for Lt. Gov. Frank O'Bannon to seek the position. Bayh, son of former U.S Senator Birch Bayh, has been active in national politics as well and may have his eye on Washington.

You can contact Gov. Bayh and Lt. Gov. O'Bannon at the Statehouse, 200 W. Washington Street, Indianapolis 46204 or by calling 232-4567 for the governor's office, 232-4545 for the lieutenant governor's office.

Indiana General Assembly

Indiana state senators are elected to staggered four-year terms so that half the members are elected each even-numbered year. Members of Indiana's House of Representatives are elected to two-year terms in even-numbered years. All senators and representatives can be contacted at the Statehouse, 200 W. Washington Street, Indianapolis 46204, or by calling 232-9400 for the Senate and 232-9600 for the House of Representatives. For information on the status of a particular bill, call 232-9856.

Listed below are the names, addresses, phone numbers and districts of all state legislators who represent parts of Marion, Hamilton, Johnson, Hendricks, Boone, Morgan, Hancock and Shelby counties. To find out which is your district, call the League of Women Voters, 925-4757, or the Marion County Election Board, 327-5100.

Photo: The Indianapolis Star & News

Mayor Stephen Goldsmith was first elected in 1991. He has gained national attention for his emphasis on privatization.

Senators

LAWRENCE BORST (R)
District 36 (parts of Johnson and Marion counties)
1725 Remington Dr.
Indianapolis 46227

Home	881-1761
Work	787-5323

BILLIE BREAUX (D)
District 34 (part of Marion County)
4123 E. 35th St.
Indianapolis 46218

Home	546-5136
Work	226-4227

J. MURRAY CLARK (R)
District 29 (parts of Marion and Hamilton counties)
601 W. 91st St.
Indianapolis 46260

Work	637-1321

BEVERLY GARD (R)
District 28 (parts of Hamilton, Hancock, Delaware, Fayette, Henry and Madison counties)
1735 Hickory Ln.
Greenfield 46140

Home	462-2527

ROBERT GARTON (R)
District 41 (parts of Johnson, Shelby and Bartholomew counties)
4024 S. Woodlake Dr.
Columbus 47201

Home	(812) 342-3984
Work	(812) 379-9509

GLENN HOWARD (D)
District 33 (part of Marion County)
1005 W. 36th St.
Indianapolis 46208

Home	923-1101
Work	261-8999

STEVEN JOHNSON (R)
District 21 (parts of Boone, Hamilton, Howard and Tipton counties)
2515 Greentree Ln.
Kokomo 46902

Home	453-1485
Work	452-9478

HOWARD "LUKE" KENLEY (R)
District 20 (parts of Grant, Hamilton, Howard, Madison and Tipton counties)
P.O. Box 809
Noblesville 46060

Home	877-1171
Work	776-7575

TERESA LUBBERS (R)

District 30 (parts of Hamilton and Marion counties)
5425 N. New Jersey St.
Indianapolis 46220
Home 253-5078
Work 251-0757

JAMES MERRITT (R)

District 31 (part of Marion County)
10327 Tarpon Dr.
Indianapolis 46256
Home 849-6310
Work 232-9493

PATRICIA MILLER (R)

District 32 (parts of Johnson and Marion counties)
1041 S. Muesing St.
Indianapolis 46239
Home 894-7023

MORRIS MILLS (R)

District 35 (parts of Johnson, Marion and Morgan counties)
7148 W. Thompson Rd.
Indianapolis 46241
Home 856-5690
Work 232-9465

Representatives

ROBERT BEHNING (R)

District 91 (parts of Marion, Morgan and Hendricks counties)
3315 S. Tibbs Ave.
Indianapolis 46221
Home 244-2190
Work 243-4245

BRIAN BOSMA (R)

District 88 (parts of Marion County)
8971 Bay Breeze Ln.
Indianapolis 46236
Home 845-9129
Work 634-6328

LAWRENCE BUELL (R)

District 89 (part of Marion County)
2502 Silver Lane Dr.
Indianapolis 46203
Home 322-5930

WOODY BURTON (R)

District 58 (parts of Johnson and Shelby counties)
147 Monticello Dr.
Greenwood 46142
Home 881-0400
Work 881-9300

WILLIAM CRAWFORD (D)

District 98 (part of Marion County)
3731 N. Station B9
Indianapolis 46218
Home 545-4175

MAE DICKINSON (D)

District 95 (part of Marion County)
5455 N. Arlington Ave.
Indianapolis 46226
Home 547-0668

RALPH FOLEY (R)

District 47 (parts of Brown, Johnson and Morgan counties)
400 Byram Blvd.
Martinsville 46151
Home 342-3031
Work 342-8474

DAVID FRIZZELL (R)

District 93 (parts of Johnson and Marion counties)
8310 Hill Gail Dr.
Indianapolis 46217
Home 882-2146
Work 635-8885

NICK GULLING (R)

District 53 (parts of Hancock and Rush counties)
1640 E. County Rd. 300 N.
Greenfield 46140
Home 462-7520
Work 462-1158

Photo: The Indianapolis Star & News

Gov. Evan Bayh was elected to the state's top post in 1988. He won re-election in 1992, but is prohibited by state law from another term in 1996.

JOHN KEELER (R)

District 86 (part of Marion county)
1620 E. 75th St.
Indianapolis 46240
Home   255-9974
Work   639-6571

JEFFREY LINDER (R)

District 57 (parts of Shelby, Rush and Bartholomew counties)
416 S. Harrison St.
Shelbyville 46176
Home   525-6493
Work   835-7669

PAUL MANNWEILER (R)
District 87 (part of Marion County)
201 N. Illinois St.
Indianapolis 46202
Home	251-2825
Work	237-3862

CANDY MORRIS (R)
District 94 (part of Marion County)
6721 Latona Dr.
Indianapolis 46278
Home	298-8072

MICHAEL MURPHY (R)
District 90 (part of Marion County)
8320 Lynn Dr.
Indianapolis 46237
Home	881-4798

GREGORY PORTER (D)
District 96 (part of Marion County)
3614 N. Pennsylvania St.
Indianapolis 46205
Home	926-1179

KATHY KREAG RICHARDSON (R)
District 29 (parts of Hamilton, Hancock and Tipton counties)
1427 Harrison St.
Noblesville 46060
Home	773-6123
Work	776-9632

VANESSA SUMMERS (D)
District 99 (part of Marion county)
3035 N. Capitol Ave.
Indianapolis 46208
Home	925-1214
Work	924-5329

SAMUEL TURPIN (R)
District 40 (parts of Hendricks and Morgan counties)
105 Westburne Dr.
Brownsburg 46112
Home	852-5638
Work	639-5474

KATHERINE WILLING (R)
District 39 (parts of Boone and Hamilton counties)
2309 Ulen Overlook
Lebanon 46052
Home	482-7595

R. MICHAEL YOUNG (R)
District 92 (part of Marion County)
3102 Columbine Cir.
Indianaplis 46224
Home	297-2544

MARTHA WOMACKS (R)
District 100 (part of Marion County)
1518 N. Bosart Ave.
Indianapolis 46201
Home	356-6402

United States Congress

Indiana's U.S. senators are elected to staggered six-year terms.

Indiana's members of the U.S. House of Representative are elected to two-year terms in even-numbered years. Indiana has nine Representatives.

U.S. Senators

RICHARD LUGAR (R)
10 W. Market St., Indianaplis 46204
306 Hart Office Bldg.	226-5555

Washington, D.C. 20510

DAN COATS (R)
10 W. Market St., Indianapolis 46204
407 Russell Office Bldg.	226-5555

Washington, D.C. 20510

U.S. Representatives

ANDY JACOBS (D)
10th District (Marion County)
46 E. Ohio St., Room 441A
Indianapolis 46204	226-7331

2313 Rayburn Office Bldg.
Washington, D.C. 20515

Dan Burton (R)

6th District (surrounding areas outside Marion County)
8900 Keystone Crossing, Ste. 1050
Indianapolis 46240   *848-0201*
2411 Rayburn Office Bldg.
Washington, D.C. 20515

Voter Registration

To be eligible to register to vote in Indiana, a person must be a U.S. citizen, 18 years old by the time of the general election and a resident of a precinct for 30 days prior to the general election. Voters can register at the Marion County Board of Voter Registration, the Bureau of Motor Vehicles, Township Trustee offices and at any Indianapolis/Marion County Library branch up to 30 days before the election.

A change of name or address requires a change in registration, and if you haven't voted at all in a four-year period preceding the most recent election, you must reregister.

For more information, call the Board of Voter Registration, 327-5040.

Political Parties and Organizations

Indiana Democratic Party

1 N. Capitol Ave., Ste. 1100
Indianapolis 46204   *231-7100*

Indiana New Alliance Party

1533 Carrollton Ave.
Indianapolis 46202   *638-2126*

Indiana State Republican Central Committee

200 S. Meridian St., Ste. 400
Indianapolis 46225   *635-7561*

League of Women Voters of Indianapolis

3808 N. Meridian St., Room 206
Indianapolis 46208   *925-4757*

Marion County Democratic Party

748 E. Bates St.
Indianapolis 46202   *236-0808*

Marion County Republican Central Committee

14 N. Delaware St.
Indianapolis 46204   *635-8881*

Inside
Service Directory

When you're new to a place, either as a visitor or as a transplanted resident, life can be confusing. What follows are addresses and phone numbers for some of the organizations that can help take the confusion out of being a stranger in a strange place.

However, be aware that despite our best efforts to provide up-to-date information, everything's subject to change. Especially in those organizations that rely on uncertain funding and volunteer staffing. We'll be updating this book annually, so let us know if you find something in this chapter that's incorrect or obsolete — or if you think there's something we should add to the chapter to make it even more user-friendly. (You'll find our contact information in the preface.)

In the meantime, welcome to Indianapolis.

General and Visitor Information

INDIANA STATE INFORMATION CENTER

302 W. Washington St.   232-3140

INDIANA CHAMBER OF COMMERCE

1 N. Capitol Ave.   264-3110

INDIANAPOLIS CHAMBER OF COMMERCE

320 N. Meridian St.   464-2200

INDIANAPOLIS CITY CENTER

201 S. Capitol Ave.   237-5200

**INDIANAPOLIS CONVENTION
& VISITORS ASSOCIATION**

One RCA Dome   639-4282

INDIANAPOLIS DOWNTOWN INC.

201 N. Illinois St.   237-2222

INDIANAPOLIS TOURISM HOTLINE

                                                    (800) 824-INDY

Indianapolis-Marion County Services

WEATHER AND TIME OF DAY
222-2362

EMERGENCY SERVICES
911

MAYOR'S ACTION CENTER
City-County Building	327-4622
TDD/TTY	327-5186

CITY-COUNTY COUNCIL
241 City-County Bldg.   327-4242

BUILDING CODES AND ZONING INFORMATION
2122 City County Bldg.   327-5053

MARION COUNTY HEALTH DEPARTMENT
3838 N. Rural Ave.   541-2000

MARRIAGE LICENSES
122 City-County Bldg.   327-4720

Police Departments

INDIANAPOLIS POLICE DEPARTMENT (IPD)
50 N. Alabama St.
Information	327-3149
Chief's Office	327-3282

MARION COUNTY SHERIFF'S DEPARTMENT
City-County Building   633-5181

BEECH GROVE POLICE DEPARTMENT
340 Chruchman Ave.   782-4949

LAWRENCE POLICE DEPARTMENT
4455 McCoy St.   549-6404

SOUTHPORT POLICE DEPARTMENT
6901 Derbyshire Rd.   787-7595

SPEEDWAY POLICE DEPARTMENT
1410 N. Lynhurst Dr.   244-9543

Fire Departments

INDIANAPOLIS FIRE DEPARTMENT
City County Bldg. E208
Chief's Office   327-6091

BEECH GROVE FIRE DEPARTMENT
330 Churchman Ave.   784-4411

LAWRENCE FIRE DEPARTMENT
4450 McCoy St. 547-4371

SPEEDWAY FIRE DEPARTMENT
1410 N. Lynhurst Dr.   244-9543

Utility Providers and Electric Services

INDIANAPOLIS POWER & LIGHT COMPANY (IPL)
25 Monument Circle   261-8261

IPL provides electricity and steam to customers inside the Indianapolis city limits, as well as to some in surrounding counties.

PSI ENERGY
1000 E. Main St., Plainfield   839-9611

PSI Energy provides electricity to customers throughout central Indiana, with the exception of those in the IPL service area.

SHELBY COUNTY REMC
1504 S. Harrison St.
Shelbyville   (800) 427-0497

This REMC provides electric service to rural customers in Shelby County.

Gas Services

CITIZENS GAS & COKE UTILITY
2020 N. Meridian St.
Information 924-3341
Customer Service924-3311, 924-4747 (TDD)

Citizens Gas provides natural gas services to residential and commercial customers inside Indianapolis and Marion County.

INDIANA GAS COMPANY
1630 N. Meridian St.
Corporate Offices 926-3351
TDD/TTY (800) 777-5144

Indiana Gas provides natural gas services to residential and commercial customers outside of Marion County.

Water Services

INDIANAPOLIS WATER COMPANY (IWC)
1220 Waterway Blvd.
Information 639-1501, 263-6308 (TDD)

IWC supplies water services throughout Marion County.

HARBOUR WATER CORPORATION
1220 Waterway Blvd. 639-1501

A subsidiary of IWC, Harbour supplies water services to portions of the Noblesville area.

HAMILTON WESTERN UTILITIES INC.
1350 Greyhound Ct., Carmel 848-6882

Hamilton Western supplies water services to the Carmel area.

INDIANA CITIES WATER CORPORATION
360 S. Madison Ave., Greenwood 881-0206
835 Wayne St., Noblesville PHONE?

Indiana Cities supplies water services to the Franklin, Greenwood and Noblesville areas.

SPEEDWAY WATER WORKS
1450 N. Lynhurst Dr. 241-2566

This utility provides water services to the Speedway area.

Sewer Services

CITY-COUNTY DEPARTMENT OF PUBLIC WORKS
200 E. Washington St. 327-4622

This department provides sewer services throughout Marion County, except to those communities that provide their own. (See separate listings below.)

Beech Grove

DEPARTMENT OF SANITATION
802 Main St. 788-4980

Lawrence

STREET-SANITATION DEPARTMENT
7699 E. 53rd St. 549-4813

Speedway

SANITATION PLANT
4251 W. Vermont St. 248-1446

Telephone Services

AMERITECH
220 N. Meridian St. 265-2266

Formerly known as Indiana Bell, this company provides telephone services through central Indiana.

GTE NORTH INC.
19845 U.S. Hwy. 31 N., Westfield 896-6464

This company provides telephone services throughout central Indiana, except within Marion County.

Cable Television Companies

AMERICAN CABLEVISION
3030 Roosevelt Ave.
Offices   632-2288
Customer Service   632-2253
    This company provides cable TV services inside the Indianapolis city limits.

COMCAST CABLEVISION
OF INDIANAPOLIS INC.
5330 E. 65th St.   353-2225
    This company provides cable TV services outside of the Indianapolis city limits.

JONES INTERCABLE INC.
516 E. Carmel Dr.   844-8877
    This company provides cable TV services in Hamilton County.

Auto License and Registration Branches

    The following sites provide auto registration and driver licensing services:

INDIANAPOLIS/MARION COUNTY
2920 Keystone Ave. (midtown)   923-3867
941 E. 86th St. (north)   255-9682
8015 Pendleton Pike (northeast) 898-4100
7770 N. Michigan Rd. (northwest) 875-8854
6351 S. East St. (south)   786-9342
3850 S. Emerson Ave. (southeast) 784-3708
4513 W. 16th St. (west)   241-0084
    For mail-in registration service, call 247-7463

BOONE COUNTY
2222 N. Lebanon St., Lebanon   482-2830

HAMILTON COUNTY
2160 E. 116th St., Carmel   846-5533
1950 E. Connor Ave., Noblesville 773-8190

HANCOCK COUNTY
21 S. Main St., Fortville   485-5250
100 S. Pennsylvania St., Greenfield 462-4778

HENDRICKS COUNTY
890 E. Main St., Brownsburg   852-2178
51 W. Marion St., Danville   745-2269
895 Andico Rd., Plainfield   839-2423

JOHNSON COUNTY
1932 Northwood Plaza, Franklin   736-7332
360 S. Madison Ave., Greenwood   881-2183

MORGAN COUNTY
1246 Morton Ave., Martinsville   342-3164
217 E. High St., Mooresville   831-4805

Library Services
(For more information, see the "Libraries" section of The Literary Life chapter.)

INDIANAPOLIS-MARION COUNTY
PUBLIC LIBRARIES
40 E. St. Clair St.   269-1700

INDIANA STATE LIBRARY
140 N. Senate Ave.   232-3675

Some neighborhoods have a curbside recycling program that allows them to place their recyclables in a box next to the curb for weekly pickup. For information about recycling drop-off sites or curbside pickup, call Rumpke Recycling, 398-6588.

Insiders' Tips

**INDIANA UNIVERSITY-
PURDUE UNIVERSITY
INDIANAPOLIS (IUPUI) LIBRARY**
755 W. Michigan St.   274-0472

BEECH GROVE PUBLIC LIBRARY
1102 Main St., Beech Grove   788-4203

GREENWOOD PUBLIC LIBRARY
310 S. Meridian St.
Greenwood   881-1953

Support Groups

For groups that deal with retirement and older adults' health issue, please see our Retirement chapter.

Alcohol/Drugs

Al-Anon/Alateen	357-9607, 776-7235
Alcoholics Anonymous	632-7864
St. Francis Counseling Center	783-8983
St. Vincent Street Center Crisis Line	338-4800
Rational Recovery Systems	357-8905
Mothers Against Drunk Driving	689-4118

Cancer

Family Support Group	929-6565
The Life Center	924-2324
Cancer Patient Support Group	776-7325
The Wellness Community-Central Indiana	257-1505

Debt

Consumer Credit Counseling Service of Central Indiana	266-1300 ex 257

Depression

Postpartum Depression Support Group	338-4800
Depression Support Group	251-0005
Manic Depression Group	251-0005

Domestic Violence

Family Service Association of Indianapolis	634-6341
Breaking Free	923-4260
The Salvation Army Social Service Center	637-5551

Infertility

Resolve	329-9519

Literacy

The Greater Indianapolis Literacy League	269-1745
Indiana Literacy Hotline	(800) 624-7585

Men's Issues

Indiana Men's Council	283-8701

Mental Health

St. Vincent Community Stress Centers Crisis Line	338-4800
The Alliance for the Mentally Ill of Greater Indianapolis	638-6127
The ARC of Indiana	632-4387

Parenting

The Family Service Assn. of Indianapolis	634-6341
Parenting Classes	846-3404
Indiana Parent Information Network	257-8683
Family Support Center	634-5050
Parents Without Partners	547-7971
	824-4269, 388-3555

Suicide

Crisis and Suicide
 Intervention Service   251-7575
National Youth Crisis Hotline   (800) HIT-HOME
Survivors of Suicide Victims   355-4743

Veterans

Indianapolis Service Office   226-7918
Disabled American Veterans   632-9266

Index of Advertisers

Index

ORDER FORM
Fast and Simple!

Mail to:
Insiders Guides®, Inc.
P.O. Drawer 2057
Manteo, NC 27954

Or:
for VISA or
MasterCard orders call
(800) 765-BOOK

Name _____

Address _____

City/State/Zip _____

Qty.	Title/Price	Shipping	Amount
	Insiders' Guide to Richmond/$14.95	$3.00	
	Insiders' Guide to Williamsburg/$14.95	$3.00	
	Insiders' Guide to Virginia's Blue Ridge/$14.95	$3.00	
	Insiders' Guide to Virginia's Chesapeake Bay/$14.95	$3.00	
	Insiders' Guide to Washington, DC/$14.95	$3.00	
	Insiders' Guide to North Carolina's Outer Banks/$14.95	$3.00	
	Insiders' Guide to Wilmington, NC/$14.95	$3.00	
	Insiders' Guide to North Carolina's Crystal Coast/$12.95	$3.00	
	Insiders' Guide to Myrtle Beach/$14.95	$3.00	
	Insiders' Guide to Mississippi/$14.95	$3.00	
	Insiders' Guide to Boca Raton & the Palm Beaches/$14.95	$3.00	
	Insiders' Guide to Sarasota/Bradenton/$12.95	$3.00	
	Insiders' Guide to Northwest Florida/$14.95	$3.00	
	Insiders' Guide to Lexington, KY/$14.95	$3.00	
	Insiders' Guide to Louisville/$14.95	$3.00	
	Insiders' Guide to the Twin Cities/$12.95	$3.00	
	Insiders' Guide to Boulder/$12.95	$3.00	
	Insiders' Guide to Denver/$12.95	$3.00	
	Insiders' Guide to Civil War in the Eastern Theater/$14.95	$3.00	
	Insiders' Guide to North Carolina's Mountains/$14.95	$3.00	
	Insiders' Guide to Atlanta/$14.95	$3.00	
	Insiders' Guide to Branson/$14.95 (12/95)	$3.00	
	Insiders' Guide to Cincinnati/$14.95 (9/95)	$3.00	
	Insiders' Guide to Tampa Bay/$14.95 (12/95)	$3.00	

Payment in full (check or money order) must
accompany this order form.
Please allow 2 weeks for delivery.

N.C. residents add 6% sales tax _____

Total _____

Who you are and what you think is important to us.

Fill out the coupon and we'll give you an Insiders' Guide® for half price ($7.48 off)

Which book(s) did you buy? _____

Where do you live? _____

In what city did you buy your book? _____

Where did you buy your book? ❏ catalog ❏ bookstore ❏ newspaper ad

❏ retail shop ❏ other _____

How often do you travel? ❏ yearly ❏ bi-annually ❏ quarterly

❏ more than quarterly

Did you buy your book because you were ❏ moving ❏ vacationing

❏ wanted to know more about your home town ❏ other _____

_____

Will the book be used by ❏ family ❏ couple ❏ individual ❏ group

What is you annual household income? ❏ under $25,000 ❏ $25,000 to $35,000

❏ $35,000 to $50,000 ❏ $50,000 to $75,000 ❏ over $75,000

How old are you? ❏ under 25 ❏ 25-35 ❏ 36-50 ❏ 51-65 ❏ over 65

Did you use the book before you left for your destination? ❏ yes ❏ no

Did you use the book while at your destination? ❏ yes ❏ no

On average per month, how many times do you refer to your book? ❏ 1-3 ❏ 4-7

❏ 8-11 ❏ 12-15 ❏ 16 and up

On average, how many other people use your book? ❏ no others ❏ 1 ❏ 2

❏ 3 ❏ 4 or more

Is there anything you would like to tell us about Insiders' Guides? _____

_____

_____

Name _____ Address _____

City _____ State _____ Zip _____

We'll send you a voucher for $7.48 off any Insiders' Guide© and a list of available titles as soon as we get this card from you. Thanks for being an Insider!

NO POSTAGE
NECESSARY
IF MAILED
IN THE
UNITED STATES

BUSINESS REPLY MAIL

FIRST-CLASS MAIL   PERMIT NO. 20   MANTEO, NC

POSTAGE WILL BE PAID BY ADDRESSEE

THE INSIDERS GUIDE
PO BOX 2057
MANTEO NC   27954-9906